THE "MATTHEW-LUKE COMMENTARY" OF PHILOXENUS

SOCIETY OF BIBLICAL LITERATURE

DISSERTATION SERIES

edited by
Howard C. Kee

Number 43

THE "MATTHEW-LUKE COMMENTARY" OF PHILOXENUS (BRITISH MUSEUM MS. ADD. 17,126): TEXT, TRANSLATION AND CRITICAL ANALYSIS

by
Douglas J. Fox

Douglas J. Fox

THE "MATTHEW-LUKE COMMENTARY" OF PHILOXENUS

TEXT, TRANSLATION AND CRITICAL ANALYSIS

Scholars Press

Distributed by
Scholars Press
PO Box 5207
Missoula, Montana 59806

THE "MATTHEW-LUKE COMMENTARY" OF PHILOXENUS (BRITISH MUSEUM MS. ADD. 17,126): TEXT, TRANSLATION AND CRITICAL ANALYSIS

Douglas J. Fox
Huron College
London, Ontario, Canada

Ph.D., 1975
University of Toronto

Supervisor:
Ernest G. Clarke

Library of Congress Cataloging in Publication Data

Philoxenus, Bp. of Hierapolis.
The "Matthew-Luke commentary" of Philoxenus (British Museum MS. Add. 17,126).

(Society of Biblical Literature dissertation series ; 43)
Syriac text: p.
Originally presented as the editor's thesis, University of Toronto, 1975.
Bibliography: p.
Includes index.
1. Bible. N.T. Gospels—Commentaries. I. Fox, Douglas J. II. British Museum. MSS. (Additional 17,126) III. Title. IV. Series: Society of Biblical Literature. Dissertation series ; 43.
BS2555.3.P5313 1978 226'.2'06 78-12852
ISBN 0-89130-266-2 pbk.

Printed in the United States of America

1 2 3 4 5

Edwards Brothers, Inc.
Ann Arbor, Michigan 48104

TABLE OF CONTENTS

ACKNOWLEDGEMENTS

In presenting this work for publication, I am deeply aware of my indebtedness to many people who supported and encouraged me in its preparation.

I wish especially to thank my thesis supervisor in the University of Toronto, Professor Ernest G. Clarke, his colleagues in the Department of Near Eastern Studies, Professor Emeritus W. Stewart McCullough and Professor David J. Lane, and my External Examiner, Dr. Carmino J. de Cantanzaro.

I would also acknowledge my profound sense of gratitude to the Trustees of the British Library (formerly the British Museum) for granting me permission to reproduce their manuscript Add. 17,126, without which permission this thesis could not be meaningfully published.

Huron College,
London, Ontario, Canada.
June, 1978

Douglas J. Fox

INTRODUCTION

In 1847, the British Museum acquired a large collection of Syriac manuscripts from the Monastery of St. Mary Deipara in the Nitrian Desert of Egypt. Among these are fourteen fragments bound together in one volume and designated British Museum Manuscript Add. 17,126. In his *Catalogue of Syriac Manuscripts in the British Museum Acquired since the Year 1838* (published between 1870 and 1872), William Wright described this manuscript as containing "Fragments of the Commentaries of Philoxenus of Mabbug on the Gospels of S. Matthew and S. Luke."[1] He continues his description as follows: "Folios 1 and 2 seem to belong to the Commentary on the Gospel of S. Matthew (18:21,22); the remainder to that on the Gospel of S. Luke (from the beginning to 3:22)."[2] While a cursory reading would lead a cataloguer to such a conclusion, the description is quite inadequate and somewhat misleading; for example, the last four fragments belong to a discourse on Luke 3:23 involving a consideration of the genealogy which that verse introduces.[3] In his list of the works of Philoxenus, Budge in 1894 adopted Wright's conclusion and assumed this manuscript preserved fragments of "the Commentary on Saint Matthew . . . (and) the Commentary on Saint Luke" which were part of a "Commentary on the New Testament."[4]

Wright's description was also accepted without question by A. Baumstark in 1902 when he published a survey of Syrian monophysite exegesis of the Gospels.[5] Concerning 'this precious fragment' (das kostbare Bruchstück), Baumstark wrote:

> Die vollständige Mattäuserklärung oder doch deren letzten Teil und die Lukaserklärung bis 3:22 scheint endlich von Hause aus die leider stark beschädigte Handschrift Brit. Mus. Add. 17,126 enthalten zu haben. Schon 511 . . . war sie entweder ein einzelner Band einer in mehrere Bände zerfallenden Gesamtausgabe seiner Evangelienerklärung oder sie wurde noch vor Vollendung der Lukasexegese nach seinem Autograph gefertigt.[6]

Baumstark simply depended on Wright's *Catalogue* not only for the above statement, but also for his brief reference to the manuscript in his *Geschichte der syrischen Literatur* twenty years later.[7]

In 1911, J. Lebon published an important article, "La version philoxénienne de la Bible," in which he critically analyzed the attempted reconstructions of the lost Philoxenian version.[8] In his concluding footnote, he suggests that the writings of Philoxenus may provide the clue, but only if their chronology has been established:

> Une chronologie exacte, obtenue par l'autres moyens, pour les oeuvres de Philoxène, serait la condition préalable de la détermination de celles qui pourraient avoir subi l'influence de la version polycarpienne et en révéler quelques traces. Encore ne doit-on pas s'exagérer les chances d'aboutir par cette voie à des résultats sûrs et considérables.[9]

While Lebon mentions no Philoxenian work except the *Discourses* published by Budge, it is clear that the principle he enunciated is a sound one, as the dissertation here presented will show.

The next important study (chronologically speaking) related to this manuscript was that of G. Zuntz, *The Ancestry of the Harklean New Testament* (1945). In his search for a pre-Harklean text, Zuntz turned to the writings of Philoxenus for evidence of the Philoxenian version. In particular, he analyzed New Testament quotations in a work published by A. Vaschalde in 1907 as "Tractatus tres de Trinitate et incarnatione." He concluded that "the text of these quotations is something like a half-way house" between the Peshitta and the Harklean.[10] The discovery was an important one, but Zuntz ignored the fact that the chronological sequences of Philoxenus' writings needed to be established in order to relate any variant patterns of biblical quotations to the Philoxenian New Testament published in 508. He did see, however, that the manuscript before us, along with the so-called "Commentary on John 1:1-17" (British Museum Add. 14,534), had such a chronological relationship:

> It is tempting to test one work of Philoxenus before all others; viz. the fragments of his commentary on the Gospels. They are preserved in two manuscripts in the British Museum, written in Mabbug, one of them certainly (A.D. 510/511), the other probably, during his episcopate and after the completion of Polycarp's

> version. . . . Unfortunately this oldest document of monophysite exegesis is still unpublished and the manuscripts are at present inaccessible.[11]

While recognizing that Zuntz's attempted solution to the problem of the Philoxenian version was in some ways unsatisfactory, A. Vööbus saw that his approach to the problem was promising. In a "Festschrift" for C. Kundziņš, *Spiritus et Veritas* (1953), he published a study, "New Data for the Solution of the Problem Concerning the Philoxenian Version," in which (following Zuntz's lead) he analyzed six quotations from John's Gospel in the unpublished manuscript of the "Commentary on the Gospel of John . . . Add. 14,534 in the British Museum."[12] His findings confirmed those of Zuntz (namely, that the Philoxenian stood between the Peshitta and the Harklean) and some of its features began to come into focus. In this study, Vööbus dismisses Add. 17,126 (the subject for our dissertation) as not being of much value for the understanding of the Philoxenian version, because in it "Philoxenus quoted a (Syriac Biblical) text influenced deeply by the Old Syriac text."[13] While this is in part true, our study will show that it too is valuable in helping us to recover some verses of the Philoxenian New Testament.

In 1963, A. de Halleux published a comprehensive study of Philoxenus, *Philoxène de Mabbog -- sa vie, ses écrits, sa théologie*.[14] In his description of all the Philoxenian writings, he analyzed and re-described the fragments of Add. 17,126 (the first to do so since Wright published his *Catalogue* in 1872), and sought to link them with the other exegetical fragments in order to reconstruct Commentaries on Matthew, Luke and John.[15] His reconstruction was impressive but premature, for he presented a detailed synthesis of Philoxenian fragments (many of which remain unpublished) within a work which was much wider and more general in its scope. My initial approach to his conclusions was one of acceptance, believing that the fragments, extracts and references which de Halleux had pieced together did in fact belong to the contents of a lost Gospel Commentary. Careful analysis, however, of the manuscript before us soon revealed de Halleux' reconstruction to be faulty and thus misleading. It then became necessary to re-examine the nature of the "exegetical" fragments (at least, those available to me), and this has been done in section C.2 of chapter 1, where de Halleux' schema is critically assessed. Chapter 3 sets forth a radically different understanding of this codex than that proposed by de Halleux.

In the last century, then, scholars have recognized the importance of this fragmentary work, but until now it has not been published. Called a "commentary" by the scribe who copied it at Mabbug while the author was bishop there, it is important in at least two ways: (1) it preserves many scriptural quotations which add to our knowledge of the history of the Syriac versions of the Bible, and (2) it gives some insight into Philoxenus' exegetical activity. After presenting a critical restatement of the historical and literary context in which British Museum Manuscript Add. 17,126 was produced (chapter 1), this dissertation provides an edited facsimile of the Manuscript (chapter 2), offers a translation with analytical notes and a proposed synthesis of its fragments (chapter 3), and examines the nature of the biblical texts it quotes (chapter 4) and the kind of exegesis it exemplifies (chapter 5).

Because the final fragment is said to belong to a "commentary," the whole manuscript has repeatedly been so designated without further definition. But the term ܦܘܫܩܐ usually translated "commentary," has a range of meanings that include the following three literary types. First, it can be used to describe an exegetical or explanatory note on a biblical text incorporated into a larger literary unit whose overall purpose may be non-exegetical; thus, some of the letters and discourses of Philoxenus contain such exegetical notes. In the second place, ܦܘܫܩܐ can encompass a series of exegetical notes extending to book size on some writing (biblical or otherwise); for example, Theodore of Mopsuestia wrote commentaries of this sort on various books of the Bible. Whether Philoxenus ever wrote this kind of work which is exclusively exegetical in nature, remains to be seen. Finally, the word can be used for a collection of homilies or sermons, each of which is based on a biblical text. I refer to this genre as "homiletical commentary." Chrysostom's expository homilies are of this order. In our examination of the so-called "Commentary" on Matthew and Luke, we shall seek to discover the sense in which that term is used in the colophon, and whether it can properly be applied to all fourteen fragments.

CHAPTER I

THE HISTORICAL AND LITERARY BACKGROUND

A. *THE CAREER OF PHILOXENUS*

Of the early life and family background of Philoxenus very little is known.[16] Ancient authorities agree that he was born in the village of Taḥil in the region of Beth-Garmai in Persia.[17] The exact location of Taḥil is not known, but Beth-Garmai was a well-defined district in the Persian Empire, being the area north of Baghdad bound by the River Tigris, its tributaries, the lesser Zab and the Diala, and the Zagros mountains.[18] By the fifth century (when Philoxenus was born), Beth-Garmai had become a metropolitan see of considerable importance with six episcopal dioceses established by canon law in 410.[19] Whether or not we can give any credence to the pious tradition that this region was initially evangelized by the disciple Addai in the first century,[20] there is no reason to doubt the statement in the *Chronicle of the Church of Arbela* that of the twenty dioceses in Mesopotamia and Persia in 225 three were in the district of Beth-Garmai.[21] It is clear, then, that Philoxenus was born in a region in Persia where, in spite of periodic persecutions, Christianity had been established for several centuries prior to his birth.

The precise date of Philoxenus' birth has been lost to history. The few hints in his own writings and in the works of others are vague, and have been variously interpreted.[22] The relevant material is as follows:

1) Eli of Qartamin in his *Memra* on Philoxenus states: "On account of the persecution (directed) against Christians because of paganism, the parents of Mar Aksenaia (i.e., Philoxenus) came from that place (Taḥil in Beth-Garmai) and travelled as far as the blessed place (called) Tur 'Abdin in the district of Haytam. They settled on a certain farm. This farm was on the north side of Beth-Sabirina, opposite [Zri^{z}a] of 'Arban."[23] The author goes on to say that Philoxenus left his family to become a hermit in a small stone cell which he

built for himself about half a mile from his home, the implication being that this event took place in his early youth.[24] Eli of Qartamin thus provides us with a reason for the family migration -- namely, persecution in Persia -- and, in so doing, he indicates a possible period for the migration. It is also evident that he believed Philoxenus was a small boy when the family fled from Persia because of the pressure of persecution.

2) In the Syriac *History of Karka of Beth-Selok*, we are told of the wave of persecution of Christians in Persia during the reign of Yezdigird II (439-457).[25] The document describes at some length the persecuting zeal of Tohm Yezdigird, a high official in the royal court.[26] The year was 446. The focus of the persecution was apparently the region of Beth-Garmai, for John (the bishop of Karka and metropolitan of that region) was put to death along with thirty-one leading Christians on the twenty-fourth of Ab, and the next day many others were martyred. P. M. Sykes, in his *History of Persia*, claims that the Christians massacred at that time numbered in the thousands, and goes on to speak of a modern (1915) witness to this ancient bloodbath:

> Karka today is known as Karkuk or Kirkuk, and it is of no small historical interest to find that every year a solemn assembly is still convened to commemorate the death of these martyrs at the little church on the hillock outside the town which was dyed with their blood.[27]

3) Simeon of Beth-Aršam, in his *Letter on Nestorianism*, describes the "School of the Persians" at Edessa under Ḥiba who was bishop of Edessa from 435 until he died in 457 (except for the years 449-451, when he was deposed for his supposed Nestorianism).[28] He claims that among those attending the school was a monophysite minority which opposed Ḥiba, including "Mar Papa from Beth-Lapaṭ, the city of the Huzaites, Mar Aksenaia (i.e., Philoxenus) from Taḥal [sic] of Beth-Garmai, his brother Addai, Mar Bar-Hadbešabba the Qardwaite, . . . and Mar Benjamin the Syrian."[29] Philoxenus was therefore old enough to be a student in the "School of Edessa" prior to the death of Ḥiba in 457.

4) Philoxenus provides a few autobiographical details in his *Letter to the Monks of Senun*.[30] De Halleux has established

that he wrote this letter in 521, two years after he was removed from his episcopal see, and two years before his death.[31] In it, Philoxenus tells us that he was a bishop for thirty-four years, and at the time of writing he was old, sick, persecuted, dispossessed of his see, and outlawed.[32] He was thus consecrated bishop of Mabbug in 485. What he meant by calling himself "old" is too imprecise to be of any help in determining the year of his birth.

From these sources we may summarily reconstruct the life of Philoxenus as follows. He was born in the village of Taḥil in the region of Beth-Garmai in Persia perhaps around the year 440. His parents fled from Persia in 446, bringing him to the district of Tur 'Abdin where they settled on a farm. While still a boy or adolescent he may have built a small stone hut on the edge of the recently acquired family property, and acquired a taste for the solitary life.[33] He enrolled in the School of the Persians during the episcopate of Ḥiba (died 457), and was a member of that school long enough to be identified with the minority which opposed the bishop's theology.[34] This would suggest that Philoxenus entered the school when he was twelve (c. 452) or fourteen (c. 454). As far as I can ascertain the minimum age for entrance into such a school is not known; but the age suggested is reasonable. In theory, he could have entered the school as late as 457 (the year of Ḥiba's death), but it is unlikely that he should have been numbered with a significant minority opposing the bishop and head of the school had he been a very junior member of the student body.

What was the nature of the curriculum to which Philoxenus may have been subjected during his formative years? The painstaking research of Professor A. Vööbus has provided a partial answer.[35] Beyond the basic skills of reading (with accurate pronunciation required for liturgical use) and writing, the student was exposed to the study and exegesis of the Old and New Testaments and the Syriac Fathers. Vööbus stresses the point that training in Biblical interpretation was at the core of the curriculum: "The exegesis of the Scriptures . . . included the responsibility to interpret, using all the resources available, such as literary, philological, lexical, and historical."[36] In the time of Ḥiba and under his guidance, most of the commentaries of Theodore of Mopsuestia were translated from Greek into Syriac and became the textbooks of biblical interpretation.[37] The School of the Persians in Edessa thus followed the Antiochian tradition of biblical interpretation.[38] Other subjects taught included history, geography, astronomy, Greek language, and Greek philosophy.[39] Indeed, the school had established a program to translate Greek philosophical writings into Syriac including the works of Aristotle, a Syriac translation of whose Hermeneutics has survived.

Given this kind of education, one would have expected Philoxenus to have become a disciple of Ḥiba, reflecting sympathetically the theology of Theodore of Mopsuestia and the Nestorian tendency of his alma mater. In his *Second Letter to the Monks of Beth-Gogal*, Philoxenus declares that he has read the books of those who created the Nestorian heresy (that is, Diodore of Tarsus and Theodore of Mopsuestia) "more than those who now preach it."[40] De Halleux sees in this brief personal reference an indication that Philoxenus reacted against "Nestorian rationalism" and opted for "Alexandrian Christology" during his student days in the Edessan School, and his reaction was strong enough to single him out as a member of the school's monophysite minority which was known to oppose Ḥiba.[41]

We know nothing of Philoxenus' career between the date of Ḥiba's death (457) and the period of the patriarchate of Calandion of Antioch (482-485). During this latter period we learn from several ancient sources that he was expelled from the see of Antioch by Calandion for disturbing the faith of the Church and creating dissension in the neighbouring villages.[42] Philoxenus, in his *Letter to the Monks of Senun*, refers to his encounter with Calandion as something which is "known and talked about everywhere."[43] It is evident that by this time his activities on behalf of monophysitism were effective enough to warrant such drastic treatment by the patriarch of Antioch. He apparently had made contact with several important monasteries and had enlisted the support of their monks. Some of his letters to these monasteries have survived in various manuscripts, providing us with an insight into Philoxenus' relationship with them and his evangelical passion in fostering the cause of monophysitism and resisting the spread of Nestorianism and the teachings of the Council of Chalcedon, which he saw as the two faces of the same heresy.[44] All in all, the general picture that comes to us of the years prior to his expulsion from Antioch is one in which Philoxenus "wanders from place to place"[45] in the area of the upper Euphrates and westward into Syria, promoting his monophysite doctrines by preaching, teaching and writing, and making staunch friends and sworn enemies in the process.

In 485, the Emperor Zeno deposed Calandion from the patriarchate of Antioch, banishing him to Egypt, and reinstated Peter the Fuller as patriarch.[46] Soon after his reinstatement, the new patriarch consecrated Philoxenus as a bishop and appointed him to the metropolitan see of Mabbug, a position which the latter held until he was deposed in 519. The year of his consecration is well attested, and the precise date, the 18th of Ab, is given by Eli of Qartamin.[47] As bishop of Mabbug, he was also metropolitan of the see of Euphratesia, comprising about a dozen dioceses.[48] Prior to his appointment, the see had been a centre first of Nestorianism (following the Council of Ephesus in 431), and then of Chalcedonianism; and Philoxenus faced much opposition as he sought to make Mabbug a stronghold of monophysitism. It appears that, while he gained fame and influence as a theologian and controversialist to be reckoned with, he never really won the hearts of the people to whom he was pastor. The anonymous chronicler of 846 states that under Flavian (498-512) he was without authority.[49] An insight into the kind of thing that chronicler meant is provided by a brief statement made by Joshua the Stylite writing in 507, who records that in the year 809 (A.D. 497-8) the bishop of Mabbug was in Edessa during a pagan festival -- "of whom beyond all others it was thought that he had taken upon him to labour in teaching; yet he did not speak with them on this subject more than one day."[50] Joshua had obviously expected Philoxenus to display his moral courage, but was disappointed. The great theologian had failed as a pastor.[51]

The years between his elevation to the episcopate in 485

and the above-quoted incident in Edessa in 497-8 are silent ones in the life of Philoxenus as far as the literary records are concerned. During this period the Emperor Zeno died (491) and was succeeded by Anastasius, who continued to reign until 518. Both emperors were sympathetic to monophysitism. In Antioch in 489, the patriarchate passed from one friend (Peter the Fuller) to another (Palladius, who died in 498). So these were years in which Philoxenus was free to pursue his episcopal duties, strengthen the monophysite hold in the east, and develop his theological acumen by writing extensively. Budge suggests that the *Discourses* were written during this time; and the fact that they contain no reference to the theological controversies in which Philoxenus was at other times involved, indicates that they were produced in a period of relative calm.[52] Since at least the last fragment of British Museum Manuscript Add. 17,126 (which is the focus of this dissertation) was copied in 511 according to the colophon, it is conceivable that that fragment along with some of the others in the manuscript, was written during this period.

The year 498 disturbed whatever calm Philoxenus had been experiencing in the preceding thirteen years of his episcopate. It was the year of Palladius' death and the subsequent appointment of Flavian II as patriarch of Antioch, who was chosen because he was reputed to be opposed to the Chalcedonian teachings.[53] Within a year of his installation, Flavian made an apparent about-face, explicitly aligned himself with the Chalcedonians, notably the patriarchs of Constantinople (Macedonius) and Jerusalem (Elias), and severed the ecclesiastical tie between the patriarchate of Alexandria and his own see of Antioch.[54] Such a radical shift in position could not go unchallenged by Philoxenus who immediately moved to force Flavian back into declaring for monophysitism. A struggle between the two men ensued which lasted until 512 when Flavian was banished to Petra.[55] These years of controversy are reflected in some of Philoxenus' writings. During this period, Philoxenus had also to face the terrible consequences of the Roman-Persian war (502-505) which wreaked havoc on the border provinces including his own metropolitan see.[56] In his *Letter to the Monks of Senun*, he complains that during the Persian

War Flavian continued to plot against him.[57]

Flavian's banishment in 512 was a victory for Philoxenus and his party, the result of which was the appointment of the monophysite, Severus, to fill the patriarchal throne of Antioch. There was no doubt about Severus' monophysitism, and the six years of his patriarchate were ones in which Philoxenus cooperated fully with him. Severus in turn constantly consulted with Philoxenus, giving due respect to the latter's seniority in years.[58] No warm friendship seems, however, to have developed between the two. Their backgrounds were quite different: Severus was a Greek-speaking Pisidian trained in Alexandria, while Philoxenus was a Syriac-speaking Persian trained in Edessa. Prior to his accession to the patriarchate, Severus was acclaimed as a writer and orator; indeed, one of his biographers (and a contemporary) says that he was considered to be a second Chrysostom.[59] It may be that their obvious differences in age, culture, status, and popular acclaim kept these two leading monophysites from establishing any close relationship with one another, in spite of their theological concord.

The scene was radically altered once more for Philoxenus when in 518 Anastasius, who for twenty-seven years had occupied the imperial throne in Constantinople and had been a good friend of the monophysites, died. He was succeeded by Justin I, whose sympathies lay entirely with the "orthodox" or Chalcedonian party. On Easter Sunday, 519, "a solemn ceremony was held in rehabilitation of the Council of Chalcedon."[60] This paved the way for reunion with Rome which came soon after. All leading monophysites were anathematized. Severus had to flee to Egypt where he remained in exile until his death in 538. Philoxenus was banished to Philippopolis in Thrace where he continued to write on behalf of his monophysite beliefs, at least in a limited way, as we see in a few of his letters.[61] The weight of written testimony and tradition indicates that he was taken to Gangra in Paphlagonia where he was martyred by asphyxiation, although de Halleux takes issue with this tradition, believing that Philoxenus first wintered in Gangra on his way to Philippopolis where he spent the remainder of his life in exile.[62] He died probably in 523.

B. *THE POLITICAL AND RELIGIOUS BACKGROUND*

In 439, about the time of Philoxenus' birth in Persia,[63] Yezdigird II (d. 457) came to the throne of that land. Almost immediately, the new king declared war on Rome because (it would appear) the latter had been strengthening its defences along the Persian frontier.[64] Yezdigird was in no position to sustain his attack on Rome across the border at Nisibis and in Roman Armenia, for the Ephthalites or White Huns were threatening him in the northeast. Peace was soon declared (c. 442), among the terms for which was the agreement on both sides not to build fortifications within a certain distance of their common frontier. This peace lasted for sixty-one years. In 503, war broke out once again with the Persian army's invasion of Roman Armenia which was laid waste. Kobad, the Persian king, then marched south, captured Amida, and made incursions into Osroene and even into Euphratesia where Philoxenus was metropolitan. Again, because of pressure from the White Huns, the Persians had to withdraw and a peace was concluded in 505. War broke out once again in 524, which was at least a year after Philoxenus' death.

During his lifetime the church in Persia was decisively separated from the church in the west (which itself was not without its schisms). The church in Mesopotamia had grown without much help from the west. In the early centuries, it had developed its own New Testament canon, its own liturgies, and its own hagiography; and its native language was Syriac. When one adds the fact that the eastern part of this Mesopotamian Christianity had its birth and nurture in a nation and culture which was outside the direct influence of the Roman Empire, it is obvious that the tie between the Persian Church and the Church of the west was never strong. Whatever bond existed was to be severed in the fifth century for two main reasons. In the first place, the Persian Christians had suffered periodic persecution partly because their religion had progressively become identified with Rome; they were, therefore, treated with suspicion.[65] The Zoroastrian priests helped to foster this suspicion. As early as 424, the Persian Christians, at a synod over which the Catholicos Dad-Isho presided, declared themselves to be an autonomous church, completely independent of the western Fathers.[66] The declaration evidently had the desired effect -- Persian Christians suffered much less persecution after 424. It was, however, unilateral, and went unrecognized by the western church.

The second reason for the separation of the Persian Church came later in the fifth century and was basically theological in nature. It is ironic that the church which had been struggling to free itself from western domination, was to be identified with a Greek theologian, Nestorius, and in that identification find its freedom. Nestorius had been condemned as a heretic at the Council of Ephesus in 431 because of his formulation of the two distinct natures of Christ. He had been a student of Theodore of Mopsuestia at the School of Antioch. In 435, Ḥiba succeeded Rabbula as bishop of Edessa, and began to introduce the writings of Theodore to the students of the Edessan School of the Persians which, while not in Persia, was an important centre of learning for the church of that country. Ḥiba thus had Nestorian sympathies, though he never admitted to being a Nestorian, and his influence on his Persian students was considerable. When Ḥiba died in 457, an anti-Nestorian bishop, Nonnus by name, replaced him. It was only a matter of time before the Nestorian scholars fled to Persia where they helped to establish a school in Nisibis, founded by Bar-Sauma, the Nestorian bishop of that city (and an alumnus of the Edessan School), with Narsai, the former head of the Edessan School, as its first principal.[67] This School of Nisibis, continuing the work of the School in Edessa which was closed in 489, was to exert a tremendous influence on the Persian Church.

When Philoxenus' family migrated from Beth-Garmai in Persia to the Tur-Abdinian region, they moved into the Eastern Roman Empire. Theodosius II was still on the throne in Constantinople.[68] His reign (408-450) began (while he was still a child) with the sacking of Rome by Alaric in 410, and was marked by external strife (two Persian wars, 421 and 441, Vandal piracy which was checked in 431, and in his last decade increasing pressure from the Huns under Attila), and internal ecclesiastical dissension.

In an effort to bring peace to a discordant church,

Theodosius called the Council of Ephesus together in 431.[69] The specific issue with which this Council had to deal was that of the controversial teaching of Nestorius who became bishop of Constantinople in 428. Nestorius had suggested that the word θεοτόκος ("God-bearer") as applied to the Virgin Mary was inappropriate, although it had been part of the language of popular Christian devotion. Cyril, patriarch of Alexandria, defended the use of the word and accused Nestorius of dividing the Person of Christ into two Sons of God, the one being the eternal Word and the other, the human Son of Mary. The conflict was more than theological, for apparently Cyril vehemently resisted the claim of supremacy for the see of Constantinople over against the ancient see of Alexandria -- a claim which was supported by Canon 3 of the Council of Constantinople held in 381. Cyril of Alexandria presided over the Council and pressed for the condemnation of Nestorius (who refused to attend the meetings) before the Patriarch of Antioch and his bishops arrived. Nestorius was deposed and sent into exile, but the Council did not resolve the dogmatic difficulties which Nestorius and his friends had raised. The christological controversy had only begun.

A power struggle ensued which was more political than theological, though fought in the arena of theology. Cyril of Alexandria continued to press for the monophysite position until his death in 444. His successor, Dioscurus, was even more zealous on behalf of the Alexandrian cause. Eutyches, an aged and influential monk in Constantinople, thought that he could resolve the quarrel by affirming that Christ had "two natures before, one after the incarnation."[70] For this, the Synod of Constantinople (at the instigation of Dioscurus) deposed him as archimandrite in 448. The following year, the "Robber Synod" of Ephesus (controlled by monophysites) reinstated him. "Eutychianism" was an extreme form of monophysitism which later monophysites like Philoxenus felt constrained to condemn.[71] In the same year (449), Eutyches appealed to Pope Leo I of Rome who responded by writing his famous "Tome" addressed to Flavian, patriarch of Constantinople, in which he condemned Eutychianism and expounded his understanding of orthodox christology in language that insisted on "two natures after the incarnation." The Council of Chalcedon two years later (451) declared Leo's Tome to be a true expression of the Catholic faith, and based its creedal statement upon it.[72]

In 450, Theodosius died and was succeeded by Marcian as Emperor of the East. The new emperor was determined to establish the unity of the Church on the basis of uniformity of religious belief.[73] To fulfil this purpose, he called a general council of the Church to meet at Nicea on September 1, 451. After the bishops were gathered there, they were ordered to proceed to Chalcedon, closer to the capital, where they were convened and where they dealt with the business of the Church in accordance with the imperial will. The outcome of the Council was a theological victory for the west with the condemnation of Dioscurus, bishop of Alexandria, and his monophysite colleagues. Both Nestorianism and Eutychianism were condemned. The Church was more divided than ever, the divisions being perhaps more political and national than theological and religious. These divisions were to continue beyond the lifetime of Philoxenus who, along with his fellow monophysites, regarded the Chalcedonian Creed as nothing more than a statement of the Nestorian heresy.[74] While Marcian lived (he died in 457), the decisions of Chalcedon were enforced; but after his death, his successor, Leo I, vacillated, and the monophysites regained ground in the east.

Zeno came to the imperial throne in 474, but soon after his accession he was dethroned and exiled for twenty months before returning to Constantinople in 476.[75] Once again, political pressure was used in an attempt to bring peace and unity to the Church. Under the influence of Peter Mongus, monophysite patriarch of Alexandria, and Acacius, patriarch of Constantinople, Zeno (in 482) issued a document known as the "Henoticon," or plan of union, in the form of a letter addressed to the churches of "Egypt, Libya, and Pentapolis."[76] Its stated object was to restore peace and unity to the Church. It emphasized the sufficiency of the first three General Councils, Nicea (325), Constantinople (381) and Ephesus (431), giving pre-eminence to the first and ignoring the formulations of Chalcedon. As R. V. Sellars has stated: "Clearly, the

Henoticon was drawn up in favour of the monophysites, who came to regard this Government Creed as 'abrogating the Synod of Chalcedon and Leo's impious Toma'."[77] Like most plans of union in the history of the church, this one both succeeded and failed. It succeeded (at least, superficially) in uniting the church in the Eastern Empire except for the extreme monophysites among the Egyptian monks and the unrepentant Chalcedonians among the Constantinopolitan monks. But it also brought schism between East and West, for the Bishop of Rome, Simplicius, intent on upholding Chalcedon, excommunicated Acacius, Peter Mongus and the Emperor Zeno in 484. This "Acacian" schism lasted for thirty-five years during which Philoxenus was most active in promoting the cause of monophysitism. His writings include explicit support of the *Henoticon*:

> We should accept the *Henoticon* which expelled all the additions and novelties which arose against the faith of the three hundred and eighteen and of the one hundred and fifty Fathers.[78]

He goes on to explain that the word "Henoticon" means "unifies," "because it brought unity to the holy churches in every place."[79]

Zeno died in 491, and was succeeded by Anastasius, who had been a financial administrator under him. Euphemius, patriarch of Constantinople, opposed the accession of the new emperor, and did not withdraw his opposition until Anastasius had signed a document accepting the Chalcedonian doctrines, swearing by fearful oaths (ὅρκων δεινῶν) that "he would maintain the faith inviolate and introduce no innovations into the holy Church of God when he became emperor."[80] However, Anastasius' sympathies were with the monophysites whom he increasingly favoured until his death in 518.

History records two occasions on which Philoxenus visited Anastasius in Constantinople. The first was in 499 when he personally protested against the elevation of Flavian to the patriarchate of Antioch, but to no avail.[81] The emperor continued his support of Flavian. In 502, the Persian War broke out, and Syria being on the border was greatly affected, both by the incursions of the Persian forces into that territory and by the settlement of monophysite refugees from

Persia where they had been identified with Rome and persecuted by the Nestorians.[82] The influx of Persian monophysites may have strengthened Philoxenus' hand against Flavian. At any rate, in 507 (two years after the conclusion of the Persian War) Anastasius invited Philoxenus to Constantinople, probably because of the mounting tension in Syria caused by the growing animosity between the latter and his patriarch in Antioch. What the immediate outcome of the visit was, is uncertain. We know that it was an occasion for the Chalcedonians of the capital to incite the populace to riot, and Philoxenus had to be smuggled out of the city.[83] We can be sure that Philoxenus pressed for the deposition of Flavian from the see of Antioch, to which pressure Anastasius finally submitted in 512 when Flavian was replaced by Severus.

The year 518 inaugurated a new era in the ecclesiastical history of the Eastern Empire.[84] It was the year of Anastasius' death and the accession of Justin as emperor. Justin was convinced that the Council of Chalcedon had to be upheld. He set about restoring the decrees of that Council and re-establishing relations with the Bishop of Rome. The reunion of Rome and Constantinople after thirty-five years of schism was consummated on Easter, 519. The new Chalcedonian policy entailed the excommunication and banishment of monophysite leaders including Severus of Antioch and Philoxenus of Mabbug. Behind the throne of the new emperor stood his brilliant nephew, Justinian, who was to succeed him in 527, and who throughout the reign of his uncle shaped the religious and other policies of the empire.[85] Eli of Qartamin blames Justin for the death of Philoxenus in 523.[86]

C. *THE LITERARY ACTIVITY OF PHILOXENUS*

1. *The Philoxenian Version of the Scriptures*

For Philoxenus, the scriptures of the Old and New Testaments were essential for a full understanding of the Christian faith and life. In his writings, which are laced with biblical proof-texts, the Bible is clearly his final court of appeal. His *Book on Selected Passages from the Gospels* expresses his concern that biblical translation be as faithful to the original as possible:[87]

> If those who translated (the biblical text) had considered that it was not right for the existence of Christ, or of God, or of the Son to be expressed in corrupted language, they ought to have known that those words do not suit each and every language. He who would translate faithfully must choose (his words) carefully, seeking only those phrases and nouns which were uttered by God or by His Spirit through the prophets and the apostles; because those things which are expressed in the Holy Scriptures are not (so much) the product of human thoughts that they will welcome any correction or reconstruction (which may be offered) by the human mind. As for the Greeks, then, each one of those verbs and nouns which, we have recalled, was spoken by the Evangelists and by the Apostle, is thus to be expressed as something said by us: 'He came into being by the seed of David in the flesh';[88] and not 'He was generated in the flesh.' And again, 'The book of the coming into being of Jesus Christ';[89] and 'The coming into being of Jesus Christ was in this way.'[90] Because the scriptures of the New Testament were spoken in their language (i.e. Greek), they (i.e. the translations) must especially be expressed to agree with them, and not with those things derived from that which was translated, that is, those things which are of its (the translation's) own opinion, and not of the teaching of the Spirit. Therefore, anyone who in a novel way changes or translates the verbs and the nouns which were uttered by the Spirit, is not only worthy of blame and reproach, but is also wicked and blasphemous, and in league with the Marcionites and Manichaeans.

It is not surprising then, that Philoxenus should speak of the need for a new translation:

> Because of this, it is also incumbent upon us at this time to translate anew the holy scriptures of the New Testament from Greek into Syriac.[91]

We have to turn to other witnesses to learn that a new Syriac translation was in fact made under Philoxenus' guidance. The earliest of these witnesses, Moses of Aggel, writing later in the sixth century, states that the chorepiscopus, Polycarp, "translated the New Testament and David from the Greek into Syriac, for Aksenaia (Philoxenus) of Mabbug."[92] Philoxenus had spoken of the need for a new translation of the New Testament, but in the above quotation Moses of Aggel indicates that the Psalms were included in the new translation made by Polycarp, the chorepiscopus under Philoxenus.[93]

The next witness, Thomas of Harkel, who issues a Syriac version of the New Testament in 616, provides the following information:

> This is the book of the four Holy Evangelists originally translated very carefully and painstakingly from the Greek language into Syriac in the city of Mabbug in the year 819 of Alexander of Macedon in the days of the holy Mar Philoxenus, the Confessor, bishop of that city. It was afterwards that I, poor Thomas, very carefully compared it with three Greek manuscripts which are highly regarded and accurate, at Enaton of Alexandria. . . . And it was written and compared in the place mentioned, in the year 927 of Alexander, in the 4th Indict. The Lord only knows how much labour and care I have (put) into it (i.e. Gospels) and into its fellows (the rest of the New Testament). . . .[94]

From this we gather that the Philoxenian version of at least the New Testament was completed in 508, and that the Harklean version published a century later was some sort of edition of it. The problem is: what sort of edition was it? What did Thomas of Harkel mean when he used the word ܐܬܦܚܡ, which I have translated "compared," but which could also be translated by "collated" or by "imitated" or "revised"?[95] Whatever the ambiguities, it is clear that the Harklean version bears witness to the fact that the Philoxenian version once existed and that the later version was closely related to it.[96]

A third important witness to the existence of the Philoxenian version is the great Syriac historian and polymath of the thirteenth century, Bar Hebraeus. In the preface to his *Scholia on the Old Testament*, after referring to the Peshitta translation of the New Testament, Bar Hebraeus writes:

> Afterward a second time it was translated more elegantly from the Greek to the Syriac in the city of Mabbug in the days of the pious Philoxenus; and it was revised a third time in Alexandria by the pious Thomas of Harkel in the holy monastery of the Antonians. The Septuagintal Old Testament, however, Paul, bishop of Tella of Mawzalat, translated from Greek to Syriac.[97]

The fact that Bar Hebraeus speaks of Thomas of Harkel's activity as a "third time" indicates that he believed the Harklean to be a version distinct from the Philoxenian; and, therefore, for him the word ܐܬܦܚܡ (the same word that Thomas had used in his colophon) had the idea of "revision" within it as Sprengling and Graham have rightly perceived.[98] It is noteworthy that Bar Hebraeus regarded the Philoxenian version as "more elegant" than the Peshitta, perhaps suggesting that a copy of it was available to him, upon which he could base such a value judgment.

From the above evidence it is clear that a distinct Syriac version of the scriptures was produced under the guidance and patronage of Philoxenus, and that the translator was probably Polycarp, his chorepiscopus.[99] Since no certain copy of this "Philoxenian" version has survived, many questions remain as to its extent and nature. In his commentary on John, Philoxenus speaks of the need to "retranslate the New Testament from Greek to Syriac," and says nothing of the Old Testament.[100] About thirty years after Philoxenus' death, Moses of Aggel states that the chorepiscopus, Polycarp, "translated the New Testament and David (i.e. the Psalms) from Greek into Syriac" for Philoxenus.[101] A century after Philoxenus, Thomas of Harkel claims that his version is a "revision" (?) of the Philoxenian version of the "book of the four holy Evangelists . . . and its fellows" -- presumably meaning the rest of the New Testament.[102] Bar Hebraeus also indicates that the Philoxenian version was limited to the New Testament.[103] However, a citation for an alternative reading of Isaiah 9:6 in a seventh-century Milanese manuscript of the Syro-Hexaplar Old Testament explicitly states that it is "from the version that was translated by the care of the holy Philoxenus."[104] If this note is accurate (as Gwynn and Ceriani before him believed),[105] then the Philoxenian version extended beyond "the New Testament and the Psalms" (as Moses of Aggel claimed) to Isaiah and perhaps the rest of the Old Testament (in which case we cannot take Eli of Qartamin more seriously on this point). But if there was a Philoxenian Old Testament, we must ask why Moses of Aggel, writing in the sixth century, limited his statement to "the New Testament and David." Beyond these two references, one to the Psalms and the other to Isaiah, there is no evidence for a Philoxenian Old Testament.

Even a Philoxenian New Testament presents problems. We cannot assume that the New Testament books which Philoxenus accepted as canonical, were the same as those received by the Western Church. Certainly, the Peshitta, the vulgate version of Syriac-speaking Christianity in Philoxenus' day, lacked the four Minor Catholic Epistles (2 Peter, 2 and 3 John, and Jude) and the Book of Revelation, which were generally received in the west before the end of the fourth century; but did the Philoxenian version include these books? Gwynn was convinced that the Syriac version of the Minor Catholic Epistles and of Revelation which he published were Philoxenian, and his conclusions in this regard are generally accepted by scholars.[106] But this is not as certain as it would appear. J. Lebon pointed out two years after Gwynn's publication that of the numerous biblical texts cited by Philoxenus in the works published to that date (1911), not one had a quotation from the Minor Catholic Epistles or Revelation.[107] Philoxenian works published since that time confirm Lebon's observations, and the same may be said of British Museum Ms. Add. 17,126, which is the subject of this dissertation.[108] We have thus no reason to believe that Philoxenus regarded these books as canonical, and it is doubtful that his chorepiscopus would have translated them without his superior's approval.[109]

A major concern of this dissertation will be to examine the biblical quotations in the unpublished manuscript before us (i.e. British Museum Add. 17,126) to see what light it may shed on the Syriac versions available to Philoxenus, including the one which bears his name. The value of this procedure was recognized by G. Zuntz in 1945, and has been reinforced by A. Vööbus and A. de Halleux.[110] Zuntz focused particular attention on the biblical quotations in Philoxenus' *Three Discourses*.[111] On the basis of his detailed study of these quotations, he provisionally concluded that "behind these Philoxenian citations there lies a definite text, different from, and intermediate between, the Peshitta and the Harklean."[112] He recognized that more work had to be done along similar lines before reaching a definite conclusion, and suggested that two unpublished manuscripts, fragments of Philoxenus' commentary on the Gospels, be subjected to such scrutiny.[113] These manuscripts are the so-called *Commentary on Matthew and Luke* (Brit. Mus. Add. 17,126 -- the subject of this dissertation) and the *Book of Selected Passages from the Gospels* (Brit. Mus. Add. 14,534). A. Vööbus, examining these and other fragments, confirms Zuntz's findings and sees also traces of an Old Syriac version; but he provides only selected examples of his comparative studies.[114] We shall attempt to provide detailed comparative tables exhibiting all the examples of the biblical texts quoted in British Museum Ms. Add. 17,126 before drawing any conclusions.

2. *The Gospel Commentaries*

Philoxenus not only sponsored a new Syriac version of at least the New Testament, he himself engaged in expository writing. It was natural for him to do so. He had a strong sense of the inspiration and authority of the Christian scriptures. Although he did not develop the notion, it is clear that he regarded the Bible as the ultimate witness to divine truth to which the councils of the Church had to bow. He could anathematize, for example, the Council of Chalcedon without compunction, which in fact he did at some length.[115] Moreover, he was educated in the School of the Persians in Edessa where the Antiochian tradition of biblical interpretation with its emphasis on the precise historico-grammatical meaning of the text, held sway.[116] In spite of his lifelong rebellion against what he regarded as the Nestorian theology of his alma mater, he never denied the validity of the basic training in biblical exegesis which he received as a student; indeed, he used it effectively in his polemics against both Nestorians and Chalcedonians.

While he ranged widely in his use of the Old and New Testaments in his writings, his expository work was apparently limited to the Gospels of Matthew, Luke and John. Even here no complete Gospel commentary is extant, though some ancient witnesses speak as if such a commentary existed. What does exist is a number of small unpublished fragments found in various manuscripts mostly belonging to the British Museum, and two very important but incomplete manuscripts (also in the British Museum), the so-called *Matthew-Luke Commentary*[117] and the *Book on Selected Passages from the Gospels*.[118] J. S. Assemanus, who did not have access to these manuscripts, cited four Syriac writers as witnesses to the existence of a Philoxenian Gospel Commentary; namely, Bar Salibi, Bar Hebraeus, an anonymous author of a "Syriac exposition of the Gospels by means of question and answer," and John of Dara.[119] De Halleux speaks of the existence of such a commentary as being "abondamment attestée . . ."

> . . . par de nombreux fragments de chaînes et d'homiliaires syriaques, arméniens, arabes ou éthiopiens; (et) par des extraits et des références chez les exégètes jacobites postérieurs,[120]

and goes on to list exhaustively all the fragments, extracts and references known to him which in any way appear to reflect something of its contents. On the basis of his extensive research, de Halleux concludes that the Philoxenian commentary was limited to the three Gospels: Matthew, Luke, and John.[121]

The available material, however, is much more limited in its scope than the last statement suggests. On the face of it, de Halleux has amassed a great deal of evidence for the reconstruction of a "commentary" by the bishop of Mabbug, but close scrutiny reveals that his conclusions are ill-founded. To establish the literary context of the so-called *Matthew-Luke Commentary*, it is necessary to re-examine de Halleux' thesis in some detail. This we propose to do in the remainder of this section. While the problem of the term "commentary" (ܦܘܫܩܐ) will be raised here, full discussion of its meaning with reference to the Philoxenian corpus will be reserved for the third chapter of this dissertation.

According to de Halleux, the extant fragments of Philoxenus' Gospel Commentary are on the following passages:
Matthew 1:17; 2:1, 14, 15; 3:1-16; 4:1-11; 5:17; 11:11(?); 13:16-17(?); 16:16-17; 22:29-32(?); 25:14-30(?); 26:26-29, 36-44; 27:45-53(?).
Luke 1:26-35; 2:7, 21, 24-39, 40, 42-46, 51-52; 3:21-38.
John 1:1-17; 2:4, 19; 3:13, 25, 27; 4:10; 6:51; 20:17.[122]

The evidence for a commentary on the whole of Matthew is the most impressive. In the first place, the distribution of the Matthean material cited above suggests it, even when the dubious fragments are discounted. Secondly, the comparative abundance of Philoxenian citations in the later Jacobite commentaries on Matthew of George of Be'eltan, Bar-Salibi, and Bar Hebraeus, are a further witness to it. Here is the list of such passages: Matthew 1:15, 18; 3:1, 4, 11; 4:1, 3, 5, 11; 8:13, 24; 9:2, 6, 37; 26:23; 27:56(?).[123] Again, as de Halleux himself admits not all of these are of unquestionable value, but together their testimony cannot be disregarded. Thirdly, the titles of some of these fragments explicitly state that they are from a Matthew commentary,[124] and some indicate that the quotation is from a given chapter in the commentary.[125] Finally, the colophon of the so-called *Matthew-Luke Commentary*, which was written during the lifetime of Philoxenus, affirms that it is "the end of the fourth book of the commentary of Matthew and Luke which was made by Philoxenus, lover of God, bishop of Mabbug; it was written in the city of Mabbug in the year 822 of Alexander of Macedon."[126]

The above-quoted colophon suggests the existence of a commentary on Luke, but all the extant material points to such a commentary's being limited at best to the first three chapters of that Gospel. The bulk of this material is found in the manuscript before us, British Museum Add. 17,126. British Museum Add. 12,145, fol. 50r, quoted "from chapter 32 of the Commentary on how our Lord was born in a cave and laid in a manger."[127] The same manuscript goes on to cite "chapter 35 against the Nestorians; a Commentary on those things which are set out below" (i.e. "in what follows").[128] De Halleux contends that such evidence indicates that the "chapter" divisions found in Matthew are continued into the first three chapters of Luke, for the last chapter cited with reference to Matthew is "chapter 29" on Matthew 26:36-44 or 27:45-53.[129] Moreover, a note in the colophon of our "*Matthew-Luke Commentary*" states, "In this book is a commentary on five chapters taken from the Evangelist, Luke"; although the contents make no mention of such a chapter division.[130] These notes appear to substantiate the bald statement of the colophon which speaks of a (single) commentary on Matthew and Luke, and which after all was written when Philoxenus was very much alive and active as a writer and preacher of considerable influence.

The evidence for a Philoxenian commentary on John's Gospel is meagre. The largest of the extant expository works is found in British Museum Add. 14,534 and is one hundred and ninety-nine folios long. De Halleux refers to it as "Commentaire de Jean 1:1-17";[131] though he recognizes that while the work contains short expository passages on John 1:10-13 (fols. 284-294) and John 1:14-17 (fols. 195v-197r), it is supremely a theological and polemical treatise on the

Incarnation, "le 'devenir' du Verbe . . . où le verset Jean 1:14 forme le pivot de l'argumentation."[132] Nowhere in the manuscript itself is there the suggestion made that it is a commentary on John's Gospel as such.[133] The colophon provides a much more general title: "The end of the writing of this book on chapters selected from the Evangelists, made by the holy Philoxenus, bishop of Mabbug."[134] It is noteworthy that no mention is made of the term "commentary" (ܦܘܫܩܐ). There is also no suggestion of a "chapter" division in this work such as we find in some of the Matthew-Luke material -- a fact which surely indicates that the English word "chapter" is an inadequate translation of ܪܫܐ in this colophon and perhaps elsewhere. The use of this and other terms will be considered below. Suffice it here to observe that to call this long work by Philoxenus a commentary is unwarranted and misleading. It is a theological treatise on the Incarnation hammered out in the heat of controversy.

De Halleux has isolated twelve fragments of what he regards as Johannine commentary, apart from the work discussed above (which is Fragment 2 in his analysis). Close scrutiny of these, however, reveals the following facts.[135] Fragment no. 1, from the so-called *Matthew-Luke Commentary* (British Museum Add. 17,126), is considered by de Halleux to be part of the large work on "John 1:1-17" (Add. 14,534), and therefore need not be regarded as "commentary."[136] Fragments 3, 4, 6, 7, 8, and 9 (on John 2:4, 2:19, 3:13, 3:25, 3:27, and 4:10) are all passages in Bar Salibi's Commentary on John in which Philoxenus is quoted or alluded to, but in none of them does Bar Salibi suggest that he is quoting from a Philoxenian "Commentary" on John.[137] He could just as well be quoting from some other type of literature. Fragment 5 (perhaps on John 2:19) is found in a catena of ecclesiastical authorities written in the tenth century, and is introduced by the words, "from the second 'memra' of the Commentary on John."[138] Here the word "commentary" is used, but it cannot have the sense of exegetical commentary when the title speaks of the second "memra" (homily or discourse), suggesting that it is one of a series of sermons on John. "Memra" is used again in Fragment 10, this time without any reference to "commentary" (though it is inferred): "From the 'Memra' on what our Lord said, I am indeed the bread of life for I have come down from Heaven." (John 6:51)[139] Again, it would appear as if the quotation is taken from a sermon or other discourse rather than a commentary. The same may be said for Fragments 11, 12 and 13 (on John 20:17).[140] The title of Fragment 11 states that it is "from the seventeenth 'memra' on (this) saying; I am ascending to my Father"; that of Fragment 12, "from the commentary of the holy Gospel according to John"; and that of Fragment 13 simply identifies Philoxenus as the source of the quotation. One can only conclude that if a Philoxenian commentary on John ever existed (as the titles of two out of thirteen fragments state), the nature of that commentary was homiletical and polemical rather than exegetical.

Philoxenus rarely alludes to Mark's Gospel in his writings, and no one has ever suggested that he wrote a commentary of any sort on it. In his "Index of Biblical Quotations" in the *Discourses*, Budge lists some seventeen passages in which he sees quotations from Mark's Gospel.[141] Actually, only four of these can be shown to be peculiarly Marcan (Mark 7:33f, 9:25, 9:46, 10:17f), while the others could equally be from Matthew or Luke. De Halleux sees two allusions to Mark's Gospel in Philoxenus' *Letter to the Monks of Senun* (Mark 3:17 and 4:38), but the second one has its Synoptic equivalents in Matthew and Luke.[142] Mark is not cited or alluded to in either of the so-called Gospel Commentaries.[143] One clear and explicit reference to Mark is found in the third of Philoxenus' *Three Discourses on the Trinity and the Incarnation* in which Mark 1:1 is quoted and identified by the author.[144] The paucity of references to Mark may be explained (a) by assuming a personal preference entirely due to Philoxenus' taste, or (b) by "the low estimate of Mark held commonly after the fourth century,"[145] or (c) by the fact that about ninety per cent of the subject matter of Mark is found in Matthew and over fifty per cent is in Luke leaving very little to be identified as peculiarly Marcan when one comes to consider the sources of isolated Synoptic quotations in an author like Philoxenus;[146] or (d) by the christological concerns which loom large in the Philoxenian corpus and which find their "proof-texts" in the explicit affirmations of Matthew, Luke and John on the Incarnation. Probably a combination of all these factors has produced the apparent lack of Marcan material in Philoxenus.

In examining the evidence for the existence of Philoxenian Gospel Commentaries, consideration must be given to the Syriac vocabulary used to indicate their nature. The most common word in this connection is ܦܘܫܩܐ, usually translated "commentary." *The Thesaurus Syriacus* provides the following range of meanings for ܦܘܫܩܐ: "interpretatio, ἑρμηνεία, commentario, ἐξήγησις, expositio, commentarius, versio, translatio."[147] Philoxenus uses the verb ܦܫܩ to mean "translate" in the excerpts already provided from the *Book on Selected Passages from the Gospels*.[148] In the document before us, he uses the verb and the noun to mean "interpret or explain" and "interpretation or explanation" respectively.[149] In its colophon (written during Philoxenus' lifetime), ܦܘܫܩܐ occurs twice and may be translated "commentary," but in a rather loose sense for the contents of the manuscript do not reflect the work of a biblical "commentator."[150] This loose or ill-defined use of ܦܘܫܩܐ also obtains in the titles of some of the fragments of Gospel "commentaries" as outlined by de Halleux.[151]

Of the thirty-six fragments of commentary on Matthew and Luke listed by de Halleux, seven are found in the so-called *Matthew-Luke Commentary*, the character of which will be examined in detail below.[152] Of the remaining twenty-nine, fourteen are designated as coming from a Philoxenian "commentary" and four of these are further qualified as being "from the chapters against" either Diodore, the Nestorians, or Theodore. The titles of the fragments on Matthew-Luke may be analyzed as follows:

By Philoxenus			6
" "	Commentary (ܦܘܫܩܐ)		10
" "	"	chapters against Diodore	1
" "	"	chapters against Nestorians	2
" "	"	chapters against Theodore	1
" "	from chapter(s) (ܪܫܐ)		1
" "	" "	against Diodore	1
" "	" "	" Nestorians	3
" "	from the section (ܦܘܠܓܐ)[153]		1
" "	from the essay (ܫܪܒܐ)		1
" "	from the discourse (ܡܐܡܪܐ)		2

Total fragments of "Matthew-Luke Commentary" (excluding the fragments in Brit. Mus. Add. 17,126)[154] 29

Only ten out of twenty-nine fragments speak of a Philoxenian "commentary" in an unqualified way, and when the contents of those ten fragments are examined it becomes clear that what has been called Philoxenian commentary is something other than the systematic exegesis of a biblical book. For example, de Halleux identifies the first such fragment with the seventh chapter (probably) of the commentary on Matthew dealing with Matthew 3:1-16.[155] Now this fragment contains four extracts on the following subjects: (1) how the Incarnation fulfils the original intention of creation; (2) how the spiritual life is developed (baptism is one of the steps); (3) how the baptism of Jesus marked the beginning of the reconciliation of the world to God; and (4) how the Christian grows in spiritual understanding after baptism. It is obvious from this summary that the only relation between this fragment and Matthew 3:1-16 is that the former contains selections of a theological work in which baptism has a prominent place while the latter is a Gospel account of Jesus' baptism by John the Baptist. In the latter, John's message and ministry are described, Pharisees and Sadducees are denounced, the Baptist's reaction to Jesus' request for baptism is recorded, and the descent of the Spirit upon Jesus in the form of a dove with the voice from heaven confirming His divine sonship is narrated; but none of these important details is even mentioned in these selections which are long enough to include at least some of them, yet in this fragment they are said to be taken "From the book of the commentary of Matthew by the holy Mar Aksenaia" (i.e. Philoxenus).[156]

The issue is brought into sharper focus when one considers the fact that only one quotation from Matthew is found in this fragment and it comes at the end of the fourth extract where Matthew 3:12 (fol. 172v) occurs without further exegetical comment. On the other hand, the following New Testament passages are quoted in the fragment: John 3:3, 5 (fol. 171v); 14:28 (fol. 162v); 16:12, 13 (fol. 165r); 1 Corinthians 3:12-15 (fol. 172r); 11:3 (fol. 162v); 13:13; 15:24-26 (fol. 167r); 15:28 (fol. 163r); and 2 Corinthians 12:2-4 (fol. 164v).[157] More commentary is provided on some of these than on anything from Matthew. For example, Philoxenus quotes from 1 Corinthians 3:12-15, then proceeds to explain that "the gold, silver, and precious stones" to which Paul refers, are related to the spiritual strengths of the soul; "error, evil and demons are compared to wood, hay and stubble."[158] This is followed by the quotation from Matthew 3:12. Precisely the same order is given to a similar passage in the prologue to Philoxenus' "Discourses on the Discipline of Life and Character,"[159] where he quotes from 1 Corinthians 3:12, 13, comments on the meaning of "gold, silver, precious stones, wood, hay, stubble" in a way that is similar to the above-mentioned fragment, and then cites Matthew 3:12. Because this passage is found in the *Discourses*, no one thinks of calling it commentary. Similarly, in spite of its title within a very long anthology of theological extracts, this fragment should not be called a "commentary."[160]

The next two fragments which are listed by de Halleux as coming from a Philoxenian commentary on Matthew and which in their titles refer explicitly to Philoxenus as the commentator, are found in an Ethiopic manuscript of the seventeenth century containing a "catena patrum" or commentary on Matthew's Gospel.[161] De Halleux is silent concerning the fact that the other two Ethiopic manuscripts containing the same catena on Matthew make no mention of the names of the several commentators quoted including that of Philoxenus.[162] Even if such a late manuscript preserves genuine Philoxenian fragments, the question still remains: are these in fact "commentary"?

De Halleux sees Fragment "7" as part of a commentary on Matthew 4:1-11, and gives the following résumé of the fragment: "L'épreuve satanique du Christ, qui consistait dans les trois passions de l'avarice, de la vaine gloire et de la gourmandise, ne troubla pas son intellect."[163] He goes on to indicate that parallel passages are found in "Commentaire de Luc 2:42-46, f.17-18"[164] and in "*Memre parénétiques*, XIII, p. 620."[165] We shall return to the "Commentaire de Luc" when considering in detail below the fragments of Brit. Mus. Add. 17,126. It is enough at this juncture to say that the "Lucan" fragment deals with the nature of Christ's coming of age at twelve, and the parallel is only indirect at best. The second "parallel" is found in the thirteenth *Discourse*, the subject of which is fornication, and it says nothing about Christ's temptations. Rather, it deals with the way in which the Christian can overcome the desire for sexual indulgence -- not one of the three wilderness temptations recorded in Matthew 4:11 and Luke 4:1-13 is mentioned! A better parallel is found in the eleventh *Discourse*, "on Abstinence."[166] There, at least, Philoxenus deals with the first temptation ("Command these stones to become bread") which He overcame by citing Deuteronomy 8:3, "Man shall not live by bread alone, but by every word that proceeds from the mouth of God" -- a verse which Philoxenus both quotes and comments on. If this passage in the *Discourses* existed only in fragmentary form, it would be easy to conclude that it belonged to a lost commentary on Matthew 4:1-11 or Luke 4:1-13. Because the *Discourses* have been preserved in full, it is patently clear that such a conclusion is untenable.

Similarly, there is no compelling reason why "Fragment 8" (belonging to the same Ethiopic catena as "Fragment 7") should be considered part of a formal commentary on Matthew 5:17 as de Halleux suggests.[167] The latter tells us that this fragment is on how Christ abrogated the Law by obeying it. He then provides references to parallel passages in "*Memre contre Habib*, VIII, f. 76va-81va,"[168] and in "*Memre parénétiques*, VIII, p. 249-255, etc."[169] The former parallel is an extended comment on Galatians 3:13 in which Philoxenus seeks to explain how Christ "became a curse for us" in that he accepted the sentence of the Law on sin. The other parallel, which is from *Discourse 8*, "On Poverty," illustrates Philoxenus' thesis that Christ was subject to the Law until His baptism, after which "He was delivering a rule of life which was more perfect than this to the children of men."[170] To make his point he comments on Matthew 12:48, John 5:30, and especially John 2:1-4 where an extended exposition is given. But nowhere does he mention Matthew 5:17, though the thought is closely related.

The next fragment in de Halleux' list is found in Brit. Mus. Add. 12,154, a long manuscript from the eighth or early ninth century containing a miscellaneous collection of quotations from Church Fathers in support of monophysite theology.[171] The title of the fragment (fol. 64r) explicitly states that it is from a commentary of Philoxenus on Matthew, the Evangelist. De Halleux tentatively suggests that it belongs to Philoxenus' commentary on Matthew 11:11, though in a footnote he thinks that it might equally come from a commentary on Matthew 3:14-15. Certainly, it contains a quotation from Matthew 11:11 (or Luke 7:28) with some comment on it.[172] A parallel passage noted by de Halleux is found in *Discourse 9* where, after citing Matthew 11:11 (or Luke 7:28), Philoxenus comments on John the Baptist's relation to Christ, the Apostles and the Christian life.[173] Once again, we must note that the *Discourse* passage is as much "commentary" as the fragment cited by de Halleux.

Having considered the value of four of the fragments designated as coming from a Philoxenian commentary, the pattern is clear and it is unnecessary to analyze here the contents of the other six.[174] What is called "commentary" apparently need not mean that these fragments belonged to a formally organized exposition of the Gospels. They could and probably did belong to other writings of Philoxenus such as his discourse or his letters. It is difficult to avoid the conclusion that the term ܦܘܫܩܐ (commentary) was used only in a general sense when applied to Philoxenus' comments, and not in any narrow sense of a formally organized exegesis of scripture. Whether the manuscript called "A Commentary on Matthew and Luke" is "commentary" in the narrower sense, will become clear when it is analyzed in detail in chapter 3 of this dissertation.

It will be noted from the table on page 29 that, besides the ten fragments called unqualifiedly "commentary," a total of eight fragments are said to be from chapters against Diodore, the Nestorians and Theodore.[175] Four of these are also called "commentaries," thus substantiating our conclusion above. All of them are patently from polemical works, and the attempt to make them fit into a postulated Gospel commentary is doomed to failure.

At this juncture it is well to return to the "chapter" divisions used in some of the fragmentary Matthew-Luke titles to which reference has already been made.[176] Of the twenty-nine fragments (excluding those in Add. 17,126), twelve say in each instance that the quotation is from some Philoxenian "chapter" (ܪܺܫܐ is used in all cases), and eight of these cite the chapter by number.[177] The fragments from the polemical works ("against Diodore" etc.) are always said to have come from a "chapter" or "chapters," and four of these provide the chapter numbers, 5th, 6th, 7th, and 35th. These four are all directed against the Nestorians. The scant evidence of the fragments suggests either that Philoxenus wrote three polemical works, called "commentaries," against Diodore, against the Nestorians and against Theodore, or (less likely) that he wrote one such work which is variously referred to by these three names. In any case, this work or these works had a distinctive "chapter" division. The word "chapter" usually translates the word in this context, but is this an adequate translation? The basic meaning of ܪܺܫܐ is that of "head," and in relation to a written work it is used to indicate a division of varying lengths -- "heading, chapter, treatise."[178] Several Philoxenian polemical works are extant each of which is divided into ܪ̈ܫܐ.[179] In these, a chapter may be as short as six lines or as long as about fifty lines; that is to say, about a paragraph in length. But they are not simply paragraphs as distinct from sentences in an ordinary literary composition. The fact that the titles of all these polemical works contain the word ܪܺܫܐ and each ܪܺܫܐ is numbered in the body of the work indicates that these are more than paragraphs.[180] Each ܪܺܫܐ contains a very distinct assertion or point of dispute in the building of the total case which Philoxenus is constrained to defend. "Chapter" may be used in English to signify this kind of terse statement and will be retained to translate ܪܺܫܐ and its Greek synonym ܩܦܠܐܘܢ, though ordinary English usage applies the word to a literary unit that is usually longer than a paragraph.

The fact that six polemical works exist having the same form provides a new approach to the fragmentary "commentaries" said to be against Diodore, the Nestorians, and Theodore, especially when some of these fragments refer to specifically numbered chapters from which they are taken. Only one of these works can be said to have any exegetical content, basing its polemic on the interpretations of certain biblical passages, and that is *The Ten Chapters against Those Who Divide Our Lord.*[181] It poses ten rhetorical questions, each making specific reference to an explicit biblical statement, intended to demolish the theological position of the dyophysites. The ten passages are (1) Matthew 1:23a, (2) Matthew 1:23b, (3) Matthew 2:11, (4) Matthew 3:16 (Mark 1:10, Luke 3:22, or John 1:32), (5) 1 Corinthians 1:25b, (6) Isaiah 63:9,[182] (7) Matthew 3:17, (8) Matthew 17:2 (or Mark 9:2),[183] (9) Luke 7:12 ff, and (10) Matthew 27 (Mark 15, Luke 23, or John 19). Except for chapters 5 and 6, all the other chapters are based on the Gospel narratives, and it would be comparatively easy to call these, "chapters from the commentary on the Gospels against those who divide our Lord (i.e. the dyophysites, Chalcedonians, or Nestorians)." We can therefore conclude that the fragments called "commentaries" written against Diodore, the Nestorians, and Theodore should not be classed as commentaries but as polemics.

Words in the titles of the remaining fragments classified by de Halleux as commentary, may be dealt with briefly. Matthean fragment 11 is said to be from the "section (ܦܘܠܓܐ) or note (ܦܘܗܪܐ) of Philoxenus of Mabbug."[184] There is no real suggestion here that this "section" belonged to a commentary. The larger context of the manuscript does not suggest it. In fact, it occurs between Philoxenus' "Profession of Faith" and a Memra by Ephrem on faith. The fragment deals with some aspects of christology, and in that context Matthew 16:16, 23 are used as illustrative texts.[185]

The title of Lucan fragment 4 states that it comes "from the essay (or treatise, ܫܪܒܐ) concerning the scripture: 'The time came for her to give birth, and she gave birth to her first-born son', where he talks about the circumcision of our Lord."[186] This fragment has four quotations from the "essay," the word being repeated in the introduction to the last one: "And again at the end of the essay." De Halleux suggests that this belongs to a comment on Luke 2:21 (on the circumcision of Christ) in spite of the fact that the title cites Luke 2:6-7 as the subject of the essay. The use here of the term ܫܪܒܐ is almost unique in the long catena patrum in which the fragment is found.[187] The only other occurrence of the word in this particular catena is in the title of a quotation from Severus of Antioch: "From the essay (ܫܪܒܐ) concerning the Henoticon."[188] From this rare usage in a plethora of all sorts of citations, it may be assumed to have a technical meaning which is by no means clear from the context of the catena in which it occurs. We have settled on "essay" as perhaps a suitable but tentative translation. At any rate, the author of the catena was constrained to use it rather than ܦܘܫܩܐ or ܡܐܡܪܐ, both of which are commonly used elsewhere in his volume. Wherever this fragment came from, it was not extracted from a commentary -- a conclusion which is confirmed by the fact that Philoxenus' thirteen *Discourses on the Ascetic Life* are called ܫܪܒܐ.[189]

In this same catena the word used most commonly to describe the kind of writing from which passages are quoted, is ܡܐܡܪܐ, sometimes translated "discourse," but often simply transliterated "memra." It is used in the titles of two fragmentary "commentaries" on Matthew and Luke listed by de Halleux.[190] Lucan Fragment 1 is called "Memra on the annunciation of Mary, the Bearer of God" and the attempt to fit it into a supposed Gospel commentary is surely artificial.[191] So with Lucan Fragment 11, which comes from Philoxenus' "Fourth Memra on the Spirit." In these two fragments we are not dealing with works which are primarily exegetical. They are discursive in nature.

We begin this section by saying that Philoxenus engaged in expository writing. This is self-evident from his works. What is not clear is that he ever wrote a distinctive work which systematically dealt with a Gospel or other biblical book and which can be called a commentary. The evidence from the fragments so diligently gathered together by de Halleux is at best inconclusive in this matter; rather, it seems to deny the existence of such a commentary. The question remains: is the "Matthew-Luke Commentary," which will be examined in detail in the following chapters, really a "commentary" after all?

3. *The Discourses*

Prominent among the writings of Philoxenus are discourses on various subjects. Probably the most widely known of these are the "essays (or discourses -- ܫܪܒܐ) which are concerned with giving instruction in the ascetic life, dictated by the blessed Mar Philoxenus, bishop of Mabbug."[192] The first discourse is introductory, written (as Philoxenus himself says) "to encourage the reader [to go on] to the wealth of the essays which are to follow."[193] The essays or discourses which follow come in pairs, each pair dealing with a specific subject: "Faith" (Discourses 2 and 3), "Simplicity" (4 and 5), "The Fear of God" (6 and 7), "Poverty" (8 and 9), "Greed and Abstinence" (10 and 11), and "Fornication" (12 and 13). It will readily be seen that the work as it stands can be divided into two parts: *Discourses* 2-7 are on God, while *Discourses* 8-13 deal with the practice and pitfalls of asceticism. De Halleux produces evidence to indicate that a third part of the work is lost.[194] He sees the three parts as corresponding to the three-stage programme of spiritual development outlined by Philoxenus in the Prologue.[195] If this is so (and de Halleux' evidence is convincing), then it may be that some of the fragments classified as "commentary" belong to these lost discourses. We shall consider this possibility when we come to deal with the so-called "Matthew-Luke Commentary."

A second sizable collection of memre is found in the volume (ܦܢܩܝܬܐ) entitled: "Ten Memre on [the Doctrine] that One of the Holy Trinity Became Flesh and Suffered."[196] By inference from the colophon, de Halleux concludes that the work was written to refute an opponent named Ḥabib who had challenged Philoxenus' monophysite theology.[197] Four documents (including the "Ten Memre") have come to us from this particular controversy, giving us a glimpse of the kind of polemic in which the bishop of Mabbug was engaged. De Halleux suggests that they were written in the following order:[198] (1) a circular letter addressed to monks and monasteries in an unspecified area in which he warns them against "the enemies of the truth";[199] (2) a "mamlela" written by a certain monk named Ḥabib which takes issue with Philoxenus' letter;[200] (3) the "Ten Memre" answering the "mamlela";[201] and (4) a shorter response in which Philoxenus gathers the testimonies of Church Fathers to support his views and concludes with some general remarks.[202] Judging on the basis of the first two discourses of the "Ten Memre" (for they alone are published), it would appear that while proof-texts are quoted to support the author's point of view, no real exegetical comments are provided in this work. It is dogmatic and polemical in nature.

Another important work in the general category of memra is "Three Discourses (Memre) on the Trinity and on the Incarnation."[203] It is less polemical in its form and contents than the "Ten Memre," but its themes have many parallels in the latter as de Halleux has well illustrated.[204] The second and third memre are divided into sub-sections each of which is numbered, and a few of which also carry a title. Many quotations from the Bible occur making this work valuable for comparative textual studies, and Zuntz has used these to develop his views on "the ancestry of the Harklean New Testament."[205] The "Three Discourses," however, are basically dogmatic rather than exegetical.

Two other works are extant which are called "memre" in the context of the manuscripts in which they are found. One is called "Memra on the Annunciation of Mary, the Bearer of God."[206] It is quite a short work (four printed pages long), so much so that de Halleux suggests that it is a fragment of a commentary on Luke 1:26-35 "sous forme d'homélie."[207] But it is quite complete as it stands except for a lacuna of a word or two in the middle of the text.[208] It has the form of a homily in that it commences with the word ܚܒܝܒܝ ("my beloved people") and ends with a doxology, its content is homiletical, and it was incorporated into a long collection of homilies by the Church Fathers.[209] To classify it, therefore, as commentary without any further qualification is misleading.[210] It may, however, have some relationship to the *Matthew-Luke Commentary* as we shall seek to show in chapter 3 below.

The remaining memra extant in a complete form is called, "A memra on the question someone asked: Does the Holy Spirit leave a man when he sins and return to him when he repents?"[211] While the title contains a question and questions are asked irregularly throughout the text, it is not a catechism, a "memra sur la foi par questions [et réponses]," as the title created by de Halleux suggests.[212] In spite of its title, the genre of this work remains uncertain. Budge and others, taking the title at face value, call it a discourse.[213] Tanghe suggests in a footnote that it is like the *Letter to Patricius* but lacks an "introduction épistolaire,"[214] and Ortiz following this suggestion includes it with the "Epistulae."[215] The contents could be those of a discourse, a letter, or a homily.

Besides these complete copies of memre, some fragments clearly indicate that Philoxenus wrote a number of works which have not survived. The colophon of the fragmentary manuscript to be examined in this dissertation illustrates this fact. It states that it is "the end of the fourth book of the commentary of the Evangelists, Matthew and Luke, which was made by Philoxenus," -- thus suggesting that at least three other books existed of which nothing more is positively known. We have already noted the fragmentary memre from which de Halleux has reconstructed a hypothetical Philoxenian commentary. These fragments refer to some of the lost works in their titles, but their meagre contents are not enough to tell us how extensive these works were. Such fragments witness to the following discourses: "Memra on the Tree of Life" cited only by Moses Bar-Kepha in his *Hexameron: On Paradise*;[216] "Fourth Memra on the Spirit" (implying that there were at least three others on the same subject);[217] "The First Memra on the Incarnation" with fragments which according to de Halleux must have come from other memre on the same subject;[218] and "Memra on the Canticle: 'You, O God, are Holy'."[219] In the preceding sub-sections of this chapter, we have already indicated something of the extent of Philoxenus "chapters" against Diodore, the Nestorians, and Theodore, and the facts concerning those need not be repeated.[220]

Allied with the polemical works are the various Philoxenian "confessions of faith." One such work is prefaced by brief statements against various heresies, and thus combines two genres. It is called, "On what distinguishes (ܦܪܘܫܐ) those heresies which are held in error."[221] It summarily deals with Mani, Marcion, Eutyches, Lantinus (? ܠܛܝܢܘܣ), Bardaisan, and eighteen others, besides the Council of Chalcedon which "says there is a quaternity for it brings Christ in after the Trinity."[222] Then follows a short statement on what "orthodox Christians" confess. In another fragment ambiguously entitled "The Faith which has anathematized what the Synod of Chalcedon has corrupted," the Chalcedonian doctrines are condemned in ten statements.[223] A positive confession of faith is found in the fragment entitled, "The reply of a man who is asked, 'How do you believe?'"[224] Several other Philoxenian confessions of faith of a similar tenor exist in fragmentary form in various manuscripts, and are listed by Budge and by de Halleux.[225]

4. *The Letters*

The ancient eulogist, Eli of Qartamin, tells us that Philoxenus "produced twenty-two books of letters addressed to all kinds of Christians that they might profit by them."[226] Budge lists twenty-three, and de Halleux describes twenty-six or twenty-seven.[227] Not all of these are extant in a complete form, and there is reason to believe that some important letters have been lost.[228] We may certainly assume that Philoxenus carried on a much more extensive correspondence than the above numbers suggest, but those which are preserved apparently have been preserved because their contents were of enduring interest to the monophysite church and became part of its patristic tradition. While some of them are addressed to individuals (e.g., the *Letter to Patricius*)[229] and others to groups of monks (e.g., the *Letter to the Monks of Senun*),[230] all are of a general character, making little or no reference to the immediate occasion for writing.

The letters reflect the same two areas of concern found in the discourses or memre: the nature and development of the ascetic life, and the defence of monophysite christology with its attendant polemic against the dyophysite christologies of Chalcedon and Nestorius, and also against other heresies. The *Letter to Patricius* is a good example of the first, while the *Letter to the Monks of Senun* exemplifies the second. However, these two concerns are not kept strictly separate. The *Letter to Patricius* contains a short passage in which some of the arch-heretics are named: "Valentinus, Bardaisan, Marcion, Mani and John the Egyptian."[231] And in the opening paragraph of his *Letter to the Monks of Senun*, Philoxenus commends them for their known faithfulness to the ascetic ideal and encourages them to persevere for "through many tribulations we must enter the kingdom of God."[232]

We have already noted Philoxenus' penchant for providing exegetical notes on passages from the Bible in his memre. The same is true of his letters, of which we draw only on those which have already been published.[233] Two examples will be sufficient to illustrate this assertion. In the *Letter to the Monks of Senun*, Philoxenus' purpose in writing is that of promoting monophysite doctrine and combatting its opponents. At a certain point in his theological discussion, he provides an extended commentary or exegetical note on Luke 1:28-35 (the "annunciation").[234] A second example may be taken from the *Letter to Patricius* which is concerned with the development of the ascetic life. Paragraph 106 of that letter is simply an exposition of 2 Corinthians 12:2, from which he concludes that the so-called revelations of the heresiarchs are false.[235] If these examples were only extant as isolated fragments, they could erroneously be called "commentary." We, thus, take issue with de Halleux who inaccurately gives the impression that Philoxenus sets aside his exegetical activity in his ascetic writings: "Dans les écrits ascétiques de Philoxène, l'exégète et le polemiste monophysite fait place au directeur de conscience et au théoricien de la vie spirituelle."[236]

5. *Other Extant Writings*

To complete this account of Philoxenus' literary activity, mention should be made of extant liturgical works attributed to him, as well as "Rules for the Monastic Life." Some six Philoxenian prayers are listed by Budge and de Halleux; but, since none of these has been published one can only echo the references to them in secondary literature.[237] Ortiz de Urbina considers that their genuineness has not been established, although it would appear that de Halleux' study was not available to him.[238] Several anaphorae have also been associated with Philoxenus' name, but how directly involved he was in their composition is not clear.[239] Budge lists a "hymn on the nativity of our Lord" as Philoxenian, but notes that it is also attributed to John Bar-Aphthon.[240] Finally, Vööbus has published a document purporting to come from Philoxenus' hand called "Rules for the Monastic Life based on six manuscripts,"[241] but de Halleux considers it to be a fragment of a "Letter to the Monks of Amid."[242]

This examination of the Philoxenian literary corpus available to us, leads us to the conclusion that our author limited himself to two main types of literature: discourses or memre, and letters. In both the memre and the letters, Philoxenus has two main concerns, the defence of monophysite christology and the development of the ascetic life; some memre and letters are devoted to the first and others to the second. Apart from the ill-defined use of the term in the titles attached to various fragments, we have no real evidence in the literature surveyed above for a Philoxenian commentary on any book of the Bible. We have deliberately excluded from this survey the fragments of British Museum Add. 17,126 and it remains to be seen whether they contain evidence to contradict or support the above conclusion. We have noted, however, that Philoxenus engaged in exegetical activity in supplying his readers with expository notes, liberally sprinkled throughout his memre and letters, which could be extracted and quoted in later commentaries and "catenae patrum."

CHAPTER II

THE TEXT OF BRITISH MUSEUM MANUSCRIPT ADD. 17,126

A. *THE PROVENANCE AND CONDITION OF THE TEXT*

British Museum Manuscript Add. 17,126 is unique; that is to say that, as far as it can be ascertained, its contents are not duplicated in whole or in part in any other manuscript.[243] It consists of fourteen fragments, thirty-eight folios in all, most of which are related to each other in style of handwriting, quality of vellum, and literary style and content. The colophon of the concluding fragment tells us that "it was written in the city of Mabbug in the year 822 of Alexander of Macedon" (i.e., A.D. 511). Thus, it comes from the lifetime of its author, Philoxenus, and there is no reason to doubt that all the fragments were originally composed by him.

The story of its preservation and travels during the last fourteen and a half centuries is not known except for the following facts. Between A.D. 927 and 932, the abbot of the Syrian monastery of St. Mary Deipara in the Nitrian Desert of Egypt, Moses of Nisibis by name, made an extended visit to Syria and Mesopotamia in which he collected some two hundred and fifty volumes for his monastery library.[244] It is assumed that the manuscript before us belonged to Moses the Nisibene's collection. Certainly, it was in the possession of the monks in that monastery in the nineteenth century when it was purchased from them (along with many others) by Auguste Pacho on July 31, 1847, who acted as agent for the British crown.[245] It thus became the property of the British Museum on November 11, 1847, and has been preserved there ever since.

What the precise condition of this document was when acquired by the British Museum is not recorded. We are dependent on W. Cureton for the general description of the Pacho manuscripts when the cases containing them were first opened:

> The day after their arrival I went to inspect them. At the first view I could almost have imagined that

> the same portion of the library as had been brought nearly five years previously by Dr. Tattam was again before me in the same condition as I found it when the books were first taken from their cases in which they had been packed, as if the volumes had been stripped by magic of their russia, and clad in their original wooden binding; and the loose leaves and fragments, which had cost me many a toilsome day to collect and arrange, had been again torn asunder, and scattered in almost endless confusion.[246]

Since Ms. Add. 17,126 was apparently one of the manuscripts which had to be bound in the British Museum, and some of its papers have obviously been repaired there, it is reasonable to assume that its folios were among those "loose leaves and fragments . . . . scattered in almost endless confusion."[247]

The thirty-eight vellum folios of the manuscript contain fourteen fragments. For convenience, we have numbered them as follows:

Fragment 1 = folios 1-2
Fragment 2 = folios 3-10
Fragment 3 = folio 11
Fragment 4 = folio 12
Fragment 5 = folio 13
Fragment 6 = folio 14
Fragment 7 = folio 15
Fragment 8 = folio 16
Fragment 9 = folios 17-18
Fragment 10 = folios 19-29
Fragment 11 = folio 30
Fragment 12 = folio 31
Fragment 13 = folio 32
Fragment 14 = folios 33-38

Fragments 2, 3 and 10 (except for its last folio [29] which is stained) are in an excellent state of preservation. Fragments 4, 5, 7, 8, 11 and 12 are stained but legible. The rest have stains and tears which make portions of them illegible (the lower eight or nine lines of Fragment 13 have been torn off and lost, and the last four folios of Fragment 14 are so badly stained that they could only be partially read under ultra-violet light).

There is clear evidence for the fact that those who gathered the fourteen fragments of our manuscript together were uncertain about the order in which to bind them. Indeed, they initially felt that some of the fragments should be bound with another manuscript. In the upper left corner of the recto side of each folio, three sets of Arabic numerals appear, written in pencil by two different scholars responsible for arranging the folios.[248] Two sets of figures in the same handwriting are stroked out, and a third set in a different hand represents the foliation of the codex as it was finally bound. Additionally, a fourth set of Arabic numerals appears in tiny unobtrusive writing on a few pages, inserted between the first and second lines of Syriac script, about the space of four or five letters to the right of the left margin.[249]

The first set of figures to be stroked out is found on sixteen folios. Since this numbering runs from 61 to 77 and the present manuscript has thirty-eight folios, we may conclude that the first "arranger's" initial decision was to include some of the fragments with another manuscript (as yet unidentified). Thus, the foliation in this set appears as follows:

nos. 61-71	=	folios 19-29	=	Fragment 10
no. 73	=	folio 32	=	Fragment 13
no. 74	=	folio 1	=	1st folio of Fragment 1
no. 75	=	folio 33	=	1st folio of Fragment 14
no. 76	=	folio 18	=	2nd folio of Fragment 9
no. 77	=	folio 34	=	2nd folio of Fragment 14

The tiny numerals seem to have come next in the process of sorting the fragments, and occur in the following order:

nos. 1-8	=	folios 3-10	=	Fragment 2
no. 9	=	folio 11	=	Fragment 3
no. 10	=	folio 12	=	Fragment 4
no. 11	=	folio 13	=	Fragment 5
no. 12	=	folio 14	=	Fragment 6
no. 13	=	folio 17	=	1st folio of Fragment 9
no. 14	=	folio 31	=	Fragment 12
no. 15	=	folio 30	=	Fragment 11
no. 17	=	folio 15	=	Fragment 7

The second set of "stroked-out" numerals represents the third stage in arranging the folios, and follows the present order except that the first two were made the last two; that is -- in this set, folios 1-36 are folios 3-38 in the present codex, and folios 37 and 38 are 1 and 2. Perhaps the first three tentative foliations were done by W. Cureton, who resigned from the British Museum in 1850, and the final foliation by W. Wright, who began his work there in 1861 and was responsible for compiling the *Catalogue of Syriac Manuscripts* published in 1871.[250]

Syriac quire numbers are found at the foot of a few pages. Folio 17v has a large well-marked beth and the next page (folio 18r) has an equally large gamal, apparently indicating that folio 17 concludes one quire and folio 18 begins the following one. Fragment 10 contains a full clearly marked quire, because folio 19r has a ḥeth (= "8") in the bottom right-hand corner written in the same script as the text, and 29r has a ṭeth (= "9") of comparative size in the same position. Thus, a quire in this fragment consists of ten folios. Similarly, a yudh (= "10") appears in the bottom corner of folio 33r, the beginning of the last quire of the original volume.[251] Since the scripts of Fragments 10 and 14 are identical, we conclude that they were written by the same scribe and belong to the same original manuscript. The quire numbers indicate that almost a complete quire is missing (that is, quire number ṭeth except for folio 29) between Fragment 10 and Fragment 14. The three single-folio fragments inserted by the British Museum may indeed be part of the missing quire for their handwriting is the same as that of Fragments 10 and 14.

Some fragments differ from others in their style of handwriting and size of margins. Fragments 2 and 6-14 have the same kind of carefully formed Estrangela, and belong in some way together. This is also borne out by the fact that the margins in these fragments invariably have the same dimensions. The scribe drew a rectangle on the recto side of the folio approximately 6 5/8" x 4 1/8", then pin-pricked the corners to draw the same rectangle on the verso side. He wrote on top of the upper horizontal line, maintained his vertical margins throughout the page, but did not feel compelled to stay within the lower horizontal line, often writing a line of text below it (in folio 28v he went three lines below it, perhaps because it was the last page of the quire and he was attempting to retain the contents of the quire he was copying). The average number of lines to a page is twenty-seven. While its script and margins are the same as the others in this group, the vellum of Fragment 6 is less well preserved than (and/or inferior to) that of the others.

Fragment 1 is in many ways similar to the majority of the fragments described above, and no doubt came from the same scriptorium in Mabbug as they, but its scribe was not the same. The horizontal lines of the margins are 1/8" shorter, the dimensions of the rectangle in both folios being approximately 6 5/8" x 4". The letters in this fragment have the same general form as the others, but are subtly bolder and larger; the lamadhs and ṭeths, for example, are longer, and the 'es and shins extend beyond the right margin. It is unlikely that it belonged to the same original codex as the others, although without doubt it is a fragment of a Philoxenian work.

Fragments 3, 4 and 5 are noticeably different from the others. They are written on an older or less well-preserved vellum, and the penmanship is more angular. Wright noticed this and thought they might "belong to the missing portion of Add. 14,534."[252] De Halleux, following Wright's suggestion, categorically states that these three fragments (which he treats as one) "proviennent du commentaire de *Jean* de l'Add. 14,534, comme l'indique clairement le style de l'écriture."[253] But this is not so for the following reasons:

1) The style of writing is not precisely the same as is found in Add. 14,534. The latter sustains the same script throughout its 199 folios which is more angular than Fragments 3-5 of our manuscript. Distinctive differences are seen in forms like he, final nun, pe, and taw.

2) While the size of the folios of both is about the same, the dimensions of the margins drawn by the scribes for each are noticeably different. Each folio of Add. 14,534 has a lightly drawn rectangle (uniform throughout) measuring approximately 7¼" x 4"; but each of our three fragments has a rectangle of about 6 9/16" x 3 7/8".

3) There is no apparent context for our fragments in Add. 14,534, apart from the unsubstantiated suggestion that they may belong to the missing introduction as noted above. From this we must conclude that Fragments 3, 4 and 5 of Add. 17,126 are orphans, belonging neither to the manuscript they are bound with nor to Add. 14,534, though they are contemporary with both and all belong to the same scribal school.[254]

Other minor features of the manuscript before us may be

summarized briefly. Quotations are usually marked in the right margin with the sign /<̇/ opposite each line in which words quoted occur; sometimes the arrowhead is in red and its dot black, and sometimes they are both black. The punctuation mark that ends a "paragraph" /... ܝ ../ occurs usually in red and black, but once in red and silver (folio 17r).[255] Erasures are in evidence in folios 5v, 9v, 10r, 12v, 14r, 24v, 26v, 27r, and 28r. The meaning of the following signs in the right or left margins is not known: /+/ (folios 17v, 23v, 25v, 28r), /X/ (folio 13r), /ܒ/ (like a beth turned on its side -- folio 23v), and /ܬ/ (folio 28v). These have all been retained in the edited text of this dissertation. Not included are the various attempts at foliation described above; three English notes on quotations, "Luke II 40" (folio 15v), "Luke II 42" (folio 17r), and "Luke III 23" (folio 15v); and the word "End" written lightly (and enigmatically) between lines 6 and 7 of folio 34r, above and to the right of the word ܫܠܡ.

B. *THE RESTORATION OF THE TEXT*

That many of the folios of our manuscript are in a deplorable condition has already been described.[256] In this edition the text has been restored as much as possible without unnecessary editorial additions. Corrections and comments will be found in the next chapter. Only the following additions have been made to it:

1) folio numbers at the top of each page and line numbers in the left margin for easy reference;
2) square brackets [ ] indicating a lacuna in the text caused by irremediable damage;[257] and
3) words and/or letters within the square brackets suggested by the context and proposed by the present editor.

Apart from these additions, the text stands uncorrected.

To restore the text, a photostat copy of the manuscript was xeroxed. Three typical pages (folios 2r, 22r and 38v) of the resulting, unrestored, xerox copy are found in Appendix B, and a comparison of them with the final edited text will illustrate the method of restoration. Folio 22r is an example of a clean page whose blemishes were removed and faded letters "touched-up" with black ink, care being taken not to eliminate diacritical points. Folio 2r required more "touching-up" and its last five lines were rewritten by the editor. Under ordinary light, much of folio 38v is illegible in the manuscript. The restored text in the editor's handwriting is his reading of the page under ultra-violet light. Folios 35 to 38 had to be read and reproduced in this way. Many doubtful or illegible words in the stained folios of the manuscript were clarified by the use of ultra-violet light, and where these readings are unambiguous they appear in this edition unmarked.

The text of British Museum Manuscript Add. 17,126 as thus restored is reproduced in the pages that follow.

C. THE RESTORED TEXT (REPRODUCED)

Folio 1r

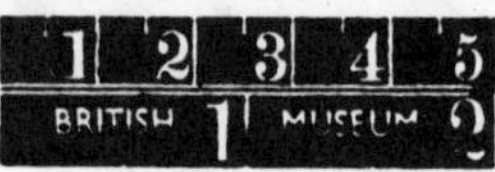

Folio 1v

ܗܕܐ ܒܡܪܗ ܕܠܘ ܗܘ ܡܫܬܐ ܒܡܫܝܚܘܬܗ
ܕܡܠܬܐ ܐܠܗܐ ܠܓܒܠܐ ܕܐܬܝܠܕܐ ܐܟܚܕ
ܗܘ ܕܡܬܠܬܗ ܐܬܚܙܝ ܒܡܫܝܚܐ. ܕܒܟܝ
ܦܫܝܛܐ ܡܠܬ ܐܠܗܐ ܗܘ. ܘܒܡܫܪܝܐ
ܠܗ ܩܢܘܡ. ܘܒܝܘܡܢ. ܐܝܟ ܕܠܗܘ ܕܐܬܝܠܕ.
ܦܠܓܐ ܒܡܠܬܐ ܚܕ. ܒܒܪ ܦܘܩܕܢܐ.
ܐܝܟ ܕܠ ܡܫܬܐ ܕܡܠܬ ܠܗܘܠ. ܚܕ.
ܩܢܘܡ. ܘܗܠܝܢ ܕܐܡܪܢ ܚܕ ܗܘܐ ܐܟܠ
ܒܡܠܬܐ ܕܠ ܐܢܫܝܢ ܕܐܡܪ ܚܕ ܩܢܘܡ
ܡܠܬ ܠܗܘܠ. ܘܡܠܬ ܗܠܝܢ ܕܠܒܫ ܐܢܫ
ܕܒܟܝܢ [ܐܬܝܠܕ]ܬ.. ܦܝܣܐ ܗܘܠ ܡܢ
ܒܬܪ ܕܡܠܬ ܡܠܠ ܒܩܢܘܡ ܒܪܢܫܐ ܗܠܝܢ
ܕܒܬܗܘܢ ܘܐܬܬܝܕܥ ܒܗ ܐܝܟ ܐܠܗܐ
ܕܠܐ ܡܬܚܫܚ ܡܢ ܡܢܗ ܠܗ ܒܠܚܘܕ ܡܢ ܒܪ
ܐܢܫܐ ܐܝܟ ܡܢ ܚܕܘܬܐ ܐܠܗܐ ܐܝܟ ܐܠܗܐ
ܡܢ ܝܘܡܐ ܢܐܡܪ. ܘܠܐ ܒܟܝܢܐ ܡܬܚܫܚ
ܕܕܒܝܫܐ ܕܠܗ ܒܝܘܡܐ ܐܝܟ ܒܟܝܢܐ
ܫܪܝܪ ܗܘܐ [ܡܫܝܚܐ]. ܕܫܡܗ ܡܢ ܫܘܒܚܐ
ܕܒܗܘܦ ܐܝܬܘܗܝ ܗܘܐ ܘܐܬܬܝܕܥ
ܒܗ ܐܠܗܐ ܕܐܦܠܐ ܡܢ ܗܠܝܢ ܒܬܪܬܐ
ܡܬܚܫܚ. ܘܒܫܬܘܬܦܢ ܗܘܘ ܐܦ ܒܢܝܐ
ܕܠܐ ܡܠܬܐ ܐܝܬܝ ܕܠܗܘܢ. ܗܘ ܕܐܦ
ܕܡܢ ܐܠܗܐ ܒܒܪܐ ܕܢܦܠܬܗ ܠܟ ܗܢ
ܕܡܫܝܚ ܠܗ. ܠܐ ܡܬܪܝܩ ܠܓܫܡܗ
ܒܡܒܝ ܗܘܐ. ܘܐܦܢ ܐܬܡܪܘܬ ܐܝܬܐ
ܠܐ ܡܬܚܫܚܬܐ ܕܐܬܬܝܕܥܬ ܒܗ
ܐܢܫܐ ܒܪ ܠܗ ܕܡܬܚܫܚܬܐ ܗ[—]
ܕܢܦܠ ܒܦܘܪܫܐ ܒܝܢܬܐ ܕܠܗܐ ܫܐ[ܪ]

Folio 2r

Folio 2v

Folio 3r

Folio 3v

Folio 4r

Folio 4v

ܒܬܪ ܕܒܥܘܬܐ ܕܦܘܪܫܢܐ ܕܐܬܟܫܦܘ܆ ܒܗ.
ܦܘܪܫܢܐ. ܡܛܠ ܕܠܗܘܢ ܘܕܒܢܝܗܘܢ. ܥܡ ܡܛܠ
ܕܠܗܘܢ ܟܠܗܝܢ ܥܠ ܦܘܪܫܢܗ܂ ܘܐܝܟ
ܕܘܪܫܐ ܕܡܫܡܠܝܐ ܠܚܘܕ ܐܬܦܫܩܘ܆ ܒܗ
ܠܡܫܡܠܝܘܬܐ ܕܦܘܪܫܢܐ ܐܝܟ ܕܐܡܪܝܢ ܠܐ
ܐܢܫ ܚܕ ܐܠܗܐ ܟܠܗ ܠܚܘܕ܃ ܗܘ ܚܢܢ.
ܒܡܫܡܠܝܘ ܕܝܢ ܟܠܗ ܚܟܝܡ ܗܘܐ ܘܒܦܘܪܫܢܗ
ܘܒܦܘܪܫܢܘܗܝ܆ ܘܒܝܕܥܬܗ܆ ܥܠ ܟܠܗܝܢ
ܡܬܠܟܢܝܢ ܗܘܘ܆ ܘܒܡܫܡܠܝܘܬܗ ܥܡ ܦܘܪܫܢܗ
ܠܗܘܢ ܟܠܗܘܢ ܕܡܬܬܘܡܢܐ ܐܝܟ ܕܐܢܫܐ ܗܘܬ.
ܘܟܠ ܕܐܬܒܥܝܬ ܦܘܪܫܢܐ ܕܠܐ ܬܗܘܐ
ܘܡܫܡܠܝܘܬܐ ܕܚܝܠܗ. ܐܝܟ ܕܝܢ ܗܘܐ
ܐܬܬܕܝܢ ܠܗܘܢ܂ ܘܐܬܒ ܕܝܢ ܕܡܬܡܬܐ
ܗܝ ܦܘܪܫܢܗ ܕܐܠܗܐ. ܕܡܬܬܐ ܐܝܟ
ܐܦ ܠܡܠܬܐ ܕܐܬܟܬܒܬ. ܒܐܝܕܗ ܠܟܢ
ܐܢܫܐ. ܟܠ ܗܘܕܐ ܠܗ ܗܘܝܐ ܒܝܕܥܬܐ
ܕܢܗܘܘܢ ܒܢܝܐ ܠܐܒܘܗܝ܆ ܘܐܬܚܫܒ ܦܘܪܫܢܐ
ܕܢܣܠܩ ܠܦܘܪܫܢܗ. ܘܐܬܬܠܝ ܡܢ ܐܢܫܘܬܐ
ܕܢܗܠܟ ܡܢ ܦܘܪܫܢܐ ܕܡܫܡܠܝܐ. ܘܟܠ
ܠܦܘܪܫܢܐ ܘܬܢܝܢ ܒܡܫܡܠܝܐ ܕܢܫܪܐ ܡܢ
ܡܫܡܠܝܘܗܝ ܘܡܢ ܠܘܬܗ. ܘܐܬܦܪܫ
ܒܡܫܡܠܝܘܬܐ ܕܢܬܠ ܠܡܫܠܡܢܘܬܐ ܦܘܪܫܢܐ
ܘܐܬܡܠܝ. ܠܐܢܫܐ ܠܡܫܡܠܝܘܬܐ ܕܢܦܩ
ܦܘܪܫܢܐ ܘܡܠܘܐܐ ܠܐܢܫܐ ܕܢܗܘܐ.
ܠܥܠܡ. ܡܢ ܗܘܝܢ ܐܝܟ ܕܐܢܫܐ. ܕܢܬܠ
ܠܝ ܦܘܪܫܢܐ ܐܢܫܘܬܐ ܕܡܫܡܠܝܐ ܒܢܝܐ
ܕܐܠܗܐ. ܘܡܢ ܘܟܠ ܘܐܬܢܝܚܘ܆ ܕܢܬܠ

Folio 5r

ܠܗ ܪܒܘܬܐ ܥܠ ܟܠܗܘܢ ܢܒ̈ܝܐ ܕܢܡܘܣܐ.
ܘܗܘܐ ܠܟܗܢܘܬܐ ܒܫܪܒܬܐ ܕܠܐ
ܡܛܠ ܕܗܘܐ ܡܫܡ̈ܫܢܘܗܝ ܐܠܐ ܟ̈ܠܗ
ܠܟܗܢܘܬܗ ܘܗܘܝܘ ܢܒ̈ܝܐ ܩܕܡ ܡܫܝܚܘܬܐ.
ܕܡܫܝܚܘܗܝ ܠܗ ܡܫܝܚܘܬܐ ܢܛܠ
ܘܡܠܟܘܬܗ ܫܠܚ ܠܗ ܡܪ̈ܘܬܐ ܢܦܫ
ܘܡܘܬܐ ܕܢܦܠ ܥܠܘ ܐܝܟ ܕܢܦܫ ܒܪ̈ܘܚ
ܫܡܥܐ. ܘܐܬܬܢܝܚ ܒܗ̇ ܒܚܝ̈ܠܐ
ܕܢܝܚܝ ܒܫܠܐ ܕܦܫܛܐ. ܘܒܠ ܒܪ̈ܘܟܬܐ
ܕܐܬܝܗܒ ܠܗ ܡܢ ܕܡܫܝܚܘܬܐ ܡܛܠ ܐܝܟ ܕܒܠܗܘܢ
ܕܗܘܘ ܩܕܡܘܗܝ ܫܝ̈ܢܚܐ ܐܝܟ ܘܡܢܗ
ܗܘ ܕܒܠܐ ܦܪܨܘܦܐ ܕܡܫܝܚܐ ܡܢܝܢ
ܠܟܠܗ̇ ܒܪܘܟܬܐ ܢܦ̈ܫܬܐ
ܕܡܫܝܚܘܗܝ. ܘܐܬܝܗ ܡܛܠ ܦܠܓܘ
ܦܘܪܩܢܐ ܗܘ ܕܒܘܪܟܬܐ ܕܟܠܗܝܢ
ܘܡܫܝܚܘܬܐ ܕܦܘܠܚܢܐ. ܕܟܠ ܟܠܗܘܢ
ܕܦܠܚ̈ܬܐ ܕܡܫܝܚܘܬܐ ܗܘ ܡܢܗܘܢ ܐܝܟ ܟܢܐ
ܢܦܫܗܝܢ. ܠܗ ܐܦܠܐ ܗܟܢܐ. ܐܠܐ
ܒܪܡ ܕܡܫܝܚ ܘܡܫܡܫ ܒܗ ܗܘܐ. ܘܗܢܐ
ܕܗܢܐ ܠܗ ܠܒܢܝܐ ܕܦܘܪܫܢܐ ܐܠܐ
ܟܠܢܫܐ ܠܟܢܫܐ. ܐܝܟ ܕܒܟܢܘܫ
ܗܘܘ ܚܝܝ ܐܦ ܢܒ̈ܝܐ ܒܡ̈ܫܝܚܐ. ܐܝܟ ܗܢܘܢ
ܕܚܢܘܟ ܠܟܗܢܐ ܕܢܦܠ ܥܠ ܟܗܢܘܬܐ
ܟܗܢܐ. ܘܠܗ ܚܠܦܐ ܕܡܫܝܚܐ ܟܗܢܐ
ܠܠ ܡܫܝܚܐ. ܘܐܝܟ ܕܡܫܝܚܘܬܐ ܕܟܗܢܘܬܐ
ܕܗܘܐ ܒܠܒܘܫ. ܚܢܘܟ ܠܟܗܢܐ ܕܢܦܠ
ܥܠ ܟܗܢܘܬܐ ܟܗܢܐ. ܘܡܫܝܚܘܬܐ.

Folio 5v

[illegible]

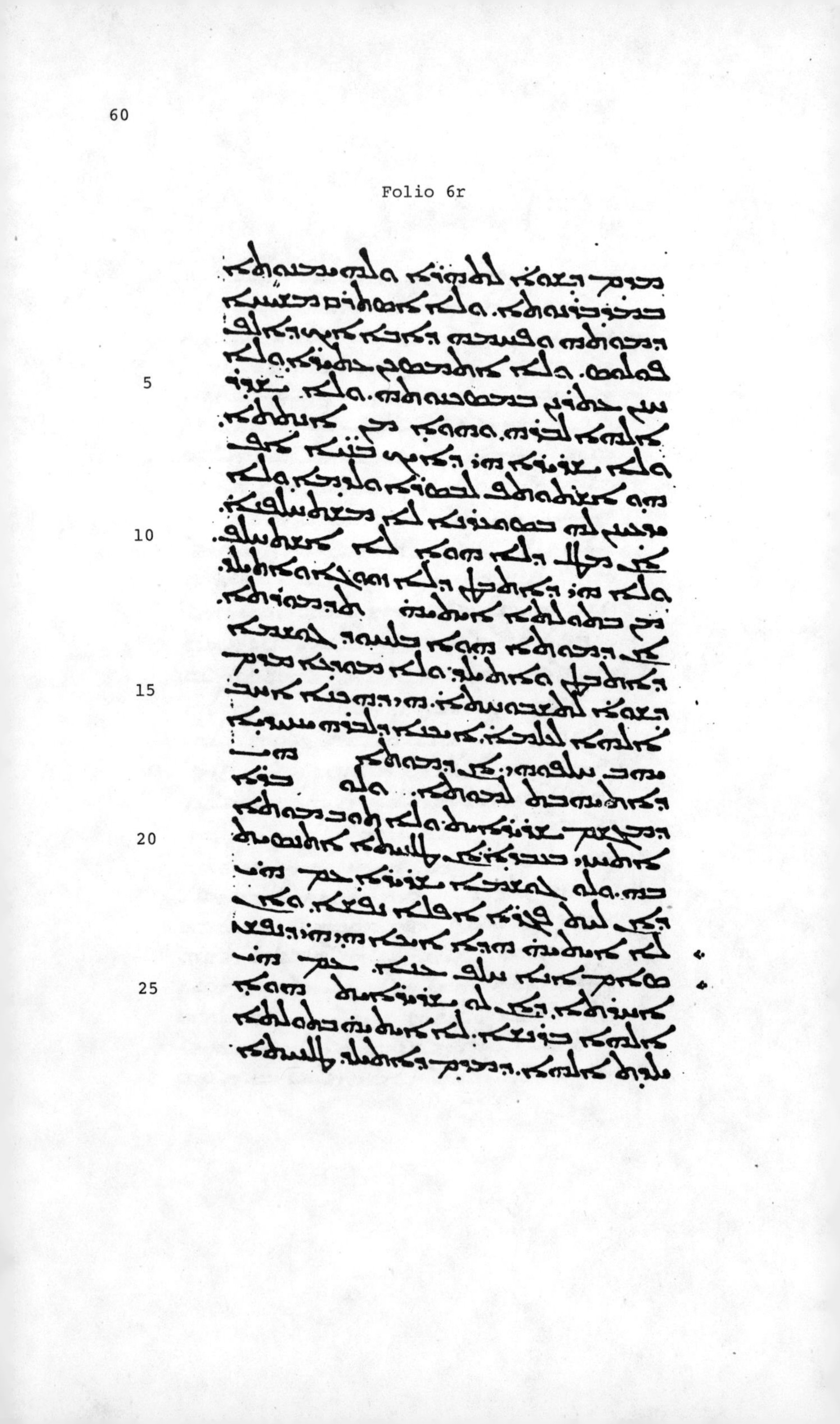

Folio 6r

Folio 6v

ܗܘܐ. ܥܠ ܐܠܗܘܬܐ ܕܟܝܢܗ ܕܒܗ. ܒܪܘܚ
ܐܢܫܘܬܗ ܡܢ ܦܓܪܐ ܕܡܠܟܘܬܗ ܕܒܬܘܠܬܐ.
ܟܕ ܗܘ ܗܘ ܢܦܫ ܐܢܫܘܬܗ ܕܝܠܗ. ܐܡܪ
ܕܠܐ ܐܠܗܘܬܐ ܐܬܓܫܡ ܘܐܬܚܠܛ. ܐܠܐ
ܒܡܪܢ ܗܘܐ ܒܒܪܢܫܐ ܕܐܬܚܠܛ. ܘܢܣܒ
ܠܗ ܠܒܘܠܒܐ ܕܗܘܝܐ ܥܠ ܕܡܠܟܐ.
ܘܒܒܪܢܫܐ ܥܠ ܕܐܠܗܐ. ܘܐܬܚܫܒܬ ܠܗ
ܕܗܘܐ ܐܝܬܘܗܝ. ܟܠ ܕܟܦܪ ܒܡܫܝܚܐ ܘܠܐ
ܒܗܘܝܐ ܕܐܠܗܐ. ܡܛܠ ܕܠܗܘ ܕܡܬܚܠܛ
ܗܘܝܐ ܠܒܪܢܫܐ ܕܗܘܝܐ ܒܡܫܝܚܐ ܘܠܐ.
ܘܐܠܐ ܗܘܐ ܐܠܗܐ ܒܡܬܚܠܛ. ܘܟܠ
ܕܠܝܬ ܢܣܛܘܪܝܣ ܗܘܝܐ ܕܗܘܝܐ ܐܠܗܐ
ܒܪܢܫܐ. ܘܡܢ ܒܪܝܗ ܐܦ ܗܘ ܕܐܬܚܠܛ.
ܡܢ ܒܬܘܠܬܐ ܘܡܫܝܚܐ ܠܒܘܠܒܐ ܐܡܪ
ܕܐܬܓܫܡ ܒܒܢܝܐ ܘܒܪܝܬܐ ܕܒܪ ܐܢܫܐ.
ܘܒܒܪܢܫܐ ܘܒܒܪܐ ܥܠ ܕܐܠܗܐ. ܕܐܦ
ܐܢܫܘܬܗ ܥܡ ܐܠܗܘܬܗ ܝܠܝܕܐ ܕܢܣܒܘܗ
ܠܗܘ ܝܠܕܐ ܐܢܫܘܬܗ ܕܠܐ [illegible] ܟܕ ܗܘ
ܐܢܫܘܬܗ ܒܡܫܝܚܐ ܕܗܘܝܐ ܐܠܗܐ
ܝܬܝܪܘܬܐ ܒܪܢܫܐ. ܕܒܗܘܢ ܢܣܛܘܪܝܣ
ܒܗܠܝܢ ܐܠܐ ܦܘܫܩܗ ܠܗܘ ܠܒܘܢܝܗ
ܕܡܠܬܐ ܥܡ ܕܒܗܘܬܐ ܕܒܝܬܐ ܕܐܢܘܫ
ܒܗ ܕܒܝܬܐ. ܘܐܝܬܝܗ ܐܢܫܘܬܗ ܒܒܪܢܫܐ.
ܕܐܝܟ ܕܐܬܢܣܒܬ ܒܒܘܢܝܐ [illegible] ܕܒܪܢܫܐ
ܒܡܘܬܗ ܗܘܝܐ. ܐܠܐ ܒܪܐ [illegible] ܐܬܢܣܒ
ܒܡܘܬܗ ܕܒܪܢܫܐ. ܘܠܒܪܢܫܐ ܒܡܬܚܠܛܐ
ܗܘܬ ܒܪܘܚܐ ܕܒܒܬܘܠܬܐ ܘܐܬܒܪܢܫܬ

Folio 7r

Folio 7v

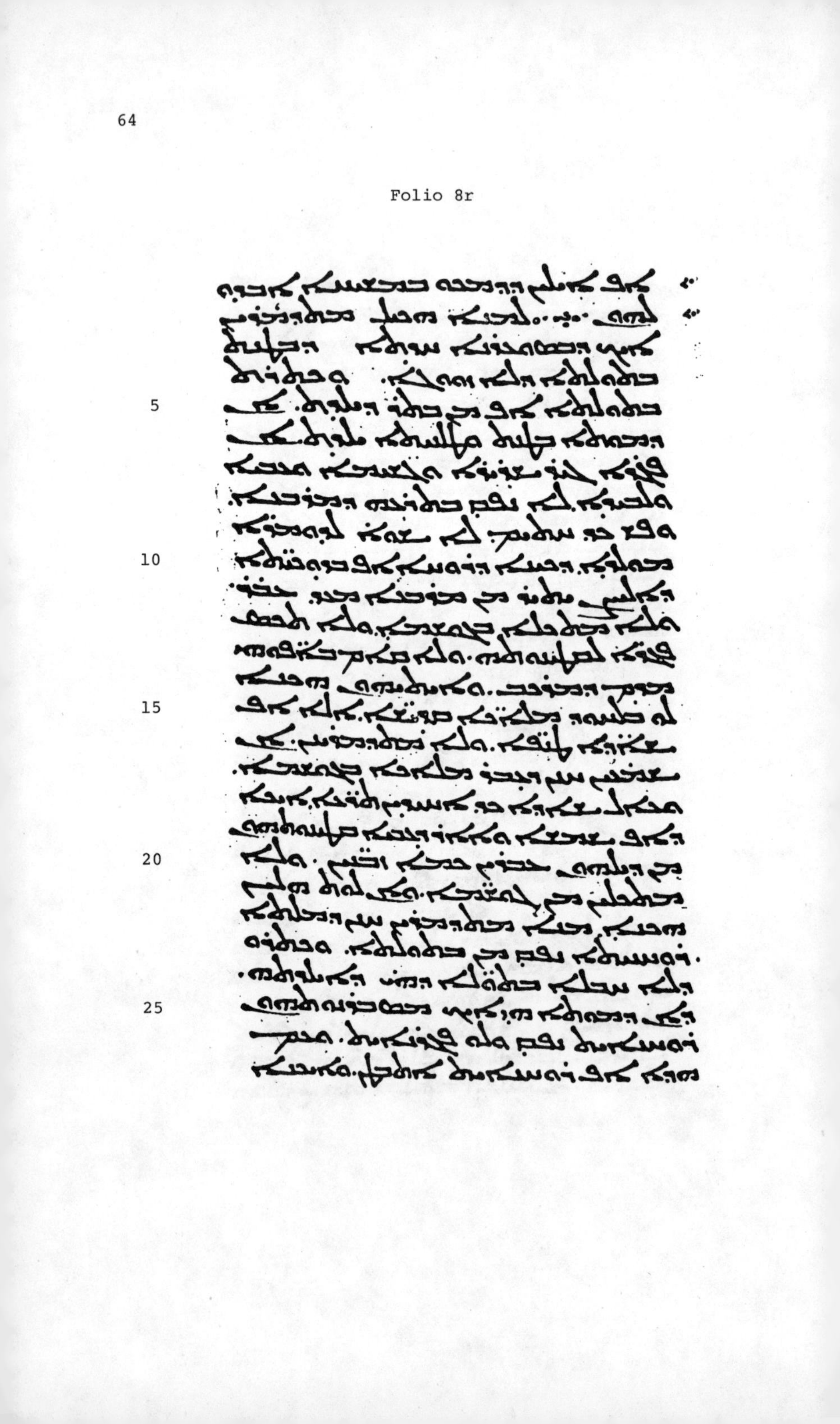

Folio 8r

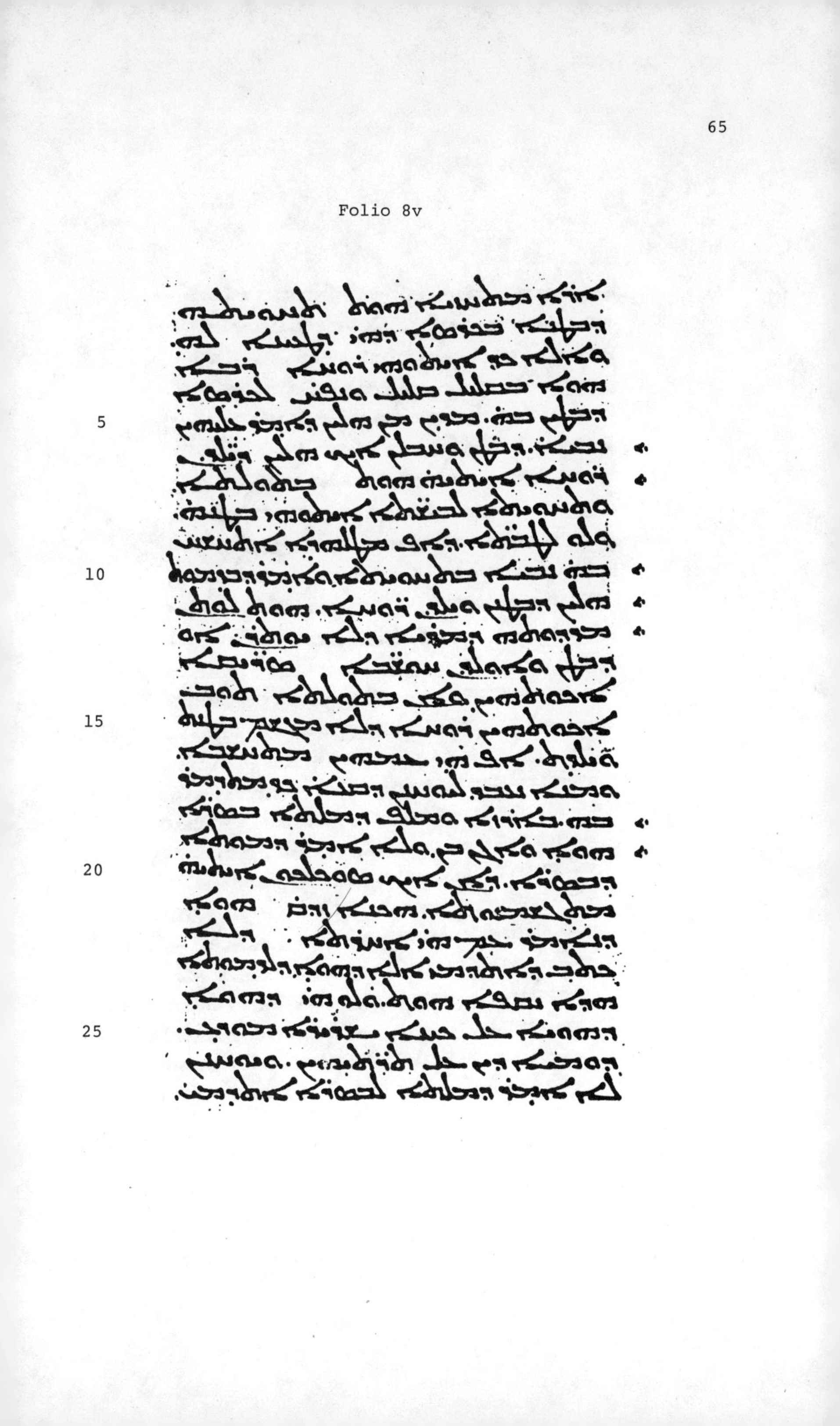

Folio 8v

Folio 9r

Folio 9v

Folio 10v

Folio 10v

Folio 11r

ܠܒܢܝܢܫܐ ܘܠܒܥܝܪ̈ܐ. ܐܝܟ ܕܒܢܐ ܕܡܢ
ܦܘ̈ܩܕܢܐ ܕܐܬܝܪ̈ܘܬܗ. ܒܗܢܐ ܐܝܟ
ܡܬܝܕܥܝܢ ܠܒܢ̈ܝܢܫܐ. ܕܪܘܚܐ ܩܕܝܫܐ
ܦܫܝܩܘ ܕܒܪ̈ܝܬܐ. ܠܗ ܠܗܘܢ
ܠܡܫ̈ܡܫܢܐ ܕܒܪܝܬܐ ܘܪ̈ܘܚܢܐ ܐܬܚܙܝܬ.
ܐܠܐ ܠܡܫܡܫܢܘܬܐ ܕܠܗܘܢ ܕܪ̈ܘܚܢܐ.
ܘܠܡܫܡܫܢܘܬܐ ܕܒܪܝܬܐ. ܒܗ ܗܘ ܕܪ̈ܘܚܢܐ
ܡܫܡܫܢܐ ܒܢܬܐ. ܟܠ ܕܗܘܐ ܒܗܢܐ.
ܠܡܫܡܫܘ ܐܬܪ̈ܐ ܒܠܗܘܢ. ܕܐܝܟ
ܗܠܝܢ ܐܡܪܢ: ܗܘ ܕܐܝܟ ܕܐܡܪܢ ܠܥܠ
ܐܦ ܗܟܢܐ ܠܒܪ ܡܢ ܗܢܐ ܠܒܪܢܫܐ
ܡܬܚܙܝܢ ܒܬܫܡܫܬܐ. ܗܘ ܕܝܢ ܕܚܝܠܘ
ܕܥܠܡܐ. ܦܫܩ ܟܠ ܡܫܡܫܢܘܬܐ ܕܒܪܝܬܐ
ܐܠܗܝܬܐ. ܠܗܿ ܒܠܗܝܢ ܐܝܠܝܢ ܕܒܪ̈ܝܬܐ
ܠܒܢܝܢܐ. ܐܝܟ ܗܘ ܕܒܪܝܬܐ ܒܒ̈ܬ ܐܪ̈ܒܥܐ
ܒܚܝܠܘ. ܘܐܝܟ ܗܘ ܕܡܒܢܐ ܐܪܒܥ
ܒܪ̈ܝܬܐ ܫܠܡܘܬܐ. ܘܒܗ ܐܬܒܪܝܬ ܐܫܬܟܚܬ
ܒܠ ܡܫܡܫܢܐ ܐܠܗܝܐ. ܕܐܝܟ ܒܬܫܡܫܬܐ
ܫܠܡܐ ܘܡܫܡܫܢܘܬܐ ܕܟܠ ܚܕ ܒܡܫܡܫܘ
ܐܡܝܢ. ܕܗܘܐ ܕܝܢ ܡܫܡܫܢܐ ܐܝܟ
ܠܬܫܡܫܬܐ. ܐܝܟ ܕܡܢ ܐܪ̈ܒܥ ܕܠܐ
ܦܫܝܩܐ ܠܗܘܢ ܐܫܬܟܚ ܠܒܢܝܢܐ.
ܐܠܐ ܘܐܦ ܟܠ ܗܠܝܢ ܐܫܬ̈ܝܢ
ܡܫܡܫܢܐ ܐܝܟ ܕܐܡܪܝܢ ܪܘܚ. ܒܪܝܬ
ܕܝܢ ܠܗܘܢ ܕܐܬܚܙܝ ܒܪܝܬܐ ܕܐܠܗܐ
ܡܠܬܐ ܡܢ ܢܦܫܗ. ܠܐ ܡܫܡܫܝܢ
ܒܬܫ̈ܡܫܬܗܘܢ ܕܡܬܩܪܝܢ. ܘܠܒܪ ܡܢ ܗܢܐ

Folio 11v

ܕܡܬܩܪܝܐ ܐܬܘܪܝܐ. ܘܐܬܘܪܝܐ ܒܠܫܢܐ ܐܪܡܝܐ ܐܡܪ ܠܐܬܘܪܝܐ ܐܝܟ ܕܢܦܩܘܢ. ܕܒܢܝܢܫܐ ܕܟܢܥܢܝܐ ܘܕܝܘܢܝܐ. ܘܕܡܨܪܝܐ ܘܕܗܢܕܘܝܐ. ܒܠܫܢܐ ܐܚܪ̈ܢܐ: ܕܡܠܬܐ ܕܝܢ ܘܕܐܠܗܘܬܐ ܦܘܫܩܐ. ܘܠܥܒܪܝܐ ܗܘܐ ܕܝܢ ܗܘ ܐܬܐܡܪ ܦܘܫܩܐ ܠܗ ܡܢ ܐܬܘܪܝܐ ܗܘܝܐ. ܕܝܢ ܗܘܪܝܐ ܐܘ ܗܘ ܕܠܘܬ ܣܓܝܐܐ ܦܘܫܩܐ ܡܦܩܢܐ ܐܝܟ ܕܗܘܐ ܕܠܐ ܢܬܦܫܩ ܐܘ ܕܐܦ ܣܓܝܐܐ ܕܡܠܬܐ ܐܝܟ ܣܓܝܐܐ ܕܗܠܝܢ ܐܚܪ̈ܢܐ ܒܠܫܢܐ ܢܬܬܪܓܡ: ܒܗܢ ܕܐܝܟ ܕܟܬܒ ܡܪܩܘܣ ܘܠܘܩܐ. ܠܗܘܢ ܗܘܢ ܫܡܥܘܢܐ ܕܗܘܝܐ. ܘܥܠ ܡܢ ܗܘ ܕܐܬܦܫܩ ܒܫܪܪܐ ܡܢ ܐܠܗܐ: ܢܬܬܪܓܡ. ܣܓܝܐܐ ܕܒܪܝܐ ܗܘ ܕܒܥܒܪܝܐ ܒܠܫܢܐ. ܒܠܫܢܐ ܗܘ ܕܝܢ ܐܡܪ ܕܝܘܚܢܢ ܕܐܝܬܘܗܝ: ܐܦ ܗܢܐ ܫܡܥܐ. ܡܛܠ ܕܠܘܬ ܡܢ ܗܢܐ ܕܒܪܫܝܬ ܗܘܐ. ܠܗ ܠܡܠܬܐ ܐܡܪ ܕܝܢ ܒܪܫܝܬ ܕܡܠܬܐ ܕܐܝܬܘܗܝ ܐܠܗܐ. ܒܪܫܝܬܐ ܠܡ ܐܝܬܘܗܝ ܗܘܐ ܡܠܬܐ. ܘܗܘ ܡܠܬܐ ܐܝܬܘܗܝ ܗܘܐ ܠܘܬ ܐܠܗܐ. ܘܐܠܗܐ ܐܝܬܘܗܝ ܗܘܐ ܗܘ ܡܠܬܐ. ܘܗܢܐ ܡܠܬܐ ܐܝܟ ܕܐܡܪ ܐܘܢܓܠܝܣܛܐ ܐܠܗܐ ܗܘ: ܗܢܐ ܕܝܢ ܗܘܐ ܒܪܫܝܬܐ ܡܢ ܒܪܫܝܬܐ ܕܠܐ ܫܘܪܝܐ ܐܠܐ ܕܐܠܗܐ ܐܝܬܘܗܝ. ܗܘܐ. ܒܪܗ ܕܐܒܐ

Folio 12r

ܡܢ ܒܪ ܐܢܫܐ ܠܐ ܡܫܟܚܐ ܕܬܬܚܙܐ.
ܗܘ ܕܝܢ ܐܬܪܐ ܟܠ ܗܘ ܕܪ̈ܚܡܐ
ܠܟܠܗܘܢ: ܕܗܘܐ ܡܚܘܐ ܕܢܚܙܐ ܠܐܠܗܐ.
ܐܬܚܙܝ ܕܐܬܘ ܟܠ ܗܘ ܕܟܠ ܢܚܙܐ
ܠܗ ܒܥܝܢܐ. ܡܫܬܘܕܥ ܠܗ ܡܟܠܗܘܢ.
ܐܝܟ ܡܟܐ ܕܐܬܐ ܕܢܚܘܝܢ ܒܗ ܐܚܘܝ
ܠܬܠܡܝܕܐ ܗܘ ܕܩܛܠܘܗܝ ܕܢܚܘܐ ܠܗ
ܒܥܝܢܐ. ܕܟܕ ܠܒܪ ܐܢܫܐ ܢܚܙܐ ܗܘܐ.
ܐܘܕܥܗ ܕܐܠܗܐ ܠܗܘܢܐ ܢܬܚܙܐ.
ܘܠܐ ܕܐܠܗܐ ܚܙܝ ܒܗ ܢܬܒܪ ܐܝܟ
ܗܘ ܕܐܬܝܕܥ ܗܘ ܠܒܪ ܡܢܗ. ܐܬܟܠ
ܚܙ ܗܘ ܕܡܢܗ ܒܦܘܪܩܢܐ ܕܐܠܗܐ ܕܢܚܘܐ
ܒܗ. ܘܟܠ ܗܘ ܠܬܠܡܝܕܘܗܝ. ܕܢܚܘܝܘܗܝ
ܘܗܘ ܕܡܡܠܠ ܥܡܢ ܗܘ ܐܬܚܙܝܘܗܝ.
ܕܒܪ ܚܝܐ ܕܗܘܐ ܕܐܬܐ ܕܐܬܒܪܝ ܐܠܗܐ
ܠܟܠ ܡܢ ܕܐܬܐ ܕܢܗܘܐ ܒܦܘܪܩܢܐ.
ܕܠܗܘ ܕܡܫܬܘܕܥ ܗܘܐ ܡܢ ܒܢܝܢܐ.
ܒܪܢܫܐ. ܘܡܬܚܙܐ ܗܘܐ ܒܦܘܪܩܢܗ.
ܘܟܠ ܘܗܘ ܒܡܫܝܚܐ. ܘܐܬܠ ܡܢ
ܘܦܘܪܩܢܐ. ܘܐܬܚܙܝ ܟܠ ܕܝܢ ܦܪܘܩܐ.
ܘܟܠ ܐܝܟ ܒܢ ܘܦܘܪܩܢܐ. ܕܢܚܘܝܢ
ܕܐܬܚܙܝ ܐܠܗܐ ܕܡܬܚܙܐ. ܗܘ ܕܐܬܚܙܝ
ܐܬܚܙܝ ܕܠܐ ܚܙܝܬܐ ܒܥܝܢܐ
ܠܢܫܐ. ܟܕ ܒܗ ܐܝܟ ܠܐ ܠܗܘܢܐ
ܒܬܚܙܝܬܐ. ܘܠܐܦ ܕܡܬܚܙܐ ܐܝܟ ܡܢ
ܢܫܐ ܕܒܚܙܝܢ. ܐܬܚܙܝ ܐܝܟ ܕܠܐ

Folio 12v

Folio 13r

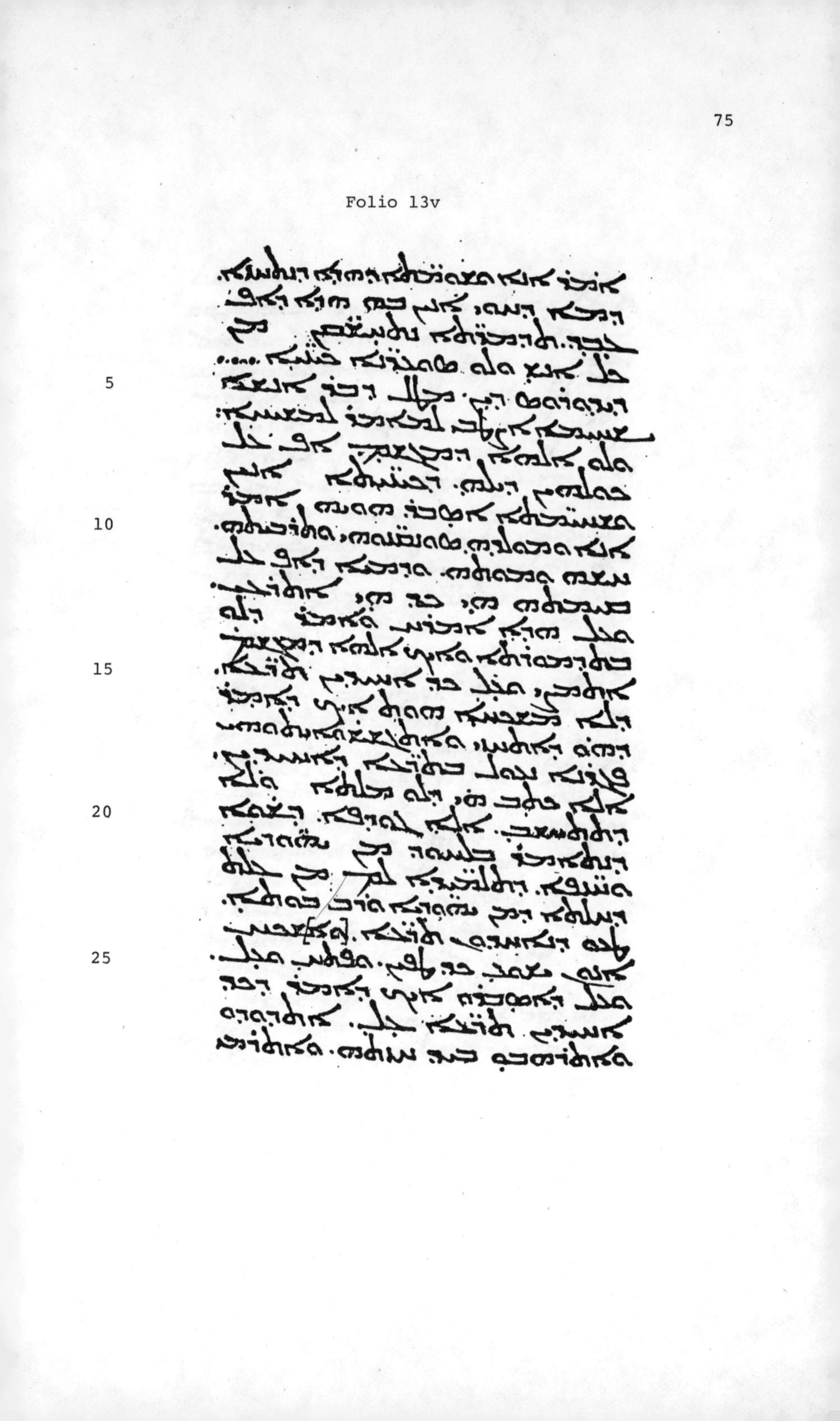

Folio 13v

[illegible]

Folio 14r

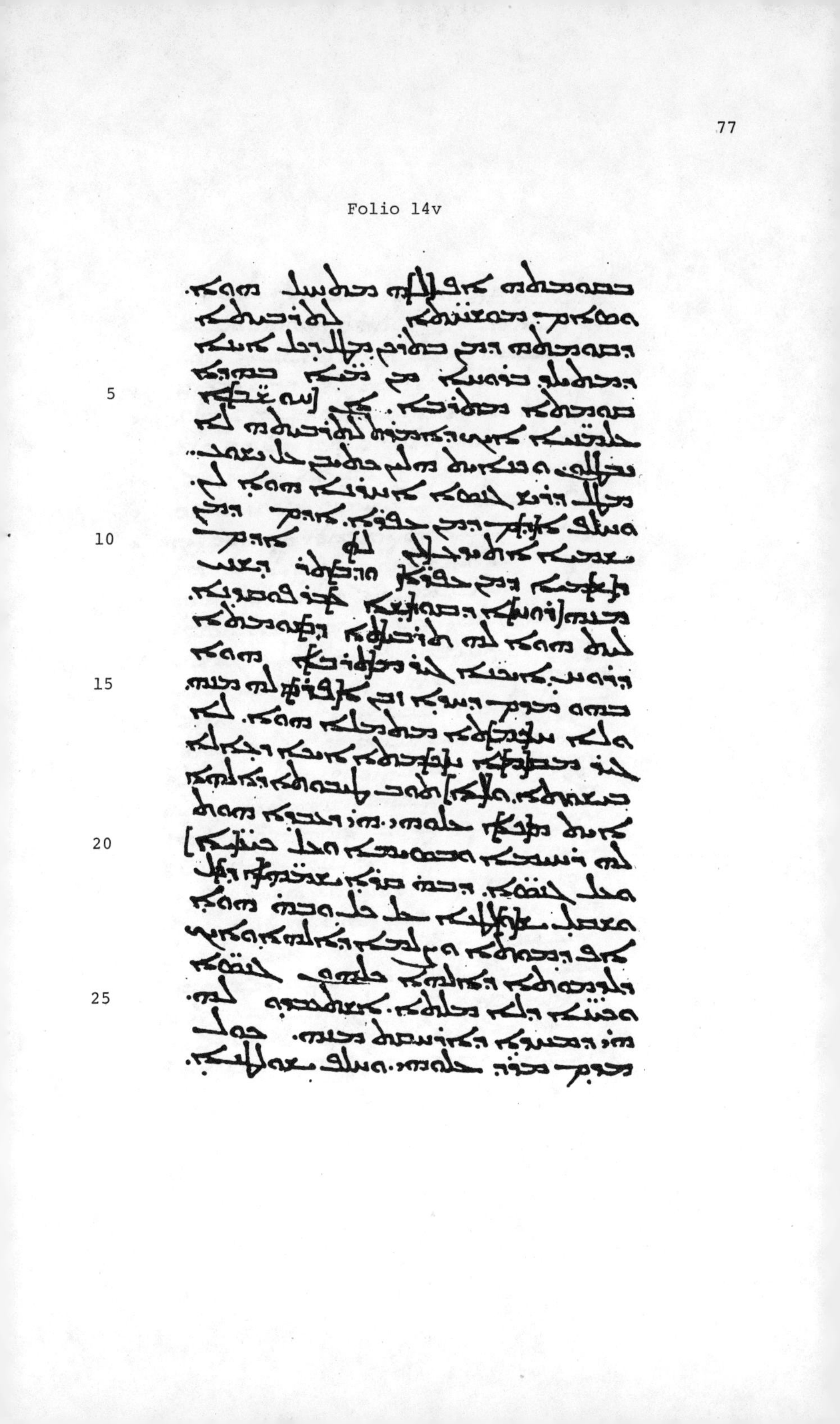

Folio 14v

Folio 15r

[illegible]

Folio 15v

[illegible]

Folio 16r

ܕܒܫܠܡܘܬܗ ܕܐܠܗܘܬܐ ܫܠܡܘܬܐ ܗܘܐ ܗܘܬ
ܒܢܝܢܫܐ. ܘܡܨܥܝܘܬܗ ܡܫܝܚܐ ܗܘ ܗܘ
ܒܝܢܝ ܐܢܫܐ. ܘܥܠ ܫܠܡܘܬܐ ܕܒܫܠܡܘܬܗ
ܡܢ ܫܠܡܘܬܗ ܕܒܢܝ ܐܢܫܐ ܠܐ ܡܬܦܪܫܐ
ܒܠܚܘܕ: ܐܠܐ ܫܘܬܦܘܬܗ ܡܬܚܘܝܐ ܡܢ
ܡܨܥܝܘܬܗ: ܕܠܐ ܦܠܓܐ ܕ̈ܒܪܢܫܘܬܐ
ܕܡ̈ܠܟܐ. ܕܢܦܩܘܢ ܙܒܘܪ̈ܝܘܬܗ ܕܐܠܗܐ.
ܘܥܠ ܕܒܫܠܡܘܬܐ ܡܫܝܚܐ ܠܗ ܗܘܐ ܕܒܪܢܫܐ
ܗܘܐ ܒܡܨܥܝܘܬܗ ܘܦܘܪܩܢܘܬܐ
ܕܡܨܥܝܢܘܬܐ ܗܘܐ ܒܡܨܥܝܘܬܗ. ܗܘܐ ܐܝܟ
ܫܠܝܚܐ ܕܠܐ ܡܬܦܪܫ ܡܢ ܒܝܢܝ ܐܢܫܐ.
ܬܘܒ ܠܗ ܒܗܝܢ ܠܡܬܒܥ ܕܒܗܘ ܗܘ ܕܪܒܐ
ܗܘܐ. ܘܠܐ ܬܘܒ ܟܠܐ ܕܐܡܝܢܐ. ܢܫܡܫ ܠܗ
ܪܒܐ ܗܘܐ ܒܡܨܥܝܘܬܐ ܘܒܡܫܡܫܢܘܬܐ
ܘܒܬܘܒܘܬܐ. ܘܕܢܫܡܫ ܗܘܐ ܒܡܫܝܚܐ
ܘܡܢ ܐܝܟܐ ܕܒܗܘܬܗ ܡܫܝܚܐ ܒܝܢܝ.
ܘܕܒܡܫܝܚܐ ܫܠܡ ܗܘ ܕܐܠܗܐ ܘܡܫܡܫܢܘܬܗ.
ܗܘܐ ܦܠܘܣ ܡܢܐ ܠܗ. ܫܠܡܐ ܒܢܝ̈
ܪܒܐ ܗܘܐ ܒܡܨܥܝܘܬܐ ܘܡܫܡܫܢܘܬܐ
ܗܘ ܕܒܗ. ܪܘܚܐ ܠܡ ܕܒܩܘܕܫܐ ܢܚܬܬ
ܘܫܠܡ ܕܠܚܡܐ ܠܗ ܥܠܝܗ. ܘܫܠܡܐ ܕܐܬܠܗ
ܗܘ ܕܐܬܠܒܫ. ܘܗܘ ܕܐܬܠܒܫ ܒܦܓܪܐ
ܒܫܠܡܐ. ܘܡܟܠ ܢܦܫܐ ܕܠܠܡ̈ܠܬܐ. ܗܘ ܗܘ
ܪܒܐ ܗܘܐ ܒܬܪܥܘܬܗܘܢ ܒܡܫܡܫܢܘܬܐ
ܕܪ̈ܘܚܐ ܘܒܡܫܡܫܢܘܬܐ ܕܢܦܫܗ. ܘܐܠܐ
ܒܡܫܝܚܐ ܠܡܫܡܠܝܘ ܐܝܪ̈ܐ ܕܬܪ̈ܥܘܬܗ.
ܠܗ ܡܬܕܡܝ ܕܒܐܠܗܐ ܐܬܚܙܝܢ ܗܘܐ ܘܠܐ
ܕܠܐ ܡܬܦܫܩܢ ܘܠܐ ܗܕܐ ܐܢܫܐ. ܘܥܠ

Folio 16v

Folio 17r

[illegible]

Folio 17v

ܐܠܐ ܐܝܟ ܐܝܬܘܗ̇
ܕܡܫ[ܬܟ]ܚ] ܒܗ ܒܢܝ ܐ[ܢ]ܫ
[ܥܡܗ ܘܐܢܫܘܬܐ ܒܢ[ܝ ܐܢܫܐ]. ܘܡܛܠ ܕܒܢܝ
ܡܛܠ ܕܡܢ ܗܠܝܢ ܕܟܠ ܗܠܝܢ ܐܝܟ ܐܢܫܐ ܒܠܚܘܕ:
ܘܡܠܘܬܐ ܡܥܒܕܢܘܬܐ ܕܝܠܗܘܢ ܡܢ ܡܫܡܫܢܘܬܐ
ܗܝ ܕܐܬܝܠܕܘܬܐ ܥ̈ܠܝܢ ܘܠܟܠ ܐܦ̈ܝ ܡܫܝܚܐ
ܐܠܗܘܬܐ ܕܒܪܐ ܕܢܣܒ ܒܪܢܫܐ ܘܢܦܫܐ
ܘܒܟܠ ܡܠܐ ܕܠܐ ܡܬܒܥܝܢ. ܘܡܛܠܗܕܐ
ܠܝܘܬܐ ܕܡܫܡܫܬܐ ܕܡܫܝܚܘܬܐ ܕܠܠ ܡܢ
ܠܥܠܡܐ. ܐܝܟܢܐ ܕܐܡܪܢ ܕܡܫܬܘܕܝܢ ܠܗ
ܐܬܝܠܝܕ ܡܢ ܡܪܝܡ ܐܦ ܠܗ ܡܢ
ܡܫܡܫܢܐ. ܡܛܠ ܕܐܬ[ܒܣܪ] ܡܢ ܪܘܚܐ
ܕܩܘܕܫܐ. ܘܡܬܝܕܥܐ ܡܢ[ܗ] ܕܝܢ. ܗܘܝܢ
ܬܪܥܘܬܐ ܕܩܢܘܡܘܬܐ ܕܝܠ[ܗ] ܕܝܢ ܗܘܘ
ܢܦܫܗ ܐܦ ܒܡܫܝܚܐ ܐܝ[ܬ]ܝܗ ܘܗܘܬ
ܕܠܐ ܐܬܝܠܕ ܒܗܘ ܕܡܫܝܚ ܕܠܐ
ܐܬܒܛܠܬ ܬܪܝܢܘܬܐ ܕܩܢܘܡܝܢ.
ܐܬܬܪܝܡܬ ܒܬܪܥܘܬܐ ܕܡܫܝܚܐ. ܕܠܐ
ܐܝܟ ܕܐܡܪܝܢ ܠܒܠܚܘܕ. ܕܠܐ ܐܘ ܐܠܐ
ܠܦܘܠܐ. ܗܘ ܕܐܡܪ ܒܗܠܝܢ ܕܡܬܪܥܝܢ ܗܟܢ
ܠܥܠܡܐ. ܕܒܠܥܕܝ ܦܘܠܘܣ ܐܝܟ
ܕܡܬܚܙܐ ܠܗ ܠܒܪܢܫܐ. ܕܠܐ ܢܬܬܠܐ
ܠܬܪ̈ܝܢܘܬܐ ܕܩܢܘܡܝܢ. ܐܝܟܢܐ ܠܗ
ܢܦܫܐ ܒܗܘ ܡܫܝܚ ܕܠܐ ܡܬܬܪܝܡܐ ܒܗ.
ܕܗܘܝܐ ܕܒܪܢܫܐ ܐܠܗܝܐ ܕܒܗܘܐ
ܐܬܬܚܝܗ ܘܢܦܫܐ ܠܗ ܒܠܚܘܕ: ܒܗܝ
ܕܒܐܠܗܘܬܐ ܘܒܐܢܫܘܬܐ. ܐܠܐ ܐܦ

Folio 18r

ܒܢܫܐ ܐܢܫ̈ܐ ܘܒܝܫ̈ܘܬܐ ܕܒܢܝܢܫ ܬ̈ܪܥܝܬܐ. ܘܐܝܠܝܢ ܕܒܡܕܒܪܢܘܬܐ ܕܫܘܠܛܢܘܬܐ ܡܬܕܒܪܝܢ. ܐܦ ܒܗܢ ܒܕܘ̈ܟܬܐ ܠܐ ܐܫܬܘܕܥܘ̱. ܐܠܐ ܠܬܘܬܒܘ̱ ܐܬܝܢ. ܟܠܗ ܕܟܠܗ ܚܝܘܗ ܕܥܠܡܐ ܘܕܒܪ̈ܝܬܐ ܐܢܫ̈ܐ ܠܘܬ ܬ̈ܪܥܝܬܐ ܕܡܬܪܒܝܢ ܘܪ̈ܒܝܢܐ ܡܢܗܘܢ ܘܒܡܚܫܒܬܐ ܚܫ̈ܝܟܬܐ. ܘܟܕ ܟܠ ܒܒܢܝܐ ܕܐܒܪܗܘܢ ܠܐ ܡܬܪܥܐ ܐܢܫ ܡܬܪ̈ܥܝܬܐ ܟܠܗ ܕܕܡܝܢ ܒܗ. ܡܟܐ ܕܟܠܗ ܠܡܫܘܚܬܐ ܕܫܘܠܛܢܐ ܕܝܠ ܒܗ. ܐܦ ܟܕ ܠܐ ܚܙܐ. ܘܡܫܘܚܬܗ̱ ܗܪ̈ܝܢܐ ܘܐܝܟ ܚܫ̈ܝܟܐ. ܘܚܝܠܐ ܕܗܪܓܐ ܗܘ: ܬܪܒܝܬܗ ܘܡܫܚܗ. ܠܐ ܡܣܒܪ ܠܬܪ̈ܥܝܬܗ ܕܦ̈ܘܫܚܬܐ ܒܒܫܘܚܬܐ ܕܬܪ̈ܥܝܬܐ ܡ̈ܢܝܢ ܐܠܗܐ ܒܠܘܬ ܒܐܝܠܝܢ ܕܒܡܢܗܘܢ ܐܬܪܒ ܘܐܬܚܙܝ. ܠܘܬ ܢܗܘܐ ܕܝܢ ܕܠܡܫܘܚܬܐ ܕܟܠ ܕܠܐ ܐܬܚܙܝ ܒܗ ܬ̈ܪܥܝܬܐ ܒܟܠ ܕܒܫܘܚܬܗ. ܠܐ ܗܘܘ ܠܗܘܢ ܒܒ̈ܝܫܬܐ ܒܢܫܐ ܕܡܢ ܠܒܪ. ܘܠܐ ܐܫܬܪܝܘ ܚܝܘ̈ܬܐ ܐܢܫ̈ܐ. ܐܠܐ ܒܡܫܘܚܬܐ ܗܘ̈ܝܐ ܕܬܪ̈ܥܝܬܐ ܡ̈ܢܝܢ ܐܘܟܝܢ ܠܟܠ ܐܢܫ ܕܡܬܒܝܢܐ ܐܬܚܘܝܘ ܗܘܘ ܬܪܥܝܬܐ ܒܡܫܘܚܬܐ ܕܡܫܒܚܬܗ. ܘܡܬܠ ܒܗ. ܗܘܝܐ ܬܫܒܘܚܬܐ ܠܐܠܗܐ ܕܒܬܪܥܝܬܐ ܕܒܡܫܟܠܐ [ܐ]ܡܝܢ. ܘܫܠܡܬ ܗܝ ܕܡܫ̈ܒܚܬܐ. ܐܠܐ ܡܠܝܢ [ܡ]ܦܩܢ ܐܢܘܢ ܒܡܫܘܕܥܢ ܒܫܘܚܬܐ ܘܡܢܗܘܢ [ܐ]

Folio 18v

ܠܐܠܗܐ ܕܟܠ ܕܡܫܝܚܐܝܬ ܐܠܗܘܬܐ
ܕܦܓܪܐ ܡܬܬܚܡܐ ܒܒܢܝ̈ܢܫܐ. ܘܗܘܝܘ
ܡܢ ܒܬܪܗ ܡܫܬܡܥܝܢ ܡ̈ܠܦܢܐ
ܘܡܬܐܡܪܢܐ. ܘܐܬܒܣܡܬܐ ܠܐܠܗܐ ܕܐܠܗܘܬܐ
ܕܐܘܣܝܐ. ܒܫܡܥ ܕܝܢ ܠܗ ܗܟܢܐ. ܐܠܗܐ
ܐܠܗܘܬܐ ܦܓܪܢܝܬܐ ܕܐܠܗܐ ܡܫܝܚܐ
ܗܘܬ ܐܘܣܝܐ ܕܡܫܬܘܕܥܢܘܬܐ ܗܕܐ
ܕܡܬܡܠܠܐ ܐܬܓܠܝܬ. ܘܠܐ ܡܢ ܒܬܪ ܕܐܬܝܠܕ
ܠܐܠܗܘܬܐ ܠܒܪ ܠܐܠܗܐ. ܐܝܟܢܐ ܕܝܢ
ܡܟܠܐ ܗܘܐ ܠܡܣܒ ܕܠܦܓܪܐ ܠܐ ܢܩܒܠ.
ܐܝܟ ܕܡܬܡܠܠ ܕܡܠܬܐ ܢܦܠ ܠܦܓܪܐ
ܠܡܦܠܚ ܡܫܝܚܐ ܦܓܪܐ ܠܐܠܗܐ. ܘܡܢ
ܡܟܠ ܠܐ ܐܫܬܠ ܘܡܢ ܦܓܪܐ. ܐܠܐ ܢܘܚ
ܟܠܗܘܢ ܕܐܝܬܝܗ ܗܘܬ ܕܡܬܝܕܥܐ ܘܦܓܪܢܝܐ
ܠܗ. ܘܐܫܬܠܡ ܡܠܦܢܘܬܐ ܕܦܓܪܐ. ܠܟܠܗܘܢ
ܕܒܗܕܐ ܡܣܒܪܢܘܬܐ ܐܝܬܝܗܘܢ. ܕܟܠ
ܗܕܐ ܢܦܠܬ ܟܝ̈ܢܐ ܘܦܓܪܐ ܠܐܠܗܐ.
ܘܢܦܠܘ ܒܢܫܐ ܕܠܒܪܐ ܒܒܢܫܐ ܕܒܗ
ܐܠܗܐ. ܘܠܐ ܠܐ ܦܫܛ ܠܗܝܢܐ ܒܗ ܕܬܐ
ܘܡܫܬܡܥܐ ܘܡܬܪܓܪܓ ܢ̈ܫܐ ܕܐܝܟ ܕܫܪܝܐ
ܘܢ ܐܬܓܠܝܬ. ܟܠ ܕܝܢ ܕܐܠܗܐ
ܐܬܗܘܝ ܐܘ ܕܢܫܒܚܘܢ ܐܘ ܕܦܓܪܢܝܐ
ܐܘ ܕܢܫܐ ܐܦܝܢ ܦܓܪܐ ܕܡܫܝܚܐ
ܠܡܫܬܘ ܡܫܬܡܥܢܐ ܗܕܐ. ܘܐܬܐܡܪ
ܡܢ ܐܝܟ ܕܐܬܐܡܪ ܐ̈ܢܫܘܬܐ. ܐܝܟ
ܕܝܢ ܐܢܫ̈ܝܢ ܕܐܬܦܩܕܘ ܟܠ ܕܝܢ ܡܫܝܚܐ
ܕܡܫܬܘܕܥܢܘܬܐ ܗܕܐ ܕܐܬܦܩܕܬ ܢ̈ܫܐ

Folio 19r

ܐܠܐ ܠܘܬ ܗܘ ܕܒܪ ܓܢܣܗ ܐܬܩܪܒ
ܘܗܘܐ ܒܪܢܫܐ. ܘܐܬܬܠܒ ܕܢܣܒ ܠ ܢܫܐ.
ܕܢܬܩܪܒܘܢ ܠܘܬ ܐܠܗܐ ܢܦܪܩܐ ܠܒܪ̈ܝܬܐ.
ܘܢܗܘܐ ܠܘܬ ܒܢܝ̈ ܐܢܫܐ. ܘܐܬܬܩܒ ܗܘ̇ ܕܠܘܬ
ܐܠܗܐ ܕܗܘܐ ܐܝܟ ܐܟܚܕܐ ܥܠ ܕܐܝܬܘ
ܒܗܘ ܕܟܠ ܕܗܘܐ ܒܪܢܫܐ. ܘܐܬܬܒ ܕܠܘܬ
ܗܘܐ ܠܒܢܝ̈ ܐܢܫܐ ܗܘܐ ܕܢܬܩܪܒܘܢ
ܒܡܫܠܡܢܘܬ ܠܘܬ ܐܠܗܐ ܐܠܐ ܐܦ ܠܟܠܢܫ.
ܒܒܢܘ̈ܬܐ. ܠܘܬ ܡܫܝ̈ܚܐ ܕܟܗ̈ܢܐ ܘܢܒܝ̈ܐ.
ܐܬܪܒܝ ܗܘ ܡܫܝܚܘܬ ܘܗܕܪܐ ܐܬܩܪܫܢܐ
ܠܟܠܢ. ܕܐܝܟ ܕܒܟܬܒܐ ܡܚܘܝܐ ܠܒܝܬܐ
ܕܒܪ̈ܝܬܐ ܢܦܪܩܐ. ܘܢܬܩܪܒܘܢ ܐܦ ܠܘܬ ܗܘ
ܕܒܗܘܢ ܒ ܚܕ. ܗܝ ܕܥܠ ܒܪܢܫܐ ܐܝܬܘܗܝ
ܒܪܘܚܗ ܢܘܬܒܠܗ ܠܫܠܝ̈ܚܐ ܘܠܢܒܝ̈ܐ
ܕܟܠ ܕܗܘܐ ܒܪܢܫܐ ܪܒܐ ܗܘܐ
ܡܫܝܚܘܬ. ܠܘܬ ܐܠܗܐ ܠܒܪ̈ܝܬܐ ܘܡܢ
ܠܘܬ ܒܢܝ̈ ܐܢܫܐ. ܐܦܠܐ ܗܘ ܕܡܫܝܚܐ
ܡܢ ܫܪܪܐ.÷.. ܠܘܬ ܗܘ ܕܡܫܠܡܢܘܬܐ ܗܘ
ܕܐܡܪ ܗܘ ܕܒܪܢܫܐ ܗܘܐ ܫܡܫܐ
ܐܡܪ ܗܘ. ܒܟܢ ܗܘ ܕܪܒܐ ܗܘܐ ܒܡܫܡܫܢܘܬܐ
ܘܒܫܘܠܛܢܐ ܒܡܫܡܫܢܘܬܐ ܘܒܫܘܠܛܢܘܬܐ
ܕܒܢܝ̈ ܐܢܫܐ ܕܐܬܦܢܝ ܠܗ ܒܫܠܝ̈ܚܐ
ܠܒܪ̈ܝܬܐ. ܘܐܫܬܠܡ ܒܗ ܗܝ ܕܒܡܫܝܚܘܬ
ܕܒܝܬ ܐܒܘܗܝ ܕܐܬܝܠܕ ܡܢܗ ܒܪܢܫܐ
ܕܒܗ ܐܝܬܘܗܝ ܕܐܝܬܘܗܝ ܗܘܐ ܒܪܢܫܐ. ܘܐܠܐ ܗܘ
ܚܠܦ. ܠܗ ܐܠܗܐ ܘܒܪܢܫܐ. ܘܟܠ ܗܘ
ܡܫܝܚܘܬܐ ܠܐ ܡܢܗ ܢܣܒ. ܠܡܫܡܫܬܐ
ܕܒܠܥܕܝܢ ܠܥܠܡ ܐܠܗܐ ܡܢܗ ܘܒܪܘܚܗ

Folio 19v

Folio 20r

Folio 20v

[illegible]

Folio 21r

Folio 21v

ܕܐܬܟܬܒܘܗܝ. ܘܡܛܠܐ ܐܝܟ ܚܕ ܡܢ ܒܢܝܢܫܐ ܚܝܘܬܐ
ܢܦܠܝ. ܗܘܘ ܕܝܢ ܠܗ ܠܐ ܕܡܘܬܐ ܐܦ
ܒܢܝܐ. ܘܠܐ ܦܐܝܐ ܗܘܬ ܕܢܬܕܡܐ
ܒܡܘܬܐ ܢܗܘܘܢ. ܗܘܝܬܐ ܕܦܬܓܡܐ ܚܝܐ
ܕܡܫܝܚܐ. ܘܠܐ ܒܡܟܠ ܐܠܗܐ ܕܢܗܘܘܢ
ܠܗ ܒܢܝܐ ܘܝܪܬܐ ܕܡܠܟܘܬܗ ܠܚܘܕܬܐ.
ܐܠܐ ܕܐܬܛܥܝܘ. ܢܫܐ ܘܠܐ ܒܡܘܬܐ
ܒܟܘܠܗܘܢ ܦܬܓܡܝܢ ܒܟܠ ܥܠܡܐ. ܘܡܛܠ
ܕܢܫܡܥܐ ܐܡܪ ܕܐܢܐ ܐܢܐ ܐܢܐ ܐܠܗܟܘܢ
ܕܐܬܒܪܝܘ ܘܕܐܝܬܘܗܝ ܘܕܡܚܝܐ
ܘܐܠܗܘܬܐ ܠܐ ܗܘܬ ܕܡܘܬܐ ܐܠܐ
ܕܚܝܐ. ܠܟܘܢ ܕܝܢ ܚܝܝܢ ܐܢܘܢ ܠܗ ܕܟܠ
ܒܢܝܐ ܐܘܦ ܕܡܕܪ ܠܗ. ܝܗܒܐ. ܕܐܢܐ ܐܢܐ
ܐܠܗܗ ܕܐܒܪܗܡ ܐܝܣܚܩ ܘܕܝܥܩܘܒ
ܕܡܬܪܢܝܐ ܠܗܘܢ ܒܟܠ ܐܦܝܢ ܕܝܢ
ܒܗ ܐܝܟܐ ܕܡܘܬܐ ܘܗܘܐ ܕܚܝܝܐ
ܕܡܘܬܐ ܠܐ ܐܬܟܢܫܘ ܒܢܝܐ ܘܐܝܠܝܢ
ܕܒܥܬܐ ܠܐܢܫܐ ܕܒܢܝܐ ܠܐ
ܐܬܟܢܫܘ ܒܡܘܬܐ. ܠܐ ܕܝܢ ܒܢܝ
ܐܢܫܐ ܚܝܝܐ ܘܠܐ ܡܠܐܟܐ
ܒܠܚܘܕܝܗܘܢ ܡܢ ܥܡܐ ܒܢܝܐ ܕܐܠܗܐ.
ܐܠܐ ܗܘ ܠܟܠܗ ܕܗܘܝܢ ܡܢ ܒܢܝܐ
ܒܢܝܐ ܗܘ. ܒܡܘܬܐ ܘܒܚܝܘܬܐ. ܘܡܛܠ
ܕܗܘܘ ܐܢܫܐ ܠܒܪܐ ܕܗܘܐ ܒܪܢܫܐ
ܒܟܘܠܗ ܚܝܘܬܐ ܕܝܢ ܒܡܫܝܚܐ ܕܡܬܝܐ.
ܐܬܓܠܝܬ ܒܬܘܚܡܝܢ ܐܝܟ ܒܢܝܐ ܕܐܬܐ.
ܕܝܠ ܦܘܪܩܢܐ ܕܐܚܘܬܐ ܕܢܦܩ ܗܘ.
ܐܝܟ ܫܒܝܐ ܕܐܬܟܬܒܘܬܐ ܕܐܬܪܚܩܘ

Folio 22r

[illegible]

Folio 22v

ܠܚܘܝܐ ܐܡܘܪܝܐ. ܘܡܢ ܐܘܝܐ ܘܐܡܘܪܝܐ ܐܬܚܫܒ. ܘܐܦ ܡܢ ܡܫܡܫܢܘܬܗ ܕܟܗܢܘܬܐ ܗܘ̇ ܕܐܬܚܫܒ ܦܛܪܘܣܐ ܕܟܗܢܘܬܐ ܘܕܡܫܝܚܘܬܐ. ܢܣܒܘܗܝ ܒܒܢ̈ܝܗ̇ ܐܚܪ̈ܢܐ ܐܝܟ ܕܟܠܗ ܫܠܝܛܐ. ܗܘ ܒܪܢܫܐ ܡܢ ܐܚܝܢܐ ܡܠܟܘ̈ܗܝ. ܕܐܬܝܗܒ ܡܢ ܟܗܢܘܬܐ ܘܡܫܝܚܘܬܐ ܕܠܗܘܢ. ܠܘܬ ܠܗ ܦܛܪܘܣܐ. ܐܝܟ ܕܐܦ ܠܐ ܒܢ̈ܝܢܐ ܡܢ ܟܗܢܘܬܗܘܢ ܘܡܫܝܚܘܬܗܘܢ ܐܫܬܘܕܝ ܠܗ̇. ܡܬܠܡܕܢܐ ܕܡܢ ܟܗܢܘܬܐ ܘܡܫܝܚܘܬܐ ܕܐܫܬܪܝܬ. ܗܟܢ ܡܫܬܘܕܥܐ ܠܗܘܢ ܒܢ̈ܝܢܐ ܗܘܘ ܒܢ̈ܝܐ. ܘܡܫܬܘܕܥܝܢ ܕܐܠܗܐ ܡܠܟܘܬܐ ܐܬܝܗܒܬ ܒܟܠܗܝܢ. ܗܟܢ ܫܘܬܦܘܬܐ ܕܠܘܬ ܢܫܘܗ ܘܡܫܝܚܘܬܗ ܐܫܬܘܕܝ ܒܢ̈ܝܢܐ ܠܡܫܝܚܗ. ܗܟܢ ܡܠܟܐ ܗܘ ܦܛܪܘܣܐ ܠܐܠܗܐ ܡܢ ܢ̈ܒܝܐ. ܫܬܐܪܘܬ ܒܢ̈ܝܢܐ ܡܢ ܠܗ ܒܗ ܕܡܫܝܚܘܬ ܕܐܢܫܐ ܐܬܝܠܕ ܘܐܬܬܠܝ. ܦܪ̈ܝܫܝܢܬ ܘܡܢ ܚܕ. ܕܡܠܟܘܬܐ ܗܘܝܐ ܥܠ ܒܢ̈ܝܢܐ ܢܦܩ ܠܗ. ܘܐܦ ܕܡܘܬ ܡܢ ܗܘ̇ܝܐ ܢܒܝܘ. ܕܒܢ̈ܝܢܐ ܟܠܗ̇ ܢܫܡܫܘܢ ܠܐܒܘܗܝ ܘܢܩܕܫܘܢ ܐܠܗܐ ܕܡܫܝܚܘܬ ܐܝܟ ܒܗܘܢ ܐܠܗܐ ܘܒܢ̈ܝܢܐ. ܢܬܒܣܡܘܢ. ܐܡܪ ܐܒܘܢܐ ܡܢ ܬܪ̈ܝܨܘܬܐ ܪܒܐ ܗܘܐ. ܘܐܦ ܢܬܒܪܟ ܕܕܠܗܐ ܐܬܬܪܝܡ ܗܘܐ ܬܪܝܨܘܬܐ. ܟܠ ܕܟܬܒܝܢ ܕܢܫܡܥ ܪܒܐ ܗܘܐ ܕܐܦ ܗܘܐ ܢܦܫܬܐ ܕܡܫܝܚܝܢ ܐܠܗܐ. ܘܐܦ ܟܠܗܘܢ ܕܗܘܢ ܢܬܪܒܐ ܘܐܦ ܡܢ ܒܢ̈ܝܢܐ

Folio 23r

ܐܚܪ̈ܢܝܬܐ. ܟܠ ܚܕܐ ܡܢܗܝܢ ܕܠܐ ܐܬܬܚܡܘ
ܡܫܝܚܐ ܡܬܝܚܕ. ܒܗܝ ܗܝ ܐܚܪ̈ܢܝܬܐ.
ܕܡܫܝܚܐ ܐܝܬ ܒܡܫܘܚܬܐ ܡܬܝܕܥ ܟܠܗܘܢ
ܕܪ̈ܟܝܐ ܗܘܘ. ܘܟܠ ܠܐ ܐܬܬܚܡܘ ܗܘܘ.
ܡܫܝܚܐ ܐܝܟܢܐ ܪ̈ܟܝܐ ܗܘܘ. ܕܗܘܐ ܐܦ
ܚܕ ܕܡܢ ܡܫܝܚܝܢ ܕܟܠ ܐܠܗܘܬܐ ܡܬܝܕܥ
ܡܢܗ ܩܢܘܡܐ ܗܠܝܢ ܡܢܗܘܢ ܡܫܝܚܐ ܐܝܬ
ܕܗܘܐ ܘܡܫܚ ܡܫܘܚܬܐ ܕܟܠ ܐܝܟܢܐ.
ܘܗܝܟܢ ܡܬܝܕܥ ܟܠܗܘܢ. ܠܐܪ̈ܟܝܘܬܐ
ܐܝܟܢ. ܕܝܢ ܒܡܫܘܚܬܐ ܕܟܠ ܡܫܝܚܐ
ܐܬܡܫܚ ܐܝܟܢ. ܕܪ̈ܟܝܐ ܗܘܘ. ܐܝܟܢ
ܐܠܗܘܬܐ ܕܠܐ ܡܬܚܡܐ ܗܘܬ ܕܟܠܗ ܐܝܬ
ܐܝܬܘܗ̇ܝ ܟܕ ܦܫܛܐ. ܘܬܘܒ ܕܠܐ ܡܬܬܚܡ
ܕܝܢ ܗܘܘ. ܐܠܐ ܕܡܫܚ ܪ̈ܟܝܐ ܗܘܘ.
ܘܐܝܟ ܐܝܟܢ ܐܬܚܠܛܬ ܡܫܝܚܘܬܐ ܕܗܘܐ.
ܐܝܬܘܗ̇ܝ ܠܐܪ̈ܟܝܘܬܐ. ܠܐ ܟܕ ܐܝܟܢܐ
ܬܬܝܚܕ ܘܟܠ ܐܠܗܘܬܐ. ܗܘ ܒܟܝܢ ܕܒܟܠܗ̇ ܐܝܬ
ܡܫܚ ܒܟܝܢܐ ܐܠܗܘܬܐ ܘܒܪ̈ܢܫܐ ܒܟܠܗ̇ ܐܝܬ
ܗܝ ܦܪ̈ܝܫܘܬܐ ܘܡܝܬܘܬܐ. ܕܡܬܝܕܥ ܒܟܝܢܐ
ܠܡܫܝܚܘܬܐ ܕܒܦܪ̈ܨܘܦܐ. ܗܘ ܦܫܝܛܘܬܗ
ܕܢܦܫܐ ܠܐ ܡܡܫܚܐ. ܕܗܝ ܡܪ̈ܟܝܐ ܐܝܟ ܘ
ܐܠܗܘܬܐ ܡܬܚܫܒܐ ܠܫܘܐ. ܐܬܚܫܒܬ ܗܘܐ
ܡܫܚ. ܐܝܟܢ ܕܗܘܝܢ ܡܢܗ ܡܫܝܚܝܢ. ܐܦ ܪ̈ܟܝܐ
ܕܡܫܝܚܐ ܐܝܟܢ ܕܐܬܐ ܕܗܘܐ ܘܦܫܝܛܘܬܗ
ܡܫܬܟܚ ܘܗܘܐ ܕܐܠܗܘܬܐ ܘܪ̈ܟܝܐ.
ܕܐܬܝܠܕܬ ܐܝܬܘܬܗ ܡܢ ܗܘ ܦܫܝܛܘܬܐ
ܐܝܬܘܗ̇ܝ ܕܠܐ ܡܬܚܫܒܐ. ܐܦ ܟܠ ܗܘ

Folio 23v

ܕܐܒܗ̈ܬܐ ܒܪܬ ܩܠܐ ܗܘܐ ܒܒܢ̈ܬܐ
ܕܐܒܗ̈ܘܬܐ ܒܟܘܬܒܝܗܘܢ. ܢܘܚܡܢܗܘܢ
ܒܡܪܟܒܬܐ ܐܬܒܗܬܘܢ. ܕܐܠܗܘܬܐ ܗܘܬ
ܒܪܢܫܐ ܕܠܐ ܚܘܠܩܐ. ܘܗܘܝܘ ܒܬܪܝܢ
ܒܡܠܬܗܘܢ. ܕܗܢܘܢ ܠܐ ܐܚܪܢܐ ܘܐܚܪܢܐ
ܐܬܬܚܠܠ ܒܪܗ ܕܐܠܗܐ ܘܒܪܢܫܐ.
ܐܠܐ ܕܠܘܬ ܕܢܬܝܪܬ ܐܬܚܝܕ
ܘܠܐ ܐܠܗܘܬܗ ܐܬܚܠܦܬ ܒܒܣܪܢܘܬܗ
ܘܠܐ ܦܓܪܢܘܬܗ ܐܬܚܠܦܬ ܘܐܬܬܪܝܡܬ ܡܢ
ܡܢ ܒܬܪ ܕܐܬܚܝܕ. ܐܠܐ ܐܝܟ
ܕܡܬܗܝܡܢ ܐܠܗܐ ܒܪܗ ܕܐܝܬܘܗܝ.
ܒܡܬܘܡܝܘܬܐ ܐܦ ܒܪܢܫܐ ܒܡܘܬܐ ܕܗܘܐ.
ܘܚܘܠܦܐ ܒܡܣܒܐ ܒܚܝܘܗܝ ܠܐ ܒܨܒܘܬܐ
ܕܠܝܬ ܗܘܐ ܗܝ ܬܪܝܢܘܬܐ. ܕܠܝܬ
ܗܝ ܐܚܪܬܐ ܕܠܘܩܒܠܐ. ܕܗܟܢܐ ܗܘܐ
ܢܩܝܦܘܬܐ ܟܝܢܝܐ ܘܐܝܬܘܬܐ ܕܨܒܝܢܐ
ܕܐܠܗܐ ܘܕܒܪܢܫܐ. ܠܐ ܕܝܢܐ ܒܡܠܬܗܘܢ
ܠܝܠܦܢ ܕܝܗܒܘ ܠܢ ܐܒ̈ܗܐ ܒܟܬܒܝܗܘܢ.
ܐܠܐ ܠܝܠܦܘܬܐ ܕܐܬܬܠܝܗܘܢ ܘܐܬܐܡܪ ܠܗ
ܒܪܢܫܐ ܠܡܪܟܒܬܗ ܕܐܠܗܘܬܐ ܒܠܚܘܕ
ܐܠܦܢ. ܕܐܬܬܢܣܒ ܡܢ ܐܠܗܐ ܒܠܚܘܕ
ܒܒܝܬ ܕܒܪܢܫܐ ܒܦܪܨܘܦܗ. ܘܐܝܟ
ܐܠܦܢ ܕܠܐ ܒܘܚܢܐ ܒܬܪ ܒܠܚܘܕ
ܦܫܝܛܘܬܐ ܕܢܩܘܛܪܘܢ ܗܘ ܕܒܒܪܐ
ܠܬܡܢ ܚܢܢ. ܘܬܘܒ ܐܡܪ ܠܗܘܢ ܚܕ. ܚܠܐ
ܘܚܕ. ܝܡܝܢܐ ܘܚܕܐ ܣܡܠܬܐ ܘܚܕ.
ܣܘܓܠܐ. ܘܟܠ ܗܢܘܢ ܢܩܛܠ ܠܟܠ
ܚܕ ܡܢ ܚܢܢ ܗܠܝܢ ܕܐܬܚܙܝܘ. ܘܠܐ

Folio 24r

Folio 24v

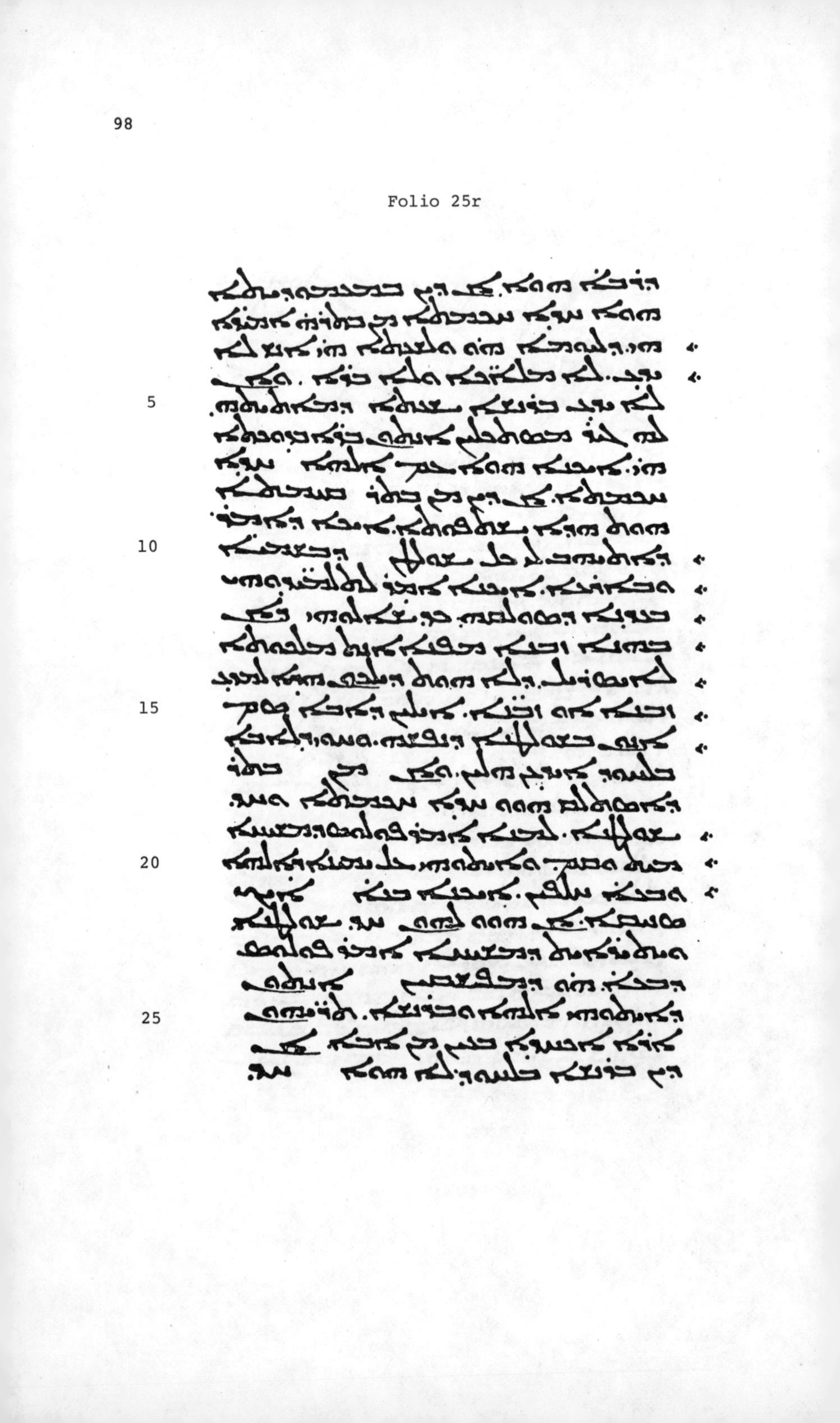

Folio 25r

Folio 25v

Folio 26r

Folio 26v

[illegible]

Folio 27r

[illegible]

Folio 27v

Folio 28r

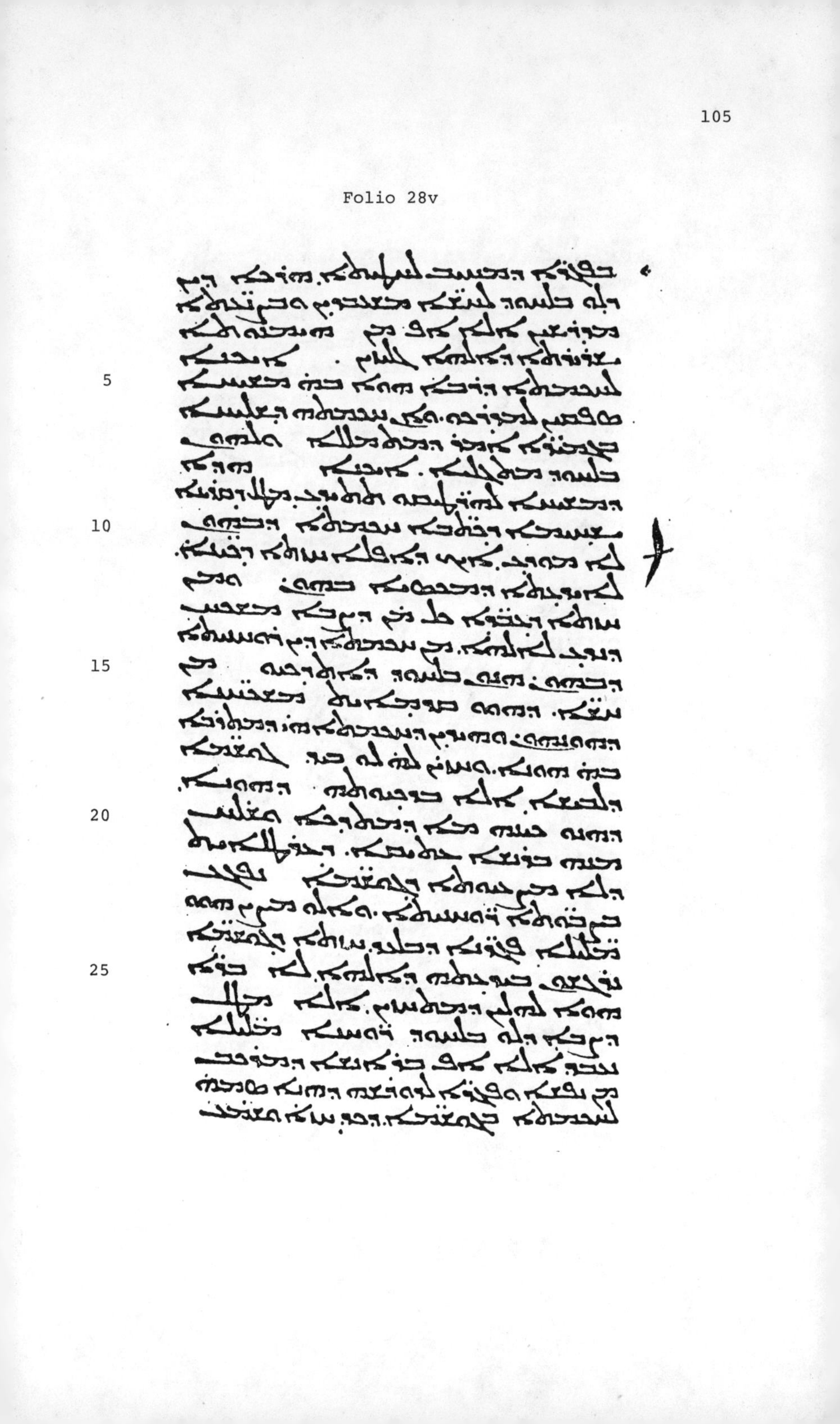

Folio 28v

Folio 29v

[illegible]

Folio 29v

ܕܒܠܚܘܕܝܗ̇. ܘܗܟܢ ܒܬܪ ܕܐܫܬܠܡ ܠܗܘܢ ܢܦܠܬ
ܐܢܫ ܠܚܫܬܗܘܢ ܘܠܬܘܟܟܗܘܢ ܕܐܪ̈ܬܘܬܐ
ܕܟܢܫܠ ܘܠܘ ܠܟܢܘܫܬܐ ܕܐܬܬܟܝܠܬ ܒܗܘܢ.
ܘܗܟܢܐ ܐܦ ܐܠܗܐ ܕܐܘܪܟ ܫܒܝܩܘܬܗ
ܒܐܬܘ̈ܬܐ ܕܫܪ̈ܒܬܐ ܗܟܢܐ ܕܒܟܠܗܠ
ܠܗ̇ ܠܐܘܟܟܐ. ܢܗܘܐ ܓܝܪ ܕܒܫܠܡ ܠܗ ܒܥܘܗܕܢܐ.
ܠܥܒܕܘܬܗ ܕܟܝܢܐ ܠܐ ܒܟܘܟܒ. ܐܠܐ ܐܦ
ܗܟܢܐ ܐܬܬܪܝܡ ܒܗ̇ ܕܠܐ ܠܐ ܫܘܠܛܢܐ.
ܘܒܫܘ ܕܐܬܦܩܘ ܕܫܪ̈ܒܬܐ ܕܠܐ ܠܐ ܢܟܣܐ.
ܒܢܝ̈ ܕܐܦܠܐ ܟܕ ܡܠܟܝܢ ܒܗܘܢ ܐܝܬܘܬܐ
ܒܝܘܡ. ܐܠܐ ܒܬܘܡܟܟܐ ܕܐܬܝܠܝܕ
ܒܗ ܘܒܟܪ̈ܝܬܐ. ܒܗ ܟܕ ܠܐ ܡܬܩܪܒܐ ܘܠܘܬ
ܒܟ̈ܘܬܐ ܒܐܘܟܟܐ ܘܒܫܪ̈ܒܬܐ. ܘܟܠ
ܕܠܐ ܐܬܬܠܝ ܦܘܪܫܢܐ ܕܒ̈ܢܝ ܐܢܫܐ
ܕܒܠܒܗ ܡܢܝܢܐ ܕܗܘܠ ܐܬܬܘ̈ܬܐ ܢܦܫܢ
ܠܬܘܟܟܗܘܢ. ܘܢܦܠ ܐܦ ܐܢܫܒܬܐ
ܕܒܗܘܢ. ܐܪ̈ܢܫܐ ܐܢܫܝ̈ܬܐ ܗܘܘ ܠܗ
ܐܠܗܐ ܕܝܗܒܐ ܒܗ ܠܬܗܘܢ. ܘܒܟܠܗܘܢ
ܐܢܫܐ ܐܠܗܐ ܫܒܝܩܘܬܐ. ܘܢܦܠ ܠܓܠܝܢ
ܒܟ̈ܘܬܐ ܒܪܫܝܬ ܫܒܝܩܘܬܐ ܕܒܗ ܘܬܗ.
ܗܟܢܐ ܒܐܘܟܟܐ ܕܒܢ̈ܝܐ ܫܒܝܩܘܬܐ
ܕܒܢܘܗ ܐܬܬܦܨܒܬ ܘܗܘܬ ܒܗܘܦܐ.
ܒܟܢܫܐ ܠܟ. ܐܬܬܘܗܝ ܫܠܗ ܘܫܒܝܩܘܬܗ
ܕܐܠܗܐ. ܘܗܟ ܕܬܟܠܐ ܗܘܬ ܒܗܘܕܟܬܐ
ܕܐܠܗܐ. ܘܗܟܢ ܕܐܬܦܨܒܬ. ܒܟܢܫܐ.
ܫܒܝܩܘܬܐ ܗܟܢܐ ܕܐܬܦܨܒܬ. ܒܟܢܫܐ
ܗܘܬ ܠܬܘܬܪ ܒܗ. ܬܪܥܘܬܐ ܗܝ ܫܒܝܩܘܬܐ
ܕܐܬܬܟܝܠܬ ܒܟ̈ܘܬܐ. ܘܗܝ ܕܒܬܪܝܬܐ
ܕܬܘܗܡܐ ܒܐܘܟܟܐ ܒܐܘܟܟܐ ܕܒܢ̈ܝܐ

Folio 30r

[illegible]

Folio 30v

Folio 31r

Folio 31v

ܗܘ ܪ̈ܐܙܐ ܕܐܫܬܡܠܝ ܒܗ̇ ܒܡܣܒܪܢܘܬܗ.
ܕܦܪܨܘܦܗ. ܕܠܗ ܚܙܝ ܐܦ ܐܒܐ ܒܗ.
ܠܗ ܦܪܨܘܦܐ ܒܡܫܝܚܘܬܗ. ܘܒܬܪ ܟܠܗ̇
ܕܢܫܠܡ ܡܕܒܪܢܘܬܗ. ܒܗ ܒܒܪܢܫܗ ܐܣܩܗ
ܐܒܘܢ ܠܫܡܝܐ ܒܗܝܟܠܐ ܕܐܬܬܩܢܐ ܕܝܠܗ.
ܕܢܬܒܐ ܠܘܬ ܐܒܘܗܝ. ܘܢܫܠܛ ܒܟܘܠܗܝܢ
ܘܒܡܕܒܪܢܘܬܐ. ܗܘܝ ܐܒܘܢ ܠܗ ܒܠܚܘܕܝܘܬܐ
ܐܢܫܝܐ. ܘܡܕܒܪܢܐ ܠܘܬ ܐܒܐ ܡܪܢ
ܐܒܘܢ ܀ ܠܐܢܫ ܕܝܢ ܕܥܡܠ ܡܬ ܕܡܫܬܘܬܦ
ܒܪܘܚܐ ܐܢܫܝܐ. ܕܢܣܒ ܕܡܬܩܪܐ
ܡܢ ܩܕܝܫ ܒܥܘܒܕܢܘܬܐ ܢܦܫܝܢ ܗܘܘ
ܒ̈ܢܝܐ ܕܐܠܗܐ. ܒܫ̈ܡܝܐ ܕܝܢ ܒܥܒ̈ܕܐ
ܒ̈ܢܝܐ ܕܦܠܚܘܬܐ ܘܒܥܒܕܐ ܒܥܘܒܕܢܘܬܐ
ܕܡܬܝܚܕܝܢ ܒܫ̈ܡܝܐ ܘܒܥܒ̈ܕܐ ܒ̈ܢܝܐ
ܕܐܠܗܐ. ܥܠ ܕܠܐ ܒܡܬܩܢܘܬܐ ܐܝܟ
ܒܡܬܬܣܠܩܐ ܦܢܝܢ ܒ̈ܢܝܐ ܕܦܩܠܝ.
ܐܠܐ ܐܢܬܘܢ ܒܥܘܒܕܢܘܬܗ. ܠܘܬܗ
ܥܘܒܕܐ ܕܗܘܘ ܒܗ ܡܕܒ̈ܪܢܐ. ܘܐܬܒ
ܐܝܟ ܕܠܘܬ ܒܡܥܝܢܐ ܠܘܬܒܝܬܐ ܒܟܠ
ܐܝܢܐ ܐܘܟܝܬ. ܕܡܛܠ ܕܠܘܬ ܢܦܫܗܘܢ ܒܪ
ܢܦܫܐ ܕܡܬܬܒܪ ܗܘܐ. ܘܐܒܕܗ ܠܘܬ ܒ
ܠܦܘܬ ܗܕܐ ܒܥܒܘܕܘܬܐ ܕܒܟܠܗ
ܗܘܬ ܒܟܪܗ. ܘܠܘܩܒܠ ܠܘܬ ܒܡܫܝܚܐ
ܘܠܐ ܒܠܚܘܕ ܠܐܬܠܡ ܕܐܬܡܠܠ: ܐܝܟ ܕܐ
ܕܒܢ ܕܒܠܝܢ ܠܗ ܐܒܘܗ̈ܝܢ ܠܥܡܪ ܥܠܡܐ.
ܘܬܘܒ ܕܐܒܗ̈ܘܗܝ ܒܟܠ ܚܝܠܐ ܐܝܟ ܡܢ ܗܘܐ
ܠܐܘܪܫܠܡ ܒܒܝܬ ܕܩܘܕܫܐ. ܠܐܘܣܦܢܘܬܐ
ܕܗܠܝܢ ܐܡܪ ܗܘܐ ܠܗ ܡܪܢ ܕܒܝܬ ܐܒܝ ܗܘܐ

Folio 32r

Folio 32v

Folio 33r

ܣܘܥܪܢܐ ܕܒܗܘܢ. ܘܒܬܪܗ ܐܬܚܙܝܬ
ܘܐܬܬܠܝܬ ܠܓܙܪܬܐ. ܘܡܢ ܒܬܪ ܗܕܐ ܐܬ
ܐܬܬܒܪܝܬ ܘܐܬܬܫܝܡܬ ܠܡܠܟܘܬܐ. ܟܕ
ܗܘܝܘ ܗܘܬ ܕܐܬܟܠܐ ܘܐܬܒܪܝܬ. ܘܟܕ
ܡܫܒܚ ܠܝܘܡܐ ܕܗܘܐ ܗܘ ܕܐܬܬܓܠܝ ܟܕ
ܗܘܝܘ ܗܘܬ. ܡܟܝܠ ܠܗܘ ܕܗܘܐ ܡܢ ܩܕܝܡ ܢܗܝܪܐ
ܕܒܗ ܐܝܟ ܠܝܬ. ܕܢܣܒ ܐܝܬܘܗܝ ܗܘܐ
ܐܝܟ ܡܢ ܫܡܝܐ ܐܬܚܙܝ. ܘܡܛܠ ܗܢܐ ܗܘ
ܡܠܟܘܬܐ ܕܫܡܝܐ ܡܕܝܢܬܐ ܠܗ ܐܠܗܐ
ܐܠܗܐ. ܗܘ ܕܒܟܢܘܫܝܐ ܕܢܝܫܐ ܠܥܠܡܐ
ܫܟܠܠܗ ܕܐܬܪܐ. ܘܫܘܪܐ ܕܗܘ ܠܘܩܒܠ
ܡܘܕܝܢ ܕܗܘܐ ܡܢ ܫܒܝܚܐ ....
ܐܡܝܢ ܠܗ ܡܢ ܐܬܝܕܥ ܘܡܬܝܕܥܐ ܡܢ
ܐܠܗܐ ܕܬܝܪܘܬܐ ܡܛܠ ܕܪܘܚܐ ܕܩܘܕܫܐ
ܘܡܛܠ ܕܒܪܘܬܐ. ܘܡܢ ܕܡܠܟܐ ܐܬܝܠܕ
ܡܫܝܚܐ [ܒܬܪ] ܬܘܕܝܬܐ. ܘܒܠܐ ܐܬܘܗܝ ܗܘܐ
[ܐܚܪܢܐ] ܕܐܠܗܐ ܡܢ ܟܠ[ܗ] ܫܘܠܛܢܗ
ܗܘܝܘ ܗܘ ܕܐܬܒܪܝ ܡܢ ܫܘܠܛܢܗ ܕܡܠܟܐ
ܕܐܠܗܐ ܫܒܝܚܐ ܕܠܝܬ ܒܗ ܕܢܫܬܪܐ
ܠܡܗܘܝܘܬܐ. ܘܡܢ ܗܘܐ ܗܘ ܕܐܬܓܠܝ
ܒܗܘ ܐܬܪܐ. ܕܕܡܘܬܐ ܠܗ ܡܫܬܠܛܢܐ
ܡܢ ܩܕܝܡ ܐܦܝܣܩܘܦܐ. ܘܗܘ ܗܘܐ ܕܝܠܢ ܚܝܝܢ
ܕܫܘܠܛܢܐ ܘܡܠܟܐ ܗܘ ܦܘܠܚܢܐ
ܒܗ ܐܬܚܝܠܬ. ܕܫܘܒܚܐ ܡܢ ܡܠܟܘܬܐ ܠܥܠܡܐ
ܠܥܠܡܐ ܕܐܠܗܐ ܘܒܗ ܗܘܠܝܢ ܐܬܝܕܥ
ܐܡܝܢ ܕܠܐ ܐܬܗܘܝ ܡܫܡܫܢܐ ܕܒܬܪܗ
ܕܐܠܗܐ ܡܢ ܟܠܗ ܫܘܠܛܢܗ. ܘܡܛܠ ܗܢܐ

Folio 33v

ܡܢ ܒܣܡܡܢ ܒܢܝܫܐ ܕܩܒܠ. ܘܡܢ ܗܘ̇ܝ
ܕܡܬܩܪܐ ܒܣܘܬܐ ܘܡܢ ܗܘ̇ ܕܐܬܬܠܝܠܬ
ܐܪܒܥܐ ܒܦܠܓܘܬܗ. ܘܡܢ ܗܘ̇ ܕܒܟܐܪ̈ܟܐ
ܡܟܝܠ ܩܢܘܢܐ ܠܗ ܣܘܟܪ̈ܬܐ. ܘܡܢ ܗܘ̇ ܝ
ܕܡ̈ܪ ܒܠܘܢ ܕܟ̈ܦܪܐ ܐܢܬ ܘܠܟܦ̈ܪ ܐܢ
ܬܬܦܢܐ. ܘܡܢ̈ ܗܘ̇ ܕܐܒܕ̈ ܘܫܠܝܬܘ ܟܝ
ܡܟܒܫ ܒܗ ܕܡܗܐ ܐܕܡ̈ ܡܗܘܐ ܐܢܫ
ܫܢ ܒܣܡ. ܘܡܢ ܗܘ̇ ܕܠܝܠܝܐ ܢܦܠ ܟܝ
ܐܠܝܐ ܕܫܬ̈ܐ ܘܐܟܠ ܦܣܚܐ ܠܠܡ
ܡܢ ܗܠܝܢ ܘܕܐܟܣܬܢ ܠܡܬܝܢ ܕܐܬܬܠܝܬ
ܡܢ ܐܕܡ̈ ܕܒܣܘܬܐ ܕܐܠܗܐ ܡܢ ܒܪ̈ܬ
ܝܬܘܗܝ. ܘܕܐܬܬܠܝܬ ܒܢܦܫܗ ܕܒܝܬܐ
ܐܬܩܬܐ ܕܪ̈ܕܝܐ ܣܘܡܬ ܒܪ̈ܘܣܗ.
ܐܬܩܝܬ ܡܢ ܗܘ̇ ܕܐܠܗܐ ܐܬܬܠܝܬ
ܒܡܐܢ ܒܗ ܐܬܬܠܝܬ ܠܗܐ ܒܗ ܟܠ ܕܡܢ
ܒܬܪܗ. ܘܕܡܢ ܣܘܪܒܗ ܕܒܟܠ
ܘܨܠܝܒܘ. ܗܘ̇ ܕܐܬܩܛܠ ܡܪܢܐ ܐܠܗܐ ܦܫܛ
ܠܗ. ܦܩܕܐ ܗܘ̇ ܕܠܐܬ ܫܒܩ ܐܢܫ ܒܝܬ
ܘܡܫܐ ܫܡܥܗ ܠܒܢܝܐ. ܘܡܢ ܗܘ̇ ܕܐ
ܦܟܪ ܠܒܣܘܪܐ ܒܐܒܗ ܕܒܪܐܝܬܐ. ܘܡܢ
ܗܠܝܢ ܟܠ ܕܥܒܕܐ ܗܪܟܐ ܚܘ̈ܬܐ ܕܟܠܐ
ܕܕܡܝܢ ܠܗܠܝܢ ܕܐܬܬܒܪܬ ܠܗ ܒܪ̈ܬܗ
ܕܐܬܕܟܪ ܕܗܘܐ ܒܬܠܬܐ ܕܡܘܫܐ ܕܢܫܐ
ܐܢܫܐ. ܘܬܘܒ ܒܣܘܟܐ ܕܒܝܬ ܐܠܗܐ
ܠܡܕܢܚ ܒܝܬ ܐܠܗܐ ܒܒܪܝ. ܕܝܢ
ܘܢܦܫܐ ܒܒܪ ܐܢܫ ܕܩܛܠ ܕܐܬܬܦܫ
ܠܢܫܐ ܘܠܒܢܝܐ ܐܝܣܪܝܐ ܕܐܬܦܫܒ

Folio 34r

[illegible]

Folio 34v

Folio 35r

Folio 35v

ܒܚܝܠܐ ܕܒܪܐ ܗܘ ܒܪ ܐܠܗܐ ܕܠܐ ܫܘܪܝܐ
ܡܠܐ ܠܗ· ܗܘ ܒܪ ܐܠܗܐ ܒܫܘܪܝܐ ܐܬܚܒܒܬ·
ܘܦܪܨܘܦܐ ܕܒܪܐ ܕܐܬܗܘܐ ܡܠܠܐܝܬ
ܐܬܦܪܨܦܬ ܐܝܬܘܗܝ· ܐܝܟ ܕܒܪܐ
ܕܒܟܒܪܘܗܝ ܘܠܐ ܒܬܪ ܡܠܬܗ ܐܬܝܠܕܬ
ܕܒܒܪ ܗܘ ܡܠܬܐ ܗܘܬ ܒܒܪܐ ܕܢܬܬܢܝ
ܗܘ ܐܪܘܬܐ ܕܡܠܬܐ ܗܘ ܕܒܬܘܢ ܕܢܗܘܐ
ܒܪܢܫܐ ܠܢܪܬܐ ܘܣܡ ܒܬܪ ܕܒܪܐ
ܐܠܗܐ ܠܫܒܝܐ ܘܠܐܪܬܐ ܒܝܫܗ ܘܒܒܪ
ܠܢܗܘܪܐ ܒܦܘܪܩܢܗ· ܬܘܒ ܢܬܒ ܕܐܬܒܪ
ܐܠܗܐ ܦܘܠܘܣܐ ܐܪܘܡܝܐ ܒܡܨܪܝܬ
ܡܪܝܐ ܘܢܘܗܪܐ ܦܪܫ ܒܢܬ ܡ̈ܪܝܐ ܠܡ̈ܪܝܐ
ܘܗܘܐ ܡܦܪܨܦܐ ܐܝܟ ܕܐܡܪ· ܘܠܐ
ܐܫܬܘܝ ܒܒܪܐ ܡܢ ܡܠܬܐ· ܘܬܘܒ
ܡܢ ܒܬܪ ܗܠܝܢ ܐܡܪ ܕܢܬܚܒܫܘܢ ܡ̈ܠܟܐ·
ܘܐܬܪܫܡ ܐܪܥܐ ܢܦܫܐ ܫܬܝܐ ܘܢܗܘܘܢ
ܢܗ̈ܪܐ ܒܐܪܒܥܐ ܕܫܒܝܐ ܘܢܫܚܢ
ܡ̈ܠܟܐ ܘܬܦܩܘܢ ܐܪܒܥܐ· ܘܒܒܠܒܘܟ ܢܦܠ
ܗܘܐ ܒܒܪܐ ܠܡܠܬܐ· ܕܗܘܝܐ ܫܠܡܐ
ܡܠܐ ܦܘܪܩܢܐ ܕܐܠܗܐ· ܐܝܟ ܗܘ
ܕܡܪܐ ܠܡܠܟ ܕܠܐ ܐܬܬܚܝܒܘܢ ܐܝܟ
ܐܬܬܚܝܒܘܢ ܕܡܬܚܘܘܢ ܐܬܬܚܝܒ ܐܦ
ܗܘ ܕܒܒܪ ܐܢܫܐ ܐܝܟ ܠܦܨܐ ܕܠܐ
ܘܐܝܟ ܕܒܟܘܬܗ ܕܒܒܪܗ ܕܡܠܬܐ ܗܘܐ
ܒܪܢܫܐ· ܘܐܦ ܡܫܝܚܐ ܠܗܘ ܕܗܘܘܢ
ܡܢ ܫܪܒܐ ܕܒ̈ܒܪܐ· ܘܡܢ ܠܫܪܒܐ ܐܚܪܢܐ
ܕܒܒܪ· ܐܦܠܐ ܗܘܐ ܡܫܬܘܝܐ ܗܘܐ
ܒܒܪܐ ܡܢ ܡܠܬܐ· ܐܝܟ ܕܠܐ ܦܫ ܒܗܘܪܐ

Folio 36r

ܡܢ ܗܝ ܡܠܬܐ. ܕܐܡܪܬ ܢܗܘܐ. ܘܠܐ
ܐܪܡܝܬܐ ܡܢ ܦܘܢܝܐ ܕܡܫܝܚܘܬܗ ܗܘܢܐ
ܐܦܠܐ ܬܬܘܡܢܗ ܕܒܪ ܐܢܫܐ ܡܢ ܗܘ
ܡܠܬܐ ܕܐܡܪ ܕܢܒܥ[ܐ] ܐ[ܢ]ܫܐ ܘܡ[ܢ] ܠܒܪܐ
ܦܘܡ. ܐܟܢܐ ܕܢܒܥܐ ܐܦ[ܒܪܢܫܐ] ܘܡܠܟܐ
ܬܘܗܡܝܐ ܐܬܬܚܝ] ܒܒܪܝܬܐ ܘܐ[ܬ]ܬ ܠ[ܡܠܟܐ]
ܫܘܡܠܝܐ ܕܒܪܝܬܐ. ܒܗ ܗܝ ܕܐܡܪ ܠܘܬܗ
ܐܟܢܐ ܕܢܒܥܐ. ܠܟ ܕܝܢ ܡܢ ܗܝ ܕܐܬܬ[ܚܝܠ]ܬ
ܡܠܬܐ ܡܣܬܒܪܐ ܠܗܢ[...] ܕܠܐ ܡܬܦܠܓܐ
ܐܬܝܠܕ ܒܪܢܫܐ. ܐܠܗܐ [ܡܠܟ] ܢܫܒܚܐ
ܘܡܠܟܐ ܗܘܝܢ ܐܬܚܙܝ ܟܒ[ܪܢ]ܫܐ. ܠܐ
ܫܪܝܐ ܗܘ ܡܬܚܙܐ ܕܗܘܐ ܐܕܡ
ܐܠܐ ܬܬܝܗܒ. ܡܢܝܟܐܝܬ ܒܗ. ܗܘ
ܕܒܪܝ. ܐܠܗܐ ܠܐܢܫܐ ܒܨܠܡܗ ܘܒܕܡܘܬܗ
ܒܗܝ ܕܒܨܠܡ ܐܠܗܐ ܠܐܢܫܐ ܢܫܐ
ܡܢ ܐܪܥܐ. ܘܢܦܚ ܒܐܦܘܗܝ ܢܫܡܬܐ
ܕܚܝܐ. ܡܛܠ ܕܐܡܪܝܢ ܕܗܘܐ ܒܕܡܘܬܐ
ܒܬܪܬܐ ܗܘܬ ܘܦܩܘܕܬܐ. ܕܐܬܚܫܒ
ܠܟ ܐܠܗܐ ܒܕܡܘܬܗ ܘܗܘܝܢ ܒܒܪܗ
ܠܒܪܢܫܐ. ܐܝܟ ܗܘ ܕܡܠܟ ܒܕܡܘܬܐ
ܕܠܐ [ܡܫܬܟܚܐ] ܐܬܚܙܝ. ܠܐ ܕܝܢ ܐܬܬܝܪ
ܗܘܢܐ. ܐܠܐ ܕܒܗܝ ܕܢܗܘܐ ܢܘܗܪܐ
ܐܬܟܪܝ [ܢܘܗ]ܪܐ. ܘܒܗܝ ܕܢܗܘܐ ܪܘܚܐ
ܒܡܟܬܒ ܗܕܐ. ܐܬܒܒܪ ܘܠܐ ܬܘܗܝܐ
ܗܘܝܐ ܐܦ ܒܗܘܐ ܦ[ܓ]ܪܢܝ ܐܢܫܐ
ܐܝܟ ܠܠܒܐ ܕܠܗ ܘܐܝܟ ܕܟܕܬ
ܡܬܒܪܢܐ ܕܡܠܟܘܬܗ ܘܠܐ ܚܫܘܒܐ
ܐܬܬܢ ܒܪܢܫܐ ܦܓܪܢܝܬܐ ܘܒܠܒܐ

Folio 36v

ܕܐܠܗܐ ܘܒܗܘܢ ܕܒܬܪܗ ܕܒܒܕ ܐܠܗܐ
ܠܐܢܫܐ ܒܨܠܡܗ ܒܨܠܡ ܐܠܗܐ
ܒܒܪܗ ܕܐܬܬܣܝܡܬ ܒܗ ܕܡܘܬܐ
ܕܐܠܗܐ [ܢܦܫ]ܢܝܬܐ ܒܒܪ ܒܪܐ ܕܐܠܗܐ
ܒܨ[ܠ]ܡܗ ܕܒܪܢܫܐ· ܕܒܪܐ ܘܢܬܒܠ
ܒܨܠ[ܡ]ܗ· ܗܘ ܕܝܢ ܕܐܬܠܬ ܕܡܒܠ
ܐܠܗܐ ܠܐܢܫܐ [ܢܦ]ܫܐ ܡܢ ܐܬܒܪܝ
ܘܢܦܚ ܒܐܦܘܗܝ [ܢܫ]ܡܬܐ ܕܚܝܐ ܢܦܫ
ܒܗ ܒܢܦܫܐ ܕܝܢ ܡܠܬܐ ܐܬܒܪܝ ܦܓܪܐ
ܘܡܢ ܐܢܫܐ ܐܬܝܠܕܬ ܢܦܫܐ ܐܝܟ
ܕܒܒܪ ܐܦ ܒܨܘܪܬܐ ܕܐܠܗܘܬܐ· ܕܡܢ
ܒܬܪ ܕܐܬܒ ܕܒܪܬܐ ܘܢܣܒܬܐ ܒܪܐ
ܐܒܘܢ ܐܦ ܕܐܢܫܐ ܐܬܒܒܪܬ ܗܘܐ
ܘܐܡܪ· ܕܐܡܪ ܡܪܝܐ ܐܠܗܐ ܠܡܘܫܐ
ܟܠ ܐܕܡ ܘܕܡܝܟ· ܘܢܦܩ ܫܒܩܐ ܡܢ
ܐܠܗܘܗܝ· ܘܟܠ ܒܣܪܐ ܢ[ܦܫ]ܗ ܘܒܢܫܐ
ܒܪܢܫܐ ܐܠܗܐ ܠܐܠܗܐ ܗܘ ܕܢܦܫ ܡܢ
ܐܕܡ ܠܐܢܫܘܬܐ· ܘܒܗ ܗܠܝܢ ܕܕܡܢ
ܐܢܫܐ ܐܬܒܒܪܬ ܗܘܐ ܘܒܐܢܫܐ
ܐܠܐ ܐܘܕܝ· ܘܠܐ ܬܬܪܝܢ ܐܬܝܢ ܐܬܬܒ
ܟܠ ܒܪܬܗ· ܐܦ ܕܝܢ ܒܗܘ ܕܐܬܬܢܬ
ܡܠܬܐ ܠܐܚܝܢ ܘܗܘܒܢ ܕܠܐ ܐܢܫܐ ܕܐܘܪ
ܐܠܗܐ ܕܒܒܪ ܐܢܫܐ ܒܪܢܫܝ ܠܐܕܡ
ܐܠܐ ܠܗܘܢ ܐܬܢܣܒ ܘܐܬܬܠܝܕ
ܗܘܢ ܒܬܪܝܢ ܒܒܪܗ· ܐܦ ܠܗܘܢ ܒܪܢܬܐ
ܕܡܠܝܢ ܐܢܫܝܘܬܐ ܐܝܬ ܠܗܘܢ ܕܢܣܒܪܘܢ
ܗܘܢܐ [ܐ]ܬܬܘܗ ܦ[ܠܓ]ܘܬܗ ܘܡܢܘܬܐ

Folio 37r

◆ ܘܕܒܟܠܗ ܐܪܥܐ. ܕܐܡܪ ܐܠܗܐ ܬܦܩ
◆ ܐܪܥܐ ܢܦܫܐ ܚܝܬܐ ܠܓܢܣܗ ܒܒܥܝܪܐ
◆ ܘܚܝܘܬܐ ܘܪܚܫܐ ܕܐܪܥܐ [ܠܓܢܣܗ
◆ ܘܒܠܬ ܗܘܐ ܗܟܢܐ. ܐܠܗܐ ܚܝܘܬܐ
◆ ܕܐܪܥܐ ܠܓܢܣܗܝܢ ܘܒܥܝܪܐ ܠܓܢܣܗ
◆ ܘܟܠܗ ܪܚܫܐ ܕܐܪܥܐ ܠܓܢܣܗܘܢ. ܘܚܙܐ
ܢܚܙܐ ܕܒܦܘܫܩܐ ܡܦܩܢܐ ܐܬܒܪܝ ܘ
ܐܬܬܥܝܕ ܒܟܠܗܘܢ ܕܐܬܥ[ܒܕ] ܗܘܐ ܗܘ
ܡܕܝܢ ܕܦܩܕ ܐܠܗܐ ܘܐܬܒܪܝ]ܐܦ ܡܛܠ
◆ ܢܦܫܬܐ. ܒܠܚܘܕ ܕܐܡܪ ܐܠܗܐ ܢܪܚܫܘܢ
◆ ܢܦܫܬܐ ܒܐܪܡܘܬܐ ܕܐܬܩܪܝܬ] ܠܡܐܪܘ
◆ ܥܠ ܐܪܥܐ. ܘܐܬܐ ܠܗ ܠܡܠܬܐ ܒܬܪ
◆ ܡܠܬܐ ܕܐܡܪ ܕܗܘܐ ܗܟܢܐ ܘܥܒܕ
◆ ܐܠܗܐ ܚܝܘܬ ܢܦܫܬܐ ܪܚܫܐ ܘܗܘܝܐ
ܠܦܘܫܐ ܕܡܠܬܐ ܡܬܚܫܚܝܢ ܠܗ
ܠܟܠܗܝܢ ܒܥܕܢܐ. ܕܡܢ ܒܬܪ ܒܦܘܩܕܢܐ
ܡܦܩܢܐ ܡܬܥܒܕܝܢ ܗܘܘ ܒܐܦ ܠܗ
ܒܡܠܬܐ ܕܟܠܗܝܢ ܘܡܦܩܕ ܕܗܘܐ ܗܘ
ܡܕܝܢ ܕܐܡܪ ܐܠܗܐ ܘܚܙܐ ܡܦܫܩܝܢ
ܒܟܢ ܗܠܝܢ ܐܦ ܟܕ ܝܬܗ ܕܟܪ ܐܢܫܐ
◆ ܠܦܫܝܢ ܕܒܗܘܢ ܕܐܡܪܐ ܐܠܗܐ ܢܥܒܕ ܐܢܫܐ
◆ ܐܝܟ ܨܠܡܢ ܕܝܠܢ ܘܐܝܟ ܕܡܘܬܢ ܐܬܒܪܝ
ܐܦ ܗܘ. ܘܐܢ ܟܬܒܝܢ ܬܠܬܐ ܕܕܡܝܢ
ܠܗܕܐ ܡܕܝܢ ܐܢܫܝܢ ܡܕܡܝܢ ܗܘ
ܕܚܫܝܚܝ ܒܡܠܝ ܡܦܩܢܬܐ ....
ܐܬܬܩܢܢ ܗܟܝܠ ܨܠܡܗ ܫܠܝܛܬܐ
ܕܐܡܪܐ ܒܪܐ ܕܥܡܐ ܒܕܡܘܬܐ ܕܗܘܘܬ

Folio 37v

ܠܗ ܘܪܕܐ ܕܡܬܝܗܒ ܒܒܠܚܘܕ [ܦܐ]ܪܐ
ܒܪܡܙܐ ܠܒܪܢܫܘܬܐ ܕܡܬܝܠܕܘܬܗ ܡܬܝܠܕܢܐ
ܗ[ܘ]ܝܘ ܡܢ [ ]ܕܡܬܝܠܕܘܬܐ ܕܐܒܘܗܝ
ܕܐ[ ] ܐܝܟ ܫܪܝܪܐܝܬ ܐܠܗܝܐ
ܡܛܠ ܕܐܝܟ ܕܒܡܬܚܫܚܢܘܬܐ ܠܢ ܠܘ ܡܬܝܠܕܘܬܐ
ܦܓܪܢܝܬܐ ܕܐܡܪ ܐܚܝ ܠܗ ܠܐ ܡܬܕܪܟܢܘܬܗ
ܡܛܠ [ ]ܕܒܪܢܫܘܬܐ ܐܝܬ ܒܗ.
ܘܕܝܢܐ [ܕ]ܐܒܘܗܝ [ܡ]ܛܠ ܒܗ̈ܝ. ܡܛܠ ܗܘ ܕܪܐ
ܠܐ ܐܫܬܒܩ ܠܒܢܝܢܐ ܘܐܝܟܢ ܘܐܒܐ ܡܢ
ܒܫܘܒ[ܚܐ] ܡܫܝܚܐ ܘܐܬܪܘܬ ܦܓܪܝ
ܡܢ ܫܡܝܐ ܘܐܠܗܐ [ܡܫܝܚ] ܫܪܟܐ ܡܬܝܠܕܢ
ܘܠܐ ܐܬܥܒܕ [ ] ܐܝܟ ܕܒܠܘܬܗ ܕܒܢܝܢܐ
ܡܛܠ ܦܓܪܢܝܬܐ ܫܪܝܪܬܐ ܕܐܠܗܐ ܠܐ ܗܘܐ ܒܗ.
ܘܡܛܠ ܕܐܝܬܘܗܝ ܡܢ ܟܝܢܐ ܢܦܫ.
ܘܦܓܪܢܝܬܐ ܒܢܝܬܐ ܐܠܗܐ ܗܘܐ.
ܡܬܚܠܦܢ ܟܝܢܐ ܠܘܬ ܐܒܘܗܝ
ܦܓܪܐ ܘܢܦܫܐ ܠܒܪܢܫܐ ܦܓܪܢܝܬܐ
ܠܒܪܢܫܐ ܕܡܬܠܒܫ ܒܦܓܪܢܘܬܗ ܗܘܐ
ܕܐܬܝܠܕ ܒܐܝܕܝ ܒܦܓܪܘܬܗ ܘܒܢܫ
ܡܢ ܒܬܘܠܬܐ ܒܫܠܡܐ ܕܪܘܚܐ.
ܘܒܠܘܬܗ ܠܒܢܝܢ ܕܪܐ ܕܒܢܝܢܐ ܕܠܗ.
ܘܐܒܘܢܐ ܕܡܢ ܐܝܟ ܡܬܝܠܕ ܠܗܘ
ܒܝܘܠܕܐ ܐܠܗܐ ܐܦ ܒܢܝܢܐ ܠܗܘ
ܒܒܢܝܢܘܬܗ ܡܢ ܕܒܢ. ܒܢܝܢ. ܒܢܝ
ܡܬܒܢܝܢ ܒܪܘܚܐ ܫܪܝܪܐ ܕܒܢܝܢܐ.
ܒܢܝܢܐ ܕܐܠܗܐ. ܘܐܝܟ ܕܒܢܝܢ ܒܗ
ܡܬܝܠܕ ܠܐܒܐ ܒܒܢܝܢܐ ܘܒܢܝܢܐ ܠܗ

Folio 38r

Folio 38v

ܫܒܚܝܢ ܘܡ[ܫܒܚܐ ܕܝܢ . ܒܡܠܟܘܬܐ ܘܡܠܟܐ
ܒܢ[ܒܝܘܬ]ܗ ܫܠܝܚ[ܘ]ܬܗ ܕܡܫܝܚܐ ܕܒܐܝܕ
ܗܘ ܕܐܠܗܐ ܐܫܬܘܝܬ ܠ[ܡܫ]ܬܥܝܘܬܗ ܕܫܘܒܚܗ.
[ܘ]ܡܛܠ ܕܡܫ̈ܝܚ[ܐ] ܐܬܒܣܒܣܝܢ] ܒܠ
ܫܪܒܐ ܗܘܐ [ܕ]ܐܬܚܫܚ ܠܗ ܫܘܠܛܢܐ
ܒܡܕܒܪܢܘܬܐ [ܗ]ܢܐ . ܘܠܝܬ] ܐ[
ܕܫܘܠܛܢ ܡܢ ܠܥܠܡܐ ܠܝܘܢܝܐ ܐܘܚܠܨܘܬܐ
ܡܬܚܦܛܝܢ[ܝ] ܕܐܦ ܠܟܠܢ ܒܐ[ܢ]ܘܬܐ
ܒܗ ܡܫܬܥ[ܝܐ] ܠܝ ܦܘܪܩܢܐ[ܕ]ܐܠܗܐ ܐܝܟ
.. .. .. ܥܠ ܥܠܡܝܢ .. .. ..
ܐܝܬ ܒܡܠܟܘܬܐ ܗܘܐ ܦܪܫܓܢܐ ܕܢܫܪ̈ܐ
ܚܕܫܬܐ ܕܝܘܚܢܢ ܡܢ ܠܗܘܢ ܐܘܚܠܨܘܬܐ.

ܫܠܡ ܟܬܒܐ ܕܐܘܪܒܐ . ܕܦܫܝܛܬܐ
ܕܐܘ̈ܢܓܠܝܘܢ . ܡܬܝ ܘܠܘܩܐ . ܕܡܢ
ܠܦܠܓܘܬܗ . ܝܘܚܢܢ ܐܠܗܐ ܐܦܣܩܘܦܐ
ܕܡܒܘܓ . ܐܬܟܬܒ ܕܝܢ ܒܡܒܘܓ
ܒܝܘܡܬܐ . ܒܫܢܬ ܬܡܢܡܐܐ ܘܬܠܬܝܢ
ܘܬܪ̈ܬܝܢ ܕܐܠܟܣܢܕܪܘܣ ܡܩܕܘܢܝܐ

⁘ ⁘ ⁘ ⁘ ⁘ ⁘ ⁘ ⁘ ⁘ ⁘ ⁘

ܟܠ ܡܢ ܕܩܪܐ ܢܨܠܐ ܐܦ ܥܠ ܕܟܬܒ
ܘܐܫܬܢܝ . ܕܠܐ ܢܬܟܬܒ ܫܡܗ ܒܟܬܒܐ...
ܫܒܝܚܐ ܠܡܫܝܚܐ ܢܗܘܐ ܘܐܠܗܐ
ܕܐܬܡܪܫ ܐܡܝܢ ⁘ ⁘ ⁘

CHAPTER III

THE NATURE AND CONTENTS OF THE MANUSCRIPT

The text reproduced in the previous chapter comprises fourteen fragments which the British Museum bound together into one volume and which its Catalogue describes in the following terms: "Fragments of the Commentaries of Philoxenus of Mabbug on the Gospels of St. Matthew and St. Luke."[258] Such a description assumes that all the fragments are in fact from the same work to which the final fragment with its important colophon belongs. That colophon states in part: "The end of the fourth book of the commentary of the Evangelists, Matthew and Luke, which was made by Philoxenus . . . ."[259] It is the intention of this chapter to examine these fragments inductively to discover what interrelationships exist among them and what light they shed on the nature of the "commentary" to which the colophon bears witness. In order to accomplish this, we shall first present the evidence in the form of an English translation of the manuscript followed by descriptive and analytical notes before presenting a synthesis of the available facts.

In the translation square brackets [ ] denote a lacuna in the text and words within them translate a suggested reconstruction. Round brackets ( ) contain words which clarify the meaning in English for which there is no Syriac equivalent in the text. Biblical and other quotations have been identified by quotations whether or not the equivalent mark /‹·/ appears in the margin of the text. For convenience, biblical references are placed as footnotes to the translation and are identified alphabetically to distinguish them from the numerically listed notes which are gathered at the end of this work. The foliations and lines of the manuscript are noted in the margin of the translation with the approximate beginning of the line marked by an asterisk (*) within the translation. The paragraph divisions of the translation follow the major divisions marked in the manuscript by the sign /. . . ܦ. . / or its variants.

A. *TRANSLATION OF BRITISH MUSEUM MANUSCRIPT ADD. 17,126*

Fragment 1

. . . And of forgiveness; for He will forgive *Folio 1r* wrongdoers "not only seven (times), but seventy times seven."[a] Indeed, He has proved it by means of His sufferings of old. While indicating this about Himself, He reminded Simon about *that number which was quoted for Lamech: "Because Cain was avenged seven times, Lamech (will be avenged) seventy times seven."[b]

Cain therefore enquired of God whether he would die because he had committed murder: "He said to him, '[It is] not *so, for whoever kills Cain shall release seven penalties'."[c] [That is to say,] "He who kills you will be doing you a favour, because you will escape the capital punishment which I have decreed for you. However, what happens to all murderers will not happen to you: *'He who sheds the blood of man, by man shall his blood be shed'.[d] It is you, then, who have become illustrative of the fact that 'murder will be avenged seven times'."[e] This saying may be understood in the following *senses: either Cain received seven punishments because he had committed murder; or he remained alive for seven generations while being punished; or he spared anyone who has committed murder from seven penalties; or, in the judgement to come, *his punishment will also be greater than [that of] all murderers; or the terms of his sentence were [fulfilled] after he was chastened, and he was considered worthy of mercy. Perhaps this happened to him *because he was not the author *Folio 1v* of murder, but had served the will of that other person about whom Christ has said: "From the beginning he has been killing men, and *he does not stand in the truth."[f] Now He refers either to the fact that Satan brought death by the

---

a. Matthew 18:22
b. Genesis 4:24
c. Genesis 4:15
d. Genesis 9:6
e. unidentified quotation
f. John 8:33(44)

transgressing of the command, or to the fact that he killed Abel by means of Cain. Since, in the one place, he brought death to Adam by means of Eve, in the other *he killed Abel by means of Cain. Because of these things, everyone [governs himself] as he wishes.

Now after Cain committed murder, he received those punishments which were prescribed and a mark was placed on him so that he might not be destroyed by anything -- neither by man alone, *nor by beast, nor even burned by fire, nor drowned by water; for he probably would have thrown himself either into a fire or into water in order to escape the tortures that he was in. But *a mark was put on him that he might not also be destroyed by these things. And even mute elements recognized the mark which was upon him. As it is, he who asked of God that anyone finding him should kill him, did not destroy himself again and again, *and the indelible mark which was put on him was well invoked. For, is it not a miracle that flesh should fall into a fire and not [catch fire], *and into water and not be drowned, *Folio 2r* and thrown to the beasts and not be devoured? But after these things which were told about him, it is written: "Cain went out from the presence of the Lord and dwelt in the land *of Nod opposite Eden";[a] that is, he could not settle down in the vicinity of Paradise, for Adam and those who were descendants of Seth were dwelling in that place. Now Eden is the name of that land in which Paradise was planted, while the land of Nod is that in which *Cain dwelt. So with regard to Adam it is said: "God removed Adam and caused him to dwell opposite the Paradise of Delights";[b] but with regard to Cain: "He dwelt in the land of Nod opposite Eden."[c] On the basis of these words, it is known that while Adam dwelt outside Paradise *in the land of Eden, Cain was outside it in that which used to be called the land of Nod. After Cain settled in that land, a son was born to him, and he called him Enoch. It was Cain who afterwards first built a city, *"and he called the city after the name of his son."[d] While Adam and those who (descended) from him probably dwelt in

---

a. Genesis 4:16
b. Genesis 3:24
c. Genesis 4:16
d. Genesis 4:17

tents, those who were descendants of Cain built a city for themselves [where they were held in the fear] of beasts *and destruction in that they had been forsaken by the Providence of God, or because they loved the land and the dwellings which were in it more than the house of Seth (did). Where do we see that *there happens to be even more of those *Folio 2v* who adorn every well-built structure of cities and walls and dwellings than of those who have ordinary thoughts? It is because of them that *the prophet has said: "Their mind feeds on ashes, and causes the wayward to err."[a] For, behold, the patriarch of the house of Abraham, and Isaac, and Jacob dwelt in tents; as [the apostle] said: *"They looked for [a city] which had a foundation whose [builder and maker is God]."[b] So Adam and the family of Seth, [acting on] the same conviction, did not build [a city] for themselves as the house of Cain which had [acted wilfully]. Rather they forsook him for the place in which Paradise is situated, *which is better than that land in which they (i.e., the house of Cain) settled. Scripture finds fault with Hezekiah also because he built and strengthened the walls of Jerusalem,[c] and brought water into it in a novel way.[d] (On the other hand,) with regard to what is written about David that he built the fortress *of Zion and called it by his name,[e] it seems that he did not do this by human planning; but, because Solomon was to build the temple, he also preceded him and built the city in which the temple was to be situated, and in which *that kingdom was to be established which was given to him as a type. If he had been allowed by God, he would have built the temple also. But the city . . .

Fragment 2

[. . . "and he foresaw and spoke concerning] *the *Folio 3r* resurrection of Christ that His soul was not left in Sheol,

---

a. Isaiah 44:20
b. Hebrews 11:10
c. 2 Chronicles 32:5
d. 2 Kings 20:20; 2 Chronicles 32:30; cf. Isaiah 22:9-11
e. 2 Samuel 5:7, 9; 1 Chronicles 11:5, 7, 8

nor did His body see corruption."[a] Again, it is our Lord who teaches that He not only had a human body, *but also a soul. "Because of this my Father loves me, for I lay down my soul that I may take it again."[b] Again, "I have power to lay down my soul, and I have power to take it again."[c] Again, "The good shepherd *lays down his soul for his sheep."[d] In another place it is written that He said, "Now my soul is troubled, and what shall I say, 'Father, deliver me from this hour'? But it is because of this that I have come to this hour."[e] *The books of the Evangelists relate that these things came from Him in that hour of prayer: that when the time of His passion came, He was afraid, and trembled, and was troubled as a man, and He said to His disciples, "My very soul is sorrowful, even to death";[f] and that 'He departed from them, *and fell on His face and prayed'[g] to His Father in agony like a man; that He was full of grief and sorrow and was seized by the fear of death, and terror prevailed upon Him to such a degree that He did not abstain *from saying clearly: "My Father, if it be possible, let this cup pass from me,"[h] -- not only once, but also a second and a third time. *When He understood the will of His *Folio 3v* Father, for He prayed for something far greater than that He should not die, He said to Him: "May my own will no longer be done, but yours."[i] Although He was afraid as a man, because *the reality of death frightened Him also as it does everyone else, the will of His Father was much more important than the love of human life. Again it is written in a certain place: "When He was in fear He prayed earnestly, and His sweat became *like drops of blood, and it fell to the ground";[j] "and there appeared to Him an angel strengthening Him."[k] Because it is understood that Jesus is God who became man, more than anyone else He was humiliated and afflicted by human sufferings; *for, as for the rest of men, (their)

---

a. Acts 2:31, cf. Psalms 16:10
b. John 10:17
c. John 10:18
d. John 10:11
e. John 12:27
f. Matthew 26:38
g. Matthew 26:39
h. Matthew 26:39
i. Matthew 26:39, cf. Luke 22:42
j. Luke 22:44
K. Luke 22:43

nature is enough to affirm their corporality; but as for Christ, it is with sight, the sense of touch and the true nature of the body, both (its) needs and sufferings, with which He was very deeply afflicted more than anyone else. *If this is not so, whom of men did the fear of death dominate to such a degree that his sweat fell to the ground like drops of blood?[a] In the same way He could be plunged into such a sleep that He would not be wakened from His sleep by the roar of storms, *the noise and clamour of sailors and disciples, and the violent tossing of the ship.[b]

Therefore, in order that His corporality might not be considered false because of His divinity, and His sufferings *and mortal needs be thought an illusion *Folio 4r* because of the greatness of His being,[c] He was afflicted by them in human ways more than any natural man. Indeed, *the opinion of the heretics bears witness to the fact that this providential action was wise; for, after all these things, they have denied His corporality. What is the error they would not have introduced, if one of these things which are written had been removed, even though one of our Lord's apostles has clearly said, *"Every spirit which does not confess that Jesus has come in the flesh is not of God, but is of the false christ."[d] The spirit of that quotation therefore is against those heretics who renounce the humanity of the Word, and deny *the true existence of Him by whom men have become children of God; for Simon the Sorcerer,[e] the first of the apostles of the false christ, said concerning Jesus that He was not a man in reality, but only in likeness did He appear to be *so. Because the Eutychianists, Marcionites, Valentinians, and Manicheans possess his (i.e., Simon the Sorcerer's) opinion concerning Christ, like him (they will also get) that justice which they deserve, and especially those who are our contemporaries and are with us, who are believed to be *children of the common congregation of the Faith.

---

a. cf. Luke 22:44
b. cf. Matthew 8:24
c. cf. Luke 1:49
d. 1 John 4:3
e. cf. Acts 8:9-24

How, then, O heretic, may the corporality of Christ be compared *with the likeness of the dove in which *Folio 4v* the Spirit was seen?[a] Do the Scriptures teach all of these things, or many of them, with regard to His corporality? When the Holy Spirit appeared alone, it was *in the likeness of a dove; as they say, "No one saw except only John."[b] But everyone was well aware of Jesus. All eyes observed His body, His needs and His sufferings. His stature with its differences *was known to the multitude of the Jews; and, because of His gradual growth which (was familiar) to them, and the plainness of His appearance, He was even considered by them to be the son of Joseph. Again, if the corporality of God is a likeness, *then the good things which He by Himself has prepared for men are (mere) likenesses. Indeed, because of this, He became a man to make us children of His Father. He appeared bodily to change us into His spiritual existence. He was born of a woman to give us birth by His Holy Spirit. He received *circumcision and observed the law to set us free by His obedience and redeem us by His becoming accursed. He grew in stature to bring us to perfection and full maturity. By grace He submitted Himself to the fathers to make us by nature the friends and relatives of the Father. *As a man He was baptized by John to form another womb for our birth as children of God. He fasted, became hungry and was tempted, to give *us victory over all the pains of sin. He *Folio 5r* conquered the tempter in the desert that we may not henceforth be his (i.e., Satan's) slaves but his adversaries. He endured sufferings and tasted death *to impart by His sufferings an indifference (to pain) and by His death to confirm immortal life. He dwelt in the bowels of the earth to make us inhabitants of heaven. He was reckoned with men to unite us with spiritual powers. If the corporality *which made these things possible for us is a likeness, then all of them which came into being through it are an illusion, as is the vision which revealed the salvation of Christ. But as far as the Word alone is concerned, these

a. Luke 3:22, cf. Matthew 3:16 b. cf. John 1:34

are the blessings which He promised. (If not, then) according to the word of Paul, *'The preaching of the apostles and the faith of Christians are vain.'[a] If the cause of the blessings is a likeness, why then should they be valued? Perhaps not at all, unless there is something which is lower and more unworthy than it. Now *it was not by the physical eye that the Spirit was seen, but by revelation He was perceived by the mind in the way that the early prophets were also accustomed to seeing; as it is (written): "I saw the Lord sitting upon a high throne, and all the host of heaven standing *above Him."[b] And as it is (written): "In the year that king Uzziah died, I saw the Lord sitting upon a high and lofty throne. *And His glory filled His *Folio 5v* temple, and seraphs stood beyond Him."[c] As it is written: "I looked and behold the Spirit coming from the north, a great cloud, and a fire burning and shining *all round it."[d] As it is (written): "I saw the Lord standing upon a wall of adamant and in His hand was an adamant."[e] As it is (written): "I saw and behold the thrones were placed, and the Ancient of Days sat down."[f] By this kind of revelation *the Holy Spirit was seen by John in the likeness of a dove. As in various ways it was shown in these likenesses to the prophets and not in the same appearance to all of them, so also it was seen by John in another way. As *in the former instances the variety of likenesses had taught something, although it was not made known to everyone, so also was this a vision by which the Spirit was revealed, and the impact of the visions and revelations was not lessened by the fact that the men themselves were not able *to understand them accurately; but by means of their incomprehensibility their importance was especially seen, for it is obvious to anyone that the things which are known and understood are of less importance than the things which are incomprehensible *and indescribable.

If, then, God appeared to be man in (this kind of)

---

a. Cf. 1 Corinthians 15:14
b. 1 Kings 22:19
c. Isaiah 6:1, 2
d. Ezekiel 1:4
e. Amos 7:7
f. Daniel 7:9

likeness, and He was not a man in reality but remained God, it would not be *something worthy of wonder and *Folio 6r* faith in the earthly ministry (of Christ). (If this were so) then Christ, the likeness and equal of the Father, did not empty Himself as Paul taught, nor did the One who "was rich become poor," nor *"are we enriched by His poverty,"[a] nor "did God send forth His Son and He was of a woman,"[b] nor is it true that 'like the children, He also was made a partaker of flesh and blood.'[c] We do not know Him to be unchangeable in actual fact, *if He did not change because He did not exist (in reality), nor is it a miracle that He was conceived without intercourse and born of a virgin. If the body which was conceived and born was only a likeness, and it does not make known something *which is praiseworthy, which God therefore loves forever, how is it that He gave His only-begotten Son instead of Himself? If it was the likeness which was delivered to death and not the truly incarnate Son, then even the death was not *in fact experienced. If the shadow was tempted within Him and not the true body -- besides the fact that if there was no flesh there was no soul -- if that did not exist, why is it (found in the scriptures), "I lay down my soul for the sheep,"[d] along with *the other? If God did not really become a man, the Virgin would not be the 'Bearer of God' (i.e., Theotokos); for that which was born would have been a shadow, *and not the incarnate God. Now, when you *Folio 6v* avoid the snare of Nestorian doctrine, you are at the same time falling into it; for he said that God was not incarnate and born, but *He dwelt in the man who was born. He ascribed to Him the birth of the temple but not of the Word, and of the man but not of God. It seemed to him that he had to say this because he had formerly denied the coming into existence of God. On account of the fact that He was born, *it was fitting that He should come into being for the first time. If He did not come into being, He was not also born. Because Nestorius rejected the fact that God became

---

a. cf. 2 Corinthians 8:9
b. Galatians 4:4
c. Hebrews 2:14
d. John 10:15

a man, along with it he also denied that He was born of the Virgin. He thought of the nativity, as *I have said, in nature and in truth to be that of a man, but in name and in metaphor to be that of God. If you are witnesses to your teaching, you adhere to it. Do you not first confess that God became *truly a man in order that the nativity also may be established by Him? But you have compared the incarnation of the Word to the likeness of the dove in which the Spirit appeared, and you have betrayed the Scripture (in your statement): "As the Person of the Spirit appeared *in the likeness of a dove, so the Son showed Himself in the likeness of a man." Why was the womb of the Virgin *and the *Folio 7r* nine months of development needed by Him who was not really endowed with a body? Why did He not pull the likeness out of the air or out of some other place, in the way that angels have sometimes appeared -- even demons are in the habit of *exhibiting themselves to men -- or in the manner in which the Spirit swiftly began and ended the vision of His revelation? It is clear that the time was short and swift in which the Spirit appeared to John in "the likeness of the body of a dove."[a] I suppose *that it was even swifter than the twinkling of an eye. It is not for us to say where that likeness came from, nor that the Person of the Spirit was transformed into the vision of the dove, nor that He took that likeness from the air, nor that *it had been in heaven, nor should we suppose that 'He came suddenly from nothing' is the right thing to think. But we only adhere to that which is written, and we do not penetrate into the innermost part of the Word by questioning, lest error confront us *instead of knowledge, and deception instead of truth. Now if Jesus had also appeared to men in that likeness, why was His kind of revelation not even such that the man would suddenly be revealed and then concealed, like the Spirit *in the likeness of a dove, and like the Father in various appearances, and like angels in the likeness of men? He needed the Virgin within whose womb He dwelt and remained

---

a. Luke 3:22

Folio 7v

for nine months, *because prophets had made predictions on His behalf, and the Spirit had revealed Him through preachers, and types and mysteries of Him had been formed and inscribed in the Old (Testament), and prophets and righteous men had been waiting for the appearance of *His birth, and the fathers longed to gaze upon the mystery which was created by Him: "Your father Abraham eagerly desired to see my day, and he saw (it) and was glad."[a] And again: "Many prophets and righteous men long *to see what you see and did not see (it), and to hear what you hear and did not hear (it)."[b] Not only did the ancients look for and expect the revelation of that mystery,[c] but disciples, obedient to His religion, have also *died and are dying in various ways for Him. By torments and afflictions they confess Him before rulers and judges, and fearlessly and unashamedly they preach the New (Testament) which is usually unknown, that God of His own will had become incarnate *and was born of the Virgin. Now if, as they reason, His was a likeness, the prophets are false and the apostles are liars, and the confession of those who have died for Him is worthless. Not only is faith in the mystery found to be *worthless and useless, but also that mystery (itself) and the things which occurred by means of it. Because of this, the word of the Apostle is quoted against those who deny Him: "Perhaps *even those who have gone to sleep in *Folio 8r* Christ have perished."[d]

Why, then, are they amazed as if it were something new that the Virgin conceived without intercourse and continued to be *a virgin even after she had given birth, if she had conceived a likeness and given birth to a shadow? For if a real body -- solid, and thick, and heavy -- could not come out through the opening of the womb while it remained closed, the birth would not be wonderful; *for the spiritual nature is accustomed to passing through places much narrower than the womb and is uninhibited by the body. The flesh is no barrier to its thinness, and any composite thing

---

a. John 8:45(56)
b. Matthew 13:17
c. cf. Romans 16:25
d. 1 Corinthians 15:18

does not resist it. It is *not only the holy angels who are like this, but also the unclean demons. We are not amazed if we understand that an angel can pass through a body, and a demon can enter when doors are shut where even the sun and the air, whose thinness is thicker *than theirs, can often pass through. They are not then inhibited by bodies. If it is so for them, why should we be amazed by a spiritual Word coming forth from a Virgin, and the virginity of her who gave Him birth remaining undefiled? *For if the likeness is in accordance with their opinion, it came forth spiritually and not physically; and along with this, it was also spiritually conceived. How, *then, *Folio 8v* was the appearance of the conception evident in the womb of her who bore Him? While being a spirit, did He not grow little by little, and swell the womb *in which He was conceived? Now it is on account of them that the prophet spoke concerning these things: "We have conceived and we have been in labour as those who have given birth to spirits."[a] Was it the Virgin (that the prophet was speaking of)? Was her conception a manifestation of evil things and not of good things so that because of this also the prophet had to deal *with the very manifestation and speak of the likeness of those things: "We have conceived and we have given birth to spirits?"[b] "Do we possess the instruction of the Lord in vain?"[c] Or do we conceive and bring forth worthless opinions like these? Then, too, if the Virgin *did conceive and give birth to a disembodied spirit similar to those, she would also have to be numbered with them. Why is it appropriate for John to cry aloud in amazement at the mystery as he taught: "The Word became flesh, and dwelt among us."[d] He did not say, "the likeness *of flesh." If the incarnation is in accordance with your understanding, was it therefore right for him to use that other expression? He did not write that 'He became like', but 'He became'; for the former corresponds to the likeness

---

a. Isaiah 26:18
b. Isaiah 26:18
c. perhaps paraphrases Galatians 3:4
d. John 1:14

while the latter, 'He became', does not. *(In this way) he proclaims that the supernatural birth is true. A resemblance, however, has to do with two things, and John did not say that the Word became like flesh, *but that *Folio 9r* He became flesh. We must understand that from the Word (comes) that which is consonant with all physical bodies which come into existence when they are non-existent, so that the Word truly became flesh. From the two *words in the mystery we are certain of the fact that, on the one hand, 'He became', and that on the other, 'He became flesh'.

Now if the heretics still persist in their opinion and assert that if He became He was changed, that is sufficient to condemn *those who flirt with the heretical without adhering to it. Indeed, everywhere they report that they are fighting against the Nestorians, but it is with the (same) error which they bear. If they are making use of their own words among themselves, they are being *contentious. However, if they say, "We adhere to the fact that the Word became flesh," they are abstaining from that which is likeness; but, while not acknowledging (it) in words, by (their) actions they deny (it). They cannot eliminate the one and explain the other; for utterances which are spoken *on the basis of faith do not admit explanation. "God sent forth His Son, and He was of a woman."[a] As written, it is credible, and it does not admit another meaning. "The Word became flesh and dwelt among us,"[b] -- its reading is its *explanation, and faith accepts this. "We are reconciled to God by the death of His Son."[c] -- the saying has no other teaching. *"If He did not spare *Folio 9v* His Son, but delivered Him up for all of us, how shall He not give us everything with Him?"[d] We are amazed at the grace of the Giver, and we do not divide His Gift, *but we glory in the fact that the Father delivered up His Son to death for us, and we do not exalt some other person above the Name. "God so loved the world that He gave His only Son for it."[e] We marvel at how much the Father has loved,

---

a. Galatians 4:4
b. John 1:14
c. Romans 5:10
d. Romans 8:32
e. John 3:16

*but we do not inquire into how His immortal Son died.

If, therefore, you affirm that the Word became flesh, you must not understand "likeness for "flesh," or "He became like" for "He became" as *the Nestorians do who explain (His) coming into existence as "adoption."[a] They say that the Word did not become flesh but adopted a man. If then the birth is true for you, He became flesh and not a likeness; and if it is credible to you *that the Virgin conceived and gave birth, it was a physical body that came out of her and not a shadow. For this reason, the miracle that after having given birth she remained a virgin, is credible; for, if what had come out of her had been the likeness of that which for Him was not a true body *and she had remained a virgin after her childbirth, the thing which had happened to her would not have been new, and she who had conceived *would not have been wonderful. If she *Folio 10r* had conceived a likeness and not the true body of someone conceived and born, we ought to strike at the nature of the one who gave birth to Him. Because this very thing is common to *all who are born, even the Son became primarily a man when He came to a second birth. He was related to His mother by nature, then born of her and called her Son. If He were not like her, He would also not be her Son; *or, if He is believed to be a likeness only, she who bore Him must also of necessity be so acknowledged. If, however, she was a woman by nature, and I suppose you have no *doubt about that, He who was born of her was also like her in every way, and on this basis He was a Son and she a mother. As for those things which it was right for us to have written against the Nestorians, your ignorance compels us *to say that you speak against them while adhering to their teaching. Now, if God did not become a man in reality, but only adopted the likeness or became incarnate in appearance, *His mother would not have been the Bearer of God. Again, if He adopted a man who came into being without intercourse and He did not come into being in reality, then too *the Virgin would not be known as the Bearer of God, *Folio 10v*

---

a. cf. Philippians 2:7, "He adopted the likeness of a servant."

and this very thing is said by two of the heretics with respect to the beginning of the earthly ministry (of Christ). It is clear, with regard also to those things which remain, that if *the nativity is a likeness, the needs and sufferings of our Saviour are an illusion also. In reality He did not fast and get hungry, nor did He become weary, and sit, and slumber, and sleep, and suffer, and die, as the Scriptures teach. But we adhere completely *to the way in which He was born of the Virgin. His circumcision, His growth in stature, and the fact that He became twelve and thirty years of age -- did these not exist in reality? If, however, they should say that the Apostle did indeed state: "He adopted the likeness *of a servant,"[a] and also: "God sent His Son in the likeness of sinful flesh because of sin,"[b] they are judged by their own opinion and not by the words of Paul; for in the first (biblical reference) he placed two *"likenesses" beside each other. First he called Christ "the likeness of God,"[c] and then "the likeness of a servant"; and he gave an example with each likeness separate from the other, so that he who speaks falsely of His likeness, reckoning us to be like you, *is shown to be wrong by the fact that He is "the likeness of God." He who denies this, like the Nestorians, is condemned by the fact that (He is) "the likeness of a servant." Paul, therefore, by these two likenesses . . . .

Fragment 3

. . . to think and to speak. One can clearly *Folio 11r* perceive that, according to his commentaries, Theodore did not consider the Holy Spirit and the power of the Most High to be the very *Persons of the Son and the Spirit, but only the operation of the Spirit and the activity of the Son. While it is a fact that the Holy Spirit comes because predictably He brings into full reality all the mysteries which *He has declared Himself to be like, now, as he has said, it is He who has also formed a man by the Virgin in a

---

a. Philippians 2:7
b. Romans 8:3
c. Philippians 2:6

new and extraordinary way. But "the power of the Most High"[a] he explained in terms of the authority which God possesses for everything He wishes *to do; as it is (written), "The Lord made the earth by His power,"[b] and as it (is written), "Thus says the mighty Lord."[c] So, reasoning as a human being about the divine Persons, he thought that the power and energy of them all rested upon the Virgin. *"But the Persons came to the Virgin" -- as if he refused to affirm that which was not proper for them, except that they had thought about these other names, as we say. *However, the fact that the Word is asserted to be the Son of God by John, we do not find in the writings of the heretics, who meditate upon everything except *what is read (in *Folio 11v*
Scripture). Moreover, Nestorius has evidently stated that the titles "Christ," "Son," "Only-Begotten," and "Lord" are composite, but "Word" and "God" are *simple. But the Evangelist associated Him who was born (i.e., "the Only-Begotten") with the title of Him who is said to be simple (i.e., "the Word"). So it follows that either the statement stands that the titles are not simple and composite as he thinks, or the title, *"Word," should be considered composite like the rest of them. Thus, as Saint John has written, He placed the reality of being born on Himself, even if *the title "Son" or "Christ" seemed to be composite because of the fact that the flesh was assumed by God. This title, then, has to be considered composite also; because above and beyond the fact that He became flesh, *John at the beginning of his book praised "the Word" which is God: "In the beginning was the Word, and the Word was with God, and the Word was God."[d] If, *as the Evangelist has stated, the Word is God but He became flesh by the Virgin, doubtless He was also born of God in that if . . . .

Fragment 4

. . . by man it is impossible for Him to be seen.[e] *Folio 12r*

---

a. Luke 1:35
b. Jeremiah 51:15
c. passim in Peshitta O.T. where "Lord of Hosts" is translated by ܡܪܝܐ ܚܝܠܬܢܐ.
d. John 1:1
e. allusion to John 1:18

But He did say concerning the one who is pure in his heart that he is able to see God.[a] It is evident that he means that when he sees *the flesh he recognizes the Word. As He taught the blind man to believe in Him, so it is written that He also gave him sight; for when He saw the man, He declared Himself (i.e., who He was) in order that God might be known to him.[b] *We must not think that God dwelt in Him in such a way that the other (i.e., the flesh) was beyond Him. Indeed, he asks who the Son of God is that he might believe in Him, and He answered him: "You have seen Him, and He who is speaking with you is He."[c] *Whoever wishes to be a Christian must (know) the full meaning of what was intended by the fact that He was considered to be a man by the multitudes. He had lived among them, He had come in and gone out with them, taught from *a ship and sat on the top of a mountain. He spoke also with the blind man in order that he might believe that He was God incarnate, which is what he wanted. The flesh was visible to the eye without any difference, whereas His nature was not apparent to the mind. *In a way that is even more subtle than the mind's vision, He was incarnate far *beyond the vision of *Folio 12v* the eye; because not even the [mind] of angels or of one of the [orators] would be able [to see] Him by means of that which was much too subtle, esoteric, [remote] *and distant for any mind which gives heed merely to the vision of the eye; because by becoming flesh He even went beyond it, since the physical sense of touch happens to be far more insensitive than the vision of the eye. *He who was incarnate was not only seen, but He was also touched by being seized, captured, bound, scourged, and more. On the cross He was fastened with nails. Because *man has other vision besides (that of) the physical eye, (we can say that) while the eye saw Him as a man, the mind which is within perceived Him to be God. Now even as *bread is seen by the former kind of eye, to the vision of a new man it appears to be the body of God. Because of this, he (i.e., Thomas)

---

a. allusion to Matthew 5:8

b. allusion to John 9:35-38

c. John 9:37

was also given a blessing; for when he touched the flesh, he declared that He was Lord and God.[a] *It was the Apostle Thomas, one of the Twelve (who said), "Except I see in His hands the print of the nails, and put my finger in the place of the nails, ..."[b]

Fragment 5

. . . that it is evident in every one or the other *Folio 13r* of them: the spirit along with that which is tangible, and the body with that which remains intangible.

For *Christ did not go in as a spirit when the doors were shut and afterwards show Himself in the flesh.[c] If He had gone in as a spiritual being, there would have been no miracle and things would not have happened as is supposed. *In fact, if solid bodies are not able to restrain angels and all the other spiritual ranks from passing through them, how could closed *doors restrain the Spirit of God when He is infinitely different from them? Or would He be obliged to go in through narrow chinks?

Well, then, Christ did not go through the doors which were shut as a disembodied spirit, or as an angel, *or as an ethereal body, even though He was transformed after the resurrection. However, although He arose to the spiritual life in which all of our bodies are to be, ethereal and *invisible to the sight, what we have now He keeps within Himself. Those things which became His through suffering and which He had gained formerly, (were His) also after the resurrection: *the handling, I maintain, and the *Folio 13v* scars, and the fact that He was seen. It seems that He proved them by what He did. Miracles will be valued by everyone but not natural phenomena.

*Now Diodore, because he chose to speak of Christ as an ordinary man and not as the God who became flesh entering also into all those things He had which were natural and ordinary, considered His coming into existence, I say, *His birth, His needs and His growth, His suffering and His

---

a. cf. John 20:28
b. John 20:25
c. allusion to John 20:19, 26

death (in the same way). It is likely that he also thought of His resurrection in that way. With regard to it, he dared to say that it was not by a miracle, but as God incarnate *He was able to enter while the doors were shut. "It was not possible," as he said, "for Him who was seen and handled and was in the flesh, to enter through closed doors." However, he wrote that which must not be *considered a precept but blasphemy equal to what is said only by Jews and pagans: "The disciples, for fear of the Jews and the chief of the nightwatch, were mistaken (in saying) that they fastened the doors. *Jesus found them closed and He opened (them) and went in. Because they thought, as he said, that He went in while the doors were fastened, they trembled and were terrified by His appearance, and He yielded . . . ."

Fragment 6

. . . to the souls of sinners who were seized by *Folio 14r*
Sheol; because "the soul of the righteous," it is written, "are in the hands of God."[a] Whereas he first commended their lives (to God) while they were in the flesh, the souls *of sinners on the other hand remain in Sheol with the body. Because they loved the [passions] and the lusts of the flesh, they remain with it in desolation, not in it but with it; that is, the souls of the ungodly who have denied God, or those who have not *believed at all, or those in the power of demons.

He therefore preached [with] His body, which was [also] laid inside the sepulchre, to the souls of sinners.[b] It is evident that a corpse did not proclaim the resurrection. Because the corpses *of sinners and of the ungodly are alone, how much would the body of God be recognized as being alive and giving life? Human life also leaves the bodies of the [righteous] daily. We have [testified] that the divine life *does not abandon them.[c] (Consider) the miracles which will be wrought on their bones, and (the fact

---

a. Wisdom of Solomon 3:1
b. cf. 1 Peter 3:19
c. cf. Wisdom of Solomon 1:15,16

that) it is demons who shout and teach against the divine life remaining with them. If it is so with respect to the righteous servants, how much more must it be with respect to the Lord God?

*Therefore it is well stated that that Spirit which made Jesus incarnate was amazingly united to His body. It is what Luke has said, that when he grew *in His *Folio 14v* stature, He also became strong by Himself, and He set the stages for His subsequent growth in stature because everyone who is born in the Spirit by water *grows in that stature. If ordinary [thoughts] belong to His growth, as I have said, they are not for nothing, and they are justifiably written about Jesus, because to us He has become the head of another race. Instead of Adam who is of the dust, the Adam who is from *heaven has become known [to us. It was not] the heavenly Adam who was of the dust [and who,] after the Holy [Spi]rit had departed from him, [trans]gressed the commandment. There was no growth in spiritual stature for him (i.e., Adam). How could he grow in *that which at one time [he drove away] from himself? He was not filled [with wisdom], for wisdom does not stand where evil intrudes, and the grace of God was never again upon him (from that time). That which is *lovely and sweet had appointed him over natural things and over races. By it he called the names [of everything] and received power over everything. By it he also became the likeness and image of God. As one who was in the likeness of God, all races *and dumb natural objects were subject to him. As soon as he abandoned Him, everything rebelled against him, and instead of authority. . . ..

Fragment 7

. . . from the things we say, but also from every *Folio 15r* record of the Gospel. Now Luke adds to the statement that He went down to Nazareth and was subject to them, "His mother kept *all these things in her heart."[a] It is evident that because they were not natural or customary, it is written in another place: "She kept and compared all these

---

a. Luke 2:51

things."[a] And again: "But Joseph and His mother marvelled at those things *which were uttered concerning Him."[b] If they had not seen (things) which were new and strange, they would not have marvelled at them, and furthermore Mary would not have kept and compared them with each other. If they had been natural *in a human way, she would not have needed to compare them. But, while comparing the words (spoken) about Him and the deeds (done) by Him with each other and with everything else that is human, she marvelled at the things which Jesus (did) as if *at things which were new; because up to that time the exact nature of the mystery was not even clear to her. The fact is that it was revealed after the coming of the Spirit: "The Holy Spirit had not been given because *Jesus had not yet been glorified."[c] Mary had known that she conceived and gave birth without intercourse, that it was by God then that He was made incarnate, and He became a man through her. *She *Folio 15v* gave birth without having been convinced of the fact that He had not been made incarnate through her but as by a miracle, while not knowing that she was the same as those who *conceive from semen. Although He was formed and fashioned (as if) by them (i.e., by women), she did not conceive (as) they experience (conception). If it is this way with the (divine) nature, sometimes those things which are known of the earthly ministry (of Christ) are beyond utterance, thought and perception. Because she had not clearly known *at that time that she had given birth to the incarnate God, she had marvelled at those things which she saw in Him, and heard from all the others concerning Him. Now after the Evangelist has related these things which were in Him and with Him and by Him until *the age of twelve, he gathers all of them together, both first and last, and says: "Jesus grew in stature, and in wisdom, and in favour with God and man."[d] But above (i.e., before that statement), he said: "The boy grew *and became strong in the Spirit."[e] There (i.e., in the first quotation) "Jesus grew in wisdom

---

a. Luke 2:19
b. Luke 2:33
c. John 7:39
d. Luke 2:52
e. Luke 2:40

and stature" to demonstrate that from this stage on He no longer knew Himself as a boy; but from seven to twelve years of age, He was known in this way (i.e., in that of the second quotation). *From this stage on, there is a different degree of stature along with that other; so that he did not write there (i.e., in the first quotation) that He grew and became strong in the Spirit, but "He grew in stature. . . ."

Fragment 8

Folio 16r

. . . "The weakness of God is stronger than men, and His foolishness is wiser than men."[a] If His weakness is stronger than the strength of men, it is (also) more incomprehensible *than theirs, and His foolishness is more misunderstood than their wisdom; for the great words of orators are not sufficient to understand the smallest things of God. If the fact that He grew in stature is considered weak by you (sing.) and *that He increased in wisdom is a deficiency, behold, the Apostle has said that they are not perceived by men.[b] So then, it should be enough for you to know the One who grew, and you should not ask, "How did Jesus grow in stature, and in wisdom, and in favour?"[c] *I am convinced that what must be believed by you is that Jesus is the Christ, and that "Christ is the Power and Wisdom of God"[d] -- behold, Paul has proclaimed it to you! So then, the Power grew in that stature and wisdom *within her (i.e., the Virgin). "The Holy Spirit will come, and the Power of the Most High will overshadow you."[e] The Power of the Most High was made incarnate, and He who was incarnate was weak flesh and received a rational soul. He grew both in the stature *of His body and in the wisdom of His soul. If we are not able to understand the mystery of His growth, shall we not marvel that the things which are not explained belong to God, and not to man? If *His mighty *Folio 16v* deeds cannot be examined, how can His weaknesses be investigated? Perhaps it is easier for the mighty deeds

---

a. 1 Corinthians 1:25
b. cf. 1 Corinthians 2:14
c. Luke 2:52
d. 1 Corinthians 1:24
e. Luke 1:35

of God to be expressed than for His weaknesses to be investigated; because the mighty deeds belong to His (divine) nature, *but His weaknesses belong to the miracle which happened in His Person. If the miracle is the fact that God became weak, all those things associated with it are also miracles. It is impossible for miracles to be explained, except that they persuade the mind *to be amazed and to wonder at them, not only those which were wrought by God, but also the others which were caused by the rest of (the mighty) deeds. If the signs which were wrought in the (following) deeds are not recognized, either (in) what occurred in Egypt, or in what was done *in the wilderness, or in the things which have taken place in every generation, or in those things Jesus demonstrated which were apart from Himself, or in things which have been effected by natural and physical means from the beginning of the world until now and are considered usual, how can anyone seek to understand and explain *a miracle which happened in an unusual way in the Person of the Word, who was emptied and became a man and fulfilled everything human by His birth? So I suppose *that he who pays attention to these things, whether he is an orator or not, will consider the fact that he did not know beforehand how to reckon them and which of them should be investigated by him.

If it is written that Jesus grew, and Jesus is indeed God the Word, as . . . .

Fragment 9

Folio 17r

. . . the age of twelve years according to that custom.[a] For if human ideas are not inferior, how can divine ideas be less? If they are given over to involvement *in many studies at this age, how can they not have incorruptible involvement with the Holy Spirit? The fact is that Jesus also, when He had developed and become strong in it (i.e., the Spirit), *displayed the fruit of his [education]. He chose for Himself to be in the [temple] of God, and to be listening to and questioning the teachers.[b]

---

a. cf. Luke 2:42

b. cf. Luke 2:46

Now, the Evangelist in this passage did not merely indicate what the age *of Jesus was, but what common teaching he would offer everyone through it. He would declare that from henceforth it is right for men to be ambitious by choosing the most excellent things. But for Jesus, this age was not the beginning of good works, *because He was never moved by anything, either feeling or thought, which opposed goodness. But anything which was in Him and was not known, He in fact made it known here, for He remained in the temple *of God while (being) in constant study of the teaching. Indeed, although men receive secular teaching until this age, *even if there are Folio 17v seven-year-olds and other men who [are made foolish] by it, how many times was He more humble than they? Because only the human voice and speech are complex, they are learning from the age *of twelve and on. Any man can receive divine ideas, and listen, and utter words which are not complex, and attain to the vision of (that) spiritual wisdom which is beyond (this) world which, as it seems to me, *was granted in the wilderness to John the Baptist also. Because [he was baptized] by the Holy Spirit, he grew there, and along with growth in stature his soul was also developing in divine ideas, and this *is what we did not know through John. Because His growth in spiritual things was not recorded, we have not been aware of it in the growth of Christ. No one will take account of a saying which is not worthy of confidence when he is considering things which grow in *the world; for in the world, there are many things which hinder a man from arriving at a perceptiveness in spiritual things. Indeed, how can he perceive by means of something that does not grow in him? The ways of man are known *to be fat and fleshy not only because of eating and drinking, but also *because of human pleasures and Folio 18r visions which set lusts aflame. Those who are growing up in boyhood are at least not (involved) in these things, but they are approaching them; *because all worldly effort including human customs leads to lusts, dulls the mind, and darkens the thoughts. Although in the time of his infancy one is not aware of the passions because they are dormant within him, *when they have reached within him the age of our boyhood even if he does not wish it, they entice the members (of the body), and stir the thoughts, and he is unable to recognize at the age of twelve that this is his growth and labour in spiritual things, *but only in those (other) things has he grown and (to them) become accustomed. With Jesus, however, it was the opposite; because lust had not been implanted in His incarnation, the things which fostered growth for Him were not struggles from the outside. Human visions did not impel it. *But at that age of twelve, He announced to everyone how the hidden growth of His thoughts had come into being, and because of it He set a limit for those who were going to receive *His Spirit and be members of His body. But they first (have to) recognize what is evil and then *what is good; because lust *Folio 18v* is stirred up in men first, and then (after it) are found teachers, and instructors, and a good upbringing in what the Spirit desires. *It was not so with Jesus, however. But the desire for and the choice of the good came before what was revealed at that specified age. It was not that He chose the good after He had rejected the evil; for how *could He have rejected something He did not completely know about; as it is written: "Before the boy knows how to reject evil, he will choose the good."[a] Jesus therefore did not reject and then choose, but He showed clearly what it was that was chosen first *by Him, and He completed the common education for all those who are at this stage of life; so that from henceforth they may refuse evil things and choose good things, exchanging worldly habits for habits which belong to God and not retaining the things of *infancy and childhood which have been said to be like one season. Everything which is of the world, or of thought, or of fellowship or of any other carnal desire, this stage can achieve. More and more, *therefore, (should it be able to achieve) those things which are spiritual. But there are some who have thought concerning the first Adam that at the age of twelve years . . . .

---

a. Isaiah 7:15

Fragment 10

". . . but towards Him who of His own will was *Folio 19r* emptied and became a man." Again, "He will set a sign for us, for He will grow in good things first towards God and then towards men." Again, this, regarding *God, "He will become like the Father because He was brought low by Him in that He became a man." Again, "It was not that He came to men that they might completely grow towards God, but it was only that in part. *(While) He grew towards the other righteous men and prophets, He was the first and the beginning of the way for everyone; for, as He wished and as long as He wished, He was growing and also being brought towards that which they were each to become with us." But if anyone wants a similar formulation of it, let him consider and repeat (this) statement, *"Because He became a man He grew first towards God in good things and then towards men," -- which is surely not far from the truth.

As for the heretics, however, who say that He became an ordinary man *like one of us, that He grew in stature, and increased in wisdom and favour, I agree with (them) that in that passage he has used few words, but I would ask them first what it is they are saying: that Jesus is a natural man, *or (that He is) God and man? If they are saying the first, let them listen to the Scriptures which in every place call Jesus God, and His equal, *and *Folio 19v* con-substantial with the Father, and Maker of the worlds, and He who is before all things from henceforth. Either we consider the Man to be equal with the God and Maker of all, or *that Jesus is God, the Word, which is still our (belief). Since the Scriptures discuss the Son by (divine) nature, from whom then do they say that the Man received wisdom and favour? If (He received them) from the Father, then indeed is He the Son; *but if from the Son, Jesus is not the Son of God, and if from the Holy Spirit like one of the prophets, why is He the Son and they the prophets? If from the Trinity He has become wise and received favour *like one of the servants, He is considering all of them (i.e., the servants) to be created by the divine nature, and established and sustained by Himself. If, however, He is like a favoured son, He came into being better than anyone else that (as) the Son He would be considered one of the Persons. *If they should say 'of the Father' because the name 'Son' is appropriate to 'Father', then the Word is divine. If the Son is considered to be one of the Father, the Son and the Spirit together, then every divine nature *should be called "Father," and where is the understanding of the Persons and the variation of names? But if they say that the divine nature is *a human father, *Folio 20r* following the foolish thought of Theodore whose opinion this is, and not the teaching of Scripture, there are those who in every place *give the name 'Father' to that one Person who has truly begotten one eternal Son. He is considered the natural Father of Him and of us who have been baptized in grace, because we have become brothers of the (divinely) natural Son by baptism, and from *henceforth we are called the Son's brothers, and the Father's children. As it was said by Him who is the Son of His Father: "I shall proclaim your name to my brothers."[a] And again, "He was not ashamed to call them His brothers."[b]

We are therefore *brothers of the (divinely) natural Son and children of God the Father. It is not because the Father, Son and Spirit are believed to be one in nature, for the name of fatherhood is a nature just as the Incarnation, the Birth by the Virgin, the Passion, and the Death *are also of an uncommon (nature). It is because they are one in essence. But if they give an example of our adoption as sons apart from that of the Jews, and as it is with them (i.e., the Jews) think that the nature is the Father and not the Person of the Father -- *they even think in this way about us -- they reject the Father's earthly ministry, they falsify the Son's redemption, and they consider our things *to be like those of the Jews. *Folio 20v* Indeed, their adoption as sons was a type, and all their things were shadows prefiguring the reality, but ours are the reality and the truth; *for we are not known as children apart from the Person of the Son, but He is the head and

---

a. Hebrews 2:12 b. Hebrews 2:11

we are members in His body. Because of this, He became a man to make us children of God, just as His incarnation was not only in name but *factually real, and He has made us members (of His body) and children of His Father not merely in word, as it was with the Jews; for at that time He did not become a man and then make children, nor was He humbled and then exalted, nor did He receive *shame and then honour. But as He gave the divine name to Moses, He also gave Israel the title of 'son'; and, desiring to honour the people before their enemies, He sent word to Pharaoh by Moses: "Send me my son, my first born, *Israel, and he will serve me."[a] When He had made known to Pharaoh the honour of the people, He declared to Moses his (i.e., Pharaoh's) reprobation and the election of the others whom He did not call "son" in an ordinary way. But He added that of "first-born" which teaches that others *were to come after him. The word was a sign to Moses that as Ishmael, Esau and Reuben were rejected and others came in (to the adopted sonship) in their place, (so) *Israel went *Folio 21r* out, and the Gentiles were accepted in their place. And if their expulsion was known from the beginning to be their election, how can their sonship be compared with ours?

Because, then, *the people were first honoured by the name alone, the Son was considered to be of God. But He is of the divine nature and not of the Person of the Father; for He was not known to them as Father, Son, and Spirit so that everywhere the teaching about the (divine) nature was delivered *to them in the language of one God. Here, however, it was revealed that along with faith in the (divine) nature goes also the profession of faith in the Persons; for it is only right that the sons, who were chosen for the honour of the adoption of sons, should take account of the Person of the Father. *They did not simply assume the name, but because they were brothers by the grace of the (divinely) natural Son. Even this did not happen simply in word and not in fact, but the Son first became a man, *and then He made men sons. They are born again, and then

---

a. Exodus 4:22, 23

they come into being: "You have been buried with Him by baptism into death, and into Him you were raised with Him."[a] Again the Apostle has said: "Do you not know that those of us who have been baptized *into Jesus Christ were baptized into His death? You have been buried with Him in baptism into death that just as Jesus Christ rose from the grave in the glory *of His Father; so we too shall walk *Folio 21v* in the new life."[b] So we become immortal, and then (we become) sons; for it was not right for dead persons to become members in the living body *of Christ. God does not accept sons and dear ones to be His who are subject to death, but His words testify that those who are in His image are alive and immortal. Out of mercy He has said: "'I am the God *of Abraham, and of Isaac, and of Jacob'. And He is not the God of the dead but of the living, for all live in Him."[c] Again, concerning the sons, it was proclaimed by the prophets: "I have said that you are all gods, and *sons of the Highest; therefore, like one of the men you shall die."[d] He showed that (His) sons are immortal men, and mortals are not those who deserve the honour of sons. So the Scriptures do not consider *ordinary men and angels to be sons of God, but it is only some men who become sons by death and resurrection. Because they have become brothers to the Son who became man *through the new birth which is by baptism, they are of necessity known as sons of the Father. If the matter of brotherhood is common (to both the Son and the baptized), so also does the name of fatherhood belong to both *the Head and His members, the Word who *Folio 22r* became a man and the men who have become sons. Just as we are truly born as men from the natural womb, (so) in truth and in reality, *we become sons from the womb of baptism. The first explains the second; for the former is not foolish, nor the latter presumptuous.

So there is no place for your new and strange idea *that the divine nature be considered a human father, or that those who received the glory of the adoption of sons

---

a. Colossians 2:12

b. Romans 6:3, 4

c. Matthew 22:32 + Luke 20: 37-48 conflated

d. Psalm 82:6, 7

are sons by nature and not by the Person of the Father. Is it not enough that the presumed adoption of sons should appear to our glory? *In that passage (already mentioned) the saying was for the Jews alone: "I have said that you are gods and sons of the Highest."[a] The word written is "I have said," and not "I have made." He said and He promised, but He did not make. *But in this passage (which follows) He made a promise before the foundations of the world, and He will fulfil His promise at the end of the times: "He chose you beforehand in Him before the foundations of the world."[b] Again, Jesus said to His disciples: "You were chosen by me *before the foundations of the world."[c] But if a heretic should say: "All believers along with that Man are sons of the Person of the Father," he should be asked, "Who has given him *this glory, and where and how *Folio 22v* was it received?" If it was from baptism, which is a type of death and resurrection, that the baptized received Him, *as the Apostle teaches, where did that Man receive it? There is no precedent for him to say (that it is) by means of His own death and resurrection, since men have not deserved it by means of their death and resurrection. Therefore the death *and resurrection of others are taken into account, for when someone is made to participate in them, he becomes a son and it follows that God the Word was afflicted by them. It is through participating in His suffering and resurrection that man is made worthy of His glory. When *a heretic exempts God from the sufferings, he increasingly burdens himself with sufferings; because it follows that He was not made flesh, nor was He born physically, nor did He suffer in that way. Yet it was on account of man that He assumed for Himself that birth. Again, if he avoids this *by considering Jesus to be only a man but cunningly confessing Him according to his tradition as God and man, he should be asked which of the two of them grew. If he should say that the growth was

---

a. Psalm 82:6
b. Ephesians 1:4
c. cf. John 15:16 + 17:24

common (i.e., shared by both) because *it is written that Jesus grew, how can God be incomplete? Whether He grew up alone or with another man, *in each of these *Folio 23r* (instances) it is not Christ who becomes known along with something else, for first it is written about Him that He grew in stature. If He was not incarnate and did not become *a man, how did He grow? For, behold, we who believe that these words were written about God, confess first that He came into being and had a human beginning, and then we have the basis (on which to consider) His growth. *But you yourself say that it was in fellowship with a man that He grew as God without being enfleshed. That clearly is blasphemy. Again, it is not written that they grew, but that Jesus grew; *and the Evangelist points out plainly that the growth was of a single (person). Whether He is regarded as man or as God, therefore, the fact that Jesus is called God and man by you (makes) that expression meaningless and false, for it is uttered *to deceive the common people. Now that doctrinal perversity has been exposed, let Jesus be henceforth recognized either as God incarnate, as we believe, or as a righteous man, as Theodore and Nestorius *understand (Him to be). That (Jesus) is of God and man, which recently has been found among the heretics, is nonsense. If *(they think) they are supported by *Folio 23v* the writings of the Fathers where that expression is used, they should first believe as they (the Fathers) did: that God, who is immutable, became man, and then use *their wording by which they understood that God and the Man were not separate, but that they should teach that He truly became flesh: His divinity was not changed by His incarnation, and His corporality was brought to birth and had a beginning *after He became flesh. However, just as God is believed in because He exists, so the Man is confessed because He came into being, and a change in either case did not occur. If that way of thinking is theirs (i.e., the Fathers), then yours is *quite the opposite. The joining and sharing of the name of God and of man, unlike their word, only bear witness to yours. It is not natures as you yourselves claim but characteristics which they have, and *the Man has a share in the mighty works of God. You have denied that God the Word was united with the humbler things of man, and you have senselessly followed the foolish word of Nestorius which preaches *two natures. Again, He speaks to them as one power, one will, one wisdom, and one authority. If this is so, we shall understand each of those natures which have been united. It is right *that power, wisdom and authority can come into *Folio 24r* being and that it then is the power, wisdom and authority of the Man. If He did not possess any of these (things) so that on this basis *what He did not have was received from God in order for Him to have a share in them, are not the actions of both of them one, even though a man is involved in the great works of God? If this can be maintained and they had a single wisdom, how did Jesus grow in wisdom? *If they were one (in) authority, how did He increase in grace? If the same power belonged to them, how was it that "the weakness of God is stronger than men?"[a] For God, according to what you say did not *partake of weakness, and the Man He possessed by (divine) nature had the same power as God. In what way, then, is the weakness of God stronger than men? If *weakness is not recognized early, it will not be known to be weak. When you leave God out of the lesser things, you increasingly deprive Him of the greater things. Again, if both of them were one in wisdom, how did Jesus *grow in wisdom? If He became a man who matured, they (i.e., both God and man) did not become *wisdom as you say. If the growth included both of *Folio 24v* them, God was ignorant and He needed to grow also since He would not be fully developed. Where *then was the wisdom of God which the Man shared? Why, it was discovered and acquired by growth! Therefore, either they were not one (in) wisdom as you say, or if they were *Jesus did not grow in wisdom. Yet He did grow up by means of wisdom -- He who once shared it with God the Word and was known to be one with Him (in) wisdom. Where, when and how can the wisdom of God *and of the Man be one? (Either) the Man's

---

a. 1 Corinthians 1:25

wisdom developed and became equal with God's, or God's was diminished and became co-extensive with the Man's. When and where was that Man's wisdom made known *and thus became one with God's (wisdom)? If they say that the union came into being in the womb, how could wisdom come into being for Him who had not yet become a son? If He was united to God by His creation and both of them became one, how *is it written that Jesus grew in stature and in wisdom? If it was when He was twelve years old, according to this reckoning, (how) is it written *that He grew after *Folio 25r* this number? If, then, it was at (His) baptism following which He became one (in) wisdom (with God), (how) is it said: "No one knows that day or that hour, neither the angels nor the Son?"[a] If *no man knows the hour of His coming -- for you understand the Son in that place -- how did He along with God come to be as one wisdom? If, again, it was after the resurrection that that partnership came into being, why is it that He said: *"All authority in heaven and in earth has been given to me?"[b] In the same way, at the time of His ascension when His disciples asked Him, "Will you restore the kingdom to Israel at this time?" He said to them, "It is not yours to know *the time or the dates which the Father has put in His own power."[c] He has shown that we understand these things only by the Father. If (it was) after He ascended that they became one (in) wisdom and one (in) authority, why did Paul say: "Christ *died and rose again, and is at the right hand of God, and He intercedes for us?"[d] How can He intercede as one in need if they have a single authority? It is especially of Christ that Paul said, "He intercedes," which you explain to mean that *He was God and man. Do both of them pray to the Father? But if it is only the Man, the Word then does not possess a single *authority and a single power. If *Folio 25v* there were no place in them for all those things of which it was said that there was one authority, power and wisdom, God and the Man *would not therefore be two as you suppose,

---

a. Matthew 24:36
b. Matthew 28:18
c. Acts 1:6, 7
d. Romans 8:34

and that partnership which you promote would not have come into being. But "Christ, the power and wisdom of God,"[a] emptied himself[b] by the will of the Father, and became a weak human being without being changed. *Just as it was right for His body to grow in stature, so (it was right) for His soul to increase in wisdom, and for His weakness to receive grace. While He appeared to be weak, He became known as the strong one. While wisdom was increasing in Him, *the providential source of His wisdom was being revealed more and more. We believe these things because they are written, and not because they are comprehensible to those who hear them; for the earthly ministry of God is an unutterable mystery and we are not ashamed to have our doctrine falter in its lack of description and comprehensibility. *But we especially glory in this: we hold a mystery that cannot be grasped by knowledge. While all philosophies and doctrines may be examined and comprehended, what we have continues quietly on. We believe only because *we cannot comprehend. To those who are lost we are considered foolish, but to those who believe (we are) unutterably wise: "The word of the cross *is *Folio 26r* foolishness to those who are lost."[c] In the name of the cross it is clear that he has indicated the whole earthly ministry (of Christ) beginning with the birth by the Virgin which is reckoned to be foolishness by those who are lost, for they do not *believe that God dwelt in the womb, became flesh as a man, and was born of a woman. Pagans and Jews deny the Birth completely and do not believe that Jesus was born of the Virgin. Heretics, who are supposed to accept *the doctrine of the mystery, yield themselves to the Man instead of to God. They say that a natural fetus was conceived without intercourse and born without semen; and, in a different way, they move towards what is said by Jews and pagans. *If it was not God who was conceived and born and a Man did not come into being of (the divine) nature without intercourse, they are like the Jews and pagans who agree

---

a. 1 Corinthians 1:24
b. cf. Philippians 2:7
c. 1 Corinthians 1:18

that He was born of Mary, and they limit the Man with (the divine) nature *to their own likeness, and in this alone does the blasphemy differ: while theirs (the blasphemy of Jews and pagans) is clearly articulated, that of the others (the heretics) is skilfully concealed. Truly, it does not agree with the order of nature that God should become man and be born of a woman, *for this does not suit Him and human nature is not up to it. As long as human thinking contemplates the miracle, it shuns Him. But Christians who believe *accept it, not by understanding it but *Folio 26v* because it is written. When they compare the deed with the power of God, they yield to His authority remembering the proclaimed word of the mystery: *"Nothing is difficult for God."[a] If, again, the heretic continues to argue by saying: "How is it possible for God to grow in stature and wisdom?" we grant him that He is perfect and complete in His being. *Paul called Christ "the power and wisdom of God."[b] It is clear that the Son is the power and wisdom of the Father, therefore Christ is the Son of God. Because it is written that Jesus grew, Jesus *then is Christ, that Son of God who grew in stature and wisdom. If he says that the Word, (who is) the power and wisdom of the Father, is God, he in fact is confessing that God the Word is Christ. If *Christ, (then) the Word is God. But (if) Jesus is Christ then those things written (about Him) are appropriate to God the Word, in which He was made ready for the salvation of men and for the dedication and consecration of everything, for He was called *Saviour by (His) action. Now if he says that Christ is called God the Word as a figure of speech, then (He is) Man also (as a figure of speech). (If this is so), where is the true man? *Behold, Jesus is *Folio 27r* the one who is believed by you to be a man. It is evident that He is Christ and God the Word: "Jesus grew in stature and in wisdom."[c] If He grew in stature, *it is clear that where He did not have stature He did not have growth. Where He did not have a human soul, He did not

---

a. Luke 1:37
b. 1 Corinthians 1:24
c. Luke 2:52

receive an increase in wisdom. Hold, therefore, to the physical beginning, and add to it the human actions. *By not considering the way of the earthly ministry (of Christ) or comparing His (divine) nature with His earthly ministry and His divine activities with His human activities, you (sing.) deny the common salvation. The stature was therefore of the body. The physical nature *came to Him from Mary from whom He received a human soul. Where He began (His) growth in stature, He began also (His) development in wisdom. He who has said that wisdom did not increase in Him, has clearly denied *both (His) growth in stature and His true physical nature, and is declared (to be) not only a disciple of Paul of Samosata and of Sabellius, but especially of Mani and Marcion; for they reject *the physical nature of God and His earthly ministry for our salvation.

Jesus, therefore, grew in those ways which are first written about Him: in the stature of His body and in accordance with the stages of His development, *in *Folio 27v* wisdom also as well as in the grace of God. Just as the stages in the development of His stature sprang forth one after the other, so that wisdom of His also grew *out of Him. The growth was evident by (its) appearance and by other things which were part of Him. The wisdom (was evident) by (His) teaching, and the grace by signs and wonders. Even if it is not written that miracles happened before (His) baptism, (the grace was evident) *from the fact that He loved men and was loved by them. As it (is written), "Joseph received favour before his master."[a] Again, "In the eyes of the governor of the prison,"[b] as (it says), "He found favour before Pharaoh."[c] And as it (also is written), *"The apostles received favour before all the people."[d] Now because of this, we have said that He grew partly upwards to God. If we cannot write about it accurately, there is nothing to wonder at, because even those things *which are thought to be revealed are not

---

a. Genesis 39:4
b. Genesis 39:21
c. Genesis 41:37; cf. Acts 7:10
d. Acts 2:47

clear to us. Not every spiritual insight can be expressed in a word or an oral composition, because the one involves the senses while the other (involves) knowledge brought together by doctrine. Grace communicates with the senses, *but the knowledge of ideas is acquired by discipline and study. Along with these, in a third category, faith is known *as the power which is born of a correct *Folio 28r* choice (made) by the soul. Two of them belong to us: *to acquire knowledge by discipline and exercise which is our responsibility, and to be aware of the spiritual things which the grace of God places within a word or an idea. But the other one is the gift of God to believe in those incomprehensible things which we choose. Sometimes (it is given) freely as (it was) to the apostles, and sometimes for the purity *of mind gained by victory over the passions and the senses which are like something inexpressible and not subject to intellectual ideas, because they (i.e., the ideas) have not seen it. But only by grace can it be made manifest to the mind. *It alone rejoices and takes delight in it. If this knowledge is not held in the ideas within words, how can it be put together in a word or captured in letters? *If those who are aware of it cannot transmit it in a word because the senses as I have said are not expressed in a word, how can heretics who do not even possess the faith, *offer a correct interpretation of it? "Wisdom does not dwell in a soul guilty of evil things, nor *in a body made guilty by a sinful woman."[a] Now in *Folio 28v* this place, (this verse includes) not only those who are enslaved by their passions and trained in craftiness, but also those deprived of the true faith in God. How could they understand *the wisdom in which Christ grew? If, as the apostle said, His wisdom is imparted among the mature[b] and is revealed to them alone, how could Christ's (wisdom) be understood by heretics, since a simple reading *of the Scriptures does not indicate the wisdom which is in them, just as the appearance of natural things does not (display)

---

a. Wisdom of Solomon 1:4
b. allusion to 1 Corinthians 2:6

the knowledge which is concealed in them. By the appearance of things that are made, anyone who wishes is able to know God. But by the spiritual wisdom *which is in them, they alone discover their intellect who have been cleansed of their earlier passions. Thus, it is in that wisdom that the intellect grows. They see it, not because of the bodies in which it is clothed, but by the purity of the intellect; *for this is its nature when it cleanses itself and discards the old man[a] to find the spiritual things completely devoid of the intervention of physical things. If physical words without bodily appearances were able *to make the knowledge of God known, He would not have created those things which are seen. But because He has willed to make not only rational spirits, but also man who is composed of soul and body, He has placed *wisdom in bodies for his discipline. Then, when he sees, and hears, *and smells and *Folio 29r* touches, he will gather knowledge for his soul, not spiritual (knowledge), but that which is joined to facts. As I have said, it is not acquired by discipline, but only by purity *of intellect. By it discipline is discovered and named, as is the inquiry which (is based) on everything. Even someone who lives in the old man can acquire this grace of God which is made manifest to the mind. *But spiritual (wisdom) can only be discovered by the new man who is known to be such by grace and by works; because, when this wisdom took flesh (by grace), it appeared externally by works, not on account of spiritual things, but in order that it may gather the idea of physical things to itself. *Although it (i.e., the intellect) was not able to perceive it, wisdom was not destroyed by works, but continues to be clothed with them until the end of time. It exists in the Maker and in the things made. Those who are in the flesh are not even disciplined by it *apart from physical mediation. That is to say, (unregenerate) men (gain knowledge) by means of them (i.e., physical things), but those who discard their passions (gain knowledge) by the likeness of spiritual powers. When the time of discipline

---

a. cf. Ephesians 4:22, Colossians 3:9

and learning has come to an end, and that which belongs to the inheritance and to the kingdom has been revealed, *wisdom will be gathered into its place and will not be corrupted or lost in the destruction of the elements. It is like, for example, when a man wishes to write with the letters (of the alphabet) part of the knowledge *in *Folio 29v* his soul, and after he has written the letters he blots them destroying their appearance and structure, but not the knowledge which was mingled with them. So it is with God, who has engraved His wisdom *into physical symbols which He will bring to an end with respect to (their) composition. But He will change it by making it new while not destroying the wisdom within them. So it is also unchanged within itself and in the reconstruction of the bodies (it remains) undamaged, *because even when He mingles it with them it does not desert Him, but it is believed to be in Him and in (His) works: in Him, while not being co-mingled (with Him), and with the works in fabric and in substance. Because a segment of mankind was unwilling, *without the study of these symbols, to discover their author and understand the knowledge which was in them, God demonstrated another way for it (i.e., the segment of mankind) to reach Him, and by another category He taught it wisdom. Because in the beginning He embodied *the wisdom of His creativity in things (He made), now at the end of time the wisdom of His nature has been embodied and has become flesh -- "Christ is the power and wisdom of God."[a] When the *wisdom which was embodied grew in stature, it gathered to itself by means of growth the wisdom which was embodied in the things (He made), and the fact that it shall be with the Father at the end of time. . . .

Fragment 11

. . . first; because of what (is said): "Let us make *Folio 30r* man according to our image and according to our likeness."[b] Because that likeness is uncovered in us especially by

---

a. 1 Corinthians 1:24 b. Genesis 1:26

baptism, it made a new beginning with Him *in a well-known way. Where (does it say) that we have become sons of the likeness of God and members (of the body) of His Son? It was made known to us in the description (of) both the ascending and descending (genealogies) of the two Evangelists. With the physical human genealogy, *Matthew came right down to the physical birth of the Son of God; while Luke, with the development of their new (life) which came into being by baptism, went up (the genealogy) until he brought them to God. Indeed the type of this *'coming down' and 'going up' is first described in that ladder which Jacob saw "standing upon the earth and its top reached heaven, and the angels of God were ascending and descending upon it, and the Lord was standing above it."[a] *While someone may liken it to the revelation connected with Jacob's going down to Beth-Laban and his [going up] with (his leaving) there, to those of us who understand as I do, (it means) specifically (Beth-)Lehem. Indeed, it is also evident that all those who *now deserve (to know) this mystery and all those (by whom) it was transmitted at that time are not aware of it because of baptism. It was derived from them; *for, *Folio 30v* after Adam lost the awareness (of it), Seth first became aware of it, and after him Enoch, and after him Noah, and then Shem, and after them Abraham, Isaac, *Jacob, and the rest who imitated them in faith and works. Today, for it has been granted to everyone in general, those who put off the old man by means of (ascetic) toil and separation and are alive *in the way of the new man can attain awareness of it. While goodness was first derived from one race and was not in all of it (i.e., the race), but was only achieved and handed down from one to another, (now) by means of baptism it is freely given to all *men and they receive the Holy Spirit and become sons of God because the Word became flesh and received a soul. Thus what happened to Him was well arranged, because the flesh needed *a soul and both needed the Holy Spirit. Just as the flesh on receiving a soul becomes a man, so that man who receives the Holy Spirit

---

a. Genesis 28:12-13

is declared by God to be a son. Instead of the flesh *acquiring a soul within the womb, the Holy Spirit is given to man in baptism, for He received Him first as the first fruits . . . .

Fragment 12

. . . we understand (that) just as Jesus was *Folio 31r* supposed to be the son of Joseph,[a] so also the members of His (body) were supposed to be the sons of Adam, because before baptism they exist by supposition as men *and even after it they are considered to be sons of Adam by supposition while they are in truth members (of the body) of Christ and sons of God. Again it is said that they are supposed to be sons of Adam in accordance with what he was before his *sin. He did not remain as he was, nor are those who have descended from him like the first creation. Instead of the body of men coming to life and being sustained by means of those things *which are visible, now they (i.e., the visible things) are sustained by Him and He repays them the reward of their work. Through His renewing (activity) which (changes) death to life and the corruptible to incorruptibility, they also attain an amazing restoration and transformation. Groans are changed *into shouts of joy, and the corruptible into incorruptibility. "All created things have been groaning and in labour until today."[b] While He calls this world "today" as long as it exists, all created things will groan and be in labour in it. *Baptism is a type of its (i.e., the world's) consummation in that when He was baptized Jesus fulfilled His Father's will, and He created all things new, both visible and invisible. This is *the mystery which *Folio 31v* was fulfilled in the baptism of our Saviour, which the Father affirmed by His voice and the Spirit by His descent. After He has made the members of His (body) new by means of His baptism, *Luke raises them up in the list of names which he repeats right back to Adam. Instead of mortals and corruptibles, by it (i.e., the genealogical list of

---

a. cf. Luke 3:23 b. Romans 8:22

names) he has demonstrated them (to be) in a different class, and thus he has brought them to the Father.

Then again he may be using the expression, "it is supposed," *with another meaning, since the Jews of old by supposition were thought to be the sons of God. But men who in reality are sons of grace, are known today as men by supposition but in reality as sons *of God, because the adoption of sons which they have received is not taken away or changed, but their mutability is in keeping with the Person in whom they have become members. Again, as it may otherwise be written by us about Christ: *because among the Jews He was supposed to be the son of Joseph, His mother also had spoken with Him in accordance with this supposition. Luke also wrote about these things which were spoken in this way: *"When His parents brought in the boy Jesus,"[a] again, "His people went to Jerusalem every year at the feast of the Passover."[b] In this passage, to correct these things, Luke said: "It was supposed . . . ."

Fragment 13

. . . he would pass on to us the remainder of those *Folio 32r* things which were done according to the book of Matthew, and he would understand that Christ became known in His earthly ministry by two births, one by the Virgin and the other by baptism. *Those who have become members of His (body) are also like Him, for first they are born as men from the womb and afterwards (they become) sons of God by baptism. While He was God, of the (divine) nature He was born a man from the womb. *While we are by nature men, we become sons of God from (the womb) of baptism. By repeating names (in the genealogy), Matthew goes down to the physical birth of the Word, but Luke in the series *of names goes up from the baptism (of Christ) to God. He explained the voice of the Father calling to His Son by the fact that [by repeating the names] he has followed the sequence and brought Him up to where He had been; because it is written

---

a. Luke 2:27
b. Luke 2:41

that He came from God and entered into the world.[a] [He *descended to] a physical birth from that [. . .] and He ascended [to God . . . .]

Folio 32v

*which is from true baptism, because it was not formed to be a natal womb and those who are born by it do not perish but continue (to live) endlessly as spiritual members *in the body to which they are joined. Those who have become spiritual beings must continue to exist without being destroyed or changed. When the Evangelist compares the birth of the (divine) nature with that of grace, he calls it first by a supposition: *"It was supposed that He was the son of Joseph."[b] The saying is fulfilled in Jesus because He was not the son of Joseph in truth. (It is also fulfilled) in the men who have become members of His (body) in that their first birth was not real. *Because of this, a second (birth) was needed which made them, not men by supposition, but [eternal] sons of God. Our first birth was not associated with nature in reality but [only] in appearance and in supposition. *Also, the scripture teaches: "Man is like a vapour."[c] And sometimes [. . . .] And again, ...

Fragment 14

Folio 33r

. . . the genealogies which were written. By her (i.e., the Virgin), (the Word) took flesh and was born physically, and by baptism (the Word) was clearly announced and made known through the witness of the Father and the Spirit. When *Luke relates how He was revealed through (that) witness, to (the words), "This is my beloved Son with whom I am pleased";[d] he adds, "Jesus was about thirty years old."[e] Then by repeating the names, he followed the sequence and brought Him right up to God *the Father who in the beginning established the mystery in the creation of Adam. When He came down, He bore witness to Him in the Jordan, "This is my beloved Son."[f]

---

a. cf. John 13:3, 16:28
b. Luke 3:23
c. cf. James 4:14
d. Luke 3:22, cf. Matthew 3:17
e. Luke 3:23
f. Luke 3:22, cf. Matthew 3:17

Now when Adam was first created by God he received two (things): that he would be the likeness (of God), *and that he would transmit (that) likeness. Both were taken away [from him] when he sinned. The well-known (fact) that in his youth he felt himself to be in the image of God, for he had *nothing to be ashamed of, is evidence that the [image] did not exist after his sin. And along with this is (the fact) that he hid himself among the trees, for the likeness could not be hidden from its archetype. Again, (there is the fact) that he gave (his) answers fearfully and deceitfully when he was asked, for not one of them was in keeping *with the image of God, and because of these things Adam was known not to be (in) the likeness of God after his sin. Then, again, *from the punishment he *Folio 33v* received, and from (the facts) that he became mortal, that in his labour the earth was cursed, that in toil he was to gather food for himself, *that He decreed against him, "You are dust, and to dust you shall return,"[a] that He spoke of him mockingly, "Behold, Adam has become like one of us,"[b] that (He said), "Lest he take from the tree of life and eat and live forever,"[c] * -- from these and related facts we learn that the likeness of God was erased from Adam after his sin. That other likeness, which was to continue in his family, was known to have been taken from him because it was not transmitted *by Cain or by Abel after him. That (the thing) which is a mystery (i.e., the likeness of God) [came down] to Seth is attested by (the fact) that it was found to be with him,[d] because of the offering and murder of Abel. He (Seth) gave it to Enosh and from that time *"he hoped to call on the name of the Lord."[e] Because the scripture has in this place repeated words like those used at the creation of Adam: "This is the book of the generation of men";[f] and again, "In the day in which God made *Adam, in the image of God He made him, male and female He made them";[g] that is, because the glory

---

a. Genesis 3:19
b. Genesis 3:22
c. Genesis 3:22
d. cf. Genesis 5:3
e. Genesis 4:26
f. Genesis 5:1
g. Genesis 5:1b-2

taken from Adam was restored to Seth and Enosh, *the *Folio 34r* words written because of that glory (already) mentioned accompany those (others). It is clear that Adam was (in) the likeness of God by reason of what is written: "God said, Let us make man *according to our image and according to [our] likeness, and let them rule over the fish of the sea and over the birds of the sky."[a] We understand that he was [in] the image of God from (the scripture which says), "God created Adam in His image, in the image of God He [made him], *male and female He made them."[b] Because the sons who transmitted this image were born from the marriage of both of them, it says, "Male and female He made them." In order that this understanding may strike us (forcefully) it (the Scripture) has repeated and supplemented its expression, *"God said, Let us make man according to our image and according to our likeness," with "God created Adam in His image." It has shown that not only did he become the image of God, but God put himself *in him that He might continue to be (within man) in (succeeding) generations; especially since it is unusual for the written word to have one clear meaning repeated. In this passage, however, both (verses) clearly teach that he was in the likeness of God and *received the image of God which was to be transmitted through his [seed]. By the first (statement), "[God] said, [Let us make] man according to our image, and [according to] our likeness," *we *Folio 34v* understand (it to indicate) the Person of the Father. By the second one, "God made man, in the image of God He made him," we understand the Son of God; because it is not only the Father who *is God in (His) nature, it is also the Son. The Father as the archetype said, "Let man come into being"; while the Son, as the one who fulfils the will of His Father, made man. It was [not] enough for *the Blessed Moses to write this word twice concerning the creation of man, but again concerning the birth of Seth and Enosh he remembered it and said: "This is the book of the generation of men, in the day when God made man, in the likeness of

---

a. Genesis 1:26 b. Genesis 1:27

*God He made him."[a] Now, while it was the Son who made Adam, it was the Father who made him in the likeness of God. Again, he repeats the word even with regard to Seth, not that he came into being in the likeness of God, for (it was) Adam who came into being in it, but *the likeness of God came into being in him. It was the Son, however, who dwelt within His first creation that He might be transmitted by his descendants. (The fact) that he says, "Male and female He made them," because he was born of the marriage of a man and a woman, (means) that he came into being to transmit *the likeness. Because it is written in this way, "[He created] man in the likeness of God," [it was not said] that the fact He *made [them] male *Folio 35r* and female was ordained, but only "Let us make man [according] to our image and according to our likeness."[b] After Adam came into being it was [said] *of him [also that he appeared] in the likeness of God. As its cause [was honoured, the effect] was also (held) in honour. There are those who say (that the words), "God said, Let us make man according to our image and according to our likeness," are the plan *and purpose, and that what is written after them, "God made man in His image," is the fulfilment of the plan. But it is not like that, since God is in every place with the Word who causes the deed to appear and does not [need] *to plan and purpose. So then, "Let us make" is the same as "God said, Let there be light," and along with that word it is written, "There was light."[c] The deed did not linger after the [command], not even for a moment, and the word did not need *to be repeated and thus something which came into being would be seen. But when He [began] to speak, light came into existence from nothing, without delay. It is like what is made known which is the first thing written: "In the beginning God created *the heavens and the earth."[d] Along with Him who sought to make those first natural things by His will, the deeds appeared.

---

a. Genesis 5:1
b. Genesis 1:26
c. Genesis 1:3
d. Genesis 1:1

Although *the will by which He created the *Folio 35v* creatures was His without a beginning, creation was made with a beginning. [When] He willed it to come into being, suddenly it was [made] as soon as He willed *it to be made. It was not that after His word was uttered that word eventually became a deed in order that by it the mystery of the Word which was finally to become man might be formed. After God created heaven and earth by His will and made *the light by His command, then it is written: "God said, Let there be a firmament in the midst of the waters, and let it separate the waters from the waters."[a] As soon as He said (it), it was [changed]. The deed was not slower than the word. Again, *after these things, He said: "Let the waters be gathered together,"[b] "Let lights be in the firmament of the heavens,"[d] "Let the waters swarm,"[e] and "Let the earth bring forth."[f] In every place the deed was united with the word, for *the command of God possesses that power; as it says: "He calls those things which do not exist as though they did exist."[g] These (words) are like (the text): "Let us make man according to our image and according to our likeness,"[h] for along with the word man came into being. *Then, too, his kind of origin was different from that of the rest of the things that were made. If He had said to the others, "Let us make," the deed would still not be slower than the word, just as the light did not linger *behind that word which I have *Folio 36r* quoted, "Let there be." Also, the firmament did not follow the command which would have thus delayed it. Nor was the creation of man (delayed) by that voice which said, "Let us make [man]." If *the Father had commanded the Son to make, He also [would have created] and the deed would have appeared immediately. The Person of the Son was revealed because the Father said to Him, "Let us make." If, however, because the word is repeated, it is supposed by

---

a. Genesis 1:6
b. Genesis 1:9
c. cf. Genesis 1:11
d. Genesis 1:14
e. Genesis 1:20
f. Genesis 1:24
g. Romans 4:17
h. Genesis 1:26

some that *man was not made (by) [birth] but He established the plan and the purpose and afterwards the deed appeared, it follows that Adam came into being not once but twice: in the first place, because *"God made the man in His image";[a] and, in the second place, because "God formed a man who came to life from the earth, and He breathed into his nostrils the breath of life."[b] Because they say that the first was the plan and preparation, for "God planned first and then He made *man," -- as if those first things were created without [thought]! But it is not so. [Light] was created because (He said), "Let there be light."[c] Because (He said), "Let there be a firmament in the midst of the waters,"[d] it was made. Similarly, there was no delay *also when (He said), "Let us make man according to our image and according to our likeness."[e] It is obvious that suddenly and instantly man was fashioned in the likeness and in the image *of God. Because after *Folio 36v* that (it says), "God made the man in His image, in the image of God he made him,"[f] for the likeness of God was destined to be in him, [since from the beginning] the Son of God dwelt in *created man in order to descend and be transmitted in His generation. Then because in the third place (it says), "God formed a man [who came to life] from the earth and breathed into his nostrils the breath of life,"[g] Moses has shown why the body was created *where the soul was inhaled, and how He also acted in the creation of the woman. After he wrote: "Male and female He created them,"[h] he taught how Eve was made *and said, "The Lord God caused Adam to go into a trance and he slept; and He took one of his ribs and filled in the flesh in its [place], and the Lord God built the woman out of the rib which He had taken from Adam."[i] By these (words), he has made known what Eve was made from and in what *way. It is not that he has written about her creation (occurring)

---

a. Genesis 1:27
b. Genesis 2:7
c. Genesis 1:3
d. Genesis 1:6
e. Genesis 1:26
f. Genesis 1:27
g. Genesis 2:7
h. Genesis 1:27
i. Genesis 2:21, 22

twice. Now if, because the word was repeated, they err and think that God did not create Adam where (it is written), "God said, Let us make man," but that He planned and devised in that passage *and subsequently He made him, then they must also consider the creation of those other things in the same way. Regarding the creation of beasts *and *Folio 37r* cattle (it is written), "God said, Let the earth bring forth the living creature according to its kind: cattle and beasts and [reptiles] of the earth (each) according to its kind";[a] and after that (it says), "[God made] the [beasts] *of the earth according to their kind, and [the cattle according to] their [kind], and every reptile according to its kinds."[b] When it is known that they were created by the first command, the word was repeated to [teach] what God had commanded. Once again, with regard to *the lights, it is written, "[God] said, Let there be lights in the firmament of the heavens to give light to the earth";[c] then soon after he repeated the word and said, "It was so. And God made two great lights."[d] This is *typical of the word we find regarding all the deeds. Although they were made by the first command, he duplicates the statement about them and declares that what God said came into being. When we compare *the creation of man with these things, we learn that because "God said, Let us make man according to our image and according to our likeness,"[e] he was really created. If words are written which are like one another, they make known *in the first words what they intend.

The Son of the (divine) nature was therefore destined to be the exact image of the Father in the likeness which He had. *And he continued to be *Folio 37v* transmitted through all of them, continuing right to the Virgin. Because of Him, they have been preserved [. . .] of the forethought of His Father, [. . . as in truth] Isaiah *has urged, "[As] a bunch of grapes [is found] in a cluster, and someone says, ['Do not] destroy it, because

---

a. Genesis 1:24
b. Genesis 1:25
c. Genesis 1:15
d. Genesis 1:16
e. Genesis 1:26

[there is blessing] in it,' so [shall I do] because of my servants, and because of this I shall not [destroy] them [all]. And I shall bring forth a descendant from *Jacob [and from Ju]dah, and he shall inherit my holy hill."[a] The destruction was not [therefore] retained or [perpetuated], according to the word of the prophet, because of the intermingled bunch which depends on Him. Since the cluster left the vine, *and the bunch in the cluster was dependant, we understand the vine to be the patriarchs of the race, the cluster to be their people, and the bunch to be Christ transmitted in their genealogy, who was implanted in Adam through his creation and sprang *from the Virgin in the fulness of times. All the intervening generations transmitted Him. Just as He was transmitted from Adam to the Virgin, He also went from her to that baptism by which when He was baptized, *He prepared a new womb for the birth of the sons of God. As One who has already perfected the mystery by the deed and has gained *from that womb _Folio 38r_ new members for His (body), He has been exalted to His Father through the transmission of the names (in the genealogy), as Luke has written. When He said to Him, "Behold I and the sons whom you have given to me,"[b] these then are the men *who became members since the body is substituted for the image. It is not the opposite, 'They become mine.' Therefore [. . .] they are retained and [inscribed] without beginning or change, for *Paul teaches that the [likeness] of God became known but without change: "Those (are the ones) whom He foreknew and predestined to become sons of the likeness of the image of His Son,"[c] -- where "image" (means) the name of the Person of the Son, for He is truly the exact image of God *the Father, and "sons of His likeness" (means) those who have become members of His (body) by baptism. Because they were worthy of the adoption [of sons], for as this title was given to them so His (is called) the Head and the First-born from the dead";[d] *and again, "That He might be the

---

a. Isaiah 65:8, 9
b. Hebrews 2:13
c. Romans 8:29
d. Colossians 1:18

First-born of many brothers."[a] Therefore, it is clear from these things which were said that not only did the first man come into being in the likeness of God, but he also was both the recipient and transmitter of (that) likeness.
*It is, however, the Person of the Son who is the exact 25
and natural image of God the Father, for Lamech prophesied
concerning Him that after *seventy-seven *Folio 38v*
generations He would reveal Himself and blot out by means
of His [death] Cain's sin of murder for which no repentance
had been found to atone. Because many (names) are written
in *this genealogy, the fulfilment is to be found in [this 5
place]. Along with [. . .] who are derived from the book
of Luke, the Evangelist, [we] are brought near (to Him);
for [we] also are introduced [to salvation (?)] when He
brings us, as *we maintain, the blessing of God. 10

In this book is a commentary of five chapters taken from Luke the Evangelist.

The end of the fourth book of the commentary *of 15
the Evangelists, Matthew and Luke, which was made by Philoxenus, lover of God, bishop of Mabbug. It was written in the city of Mabbug in the year eight hundred and twenty-two of Alexander of Macedon.

*Anyone who loves to read should also be careful 21
to ponder and comprehend in depth, lest he find himself labouring in vain.

Glory to Christ Jesus, the God who became man. Amen.

---

a. Romans 8:29

B. *DESCRIPTIVE AND ANALYTICAL NOTES ON THE FOURTEEN FRAGMENTS OF THE MANUSCRIPT*

Fragment 1

The two folios of this fragment are badly stained, but are almost completely legible with the aid of ultra-violet light. Fol. 1 is torn across the page from the right margin of 1r 10 to the left margin of 1r 12. The writing is in Estrangela, the style being very similar to but not identical with the rest of the manuscript.[260] A unique feature of this fragment is that an expanded paraphrase of a biblical quotation is marked in the margin as a quotation (lr 12-18). This does not occur elsewhere in this manuscript. The fragment comes from the same scriptorium as the others and is contemporary with them. There is no reason to doubt that it is part of a Philoxenian work, but it is not part of the work to which it is here attached.

lr 1-2 -- The quotation from Matthew 18:22 led Wright to state that this fragment "seems to belong to the Commentary on the Gospel of St. Matthew (18:21, 22)."[261] This is a more reasonable assumption than that made by de Halleux who attempts to fit it into a commentary on the genealogy in Luke 3:23-28.[262] Much of this fragment is concerned with the meaning of the cryptic statement that "Cain will be avenged seven times" (Genesis 4:24) in relation to his subsequent career, and Cain is not even mentioned in Luke 3:23-38. So de Halleux' suggestion must be discounted. ܒܠܚܘܕ -- "only" -- used by Aphrahat when quoting this text, but the word order is different.[263] No Greek text or Syriac version has this word or its equivalent in this context. ܫܒ̈ܥܝܢ ܠܠ ܫܒܥ -- "seventy times seven" -- the use of ܠܠ in this context is not found in the Syriac versions.[264] As far as can be ascertained, this phrase from Matthew 18:22 occurs in only one other Philoxenian work, *The Letter Sent to a Friend.*[265] *Liber Graduum* almost invariably uses the same phrase.[266] Ephrem reverses the word-order, using ܠܠ.[267] Leloir has noted that ܠܠ in this context is an older Syriac usage.[268] It appears to have been replaced later by ܐ̈ܦܝܢ, as in the Peshitta. The ܠܠ preceding the numbers in Aphrahat and in the Curetonian and Sinaitic versions is equivalent to ܥܕܡܐ ܠ in the Peshitta (= ἕως of Greek).

lr 4 -- ܫܡܥܘܢ -- "Simon" -- Peshitta read ܟܐܦܐ (= Πέτρος of Greek text), but Curetonian version has ܫܡܥܘܢ ܟܐܦܐ (Matthew 18:21). In the *Discourses*, also, Philoxenus prefers "Simon" to "Peter."[269]

lr 6 -- that Matthew 18:22 is related to Genesis 4:24 was seen at least as early as Tertullian.[270]

lr 7 -- ܫܒ̈ܥܝܢ ܠܠ ܫܒܥ -- "seventy times seven" as in lr 2. MT and Peshitta of Genesis 4:24 read "seventy-seven." The Greek of Genesis 4:24 (LXX) and Matthew 18:22 has the same phrase, ἑβδομηκοντάκις ἑπτά, which can mean either "seventy-seven times" or seventy times seven." The Syro-Hexapla follows Philoxenus' understanding of the text although the wording is different: ܫܒܥܝܢ ܙܒ̈ܢܬܐ ܫܒܥ.

1r 8 -- implies that in Genesis 4:14 Cain asked God the question: "Shall it be that whoever finds me will kill me?" This is a possible translation of MT and Syro-Hexapla and fits well with the context, but it is not the traditional understanding of the text as reflected in LXX and Peshitta where Cain simply makes a statement concerning his future.

1r 11-18 -- this passage is marked as a quotation /</ although it is the author's paraphrastic exegesis of the divine dictum in Genesis 4:15. Philoxenus uses this style of exegesis elsewhere in his writings, and its appearance in this fragment is additional evidence that he is the author of it.[271]

1r 18 -- appears to be a quotation because of the emphasis placed on it in the sentence and in what follows, although the syntax itself is ambiguous. It is reminiscent of the statement in the Greek *Ben Sirach* 40:8 f., "(There are) . . . upon the ungodly sevenfold (calamities)."[272]

1r 20-28 -- as far as can be determined, these exegetical alternatives taken together are original with Philoxenus. None is found in early rabbinic or Christian literature.[273]

1v 14 - 2r 2 -- the emphasis here on the possibility of some animal or natural force killing Cain is due to the understanding that Cain was the only man in existence apart from his father, Adam. This is also assumed by the rabbis and Josephus.[274]

2r 3-28 -- the geographical assumptions of this passage are based on Genesis 2:8, "The Lord God planted a garden *in* Eden." (גן־בעדן). The garden, or "Paradise," is contained within the larger territory of Eden. LXX stresses this by leaving "Eden" as a proper name in Genesis 2:8, and translating it where the phrase is גן־עדן, thus avoiding the ambiguity of "Garden of Eden."[275] Ephrem, Aphrahat and the Curetonian Gospels are unaware of these geographical subtleties in the context of Luke 23:43 ("Today you will be with me in Paradise") where they read "Garden of Eden" for "Paradise," thus equating the two.[276]

2v 3 -- ܚܘܫܒܐ ܥܠܡܝܐ -- "ordinary thoughts" -- this expression seems to occur also in 14v 5-6 (although it is partly illegible) where it is used in the context of Christ's human growth of which "ordinary thoughts" (or "the ideas that are common to this world") are a part.

2v 11 f. -- that Adam and the Sethites were not involved in the urbanization programme of Cain is inferred by the author. It is not explicitly stated in the Bible.

2v 16 f. -- Isaiah 22:9-11 condemns Judah (and therefore Hezekiah) for a rebuilding programme which the prophet relates to a lack of faith in God. 2 Chronicles 32:30 states that "Hezekiah prospered in all his works."

2v 19 -- ܡܨܪܬܐ -- Peshitta has ܡܨܪܬܐ which is surely a mistake.[277] The word is not found in the Syriac lexicons, but it is obviously related to the Hebrew מצרה which is used in this context in 2 Samuel 5:7, 9. The Aramaic מצרא also occurs.

2v 26 -- ܛܘܦܣܐ -- this Greek word is used throughout the manuscript. Its use will be considered in chapter 5.

This first fragment is obviously exegetical in character. Because of its fragmentary and somewhat rambling nature (going from Matthew 18:22 to Genesis 4:24 to an excursus on Genesis 4:15 to Hezekiah, David and Solomon), it is impossible to say whether Matthew 18:22 or Genesis 4:15 is the focus of the exegesis, although the former is a reasonable guess since Philoxenus seems to use the Old Testament to illumine his understanding of the New. Throughout the fragment, the author's comments on the Bible are of a literal nature in the tradition of the School of Antioch. There is no hint of allegorizing, or even of "une exégèse typologique des premières pages de la *Génèse*" as de Halleux suggests.[278] The only reference to typology is in 2v 26 where the Davidic kingdom is said to be a "type."

It is clear that, while Fragment 1 is Philoxenian, it does not belong with the bulk of the fragments which (as we shall show below) are from a "commentary" on five topics taken from Luke.[279] Whether it is from a "commentary" on Matthew must remain a moot question until more evidence comes to light. In favour of such a context is the fact that it contains no polemic and no suggestion of ascetic instruction (unless one considers his comments on urbanization to be a reflection of his ascetic bent). On the other hand, we have noted in chapter 1 that so-called "commentary" fragments which we have already examined (apart from the manuscript before us) fit well into other literary genres which we know Philoxenus did produce.

Fragment 2

The eight folios of this second fragment are well preserved and completely legible. The style of handwriting is the same as most of the manuscript including the last fragment with its colophon containing the author's name (Philoxenus) and the date of writing (A.D. 511).[280] Three erasures and corrections occur, 5v 10, 19 and 9v 24, all made by the original scribe. Quotations are clearly marked in the margin throughout. This fragment has no quire number, perhaps indicating that it belonged to a quire of ten folios as we see in Fragment 10 and in the contemporary manuscript, British Museum Add. 14,534 (*Book on Selected Passages of the Gospels*).[281] This would mean that the first and last folios of this fragment's quire are lost (i.e., the outside sheet of vellum). No unusual marks occur.

3r 1-3 -- the translation supplies the probable beginning of this quotation from Acts 2:31, viz. ... ܘܩܕܡ ܚܙܐ ܘܡܠܠ ܥܠ. The words quoted are exactly those of the Harklean version. The Peshitta omits ܢܦܫܐ along with nearly all the Greek MSS.[282] The use of ܢܦܫܐ here is necessary for Philoxenus' argument that Christ had a soul like any other human being.

3r 12 - 3v 11 -- a similar passage is found in the *Three Discourses on the Trinity and the Incarnation* where the author quotes from Matthew 26:38, John 12:27 and Luke 22:44, making reference to his source as ܐܘܢܓܠܝܣܛܐ.[283] Here, he quotes more fully from these passages, citing his source as ܟܬܒܐ ܐܘܢܓܠܝܣܛܐ.

3v 25 -- ܡܠ̈ܚܐ -- the Synoptics make no mention of "sailors" in the pericope referred to.

4r 17 -- "Simon the Sorcerer" -- Philoxenus with the Peshitta uses the form ܣܝܡܘܢ for this man's name, which is ܫܡܥܘܢ graecized, perhaps to distinguish the protoheretic from the apostle.[284] Indeed, in the *Letter to Abraham and Orestes*,

Simon Magus (ܫܡܥܘܢ ܚܪܫܐ) is contrasted with the apostle, Peter (ܦܛܪܘܣ).[285]

4r 21 f. -- ܐܘܛܝܟܝܢܣܛ̈ܐ -- "Eutychianists" -- this form is not listed in R. Payne Smith's *Thesaurus Syriacum.* It occurs also in the *Three Discourses.*[286] One Philoxenian "confession of faith" is prefaced by a catalogue of heretics and their heresies which begins: "Mani, Marcion and Eutyches deny the incarnation of God the Word etc."[287]

4r 23-26 -- Philoxenus in this fragment is combatting the teaching of those heretics or "near-heretics" who, while remaining within the monophysite fold, teach dogma that is heretical or "flirt with the heretical" (9r 10). The remaining contents of this fragment make this clear.

4r 27 -- "O heretic" -- The text clearly reads the singular, plural nouns being consistently marked by seyame; but the second person plural occurs throughout the rest of this fragment. It may have been addressed to some monks whose loyalty to Philoxenus and the monophysite cause was unquestionable. In the first two discourses of the "Ten Memre," the first person singular is consistently used, and the person addressed is called sarcastically "your wisdom," "O sage" and "O philosopher" with his work being referred to as "your heretical writings."[288] In his letter "To the Monks of Beth-Gogal," Philoxenus addresses them in warm and friendly tones, but when he deals with the heresy of his opponents in the body of the letter he apostrophizes his opponents as though they were a single adversary: "O godless one," "O false disciple," and "O disciple in name (only)."[289] In the fragment before us, the author employs the same literary device. In the rest of the fragment, he is addressing more than one person.

4v 1 -- ܕܡܘܬܐ ܕܝܘܢܐ -- "the likeness of a dove" -- Philoxenus picks up the meaning of ܕܡܘܬܐ in 4r 19 and discusses its meaning in the rest of the fragment. The translation "likeness" has been used consistently in order to retain the flavour of the author's discussion; although the word "form" could at times be substituted for it, reflecting the English translation of εἶδος in Luke 3:22 and μορφή and ὁμοίωσις in Philippians 2:6, 7 (the Syriac uses ܕܡܘܬܐ for all three words). "Likeness" is the familiar word used in the context of

Genesis 1:26, "in our image and after our likeness (דמות– ὁμοίωσις – ܕܡܘܬܐ)," and that context is prominent in Fragment 14.[290] All Syriac versions of Luke 3:22 read: ܒܕܡܘܬ ܓܘܫܡܐ ܕܝܘܢܐ -- "in the likeness of the body of a dove," but here and most often in the fragment the author omits ܓܘܫܡܐ. Only once (7r 9) is the full Lucan expression used. It is noteworthy that the Sinaitic version of Matthew 3:16 has ܒܕܡܘܬܐ ܕܝܘܢܐ for ܐܝܟ ܝܘܢܐ of the other Syriac versions, and it may well be that that version of Matthew 3:16 came more readily to the author's mind than Luke 3:22 with which he was also familiar. At any rate, what we have here is his answer to those who use this phrase to cast doubt on the real corporality of Christ. The descent of the Holy Spirit in the form of a dove was the focus of much theological controversy in the Church prior to the time of Philoxenus, but his particular development of the theme in this fragment seems to be original with him, although antecedents may be found for individual aspects of his argument.[291]

4v 5-6 -- "As they say, 'No one saw except only John'." This is a reasonable inference drawn especially from John 1:29-34, and apparently current also in the time of Chrysostom.[292]

4v 11 -- ܬܪܒܝܬܐ ܢܓܝܪܬܐ -- literally "lengthy or prolonged growth" i.e., the long period of development or gradual growth of a child.

5v 3 -- ܪܘܚܐ -- Philoxenus treats this word as a masculine noun whenever he believes it refers to the Holy Spirit, as apparently he does here. He or his scribe, however, is not consistent in this quotation for he clearly uses the 3 f. s. suffix on ܫܪܝܗ̇ (5v 5).

6r 2 -- ܡܕܒܪܢܘܬܐ -- translated here and throughout the manuscript as "the earthly ministry (of Christ)." In the context of theology, it is equivalent to the divine οἰκονομία (Philippians 1:10) fore-ordained and fulfilled in the life and work of Christ. According to de Halleux, Philoxenus has provided us with a definition of this word in his *Ten Discourses*: "L'économie, c'est la naissance, la passion et la mort."[293] "Earthly ministry" covers this quite well.

6r 27 --ܝܠܕܬ ܐܠܗܐ= Θεότοκος -- Nestorius had refused to use this term as a title for the mother of Jesus.

6v 2 -- ܐܢܬܘܢ -- here the second person plural is used, while in 4r 26 a heretic was addressed in the singular. A plurality of persons is addressed throughout the rest of this second fragment.

7r 3-4 -- "as angels have sometimes appeared" -- in his sermon on the Annunciation, Philoxenus spoke of how an angel can put off and put on likenesses when he appears.[294]

7v 4 -- ܐܪ̈ܙܐ -- "mystery" is used throughout to translate this word which in the Peshitta always translates μυστήριον. The phrase in 7v 13 ܓܠܝܢܐ ܕܐܪ̈ܙܐ is Pauline (Romans 16:25). Because it is used here in conjunction with ܛܘܦܣܐ, one is tempted to translate it by "symbol," but that term no longer contains the fulness of religious significance it once had. A variant spelling -- ܪ̈ܐܙܐ -- is found in 7v 24, 31v 1 and 33v 17, while ܐܪ̈ܙܐ occurs sixteen times in the whole manuscript.

8v 6 -- ܟܬܒ -- should be ܟܬܒܘ, but compare 8v 11, 13.

8v 11-12 -- ܗܘܬ ܠܟܘܢ ܘܐ̄ -- this is marked as a quotation, but as it is here phrased it is not biblical. It is closest in spirit to Galatians 3:4.

9r 10 -- "those who flirt with the heretical" -- the Syriac literally means "those who are familiar with the word of heresy." These are the people to whom this fragment seems to be addressed.[295]

9v 10-11 -- ". . . how the immortal Son died" -- this kind of paradoxical statement is found elsewhere in the writings of Philoxenus.[296]

The contents of this second fragment clearly indicate that it is from a letter or a sermon addressed to a group within the monophysite camp whose monophysitism was not as sharply defined as Philoxenus would have liked. In his "Seven Special Chapters, etc.," he writes "against those who say that what is bad in the teaching of the heretics should be cursed, but not the heretics themselves along with all their teaching."[297] Obviously Philoxenus believed that heresy had to be opposed wherever it appeared and by whomever it was espoused, even in its mildest form. The clear and precisely correct definition of monophysite christology had to be constantly maintained and defended. This fragment is of that order, polemical and doctrinaire.

Fragment 3

This single-folio fragment and the two following it belong together as far as their scribal style and quality of vellum are concerned. As has already been shown, they were not originally part of the manuscript before us or of any other Philoxenian manuscript we know of.[298] Although all three deal with aspects of the Incarnation, it is impossible to establish any continuity of thought which demonstrates unequivocally that these three fragments should be placed in their present order.

11r 2 -- the reference is to Theodore of Mopsuestia (died A.D. 428), the great biblical exegete of the School of Antioch. He was the teacher of Nestorius and by Philoxenus' time was considered the father of Nestorianism.[299] Theodore is also mentioned in 20r 2 and 23r 24. No commentary on Luke by Theodore is extant by which to assess the value of Philoxenus' statement in this fragment, but there is a genuine tradition here which our author is constrained to criticize. The glimpse provided of Theodore's exegesis of Luke 1:35 in 11r 13-15 is true to the kind of literal interpretation to which he strictly adhered.

11v 4 --ܟܦܝܠܐ-- translated here by "composite," it literally means "double." In this context, it is contrasted with ("simple"). It refers to the "double" or composite nature of Christ implicit in words like "Christ, Son, Only-Begotten and Lord." On the other hand Nestorius (so we are here told) said that "God, and the Word" are "simple"; that is, they can refer only to a single, unambiguous divine nature.[300] Philoxenus and the monophysites claimed that these words too must be composite for the Word was both divine and human. Whether we have here a direct quotation from Nestorius is not known.

This fragment is dogmatic and polemical in character.

Fragment 4

That this fragment belongs in some way with Fragments 3 and 5 has already been stated. Though legible for the most part, its verso is stained making a few words illegible even under ultra-violet light. A notable erasure and correction occurs in 12v 27 where the word ܛܘܦܣܐ is written over the erasure in the same style of handwriting as that of the rest of the fragment except that it is slightly larger and the waw is formed [Syriac letter] rather than [Syriac letter] . I judge it to be written by the same scribe who wrote the rest.[301] It is impossible to say what was erased.

12r 1-3 -- these three lines, though beginning in a fragmentary way, strike the keynote ot this isolated folio: what it means for the pure in heart to see God (Matthew 5:8), when the Fourth Gospel assures us that no one has ever seen Him (John 1:18). The paradox is resolved when it is understood that the eyes of faith see beyond the flesh to the Word (12r 4-5) just as the sacramental bread is seen to be "the body of God" by "the vision (or insight) of a new man" (12v 20-22).

12v 2 -- ܗܘܢܐ] -- "the mind of angels" -- only the final aleph is legible with hints of the other three letters. The phrase fits the context though it is not found elsewhere in the manuscript.

12v 3 -- ܡܡܠܠܐ -- "orators" -- only the first and last letters are visible. Philoxenus makes the same kind of reference to orators in 16r 7 and 16v 24.

12v 20-22 -- "bread . . . is seen to be the body of God" -- the sacramental reference is unique in this manuscript. Indeed, Philoxenus rarely alludes to the Eucharist.[302]

12v 27 -- ܛܘܦܣܐ -- is the Syriac equivalent of τύπος used in the Greek in this context (John 20:25). The Peshitta and other pre-Philoxenian Syriac traditions all read τόπος (=ܕܘܟܬܐ) and possibly the scribe (or was it Philoxenus himself?) first wrote ܕܘܟܬܐ before changing it to ܛܘܦܣܐ The Greek text reflected here is exactly that of Codex Alexandrinus which reads, Ἐὰν μὴ ἴδω ἐν ταῖς χερσὶν αὐτοῦ τὸν τύπον τῶν ἥλων, καὶ βάλω τὸν δακτυλόν μου εἰς τὸν τόπον τῶν ἥλων.

As it stands, there is no real indication that this fragment is other than exegetical. What its larger context was, is impossible to say. As we have noted regarding other fragments, that context could be a polemical discourse or letter, or a discourse on the nature of the ascetic life. In that case, it is more likely that this fragment would come from a theological discussion in which Philoxenus could hardly avoid his polemic against non-monophysites. On the other hand, we cannot ignore its claim to be an exegetical fragment, although what precisely the Biblical passage being exegeted would be is not clear. It could be John 1:18, Matthew 5:8, John 9:37, or John 20:25, all of which are quoted or alluded to; or it could be another passage altogether such as 1 Corinthians 2:14 to which the author alludes in 16r 11.[304] All in all, it is difficult to believe that this came from an exegetical work in any formal or technical sense. It is possible, however, that it is part of an expository homily on any of the above-mentioned passages.

Fragment 5

This is the third of the three "orphan fragments." Unlike the other two, this one contains no direct quotation from the Bible. It is concerned nevertheless with a specific Biblical passage, John 20:19, 26.

13r 13 -- ܪܘܚܐ ܐܠܗܐ -- one would expect ܕ before ܐܠܗܐ or perhaps ܪܘܚ ܐܠܗܐ. In his "Letter to the Monks of Senun," Philoxenus always uses ܪܘܚܐ ܕܐܠܗܐ.[305] It is unusual as an appositional construction which would reverse the word-order.[306] What we have here is probably a scribal omission.

13v 5 ff. -- two other Philoxenian fragments exist which attack the teachings of Diodore of Tarsus (died before 394) who was condemned by a synod held in Constantinople in 499 as the father of Nestorianism.[307] As a teacher in the School of Antioch, he had Chrysostom and Theodore of Mopsuestia as students. The quotations purporting to be from Diodore in 13v 16-18 and 22-28 are not marked as such in the margin. Whether Diodore ever wrote these words is not attested by any of his extant work, but they reflect his teaching and are true to his exegetical method.

13v 20-21 -- "Jews and pagans" -- in his "Letter to the Monks of Senun," Philoxenus again associates the idea of Christ's being an ordinary man with "the Jews and pagans."[308]

While this fragment has a biblical basis for its discussion (i.e., John 20:19, 26), it is Philoxenus the polemicist who is writing, and the focus of his attack is Diodore of Tarsus. In Fragments 3 and 4 he attacks Theodore of Mopsuestia and Nestorius respectively. We have already mentioned the fact that our author carried on a polemic against all three, and (until other evidence is produced to the contrary) it is reasonable to assign these three fragments to that lost work or works.[309] The fact that these fragments are found together and written in the same handwriting indicates that they belong to a single work rather than three separate works as the titles to other fragments assume.[310] Probably such a work was basically against the Nestorians in which it was natural for Philoxenus to denounce also the teachings of Theodore and Diodore.

Fragment 6

Although this single-folio fragment is in poor condition, it is almost entirely legible. A tear in the upper folio (repaired as well as possible by the British Museum) makes the last word of 14v 5 illegible. A hole running through lines 10 to 15 has destroyed parts of words in each line. Other smaller holes and stains have obliterated letters here and there, but in every instance reconstruction of the text has not been difficult. A crude erasure occurs in the last line of 14r for no apparent reason, the words deliberately blotted out being necessary for the meaning of the text. They were clearly legible under ultra-violet light and have been restored in this edition. The script is in the same hand as that of most of this manuscript.

14r 2-3 -- the quotation from Wisdom 3:1 is not marked in the margin as one would expect.

14r 11-24 -- this discussion concerning Christ's preaching to the dead is based on 1 Peter 3:19 and 4:6. In his "Letter to the Monks of Senun," Philoxenus includes "the preaching to those in prison and darkness" as part of the total ministry of Christ.[311]

14r 19 f. -- "while we have [testified] that the divine life does not abandon them," -- in his "Memra on the Question Someone Asked, etc.," Philoxenus maintains that once the Holy Spirit is given to a believer by baptism He never leaves his body even in death, except when he denies God or communicates with demons.[312] Thus, the Holy Spirit remained with the corpse of Christ in the tomb enabling Him to preach "to the souls of sinners."

14r 25 ff. -- the idea of the Holy Spirit's being miraculously and inextricably joined to the body of Jesus is developed in the remainder of this fragment.
14r 27 -- with the aid of ultra-violet light the words ܠܗܘܐ ܟܕ ܪܒܐ ܗܘܐ are discernible under what appears to be a crude erasure. The obliterating mark is too definite in its contour to be a mere stain. Why anyone would wish to remove these words is not at all evident.
14v 5-6 -- ܠܡܠܬܐ ܡܫܐܠܬܐ -- this reconstruction suits the context. The phrase is also found in 2v 3.[313]
14v 10-12 -- according to Philoxenus' theology, the Holy Spirit departed from Adam because he had denied God's authority and (through his wife) had communicated with the serpent (i.e., a demon).[314]

The tone and contents of this fragment suggest a discourse or memra similar to that already cited, "Memra on the Question Someone Asked: Does the Holy Spirit Leave a Man when He Sins and Return to Him when He Repents?" As Tanghe has suggested, the latter may be a letter with the "introduction epistolaire" omitted.[315] The reference to Christ's growth in stature and in the Spirit indicate that the author had Luke 2:40 in mind, and that text may have been the basis for an expository homily of which, then, we have here a fragment. Certainly, there is no hint of polemical intent in it.

Fragment 7

Fragment 7 is completely legible in spite of its generally stained appearance and a vertical tear in the lower right corner of the text. The handwriting is that of most of the manuscript. No erasures are discernible. The quotation marks in the margin of 15r 4, 5, 7, 8, 9, 10 were clear under ultra-violet light.
15r 2-3 -- "Luke adds . . . ." -- the context suggests that in the lost text which preceded this fragment, Philoxenus discussed the statement that Jesus "went down to Nazareth and was subject to them." Now he turns his attention to the meaning of the second part of that verse (Luke 2:51) relating it to the larger context of Luke, chapter 2.
15r 8 -- "Joseph" -- Philoxenus follows the Peshitta and the Greek textual tradition reflected in Codex Alexandrinus, the

old Latin, Gothic and Diatessaron. The older tradition of Codex Sinaiticus simply reads ὁ πατηρ αὐτοῦ and this is followed by the Old Syriac of the Sinai Palimpsest. Our author discusses Jesus' relation to Joseph in Fragment 12 (folio 31).

15v 7 -- for the translation "earthly ministry (of Christ)," see the note on 6r 2.

15v 19 -- ܛܠܝܐ -- "the boy" -- this term has the specific meaning of child between the ages of seven and twelve as Philoxenus explicitly states in 15v 23-24. He intends to contrast the use of ܛܠܝܐ in Luke 2:40 with that of ܛܠܐ in Luke 2:52 the latter being applied to Jesus after he was twelve years of age (according to our author's exegesis). He returns to this childhood period in Jesus' life in folio 18.

15v 20 -- "in the Spirit" -- this phrase is found in Codex Alexandrinus and the Peshitta, Old Latin and Diatessaron, while Codex Sinaiticus and the Old Syriac version omit it.

The contents of this fragment are clearly exegetical. The author considers the meaning of Luke 2:51b, then moves on into Luke 2:52a. Presumably, in the page or pages immediately preceding this folio, he had commented on at least Luke 2:51a, "(Jesus) went down with them and came to Nazareth, and was obedient to them," and beyond this folio he discussed the rest of Luke 2:52. But the fact that we have here a running commentary on Luke 2:51-52 does not in itself make this fragment part of a Gospel commentary in any technical sense. We have already demonstrated that such fragments may have belonged to some other literary genre. Fragment 7 does not provide any evidence to the contrary.

Fragment 8

Before it was repaired by the British Museum, this single-leaf fragment was torn in two with the tear running roughly from the middle of the text at the top to about an inch from the right margin at the bottom. Both sides are stained. However, the text is entirely legible except for one letter on 16v 17 which has been obliterated because of a smudge. The resh of ܐܡܪ at the end of 16r 10 lacks a dot. The second singular masculine pronoun is used in 16r 8, 12, 16, and 18, but there is no indication of the identity of the person so addressed.

16r 1-3 -- Philoxenus has reversed the two clauses in this quotation from 1 Corinthians 1:25 which (all textual witnesses agree) reads: "The foolishness of God is wiser than men and the weakness of God is stronger than men." Only in this fragment (among his available writings) does he quote the verse in full (except for shortening "the foolishness of God" to "His foolishness") so it is impossible to say whether such an inversion reflects a versional tradition on which he was drawing. He does quote the first clause of the text in 24r 12-13 of the manuscript before us, in his *Three Discourses on the Trinity* and in his discourse "On Simplicity."[316] In each instance, he writes, "The foolishness of God is wiser than men," which suggests that he was quoting from memory or was unconcerned about rendering the text verbatim when he wrote this fragment.

16r 9 -- the reference to a single reader ("you") is suggestive of a letter except for the fact that Philoxenus' style in many of his discourses employs a similar form of address. One notable example is in the discourse "On Simplicity" (cited above), where, after quoting 1 Corinthians 1:25a, he exhorts his reader to follow Christ by living a life of simplicity.[317] It must be added, however, that in this fragment our author appears to be answering an enquirer who had difficulty in reconciling divine power with the "weakness" of Christ's humanity. He is not engaged in a polemic, but is simply clarifying his understanding of the Incarnation.

16r 17 -- "Christ is the Power and Wisdom of God" -- it is necessary to capitalize "Power" and "Wisdom" because of what follows. Philoxenus sees these words as synonyms for Christ. The same understanding is found in his "Letter to the Monks of Beth-Gogal":

> He who says that He of whom it is inscribed that He was in the beginning, and He was with God and He was God, is not the Power of the Most High, concerning whom the angel said to the Virgin, "You shall conceive in the womb, give birth to a son and call His name Jesus," is excommunicated by the word of Jesus.[318]

This fragment has been inserted in the manuscript immediately after Fragment 7 presumably because the latter ended with the words, "He grew in stature," while this one is concerned with the "weakness of God" as it is seen in "the fact that He grew in stature" (16r 8-9). At first glance, the connection appears superficial. The style and content of Fragment 7 are exegetical, while in Fragment 8 they are didactic and discursive. Whether Fragments 7 and 8 belong together remains to be seen, and will be considered in the light of all evidence of the manuscript as a whole. To reach any conclusion at this juncture would be premature.[319]

Fragment 9

These two, somewhat damaged folios are legible for the most part. Folio 17 has two holes which have eliminated several letters of the text in recto 1, 2, 11, 12, 13, and verso 1, 2, 3, 10, 11, 12, 13, 14, and a tear running from the right of 17r 5 to left of 17r 8 has made the third letter of 17r 5 illegible. A smudge, or more probably an erasure, has obliterated the first word of 17r 9. A crude erasure or deliberate blot (for no apparent reason) occurs at the top of 17v, but the reading is clear under ultra-violet light. Other stains and smudges abound on both sides of the folio, but the reading is always clear. While also stained, folio 18 is on the whole much cleaner than 17. It has a tear running from the left margin of 18r 5 to the right margin of 18r 10 almost obliterating the first letter of 18r 10. The lower right corner of the text is missing, but only the initial letters of 18r 25 and of 18r 26 and the final letter of 18v 26 are lost. A smudge covers the first word of 18v 3, but the reading is clear. The large beth at the foot of 17v and the equally large gamal at the foot of 18r seem to indicate some form of numbering -- perhaps of folios or quires. These numbers are rather crude in form and have been added by a later hand. They have no relationship to the neat quire numbers found on folios 19, 29 and 33.

17r 1-2 -- the opening fragmentary phrase refers to Luke 2:42 as the following sentences show.

17r 9 -- the initial word is erased. It was probably ܐܦ erroneously repeated.

17r 12 ff. -- the style of this passage is very like that of the ascetic discourses. Philoxenus makes use of a biblical description of Jesus to commend the theory and practice of the ascetic life for which (according to our author) Jesus is the supreme example.[320]

17v 1 -- ܕܥܠ[ܡܐ] -- it is assumed that Philoxenus had 1 Corinthians 1:20 in mind: "Has not God made foolish the wisdom of this world?" Yet Christ who has the teaching of God is 'many times more humble than they'.

17v 10 -- ܒܡܕܒܪ̈[ܝܐ -- while the final two letters are obliterated, the seyame are visible, and the word should be translated "wildernesses" or "deserts." But this is very likely a scribal error.[321] The singular is used in 16v 15 with reference to the wilderness experience of Israel. In 5r 2, ܚܘܪܒܐ is the place of Jesus' temptation. The latter word occurs more often in the Peshitta, while ܡܕܒܪܐ is preferred in the Old Syriac to translate

18r 2 -- ܒܡܫܘܚܬܐ ܕܛܠܝܘܬܐ -- literally, "in the stature of boyhood"; that is, between the ages of seven and twelve.

18r 8 -- "In the time of his infancy" -- presumably the period prior to seven years of age.

18v 11-12 -- in quoting from Isaiah 7:15b, Philoxenus follows the Greek of Codex Alexandrinus: πρὶν γνῶναι αὐτὸν προελέσθαι πονηρὰ ἐκλέξεται τὸ ἀγαθόν. His exegesis requires it. The Peshitta and the Greek tradition of Codex Sinaiticus are closer to the Hebrew.[322]

18v 19-20 -- ܒܒܨܝܪܘܬ ܝܘ̈ܡܬܐ ܘܒܙܥܘܪܘܬ ܫܢ̈ܝܐ -- literally, "in fewness of days and smallness of years" which is taken here to mean "infancy and childhood," that is, prior to twelve years of age.

The style and content of this fragment have more in common with the ascetic discourses of Philoxenus than with what we find in exegetical fragments such as 1 and 7 of this manuscript. While the discussion finds its base in Luke 2:42, 46, the main concern of the writer is to highlight an aspect of Christ's life which will encourage his readers to continue in the life of asceticism. De Halleux has pointed out that Philoxenus in his introduction to the *Discourses* outlines the plan of his work in which

> il n'omet pourtant pas d'y mentionner la purification de l'intellect dans le recueillement de la solitude (I, p. 15, 16-17), la contemplation spirituelle (I, p. 8) et la prière pure (I, p. 16), et il annonce

> son intention de décrire l'ascension intérieure jusqu'au 'degré supérieur de la charité', voire jusqu'à celui de la perfection (I, p. 25). Or on ne découvrira pas la moindre trace de ceci dans les douze memre suivants.[323]

Fragment 9 could well belong to a lost discourse on "la purification de l'intellect," for in this fragment we are told something of the author's understanding of Christ's intellectual development which makes "it right henceforth for men to be ambitious by choosing the most excellent things" (17r 17, 18).

Fragment 10

Besides being the longest of the fragments in this manuscript, Fragment 10 has also a very clean text except for folio 29. It consists of a complete quire (folios 19-28) and the first folio of the quire which once followed it.[324] The recto of the first folio (19) is somewhat stained (but entirely legible) indicating that the quire has been separated from the original codex for some time. The rest of the quire (19v-28v) is in excellent condition. Folio 29 is stained and damaged, the worst stain covering about the first ten lines of 29r. However, apart from three letters on 29r 1, the folio is legible under ultra-violet light. The bad condition of 29r suggests that its quire (of which it is the first page) had a separate existence for a considerable time prior to its being incorporated into the present codex.

To all outward appearances, this fragment is closely related to Fragment 14. Not only is the handwriting the same, but together they contain a series of three quire numbers in sequence and in the same handwriting as that of the text: ḥeth (19r), ṭeth (29r) and yudh (33r). Quire ḥeth (=8) is complete with ten folios (19-28), quire ṭeth (=9) has only the first folio (29), and quire yudh (=10) is complete with six folios (33-38). Since quire yudh is the final one because it contains the colophon, we may expect it to have less than the full number of folios. If ten folios to one quire was the rule for the original codex, we can assume that nine folios are missing from quire ṭeth (that is, between folio 29 and 33).[325] The composition of the present codex places three fragmentary folios (30-32) where these presumed nine folios were and it remains to be seen whether they belong there or not.

19r 1 -- ܐܣܬܟܡ -- the Peshitta of Philippians 2:7 has ܐܣܟܡ ܐܢܫܐ. Philoxenus prefers the former in 65 2, 16v 21, and 25v 8. He never uses the latter expression in this codex.

19r 1-18 -- most of this section consists of quotations of unknown origin and marked only by the repetition of ܘܬܘܒ and the general context. It is uncertain whether the fourth quotation runs from ܕܠܝܬ (l. 6) to ܟܝ̈ܢܘܬܐ (l. 9) or to ܟܢ(l. 13). Our translation assumes the second possibility. One can only speculate on the source of these quotations. Athanasius may be their author since this fragment (as we shall show below) is like some passages in his writings and we know that elsewhere Philoxenus expressed great admiration for him.[326] The beginning of the new paragraph on l. 18 in which our author turns his attention to the teaching of his heretical opponents, suggests a contrast with the preceding paragraph containing these orthodox quotations, and who could be more orthodox than Athanasius?

19r 22 --ܬܡܢ -- literally "there" but translated "in that passage" for he is alluding to Luke 2:52.

19r 25 --ܟܝܢܐ -- where this word refers to the nature of God but is not so qualified, we have translated it "(divine) nature." It is clear that when Philoxenus writes of the nature of Christ, he means His nature as the second Person of the Trinity. To use the word "nature" alone in translation would be to blur in some contexts the clear intention of the author. The context here is a case in point. A literal translation of the phrase ܐܝܬܘܗܝ ܝܫܘܥ ܒܪܢܫܐ ܟܝܢܝܐ would be "Jesus is a natural man" which, as is evident from the sentences which follow, is far from the author's mind. The correct translation of ܟܝܢܐ and its derivatives is particularly important in this fragment.[327]

20v 3-4 -- "prefiguring the reality" -- literally, "running after the body."

20v 13 -- ܠܗܠ -- here this adverb expressing remoteness refers to Israel's experience of God in the Old Testament; so it is translated "at that time."

21r 26 -- ܐܬܒܪܝܬܘܢ -- second plural form for first plural of the Greek.

21v 6 -- the context requires the reading ܪܚܡܐ ("dear ones") for ܪ̈ܚܡܐ ("mercy"), unless one considers the latter as scripta defectiva for the former (that is, ܪ̈ܚܝܡܐ).
21v 9-12 -- Philoxenus quotes from Matthew 22:32 (omitting the repetition, "God of" Isaac and "God of" Jacob), but adds the last clause of Luke 20:38, "for all live in Him." This conflation is found also in the Diatessaron.[328]
21v 13-16 -- in his "Letter to Someone Who Asked the Question, etc.," Philoxenus quotes these lines from Psalm 82:6-7 correctly.[329] Here he omits the second clause of v. 7, ܘܐܝܟ ܚܕ ܡܢ ܪ̈ܘܪܒܢܐ ܬܦܠܘܢ, taking from it ܚܕ ܡܢ which he adds to the first making it read ܚܕ ܡܢ ܒܢ̈ܝܢܫܐ instead of simply ܒܢ̈ܝܢܫܐ.[330] This may in fact be a scribal error, but it is translated literally as it stands. These verses from the Psalter are used both here and in the above-mentioned Letter to support the idea that they apply to Jews in the Old Testament but not to Christians who have been made sons of God by adoption.
21v 22 -- ܡܢ ܒܢ̈ܝܢܫܐ is reminiscent of the supposed scribal error discussed in 21v 13-16 above.
22r 9 -- note the use of the second plural. It recurs in 23r 10, 23v 14, 24r 21, 25r 6; while the second singular is used in 27r 8, 13. It is apparently part of the author's style and does not necessarily mean that this fragment is part of a letter or discourse addressed to anyone or any group in particular.
22r 22-23 -- ܠܒܟܘܢ -- Peshitta has ܠܒܢ (= Greek). It would be easy to mistake the ὑμᾶς of the Greek text for ἡμᾶς. However, in 21r 26 he uses the second plural in place of the first plural, and it would thus appear that this is just a stylistic idiosyncrasy.
22r 23-25 -- this saying of Jesus (according to Philoxenus) appears to be a conflation of John 15:16 and 17:24. It is by no means accidental for the exact same wording appears in his *Three Discourses on the Trinity* repeated three times.[331]
23r 3 ff. -- "first it is written that He grew in stature" -- the passage that follows is reminiscent of a similar passage in Athanasius' "Third Discourse against the Arians" where he too stresses the fact that the growth in stature is mentioned

first: "The Evangelist, speaking with cautious exactness, has mentioned stature in the advance (i.e., the growth); but being Word and God He is not measured by stature, which belongs to bodies."[332]

23r 25-27 -- "(Jesus) is of God and man" -- the name of Jesus has been supplied in translation for the author understands by it the man who "grew in stature, etc.," and who "came into being" (23v 12). The "heresy" being attacked here as nonsense is that of the Council of Chalcedon as the reference to its "recentness" would substantiate.[333] In this fragment, Philoxenus is concerned to say that Christ had one divine nature which was clothed with a body when Jesus was born of the Virgin, and He was thus fully human but not "of God and man."

23v 16 -- ܢܩܝܦܘܬܐ -- "joining" -- Vaschalde has shown that the verb ܢܩܦ and its derivatives belong to Nestorian terminology and are used to describe 'the mere moral union of the two natures of Christ.'[334]

23v 22 -- an erasure occurs in the middle of the line with ܕܒܪ̈ܢܫܐ ܒܦܪ̈ܬܝܗܘܢ written over it. The second word is a misspelling of ܒܦܪ̈ܬܗܘܢ. What was underneath the erasure is lost.

24v 22 -- the second half of the line was erased and the present text written over it.

25r 3-4 -- in his "Third Discourse against the Arians," Athanasius discusses this verse (Matthew 24:36) at some length immediately before his discussion of Luke 2:52 mentioned above.

25r 9 -- ܫܬܦܘܬܐ -- a mistake for ܫܘܬܦܘܬܐ which occurs nine times in this codex (e.g., 25v 6).

27r 17 -- an erasure occurs under the word ܫܪܝ.

27r 22 -- ܦܘܠܐ -- when this name refers to the Apostle Paul, it is always spelt ܦܘܠܘܣ in this codex (nine times).

29r 25-26 -- ܘܠܐ ܘܠܐ -- this is simply a case of dittography.

Fragment 10 belongs with the theological discourses of Philoxenus. Its style, which at times borders on a dialogue with "the heretics," is discursive and dogmatic and its contents deal with certain aspects of his christology vis-à-vis that of his opponents. Luke 2:52 is the biblical basis for his discussion, but that discussion is not exegetical in the technical sense of that term. The clue to its genre is to be found in the anti-Arian Discourses of Athanasius with one of which this fragment has close affinities (as we have already noted).[335] In these discourses, Athanasius discusses certain biblical texts which were used (or could be used) by the opponents of orthodoxy to support their theological position.[336] The exposition of these texts is subordinated to the polemical intention of Athanasius. In a similar fashion, Philoxenus treats Luke 2:52 as a christological crux to promote his monophysitism and demolish the position of his enemies, the Nestorians and the Chalcedonians.

Fragment 11

This single folio is legible throughout except for two letters in a word on 30r 22. These are obliterated because of a tear running from the right margin of 30r 22 to the left margin of 30r 25. Both sides of the folio are somewhat stained. The handwriting is identical with that of most of the manuscript. In literary content, this fragment has obvious affinity with the following two single-folio fragments. The sequence in which they originally occurred will be considered later in this chapter. De Halleux reverses the present sequence without explaining why he does so.[337]

30r 7 -- ܡܣܩܬܐ ܘܡܚܬܬܐ -- literally, "the ascent and the descent." The former refers to the Lucan genealogy which begins with the human Jesus and "ascends" to God, and the latter refers to the Matthean genealogy which begins with Abraham and "descends" to the birth of Jesus. Chrysostom uses the same idea when dealing with the genealogies.[338]

30r 21, 23 -- ܒܝܬ ܠܒܢ ... ܠܚܡ -- the contrast between Beth-Laban and (Beth-)Lehem is that of 'literal' vis-à-vis typological interpretation. In Genesis 28, Jacob had his dream while on his way *down* to the house of Laban; thus the "ascending" and "descending" can be linked with the immediate and literal context.[339] Philoxenus does not deny such an interpretation of Jacob's dream at Bethel, but he sees in it a type foreshadowing the Incarnation represented here by Bethlehem.[340]

30r 23-27 -- "all those . . . are not aware of it . . . because of baptism" -- that is, the Jews do not understand their own scriptures because they have not been initiated into "the mystery" by baptism.

30v 1-5 -- "Adam . . . Seth . . . Enoch . . . Noah . . . Shem . . . Abraham, Isaac and Jacob" -- these names are all taken from the end of the Lucan genealogy (Luke 3:34-38), but in reverse order.

This fragment is based on Luke 3:22-23, being concerned with the relationship between the account of Jesus' baptism and the genealogy which immediately follows it. The same expository concern is seen in the next two fragments.

Fragment 12

The somewhat stained and torn condition of this fragment is similar to that of Fragment 11. The top left corner of the text was torn off and skilfully re-attached, the tear being in the shape of an irregular arc running from 1¼ inches to the right of the top left corner to the left margin of line 9. A hole has eliminated two letters on 31v 28. The handwriting is that of most of the manuscript.

31r 4 -- ܣܒܪܢܘܬܐ -- translated in this context by "supposition" to bring out its relation to the participle used in Luke 3:23, ܡܣܬܒܪ ("it is supposed"). Elsewhere in the manuscript this noun is translated "opinion."[341]

31r 28 - 31v 1 -- ܗܘ ܗܘ -- dittography.

31v 8-9 -- "he has brought them to the Father" -- the Lucan genealogy ends with ". . . Seth (son) of Adam (son) of God"; so in this sense they are brought to the Father.

In common with Fragments 11 and 13, this fragment deals with Christ's "supposed" filial relationship to Joseph. The biblical basis for the discussion is Luke 3:23.

Fragment 13

About twenty-five percent of the text is missing from this mutilated folio, torn below line 20. The folio was also torn in places to the edge of the margins, but fortunately what remains of the badly stained text is complete and mostly legible under ultra-violet light.

32r 15 -- ܦܫܩ -- "he explained" -- the subject of the verb is not known. The word is used in Fragment 3 (11r 13) where Philoxenus refers to an exegetical comment of Theodore of Mopsuestia in order to refute it. In this fragment he is citing a Church Father to support his conclusions (witness also [illegible] and [illegible] in lines 1 and 2), who must have been named in the preceding lost folio. In his second homily on Matthew 1:1, Chrysostom links the genealogies with the baptism of Jesus and speaks of the twofold birth of Jesus (of the Virgin and of the Holy Spirit) and His twofold baptism (by John the Baptist and by descent of the Holy Spirit) as being "of the same kind, for it partook of the old and it partook of the new."[342] Such a statement is similar to the fragmentary first sentence of this folio (32r 1-5), and when we consider that the contexts of both are the same we must conclude that either Philoxenus was drawing on Chrysostom or on a source common to Chrysostom.

32r 17 -- [illegible] -- "followed the sequence" -- in the preface to his Gospel, Luke stated his purpose in writing was to provide an "orderly account" of "the things which have been accomplished among us" (Luke 1:1-3).

32v 20-21 -- "Man is like a vapour" -- this is no doubt an allusion to James 4:14 (compare Wisdom 2:2), but it is by no means a direct quotation as Philoxenus would have us believe both by his reference to the "scripture" and his use of [illegible]. We note that in the same homily mentioned above, Chrysostom also speaks of the transitoriness of human life but he quotes from Psalm 102:4 (LXX): "My days have failed like smoke."[343]

That Fragments 11, 12 and 13 belong together is abundantly clear. They contain separate parts of a discussion on the relation of Jesus' baptism (Luke 3:22) to the Lucan version of His genealogy (Luke 3:23-38). Fragment 11 deals with the re-establishing of the likeness of God in man by baptism. We suggest that, leading up to this in folios now lost, Philoxenus had been discussing the baptism of Jesus and especially the words, "This is my beloved Son with whom I am pleased" (Luke 3:22), as they are related to the believer's baptism and his adoption into God's family. This brings him to introduce the Lucan genealogy in relation both to Christ's baptism and to the Matthean genealogy (30r 5-10). Fragment 12 is particularly concerned with the significance of the comment in 3:23 that Jesus "was supposed" to be the son of Joseph, and provides us with two points on this subject in two fragmentary paragraphs. Fragment 13 discusses the relationship between

Christ's birth and baptism and those of the believer as it is reflected in Luke 3:22-23. In the light of all this, it is evident that Fragments 11 and 13 go together in their respective discussions on the relation of verse 22 to verse 23 in Luke 3. We submit that Fragment 11 came first because it introduces the whole discussion on that relationship ("Where [does it say] that we have become sons of the likeness of God, etc.?"), and deals with it more generally than Fragment 13. Fragment 12 must be placed after 13 for it is concerned with the exposition of one word in Luke 3:23 (ܐܣܬܒܪ).[344] Thus, the order of these fragments should be 11, 13, 12.

It is also evident that these three fragments come before the final fragment of the codex. The first twelve lines of Fragment 14 contain the concluding sentences of the final paragraph of the section on Luke 3:22-23 (of which Fragments 11, 12 and 13 are parts). In those final sentences, Philoxenus sums up the main points of his exposition. We have already suggested that if the quire numbers on folios 29 (ܛ) and 33 (ܝ) mean anything, they mean that probably nine folios once existed between Fragments 10 and 14.[345] There is no doubt that Fragments 11, 12 and 13 are three folios from quire ܛ.

In these three fragments along with their conclusion in 33r 1-12, we have evidence of a sustained exposition of two verses in the Gospel of Luke. We have noted that Chrysostom, in his second homily on Matthew 1:1, developed his exposition in some ways similar to what is found here. While the evidence is not strong enough to say that Philoxenus drew directly on Chrysostom, the parallel helps us to understand the nature of these fragments called "commentaries." Just as the homilies of Chrysostom were expositions of biblical passages containing genuinely exegetical material, so (we submit) these three fragments indicate that they belong to an expository discourse, perhaps of a homiletical nature, based on Luke 3:22-23. We shall consider this further at the conclusion of this chapter.

Fragment 14

This last fragment forms a complete quire since its first page contains the quire number yudh and its final page, the colophon. Each of the six folios is damaged and stained in some way. The first folio (no. 33) is the most legible of the six, though it is stained, torn across the page from the right margin of line 6 to the left margin of line 9, and has two small holes on lines 16 and 17 which obliterate several letters. Folio 34 is less legible, particularly because of a bad stain on both sides covering the left half of 34r 1-9 and the right half of 34v 1-9. It has a tear running from the right margin of line 15 to the left margin of line 18, and about 3/4 inch is torn out of the last two lines. A stain in the middle of 34r 25 has also obliterated several letters. Most of the last four folios are so badly stained that they could only be read under ultra-violet light. The lacunae in the text of these four folios are mostly holes caused by the deterioration of the vellum. The scribe who copied most of the manuscript, was also the writer of all four notes in the colophon (which is completely legible).[346] The handwriting of the third note is noticeably smaller than that of the others, but it is without doubt by the same hand.

33r 1-2 -- ܐܬܬ ܫܪܬ ܘܐܬܓܠܝܬ -- the antecedent of these feminine verbs is ܡܠܬܐ which, while normally feminine, is usually construed in Philoxenus as a masculine when it refers (as here) to Christ, "the Word." The construction here changes to masculine in line 5 -- ܐܬܐ ܠܗ. When ܡܠܬܐ refers to Christ, it is always treated as a masculine in the Peshitta, but in the Old Syriac it is construed as the feminine word it is.[347]

33r 5-7 -- Philoxenus cites Luke for the source of his quotation, but the use of the third person, ܗܢܘ ... ܒܗ is the Matthean form (Matthew 3:17). The overwhelming evidence of the texts and versions (including Syriac) favours the use of the second person singular in Luke 3:22.[348] Our author may have been influenced by the Diatessaron, or he may simply be quoting from his memory of the text in Matthew.

33v 12-13 -- "that other likeness" -- Philoxenus is referring to the implanted likeness of God which was transmitted by heredity (as the Lucan genealogy shows) through Seth to Mary. The likeness was erased because of Adam's sin, but it was restored to Seth (so Philoxenus interprets the statement in Genesis 5:3) in such a way that he would transmit it through succeeding generations to the Virgin and thus to Christ who alone is the true image of the Father (38f 25). Our author has to explain why Abel is not mentioned in the genealogy as one who had a restored divine likeness; he was murdered by Cain before he had any offspring. Abel was murdered when Cain saw that God had accepted Abel's offering (alluded to in 33v 16-17) and rejected his.

34v 26 -- [ܒܪܐ] -- this reconstruction could also be [ܥܒܕ]. In his writings, Philoxenus uses these two words synonymously.

36r 6 -- ܬܘܡܘܣܐ -- is a misspelling for ܬܘܡܣܐ, which is spelled correctly in 36r 24.

36r 18-20 -- unidentified quotation probably from a Nestorian opponent.

36v 7 -- [ܕܚܝ]ܠܐ -- reconstructed on the basis of 36r 15.

37r 23-25 -- here Philoxenus enunciates one of his principles of biblical interpretation.

37v 1 -- "all of them" -- that is, all those named in the Lucan genealogy.

38r 12 -- ܒܢܝ̈ ܕܡܘܬܐ -- literally (as here translated), "sons of the likeness." Idiomatically, the expression means simply "like," but the literal meaning is used in our translation to retain some of the emphasis of the author as 38r 15 (where it is repeated) makes clear. The expression also occurs in 30r 5.[349]

38v 1 -- "seventy-seven generations" -- is the number of names in the Lucan genealogy. This reference to Lamech is at variance with the reference to him in Fragment 1 where Philoxenus says that Lamech will be avenged seventy times seven (1r 7). The Hebrew and Peshitta of Genesis 4:24 both read seventy-seven, but the Greek is ambiguous.[350] We note that Philoxenus does not press the numeral correspondence here, but seems only to mention it in passing. In 38v 4, he refers vaguely to the "many written in the genealogy," when he could have been more specific. This obvious discrepancy in citing the number from Genesis 4:24 could hardly have occurred in the same work and adds considerable weight to the conclusion already drawn that Fragment 1 does not belong to this manuscript.[351]

38v 2 -- [ܒܡܘܬ]ܗ -- this reconstruction is based solely on the context. There is no reference to Christ's death negating the sin of Cain in any of the extant writings of Philoxenus (as far as we can determine).[352]

38v 8 -- the reconstructions on this line are quite uncertain. The use of the first plural ending on both participles is based on its use in the next two lines. ܐ[ܣܝܘܬܐ -- the noun is used in only one other (and quite different) context in this manuscript (31v 27). It is translated here as "salvation" although its usual meaning is that of "the healing art" or "a cure."[353]

38v 11-22 -- the significance of the colophon will be considered in the next section of this chapter.

38v 14-15 -- if the present codex as the fourth volume was limited to five topics (ܪ̈ܝܫܐ) taken from Luke 1-3, we may assume that the first three volumes (now lost) were devoted exclusively to Matthew; and if they were of similar length, then together they dealt with some fifteen topics from that Gospel. Whether further volumes were written on topics from Luke 4-24 is not known.

38v 15-17 -- ܥܒܝܕ ܐܬܟܬܒ -- we have translated these words literally. They mean that Philoxenus was the author of the book which was then copied in Mabbug on the date given.

38v 18-19 -- the date is equivalent to A.D. 510/511. For the sake of simplicity, the single date of 511 has been used in this dissertation.

38v 21-22 -- this final comment is the scribe's own expression of restrained respect for the author who was his bishop. Although it reads like a copybook aphorism, it may very well be an original comment.

C. *SYNTHESIS*

This study has established that ten of the fourteen fragments in the present codex originally belonged together. Only Fragments 1, 3, 4, and 5 are intrusions. It is clear, too, that the colophon, written by the same scribe who penned the manuscript, must apply to the contents of all ten fragments. That colophon states categorically that the original codex was the fourth in a series of "commentaries" on Matthew and Luke, and that it contained five "chapters" on Luke. Our task now, on the basis of the evidence already adduced, is to present a reconstruction of the probable nature and contents of the original work by Philoxenus to which the colophon bears witness.

First, it is necessary to deal conclusively with two terms in the colophon, ܦܘܫܩܐ and ܪ̈ܫܐ, which have already been discussed in this dissertation.[354] The contents of the ten fragments clearly show that ܦܘܫܩܐ usually translated "commentary," cannot in this context mean an exegetical work in any narrow sense. The key to its meaning is well illustrated in the final four fragments to which the colophon is immediately attached. We have seen that they are based on the introduction to the Lucan genealogy (Luke 3:23) and its relationship to the preceding biblical passage on the baptism of Jesus and to the Matthean genealogy. The style is discursive. We have noted a similar passage in one of the homilies of Chrysostom. We conclude that ܦܘܫܩܐ in this context is a homiletical exposition of a biblical verse (or in this case part of a verse) into which are introduced the author's theological presuppositions. This understanding will help us to re-evaluate the other fragments of the codex.

The colophon goes on to say that the commentary consists of "five" chapters (ܪ̈ܫܐ). This last fragment, along with the isolated leaves of Fragments 11-13, presumably contains the remnants of the fifth "chapter." A "chapter," then, deals with a single topic based on a biblical verse or statement, in this case the statement that Jesus was supposed to be the son of Joseph. It is also reasonable to expect that the chapters would be approximately equal in length, especially (as we would suggest) if they were of a homiletical nature. Assuming this, and considering the fact that the codex had about ninety-six folios,[355] we can conclude that the last four fragments are all that remains of the fifth chapter which could not have been more than fifteen folios in length; that is, it was somewhat less than a fifth of the original codex, thus confirming the reasonableness of our assumption. We can then assume that the remaining eighty-one folios contained discussions of four other topics from Luke.

We are now able to work back to the other fragments and reconsider their place in the work as a whole. We have noted that Fragment 10 is tied to Fragment 14 because of the two quire numbers it contains, establishing the sequence: ܫ-ܬ-ܕ. We have also noted that, while Fragment 10 is part of a theological discourse, it is based on Luke 2:52.[356] We are inevitably drawn to the conclusion that that verse is the topic of the fourth chapter of our codex. Fragment 7 clearly belongs to this fourth chapter, since it deals exegetically with the relationship between Luke 2:51b and Luke 2:52a.[357] Since Fragment 14 has clearly demonstrated that the Philoxenian commentary can be both exegetical and discursive, we can now admit that Fragment 8 probably belonged with 7 and 10 as part of the fourth chapter on Luke 2:52.[358] Since Fragment 7 relates Luke 2:52 to its context, it must have been near the beginning of its chapter. The end of Fragment 10 must also have been near the end of the chapter, because the fifth chapter could not have been shorter than fourteen or fifteen folios without being too short. Therefore, the order of these fragments in the fourth chapter is 7, 8, and 10.

There is internal evidence in Fragments 6 and 9 to link them together and perhaps also to Fragments 7, 8 and 10 of the fourth chapter. In Fragment 6, the references to Luke and to Christ's growth in stature and "in the Spirit" point to Luke 2:40 as a possible focus for an expository discourse to which this fragment could belong.[359] Fragment 9 deals with Jesus' intellectual development in relation to His becoming strong in the Holy Spirit (17r 7-9) as His presence in the temple at the age of twelve reveals (Luke 2:42, 46). It is possible that these two fragments belonged with 7, 8 and 10 in the fourth chapter on Luke 2:52. But it is more likely that they are all we have of the third chapter, the topic of which was Luke 2:40. The reasons for assigning them to the third chapter are these: (1) the fragments of the fourth chapter are mainly concerned with the dogmatic implications of Luke 2:52, while these two fragments are parenetic and have more in common with the ascetic *Discourses*; (2) the tone of the bulk of Fragment 9 (from 17r 13 to 18v 27) suggests that it contains most of the concluding paragraph of a chapter, and the same may be said of the last paragraph (fragmentary) of Fragment 10 (from 27r 26 to 29v 28), which means that they came from two distinct chapters;

and (3) Fragments 7, 8 and 10 of the fourth chapter provide us with thirteen folios out of perhaps twenty leaving little room for the author to have introduced into them the kind of content of which Fragments 6 and 9 were a part. Since the handwriting, quality of vellum and size of page of these two fragments are the same as most of the other fragments of this codex, we conclude that they are the remains of the third chapter on Luke 2:40.

Fragment 2 presents a certain difficulty in the effort to fit it into the scheme here proposed. There is no doubt that it belongs to this "Commentary of five chapters taken from Luke the Evangelist." The external style of production (handwriting, quality of vellum, size of page) are the same. In our preliminary analysis we suggested that the contents indicated that it was part of a letter or a sermon. We now see that the word ܦܘܫܩܐ (commentary) was applied to a discourse or homily based upon a biblical text. The question is: upon what text in Luke was Fragment 2 based? If we follow de Halleux in assigning it to a "commentary" on Luke 3:22 because of the extended discussion on the statement there that the Holy Spirit appeared "in the likeness of the form of a dove,"[360] we are confronted immediately by two objections: (1) Luke 3:22 (or that portion of it quoted) is not the basis for the discussion found in the eight folios of this fragment, and (2) a discourse on Luke 3:22 would come between the discourse on Luke 2:52 and the one on Luke 3:23 and that would interrupt the sequence which the evidence of the manuscript has established.[361] The first objection is not insurmountable given the fact that there are only eight folios out of about twenty on which to base any conclusion. But the second objection cannot be so easily skirted, for it arises out of the colophon's explicit statement that the codex is the fourth in a series of expository commentaries and contains five "chapters." Given such an orderly presentation of collected expositions, it is highly improbable that the order of Luke's Gospel would be violated by placing a discourse on Luke 3:22 before that on Luke 2:52.

If this second fragment belongs with the others (and it surely must), the Lucan text on which it is based has to be one that precedes Luke 2:52. Such a text is not to be found as a direct quotation in this fragment. We have suggested that 4r 2 contains an allusion to Luke 1:49, but it is not likely this was the text for one of the five chapters of this commentary. However, it does point to the most probable text, Luke 2:14, "Glory to God in the highest . . . ." It is true that there is no direct or indirect quotation from this verse in the fragment before us, and our conjecture must remain just that; but it is not without foundation. The subject of Fragment 2 is that of the meaning of Christ's divinity vis-à-vis His incarnation. The divinity is unequivocally affirmed, and what better scriptural affirmation could there be than the angelic doxology of Luke 2:14 accompanying the announcement of Christ's birth? In this fragment, Philoxenus attacks those heretics who, in affirming His divinity, "deny His corporality" (4r 6). Moreover, one would expect an ardent spokesman for monophysitism like Philoxenus to choose the Birth narrative as the source of at least one of five topics taken from the first three chapters of Luke. Certainly, the story of the Nativity is never far from the author's mind in this fragment whether or not Luke 2:14 was the actual basis for the discourse. If it was not Luke 2:14, then it was probably some other verse from the same pericope.

Having proposed the topics for four of the chapters, we cannot avoid the question: what was the topic of the chapter that is completely missing? Since, as has been demonstrated, this volume contained expository discourses on five texts taken from the first three chapters of Luke, and since four of these were from chapters 2 and 3, we can reasonably assume that one was from the first chapter. Here the most likely verse is Luke 1:35, the climax of the Annunciation. This passage was of considerable interest to Philoxenus, as his many citations of it show.[362] Moreover, several years after the completion of this commentary, he wrote a short homily on the Annunciation;[363] which, however, must be regarded as distinct from the first chapter now lost, because it is much shorter than the probable length of that chapter (about twenty folios), having only the equivalent of five folios, because in its present form it is complete in itself and cannot be regarded as a fragment,[364] and because internal evidence points to a later date of writing than that of our codex. It is to be expected that *Annuntiatione* repeats some of the contents of this conjectured first chapter. Another reason for assuming that the Annunciation was the focus of the first chapter is that two monophysite commentators of a later age, Bar Salibi and Bar Hebraeus, cite Philoxenus when dealing with that pericope.[365]

We, therefore, conclude that the five chapters of the original volume were in all probability as follows: Chapter 1 (now completely lost) on Luke 1:35 (or another verse from the Annunciation), Chapter 2 (Fragment 2) on Luke 2:14 (or another verse from the Nativity), Chapter 3 (Fragments 6 and 9) on Luke 2:40, Chapter 4 (Fragments 7, 8 and 10) on Luke 2:52, and Chapter 5 (Fragments 11, 13, 12 and 14) on Luke 3:23.

CHAPTER IV

THE BIBLICAL QUOTATIONS IN THIS MANUSCRIPT AND THEIR RELATION TO THE TEXTS AND VERSIONS OF THE BIBLE

In his preface to the ascetic *Discourses* (published in 1894), E. A. Wallis Budge wrote of Philoxenus' habit in quoting from the Bible as follows:

> A comparison of the quotations (in the *Discourses*) with existing Syriac versions of the Bible seems to show that Philoxenus was perfectly acquainted with the Syriac text, but that he in many cases quoted from memory. The version used by him was the Peshitta, which he quoted loosely, or with such modifications as his argument required or his fancy dictated. . . . Every one of his quotations which differs from extant versions is of interest. . . .[366]

In Philoxenus' case, that interest is born of more than ordinary curiosity since our author is said to have sponsored a new version of the New Testament, published in A.D. 508 by his chorepiscopus, Polycarp, and now lost.[367] G. Zuntz in 1945 recognized the value of examining his biblical quotations more closely to see what light could be shed on the nature of the Philoxenian version.[368] He limited his examination to one published work, the *Three Discourses*,[369] but recognized the great value of the manuscript before us for such comparative studies.[370] A. Vööbus extended the enquiry to include this and other Philoxenian texts, especially as they were related to the history of the Syriac versions of the Gospels.[371] But no detailed study has been made of all the quotations in the manuscript before us.

The purpose of this chapter is to provide such a study. We shall first extract from the manuscript all the recognizable quotations, separating them into two categories: those which correspond to the Peshitta exactly (the reference to which will be merely listed), and those which in some way deviate from the Peshitta (these will be quoted in full and compared with other versions). Then, in the second place, we shall draw whatever conclusions the evidence warrants. In this analysis the following symbols will be used:

Aph--Aphrahat, cited in Burkitt, *Evangelion*

Cur--Curetonian Version (Cureton, *Gospels*)

Eph--Ephraim's quotations from the Diatessaron collected in Leloir, *Ephraem*

Gr--Greek New Testament

Har--Harklean Version (White, *Harklean N.T.*)

Heb--Hebrew Bible

Hex--Syro-Hexaplar[372]

LXX--Old Testament in Greek

P--Peshitta Version[373]

Pal--Palestinian Syriac Texts[374]

Ph--Quotation from Philoxenus in Add. 17,126

Sin--Syriac Version of Sinaitic Palimpset (Bensley, *Four Gospels*).

The notes appended will indicate where the same quotation is found in other works of Philoxenus.

A. *ANALYSIS OF BIBLICAL QUOTATIONS*

1. *Quotations Identical with the Peshitta*

Genesis--1:3 (35r 16-17),[375] 1:9a (35v 15), 1:14a (35v 16-17),[376] 1:16a (37r 13-14), 1:20a (35v 17-18), 1:24a (35v 18), 3:19b (33v 5-6), 3:22a (33v 7-8), 39:21b (27v 12-13);

Jeremiah--51:15a (11r 15-16);

Matthew--3:17b (33r 6-7, 12),[377] 13:17 (7v 9-12), 26:38 (3r 18);[378]

Luke--1:37 (26v 5),[379] 2:27 (31v 25), 2:33 (15r 8-10), 2:40 (15v 19-20), 2:41 (31v 26-27), 2:51b (15r 4), 3:22b (7r 9), 3:23a (33r 7-8), 22:44 (3v 8-10);

John--1:14a (8v 18-19, 9r 23-24),[380] 8:(45)56 (7v-7-8), 10:11 (3r 9-10),[381] 10:15 (6r 23-24);

Romans--4:17 (35v 21-22),[382] 8:3 (10v 15-17),[383] 8:22 (31r 21-22), 8:32 (9v 1-3),[384] 8:34 (25r 19-21);

1 Corinthians-- 1:18a (25v 27 - 26r 1) [385] 15:18 (7v 28 - 8r 2);[386]

Galatians-- 4:4 (6r 6-7, 9r 21-22);[387]

Philippians-- 2:6 (phrases-10v 21-22), 2:7b (10v 14);[388]

Colossians--1:18 (38r 19-20);
Hebrews--2:11 (20r 13-14),[389] 2:12 (20r 12-13).[390]

2. *Quotations Which Differ from the Peshitta*

In the following exhibits, biblical quotations in our manuscript (Ph) are set out along with the corresponding Peshitta version (P). Where the Syro-Hexaplaric version (Hex) of the same text is available, it is also quoted. Other versions are included only where their inclusion seems useful.

1. *Genesis 1:1* (35r 24-25)[391]

Ph ܒܪܫܝܬ ܒܪܐ ܐܠܗܐ ܠܫܡܝܐ ܘܠܐܪܥܐ.
P " " " ܝܬ ܫܡܝܐ ܘܝܬ ܐܪܥܐ.

2. *Genesis 1:6* (35v 10-12)[392]

Ph ܐܡܪ ܐܠܗܐ ܢܗܘܐ ܐܪܩܝܥܐ ܒܡܨܥܬ ܡܝܐ
P " " ܢܗܘܐ ܪܩܝܥܐ " "
Ph ܘܢܗܘܐ ܦܪܫ ܒܝܬ ܡܝܐ ܠܡܝܐ.
P " " " " " .

3. *Genesis 1:11* (35v 16)

Ph ܬܪܚܫ ܐܪܥܐ ܢܦܫܐ ܚܝܐ.
P ܬܦܩ " ܬܕܐܐ.

4. *Genesis 1:15* (37r 10-12)

Ph ܢܗܘܘܢ ܢܗܝܪ̈ܐ ܒܐܪܩܝܥܐ [ܕܫܡܝܐ]
P " ܡܢܗܪ̈ܢ ܒܪܩܝܥܐ "
Ph ܠܡܢܗܪܘ ܥܠ ܐܪܥܐ.
P " " " .

Heb וְהָיוּ לִמְאוֹרֹת בִּרְקִיעַ הַשָּׁמַיִם....

LXX καὶ ἔστωσαν εἰς φαῦσιν ἐν τῷ στερεώματι τοῦ οὐρανοῦ...

5. *Genesis 1:24* (37r 1-3)

Ph ܐܡܪ ܐܠܗܐ. ܬܦܩ ܐܪܥܐ ܢܦܫܐ ܚܝܬܐ
P " " . " " " "
Ph ܠܓܢܣܗ ܒܒܥܝܪܐ ܘܚܝܘܬܐ ܘܪܚܫܐ ܕܐܪܥܐ
P " " ܘܪܚܫܐ ܘܚܝܘܬܐ "
Ph ܠܓܢܣܗ.
P " .

6. *Genesis 1:25* (37r 4-7)

Ph ܥܒܕ ܐ[ܠܗ]ܐ ܚܝܘܬܐ ܕܐܪܥܐ ܠܓܢܣܝܗ̇
P " " " " ܠܓܢܣܗ
Ph ܘܒܥܝܪܐ ܠܓܢܣܝܗ̇ ܘܟܠܗ ܪܚܫܐ ܕܐܪܥܐ
P " ܠܓܢܣܗ " " "
Ph ܠܓܢܣܘܗܝ.
P " .

7. *Genesis 1:26* (34r 4-7)[393]

Ph ܐܡܪ ܐܠܗܐ. ܕܢܥܒܕ ܐܢܫܐ ܐܝܟ ܨܠܡܐ ܕܠܢ
P " " . ܢܥܒܕ " ܒܨܠܡܢ
Ph ܘܐܝܟ ܕܡܘܬܢ. ܘܢܫܠܛܘܢ ܒܢܘ̈ܢܝ ܝܡܐ
P ܐܝܟ " . " "
Ph ܘܒܦܪ̈ܚ ܚܝܘܬܐ ܕܫܡܝܐ.
P " "

8a. *Genesis 1:27* (34r 8-10)[394]

Ph ܒܪܐ ܐܠܗܐ ܠܐܕܡ ܒܨܠܡܗ. ܒܨܠܡ ܐܠܗܐ
P " " " . " " "
Ph ܒܪܝܗ. ܕܟܪ ܘܢܩܒܬܐ ܒܪܐ ܐܢܘܢ.
P ܒܪܝܗܝ. " " ܒܪܐ " .

8b. *Genesis 1:27a* (36v 103)[395]

Ph ܒܪܐ ܐܠܗܐ ܠܐܢܫܐ ܒܨܠܡܗ ܒܨܠܡ ܐܠܗܐ ܒܪܝܗ.
Pal " " ܠܒܪܢܫܐ ܒܕܡܘܬܗ ܕܐܠܗܐ ܒܪܐ ܝܬܗ.

LXX ἐποίησεν ὁ θεὸς τὸν ἄνθρωπον, κατ' εἰκόνα θεοῦ ἐποίησεν αὐτόν.

9. *Genesis 2:7* (36r 15-17)[396]

Ph ܓܒܠ ܐܠܗܐ ܠܐܢܫܐ [ܕܚ]ܠܐ ܡܢ
P " ܡܪܝܐ " ܠܐܕܡ ܥܦܪܐ "
Ph ܐܪܥܐ ܘܢܦܚ ܒܐܦܘܗܝ [ܢ]ܫܡܬܐ ܕܚܝ̈ܐ.
P ܐܕܡܬܐ " " " " .

10. *Genesis 2:21-22* (36v 14-18)[397]

Ph ܐܪܡܝ ܡܪܝܐ ܐܠܗܐ ܬܗܘܬܐ ܥܠ ܐܕܡ ܘܕܡܟ.
P " " " ܫܢܬܐ " " " .
Ph ܘܢܣܒ ܚܕܐ ܡܢ ܐܠܥܘ̈ܗܝ ܘܡܠܐ ܒܣܪܐ ܚܠܦܝܗ̇.
P " " " " ܘܐܚܕ " " .
Ph ܘܒܢܐ ܡܪܝܐ ܐܠܗܐ ܠܐܠܥܐ ܗ̇ܝ ܕܢܣܒ
P ܘܬܩܢ " " ܐܠܥܐ "
Ph ܡܢ ܐܕܡ ܠܐܢܬܬܐ.
P " " " .

11. *Genesis 3:24* (2r 10-12)

Ph ܐܦܩܗ ܐܠܗܐ ܘܐܘܬܒܗ ܠܩܘܒܠ
P " ܡܪܝܐ " ܘܐܫܪܝ ܡܢ ܡܕܢܚ

LXX ἐξέβαλεν τὸν Ἀδαμ καὶ κατῴκισεν αὐτὸν ἀπέναντι

Ph ܦܪܕܝܣܐ ܕܒܘܣܡܐ.
P " ܕܥܕܢ ܟܪܘܒܐ.

LXX τοῦ παραδείσου τῆς τρυφῆς

12. *Genesis 4:15* (1r 10-11)

Ph ܠܐ ܗܘܐ ܗܟܢܐ ܕܟܠ ܡܢ ܕܩܛܠ ܠܩܐܝܢ

Hex " " ܟܠ " " "

P " " " ܡܛܠܗܢܐ ܕܩܐܝܢ

Ph ܫܒܥ ܡܬܒ̈ܥܝܢ ܫܪܐ.

Hex " ܡܬܬܒ̈ܥܢܘܬܐ " .

P ܫ̣ ܫܒܥܥܐ ܢܬܦܪܥ.

13. *Genesis 4:16* (2r 3-5)[398]

Ph ܢܦܩ ܩܐܝܢ ܡܢ ܩܕܡ ܐܦܘܗܝ ܕܡܪܝܐ. ܘܥܡܪ

Hex " " " ܦܪ̈ܨܘܦܐ ܕܐܠܗܐ. "

P " " " " ܡܪܝܐ. ܘܝܬܒ

Ph ܒܐܪܥܐ ܕܢܘܕ ܠܘܩܒܠ ܥܕܢ.

Hex " " " " .

P " " ܡܢ ܡܕܢܚܗ ܕܥܕܢ.

14. *Genesis 4:17* (2r 20-21)

Ph ܘܒܢܐ ܩܐܝܢ ܠܡܕܝܢܬܐ ܥܠ ܫܡܐ ܕܒܪܗ.

Hex ܘܫܡܗ ܫܡܐ " " " ܕܒܪܐ ܕܝܠܗ

P ܘܩܪܐ ܫܡܗ ܕܡܕܝܢܬܐ " ܫܡ ܒܪܗ

Hex ܚܢܘܟ.

P " .

15. *Genesis 4:24* (1r 6-7)

Ph ܡܛܠ ܕܫ̣ ܫܒܥܐ ܐܬܬܒܥ ܩܐܝܢ. ܠܡܟ ܕܝܢ

Hex " ܕܫܒܥܐܝܬ ܬܬܒܥܐ ܡܢ " ܩܢ. ܕܝܢ ܠܡܟ

P " ܕܫ̣ ܫܒܥܥܐ ܢܬܦܪܥ " . ܘܠܡܟ

Ph ܫܒܥܝܢ ܥܠ ܫܒܥ.

Hex " ܫܒ̈ܥܝܢܬܐ " .

P ܠܫܒܥܝܢ ܘܫܒܥܐ.

16. *Genesis 4:26* (33v 19-20)

<u>Ph</u> ܗܢܘܢ ܗܪܟܐ ܣܒܪ ܠܡܩܪܐ ܒܫܡܗ ܕܡܪܝܐ·
<u>Hex</u> ܗܢܐ " " ܫܡܗ " ܐܠܗܐ·
<u>P</u> ܗܝܕܝܢ ܫܪܝ " ܒܫܡܗ " ·

17. *Genesis 5:1-2a* (33v 23-26)[399]

<u>Ph</u> ܗܢܘ ܟܬܒܐ ܕܬܘܠܕܬܐ ܕܒܢܝ ܐܢܫܐ· ܒܝܘܡܐ
<u>Hex</u> ܗܢܐ ܗܘ " " " " · "
<u>P</u> ܗܢܘ ܣܦܪ ܬܘܠܕܬܗ ܕܐܕܡ· "
<u>Ph</u> ܕܒܪܐ ܐܠܗܐ ܠܐܕܡ ܒܨܠܡ ܐܠܗܐ
<u>Hex</u> ܗܘ " ܒܗ " " ܐܝܟ ܨܠܡܐ ܕܐܠܗܐ
<u>P</u> ܕܒܪܐ " " ܒܕܡܘܬ ܐܠܗܐ
<u>Ph</u> ܒܒܪܝܗ· ܕܟܪ ܘܢܩܒܬܐ ܒܪܐ ܐܢܘܢ·
<u>Hex</u> " · ܕܟܪܐ ܘܢܩܒܬܐ " " ·
<u>P</u> ܒܪܗܝ· ܕܟܪ ܘܢܩܒܬܐ ܒܪܐ " ·

18. *Genesis 9:6* (1r 15-17)

<u>Ph</u> ܡܢ ܕܐܫܕ ܕܡܐ ܕܐܢܫܐ· ܒܐܢܫܐ
<u>Hex</u> ܗܘ " " ܕܒܪܢܫܐ· ܒܒܪܢܫܐ ܢܫܦ
<u>P</u> ܡܢ ܕܢܐܫܘܕ " ܕܐܢܫܐ· ܒܐܢܫܐ
<u>Ph</u> ܕܡܗ ܢܬܐܫܕ·
<u>Hex</u> ܕܡܐ ܕܝܠܗ " ·
<u>P</u> ܕܡܗ " ·

19. *Genesis 28:12-13* (30r 17-20)

Ph ܘܣܒܠܬܐ ܣܝܡܐ ܒܐܪܥܐ ܘܪܝܫܗ ܡܛܐ ܠܫܡܝܐ.
P " " " " " .
Ph ܘܡܠܐܟ̈ܘܗܝ ܕܐܠܗܐ ܕܣܠܩܝܢ ܘܢܚܬܝܢ ܒܗ.
P ܘܗܐ ܡܠܐܟܘܗܝ " ܣܠܩܝܢ " "
Ph ܘܡܪܝܐ ܕܩܐܡ ܠܥܠ ܡܢܗ.
P ܘܗܐ ܡܪܝܐ ܩܐܡ " " .

20. *Genesis 39:4* (27v 11-12)

Ph ܐܫܬܟܚ ܝܘܣܦ ܒܪܚܡܐ ܩܕܡ ܡܪܗ.
Hex ܐܫܟܚ " ܛܝܒܘܬܐ " ܡܪܐ ܕܝܠܗ.
P " " ܪ̈ܚܡܐ ܒܥܝܢ̈ܘܗܝ.

21. *Exodus 4:22-23 conflated* (20v 19-20)

Ph ܐܡܪ ܠܗ ܠܒܪܝ [ܒܘܟܪܝ ܐܝܣܪܝܠ] ܘܢܦܠܚܢܝ.
Hex " ܠܥܡܐ ܕܝܠܝ [ܒܘܟܪܐ ܕܝܠܝ "] ܕܢܦܠܚܘܢ ܠܝ.
P ܫܕܪ ܠܒܪܝ [ܒܘܟܪܝ ܐܝܣܪܝܠ] ܘܢܦܠܚܢܝ.

22. *1 Kings 22:19* (5r 23-25)

Ph ܚܙܝܬ ܠܡܪܝܐ ܕܝܬܒ ܥܠ ܟܘܪܣܝܐ ܪ̈ܡܐ.
Hex " " " " " ܕܝܠܗ.
P " " ܝܬܒ " ܟܘܪܣܝܗ.
Ph ܘܟܠܗ ܚܝܠܐ ܕܫܡܝܐ ܩܐܡ ܠܥܠ ܡܢܗ.
Hex ܘܟܠܗ̇ ܦܠܚܘܬܐ " ܩܝܡܐ
P ܘܟܠܗ ܚܝܠܐ " ܩܐܡ " " .
Hex ܠܘܬܗ ܡܢ ܝܡܝܢܐ ܘܡܢ ܣܡܠܐ ܕܝܠܗ.

23. *Psalm 82:6-7* (21v 13-16)[400]

Ph ܐܢܐ ܐܡܪܬ ܕܐܠܗ̈ܐ ܐܢܬܘܢ ܘܒ̈ܢܘܗܝ ܕܡܪܝܡܐ
P " " ܕܐܠܗ̈ܝܢ " " "
Ph ܟܠܟܘܢ. ܡܟܝܠ ܐܝܟ ܚܕ ܡܢ ܒ̈ܢܝ ܐܢܫܐ ܬܡܘܬܘܢ.
P " . " " " " "

24. *Isaiah 6:1-2* (5r 25 - 5v 2)

Ph ܒܫܢܬܐ ܕܡܝܬ ܥܘܙܝܐ ܡܠܟܐ· ܚܙܝܬ ܠܡܪܝܐ ܕܝܬܒ

P " " " " · " " ܝܬܒ

Ph ܥܠ ܟܘܪܣܝܐ ܪܡܐ ܘܡܬܥܠܝܐ· ܘܡܫܡܫܝܢ ܡܠܐܟܐ

P " " " · ܘܡܬܥܠܝܐ ܕܫܘܠܘܗܝ "

Ph ܗܝܟܠܗ· ܘܣܪܦܐ ܩܝܡܝܢ ܠܥܠ ܡܢܗ·

P " ܘܣܪ̈ܦܐ · " " " ·

25. *Isaiah 7:16* (18v - 11-12)

Ph ܕܥܕܠܐ ܢܕܥ ܛܠܝܐ ܠܡܣܠܝܘ ܒܒܝܫܬܐ ܢܓܒܐ ܛܒܬܐ·

P " " " " " ܘܠܡܓܒܐ " ·

26. *Isaiah 26:18* (8v 6-7)

Ph ܒܛܢ ܘܚܒܠܢ ܐܝܟ ܗܠܝܢ ܕܝܠܕܢ ܪ̈ܘܚܐ·

P ܒܛܢܢ " ܗܢܝܢ " " ·

27. *Isaiah 44:20* (2v 5-6)

Ph ܒܩܛܡܐ ܕܥܐ ܠܒܗܘܢ ܘܡܛܥܐ ܠܗܘܢ·

P ܕܥܐܗܘ " " " ܗܘ " ·

28. *Isaiah 65:8-9* (37v 6-11)

Ph [ܐܝܟ ܕܡܫܬܟܚ]ܐ ܥܢܒܬܐ ܒܩܛܘܦܐ· ܘܐܡܪ[ܝܢ]

P " " " " "

Ph [ܐܢܫ] ܠܐ ܬܚܒܠܝܢܗ ܡܛܠ[ܕܒܘܪܟܬܐ]

P " ܠܚܒܪܗ· " " " "

Ph [ܐܝ]ܬ ܒܗ· ܗܟܢܐ [ܐܥܒܕ] ܡܛܠ ܥܒܕܝ· ܘܡܛܠ

P " " · " " " "

Ph ܗܕܐ ܠܐ ܐܚܒܠ ܠܟܠܗܘܢ· ܘܐܦܩ ܙܪܥܐ ܡܢ

P ܘܠܐ " " · " " "

Ph ܝܥܩܘܒ [ܘܡܢ ܝ]ܗܘܕܐ ܢܐܪܬ ܛܘܪܝ ܓܒܝ̈ܐ·

P " " " ܝܪܬܐ " ·

29. *Ezekiel 1:4* (5v 2-5)

Ph ܚܙܝܬ ܘܗܐ ܪܘܚܐ ܐܬܝܐ ܡܢ ܓܪܒܝܐ.
P " " " ܕܥܠܥܠܐ ܐܬܝܐ " " .
Ph ܥܢܢܐ ܪܒܬܐ ܘܢܘܪܐ ܡܬܠܗܠܗܬܐ ܘܙܠܝܩܐ ܚܕܪ̈ܘܗܝ.
P " " " ܕܡܬܠܗܠܗܬܐ " " .

30. *Daniel 7:9* (5v 7-9)

Ph ܚܙܝܬ ܗܘܐ ܟܘܪ̈ܣܘܬܐ ܐܬܬܣܝܡܘ ܘܥܬܝܩ
P ܚܙܐ ܗܘܝܬ " " "
Ph ܘܝܘ̈ܡܬܐ ܝܬܒ.
P " " .

31. *Amos 7:7* (5v 5-7)

Ph ܚܙܝܬ ܠܡܪܝܐ ܕܡܬܩܝܡ ܥܠ ܫܘܪܐ
P ܗܟܢܐ ܚܘܝܢܝ. ܘܗܐ ܡܪܝܐ ܡܬܩܝܡ " "
Ph ܕܐܢܕܘܟܐ. ܘܒܐܝܕܗ ܐܢܕܘܟܐ.
P " . " " .

32. *Wisdom 1:4* (28r 25 - 28v 1)[401]

Ph ܠܐ ܒܢܦܫܐ ܚܟܡܬܐ ܒܦܓܪܐ ܕܡܫܬܥܒܕܐ
P " "
Ph ܒܚ̈ܛܗܐ. ܥܐܠܐ
P " . ܠܐ ܒܥܠܬܐ ܚܟܡܬܐ. ܘܐܦ ܠܐ ܒܦܓܪܐ
Ph ܒܦܓܪܐ ܕܡܫܥܒܕ ܠܚܛܝܬܐ.
P " " " .

33. *Wisdom 3:1* (14 r 2-3)

Ph ܢܦܫܬܐ ܕܙܕܝܩܐ ܒܐܝ̈ܕܝ ܐܠܗܐ ܐܢܝܢ .
P ܢܦܫܬܗܘܢ ܕܝܢ " ܒܐܝܕܘܗܝ ܐܢܝܢ ܕܐܠܗܐ.

34. *Matthew 18:22* (1r 1-2)[402]

<u>Ph</u> ܠܘ ܟܠܫܒܥ ܫܒܥ܇ ܐܠܐ ܫܒܥܝܢ ܙܒܢ ܫܒܥ܂

<u>P</u> ܠܐ.... ܥܕܡܐ ܠܫܒܥ܇ " ܥܕܡܐ ܠܫܒܥܝܢ ܙܒܢܝܢ
ܫܒܥ ܫܒܥ܂

<u>Aph</u> ܠܐ ܫܒ̈ܥ܇ ܐܠܐ ܫܒܥܝܢ ܫܒ̈ܥ ܫܒ̈ܥ܂

<u>Eph</u> ܫܒ̈ܥ ܙܒܢ ܫܒܥܝܢ܂

also <u>Eph</u> ܫܒܥ ܫܒܥ " " ܂

35a. *Matthew 22:32* (21v 9-12)

<u>Ph</u> ܐܢܐ ܐܢܐ ܐܠܗܗ ܕܐܒܪܗܡ ܘܕܐܝܣܚܩ

<u>P</u> " " " " ܐܠܗܗ ܕܐܝܣܚܩ

<u>Ph</u> ܘܕܝܥܩܘܒ ܘܐܠܗܐ ܠܐ ܗܘܐ ܕܡܝ̈ܬܐ

<u>P</u> ܐܠܗܗ ܕܝܥܩܘܒ " " " "

<u>Ph</u> ܐܠܐ ܕܚ̈ܝܐ܇ ܟܠܗܘܢ ܓܝܪ ܚ̈ܝܝܢ ܐܢܘܢ ܠܗ܂

<u>P</u> " " ܂ [= Luke 20:38b = =]

35b. *Matthew 22:32* (*Senun*, p. 31)

<u>Senun</u> ܐܢܐ ܐܝܬܝ ܐܠܗܐ ܕܐܒܪܗܡ

<u>Har</u> " " ܐܠܗܗ ܕܐܒܪܐܗܡ ܘܐܠܗܗ

<u>Senun</u> ܘܕܐܝܣܚܩ ܘܕܝܥܩܘܒ܇ ܘܐܠܗܐ ܠܐ

<u>Har</u> ܕܐܝܣܚܐܩ ܘܐܠܗܗ ܕܐܝܥܩܘܒ܂ "

<u>Senun</u> ܐܝܬܘܗܝ ܐܠܗܐ ܕܡܝ̈ܬܐ ܐܠܐ ܕܚ̈ܝܐ܂

<u>Har</u> " ܐܠܗܐ " " " "

36. *Matthew 24:36* (25r 3-4)

<u>Ph</u> ܠܝܘܡܐ ܗܘ ܘܠܫܥܬܐ ܗܝ܇ ܐܢܫ ܠܐ ܝܕܥ܂

<u>P</u> ܥܠ ܝܘܡܐ " ܘܥܠ ܫܥܬܐ " " " ܂

<u>Ph</u> ܠܐ ܡܠܐܟ̈ܐ ܘܠܐ ܒܪܐ܂

<u>P</u> ܐܦܠܐ " ܕܫܡܝܐ܂

37. *Matthew 26:39* (3r 19-20, 25-26)

Ph ܦܪܩ ܡܢ ܠܘܬܗܘܢ ܘܢܦܠ ܥܠ ܐܦܘܗܝ
P " " ܩܠܝܠ " " "
Sin ܐܙܠ ܩܕܡܝܗܘܢ . " ܢܦܠ " "
Ph ܘܡܨܠܐ ܗܘܐ . . . . . ܐܒܝ ܐܢ ܡܫܟܚܐ
P " ܘܐܡܪ . " " "
Sin " . " " ܗܘܐ (") ܐܢ ܡܫܟܚ
Ph ܢܥܒܪܢܝ ܟܣܐ ܗܢܐ.
P " " " .
Sin ܕܢܥܒܪܝܘܗܝ " " .

38. *Matthew 28:18* (25r 10-11)

Ph ܐܬܝܗܒ ܠܝ ܟܠ ܫܘܠܛܢ ܕܒܫܡܝܐ ܘܒܐܪܥܐ.
P " " " ܒܫܡܝܐ " .

39a. *Luke 1:35* (16r 20-21)[403]

Ph ܪܘܚܐ ܕܩܘܕܫܐ ܬܐܬܐ ܘܚܝܠܗ ܕܥܠܝܐ ܢܓܢ ܥܠܝܟܝ.
P " " ܬܐܬܐ " " " " .

39b. *Luke 1:35* (*Senun*, and *Tractatus*)[404]

Trac ܪܘܚܐ ܕܩܘܕܫܐ ܬܐܬܐ ܥܠܝܟܝ: ܘܚܝܠܗ ܕܡܪܝܡܐ
Sen¹ " ܩܕܝܫܐ " " . " "
Sen² " " " " . " "
Ann " " " " . " "
Har " " " " . " "
Trac ܢܓܢ ܥܠܝܟܝ. ܡܛܠ ܗܢܐ ܗܘ ܕܡܬܝܠܕ ܡܢܟܝ
Sen¹ " . " ܗܘܐ " " "
Sen² " . " ܗܢܐ ܘܐܦ " "
Ann " " . ܘܡܛܠ " "
Har " " . ܡܛܠ ܗܢܐ ܐܦ " "
Trac ܩܕܝܫܐ ܢܬܩܪܐ ܒܪܗ ܕܐܠܗܐ.
Sen¹ " " " " .
Sen² " " " " .
Ann " " " " .
Har " " " " .

40. *Luke 2:19* (15r 7-8)

Ph ܢܛܪܐ ܗܘܬ ܘܡܦܚܡܐ ܟܠܗܝܢ ܡ̈ܠܐ·

P " ܟܠܗܝܢ ܡ̈ܠܐ ܗܠܝܢ: ܘܡܦܚܡܐ ܒܠܒܗ·

41. *Luke 2:52* (15v 16-18)[405]

Ph ܝܫܘܥ ܪܒܐ ܗܘܐ ܒܩܘܡܬܐ ܘܒܚܟܡܬܐ

P " ܕܝܢ " " ܒܩܘܡܬܗ ܘܒܚܟܡܬܗ

Ph ܘܒܛܝܒܘܬܐ ܠܘܬ ܐܠܗܐ ܘܒܢ̈ܝ ܐܢܫܐ·

P " " " " " ·

42. *Luke 3:22c* (33r 6-7)[406]

Ph ܗܘ ܒܪܝ ܚܒܝܒܐ ܕܒܗ ܐܨܛܒܝܬ·

P(Mt.) " " " " " ·

P(Lk.) ܐܢܬ ܗܘ " " ܕܒܟ " ·

Let ܗܘ " ܚܒܝܒܝ·

Sen ܗܢܐ ܐܝܬܘܗܝ, " ܚܒܝܒܐ ܕܒܗ " ·

Har ܐܢܬ ܐܝܬܝܟ ܒܪܐ ܕܝܠܝ ܗܘ ܚܒܝܒܐ ܒܟ " ·

43. *Luke 3:23b* (32v 10-11)[407]

Ph ܘܡܬܬܣܒܪ ܗܘܐ ܕܐܝܬܘܗܝ, ܒܪ ܝܘܣܦ·

P " " " " ·

Har ܕܐܝܬܘܗܝ, ܐܝܟ ܕܡܬܬܣܒܪ ܗܘܐ ܒܪ ܕܝܘܣܦ·

Sin ⌈ܗܘܐ ⌈ܡܬܣܒܪ⌉ ܕܒܪܗ ܗܘ ܕܝܘܣܦ·

44. *Luke 22:42* (3v 3)

Ph ܠܐ ܗܟܝܠ ܨܒܝܢܝ ܕܝܠܝ ܢܗܘܐ ܐܠܐ ܕܝܠܟ·

Cur-Sin ܐܠܐ " " " " " ·

P ܒܪܡ " " ܐܠܐ ܕܝܠܟ ܢܗܘܐ·

45. *Luke 22:43* (3v 11)

Ph ܘܐܬܚܙܝ, ܠܗ ܡܠܐܟܐ ܕܡܚܝܠ ܠܗ·

P " " " ܡܢ ܫܡܝܐ " " ·

Cur-Sin " " " ܡܢ. " ·

46. *John 1:1* (11v 21-24)[408]

ܒܪܫܝܬܐ ܐܝܬܘܗܝ ܗܘܐ ܡܠܬܐ· ܘܗܘ ܡܠܬܐ <u>Ph</u>
ܒܪܫܝܬ ” ” ” . ” ” <u>P</u>
ܒܪܫܐ ” ” ” · ܘܡܠܬܐ <u>Har</u>
ܐܝܬܘܗܝ ܗܘܐ ܠܘܬ ܐܠܗܐ· ܘܐܠܗܐ ܐܝܬܘܗܝ ܗܘܐ <u>Ph</u>
” ” ” ” . ” ” ” <u>P</u>
” ” ” ” · ” ” ” <u>Har</u>
ܗܘ ܡܠܬܐ· <u>Ph</u>
” ” · <u>P</u>
” · <u>Har</u>

47. *John 3:16* (9v 7-9)[409]

ܗܟܢܐ ܐܚܒ ܐܠܗܐ ܠܥܠܡܐ· ܕܠܒܪܗ <u>Ph</u>
” ” ” ” · ܐܝܟܢܐ ܕܠܒܪܐ <u>Sen</u>
” ܓܝܪ ” ” ” · ” ܕܠܒܪܗ <u>P</u>
” ” ” ” ” · ” ܕܠܒܪܐ <u>Har</u>
ܝܚܝܕܝܐ ܝܗܒ ܚܠܦܘܗܝ· <u>Ph</u>
” ܕܝܠܗ ” ” · <u>Sen</u>
” ܢܬܠ· <u>P</u>
ܕܝܠܗܘܗܝ ” ܝܗܒ· <u>Har</u>

48. *John 7:39* (15r 23-25)

ܠܐ ܐܬܝܗܒ ܗܘܐ ܪܘܚܐ ܕܩܘܕܫܐ. <u>Ph</u>
” ܓܝܪ ܥܕܟܝܠ ܐܬܝܗܒܬ ܗܘܬ ” · <u>P</u>
” ܥܕܟܝܠ ܓܝܪ· ܐܝܬܘܗܝ ܗܘܐ ܪܘܚܐ ܩܕܝܫܐ ܝܗܝܒܐ· <u>Har</u>
ܡܛܠ ܕܠܐ ܥܕܟܝܠ ܐܫܬܒܚ ܗܘܐ ܝܫܘܥ· <u>Ph</u>
” ” ” ” ” ” · <u>P</u>
” ܕܝܫܘܥ ܠܐ ” ” ” · <u>Har</u>

49. *John 8:33 (44)* (lv 3-5)

Ph ܡܢ ܕܫܘܪܝܬܐ ܩܛܘܠ ܐܢܫܐ ܗܘܐ܂ ܘܒܫܪܪܐ ܠܐ ܩܡ.
P " ܒܪܫܝܬ " " . " " " .

50a. *John 9:37* (12r 13-14)

Ph ܚܙܝܬܝܗܝ ܘܗܘ ܕܡܡܠܠ ܥܡܟ ܗܘ ܐܝܬܘܗܝ.
Har " " " " " " .

50b. *John 9:37* (*Tractatus*, 45:23-24)[410]

Tra ܚܙܝܬܝܗܝ ܠܒܪܗ ܕܐܠܗܐ܂ ܘܗܘ ܕܡܡܠܠ ܥܡܟ ܗܘܝܘ.
P " " " " "

51. *John 10:17* (3r 5-7)

Ph ܡܛܠ ܗܕܐ ܐܒܝ ܪܚܡ ܠܝ܂ ܕܐܢܐ ܣܐܡ ܐܢܐ
P " ܗܢܐ " " " . " " "
Ph ܢܦܫܝ ܕܬܘܒ ܐܣܒܝܗ̇.
P " " " .

52. *John 10:18* (3r 7-9)[411]

Ph ܫܠܝܛ ܐܢܐ ܕܐܣܝܡܝܗ̇ ܠܢܦܫܝ.
P " " ܓܝܪ " .
Let " " ܠܠ ܢܦܫܝ " .
Ph ܘܫܠܝܛ ܐܢܐ ܕܬܘܒ ܐܣܒܝܗ̇.
P " " " " .
Let " " " " .

53. *John 12:27* (3r 11-14)[412]

Ph ܗܫܐ ܢܦܫܝ ܗܝ ܫܓܝܫܐ܂ ܘܡܢܐ ܐܡܪ ܐܒܐ ܦܨܢܝ
P " " " " . " " ܐܒܝ "
Ph ܡܢ ܗܕܐ ܫܥܬܐ܂ ܐܠܐ ܡܛܠܗܢܐ ܐܬܝܬ ܠܗܕܐ ܫܥܬܐ.
P " " " . " " " " " .

54. *John 15:16 + 17:24 conflated?* (22r 24-25)[413]

ܓܒܝܬܘܢ ܗܘܝܬܘܢ ܠܝ	Ph
ܐܢܐ ܗܘ ܓܒܝܬܟܘܢ	P (Jn. 15:16)
ܡܢ ܩܕܡ ܬܪܡܝܬܗ ܕܥܠܡܐ.	Ph
" " " " .	P (Jn. 17:24)

55. *John 20:25* (12v 26-28)

ܐܠܐ ܚܙܐ ܐܢܐ ܒܐܝܕܘܗܝ ܕܘܟܬܐ ܕܨܨܐ:	Ph
ܐܢ ܠܐ " " " ܠܕܘܟܬܐ " :	Har
ܐܠܐ " " " ܕܢܩܒܬܐ :	P
ܘܪܡܐ ܐܢܐ ܨܒܥܝ ܒܕܘܟܬܐ ܕܨܨܐ:	Ph
" " ܨܒܥܬܐ ܕܝܠܝ " " :	Har
" " ܒܗܘܢ ܨܒܥܬܝ:	P

56. *Acts 2:31* (3r 1-3)

[missing ——— ܥܠ ܩܝܡܬܗ ܕܡܫܝܚܐ.	Ph
ܘܩܕܡ ܚܙܐ ܘܡܠܠ ܥܠ " " .	P
ܕܟܕ ܩܕܡ " ܡܠܠ ܥܠ " " .	Har
ܕܠܐ ܐܫܬܒܩܬ ܢܦܫܗ ܒܫܝܘܠ. ܐܦܠܐ	Ph
" ܐܫܬܒܩ ܒܫܝܘܠ. "	P
" ܐܫܬܒܩܬ " ܢܦܫܗ ܕܝܠܗ. "	Har
ܦܓܪܗ ܚܙܐ ܚܒܠܐ.	Ph
" " " .	P
ܒܣܪܐ ܕܝܠܗ " ܡܚܒܠܢܘܬܐ.	Har

57. *Acts 2:47* (27v 14-15)

ܘܡܪܢ ܗܘܐ ܡܘܣܦ ܗܘܐ ܠܕܚܝܝܢ ܟܠ ܝܘܡ ܒܥܕܬܐ.	Ph
ܡܪ " " " " " .	P

58. *Romans 5:10* (9r 26-27)[414]

ܐܬܬܪܥܝܢܢ ܠܐܠܗܐ ܒܡܘܬܐ ܕܒܪܗ·	<u>Ph</u>
" " ܒܝܕ ܡܘܬܐ " ·	<u>Sen</u>
" " " " ܕܒܪܗ ܕܐܠܗܐ·	<u>Har</u>
ܐܬܪܥܝ ܥܡܢ ܐܠܗܐ ܒܡܘܬܐ ܕܒܪܗ·	<u>P</u>

59. *Romans 6:3-4* (21r 24 - 21v 1)

ܠܐ ܝܕܥܝܢ ܘܓܘ	<u>Ph</u>(v.3)
ܐܘ " " "	<u>P</u> (v.3)
ܐܬܩܒܪܢܢ ܥܡܗ ܘܓܘ	Ph(v.4)
ܐܬܩܒܪܢ " "	P. (v.4)

60. *Romans 8:29* (38r 10-12 and 20-21)

ܘ[ܠܗܘܢ] ܕܩܕܡ ܐܝܕܥ· ܘܩܕܡ ܪܫܡ	<u>Ph</u>
ܡܛܠ ܕܠܗܘܢ " ܝܕܥ· ܐܦ ܩܕܡ ܬܚܡ	<u>Har</u>
ܘܠܗܘܢ ܠܡܩܕܡ " ܝܕܥ· ܘܪܫܡ	<u>P</u>
ܕܢܗܘܘܢ ܒܢܝ ܕܡܘܬܐ ܕܨܠܡܐ ܕܒܪܗ·	<u>Ph</u>
ܫܘܬܦܐ " " ܕܒܪܗ ܕܐܠܗܐ·	<u>Har</u>
ܒܕܡܘܬܐ " ܕܒܪܗ·	<u>P</u>
ܗܘ ܢܗܘܐ ܒܘܟܪܐ ܕܐܚܐ ܣܓܝܐܐ·	<u>Ph</u>
ܠܡ ܕܢܗܘܐ ܗܘܝܘ ܒܘܟܪܐ " ܒܣܓܝܐܐ ܐܚܐ·	<u>Har</u>
ܕܗܘ ܢܗܘܐ " ܕܐܚܐ ܣܓܝܐܐ·	<u>P</u>

61. *1 Corinthians 1:24* (16r 17)[415]

ܡܫܝܚܐ ܚܝܠܗ ܗܘ ܕܐܠܗܐ ܘܚܟܡܬܗ·	<u>Ph</u>¹
" " " " .	<u>Ph</u>²
" ܐܝܬܘܗܝ ܚܝܠܗ " ܕܐܠܗܐ·	<u>Ph</u>³
ܚܝܠܐ ܘܚܟܡܬܐ "	<u>Ph</u>⁴
" " ܕܐܠܗܐ " " .	<u>P</u>
" " " " " .	<u>Har</u>

62. *1 Corinthians 1:25* (16r 1-3)[416]

Ph1	ܡܣܟܠܘܬܗ ܕܐܠܗܐ ܚܟܝܡܐ ܗܝ ܡܢ ܒܢܝܢܫܐ.
P2	ܘܫܛܝܘܬܗ " " " " " .
Har2	ܗܘ ܗܝ ܕܣܟܠܐ " ܕܒܢܝ " " ܐܢܫܘܬܐ.
Ph2	ܘܫܛܝܘܬܗ ܚܟܝܡܐ ܗܝ ܡܢ ܒܢܝܢܫܐ.
P1	" ܕܐܠܗܐ " " " " .
Har1	ܗܝ ܕܐܠܗ̈ܐ " ܕܒܢܝ " " " ܐܢܫܘܬܐ.

63. *Ephesians 1:4* (22r 22-23)

Ph	ܩܕܡ ܓܒܢ ܒܗ ܡܢ ܩܕܡ ܬܪܡܝܬܗ ܕܥܠܡܐ.
P	" ܓܒܢ " " " " " .

64. *Colossians 2:12* (21r 21-23)

Ph	ܐܬܩܒܪܬܘܢ ܥܡܗ ܒܡܥܡܘܕܝܬܐ ܠܡܝܬܘܬܐ.
P	" " " .
Ph	ܘܒܗ ܩܡܬܘܢ ܥܡܗ.
P	" " " .

65. *Hebrews 2:13* (38r 3-4)

Ph	ܗܐ ܐܢܐ ܘܒܢܝܐ ܕܝܗܒܬ ܠܝ.
P	" " " ܕܝܗܒ " ܐܠܗܐ.

66. *Hebrews 2:14* (6r 7-9)[417]

Ph	ܐܝܟ ܒܢܝܐ ܐܫܬܘܬܦ ܠܒܣܪܐ ܘܠܕܡܐ.
P	ܡܛܠ ܕܝܢ ܕܒܢܝܐ ܐܫܬܘܬܦܘ ܒܒܣܪܐ ܘܒܕܡܐ.
Tra	" " " ܠܕܡܐ ܘܠܒܣܪܐ.
Har	" ܗܟܢ " " " " .

67. *Hebrews 11:10* (2v 9-11)[418]

Ph ܡܣܟܐ ܗܘܐ ܠܡܕܝܢܬܐ ܕܐܫܬܐܣܬܐ ܐܝܬ ܠܗ̇
P ܡܣܟܐ ܗܘܐ ܓܝܪ " " "
Ph ܠܗ̇. ܕܐܪܕܝܟܠܗ̇ ܘܥܒܘܕܗ̇ ܐܠܗܐ ܗܘ.
P " . " " " " .

68. *1 John 4:3* (4r 9-12)[419]

Ph ܟܠ ܪܘܚܐ ܐܝܕܐ ܕܠܐ ܡܘܕܝܐ ܕܝܫܘܥ ܐܬܐ ܒܒܣܪ.
P " " " " " " "
Ph ܠܐ ܐܝܬܝܗ̇ ܡܢ ܐܠܗܐ ܐܠܐ ܡܢ ܡܫܝܚܐ ܕܓܠܐ.
P ܠܝܬܝܗ̇ " " " ܗܕܐ " " ܗ̇ܝ "

3. *Comments on These Variant Quotations*

1. The use of ܠܘܬ in P is a slavish imitation of Heb. Ph's use of the preposition lamadh is idiomatically correct, and the fact that Philoxenus has exactly the same wording in another work indicates his settled preference for this version. It may also reflect the influence of LXX.
2. Ph's use of ܕ to introduce a direct quotation and the alternative spelling of ܐܪܕܝܟܠܐ are not significant variants in themselves. The quotation is from P.
3. This is one of a series of phrases taken from Genesis 1 and hurriedly quoted one after the other for rhetorical effect. Although marked as a quotation along with the others, there is no textual or versional warrant for it. It is simply a misquotation.
4. In his use of the noun ܢܗܪܐ, Ph is closer to Heb than to P or LXX. The variant spelling ܐܪܕܝܟܠܐ is not significant.
5. Ph = P except for the reversing of the word-order of ܪܚܫܐ ܘܚܝܘܬܐ (P). It is probably conditioned by the word-order of the next verse (Genesis 1:25).
6. P follows Heb exactly in the use of pronominal suffixes, while Ph in his variant suffixes agrees with some MSS of LXX, but the oldest LXX witnesses have no pronoun with the

first two instances of γενος.

7. Ph's addition of ܕ and ܘ are his stylistic preference but otherwise they are not significant variants. Ph's variant conforms to LXX (κατ' εἰκόνα ἡμετέραν).
8. Ph's preference for ܓܒܠ over ܒܪܐ in 8a is complete in 8b. A comparison of the variations in this quotation in Ph with Heb and versions shows that Philoxenus was acquainted with P and LXX (or some version like Pal derived from LXX).
9. Ph's omission of ܥܦܪܐ, and his use of ܐܢܫܐ (=ἄνθρωπος) and ܐܪܥܐ (=γῆ) indicate dependence on LXX. His phrase ܐܢܫܐ ܕܚܝܐ, used in two contexts, may be his way of condensing the verse for he omits the last clause, "man became a living soul." There is no reason why he should omit ܥܦܪܐ in reference to man's origin, for in 14v 9, 11 and 33v 5 he uses it in that context.
10. Philoxenus provides us with another variant of the text in *Tractatus*, p. 235, which is closer to P than Ph is. Like Ph, *Tractatus* prefers ܬܗܪܐ (=ἔστασις of LXX) to ܫܢܬܐ (=תרדמה of Heb), and the addition of Lamadh to ܫܢܬܐ. Ph and Pal have ܢܣܒ for ܐܚܕ in P and ܒܣܪܐ for ܚܠܦ in P. Both these preferences in Ph are derived from LXX or a version (like Pal) more closely related to it than P. The variants in *Tractatus* and Ph suggest that as Philoxenus grew older he increasingly preferred LXX to P, though much more evidence is needed to substantiate such a suggestion. But it is certainly in keeping with his conviction that a new translation of the scriptures into Syriac was needed.
11. Ph depends on LXX in its modification of Heb (≡ P), except that Ph retains the nominal subject ܐܠܗܐ for ܡܪܝܐ ܐܠܗܐ of P (= Heb) and pronominal object of P (= Heb) in the first clause. Pal (not exhibited) = LXX except for the last word where ܒܢܝ is used. The author is clearly acquainted with P but prefers a translation from LXX.
12. Ph's dependence on LXX is underscored by Hex which renders ἐκδικούμενα of LXX more literally than Ph. The first clause in Ph and Hex, however, is closer to Heb than to LXX. While P on the whole follows Heb, in that same first clause P = LXX.

13. Ph = LXX (= Hex).
14. The insertion of ܗܟܝ in Ph is stylistically necessary and not significant for textual criticism; so also regarding the omission in Ph of ܢܦܫܝ. By omitting ܫܒܥܐ before ܡ̈ܢܝܬܐ, Ph shows itself to be closer to LXX than even Hex which follows P and Heb at this point.
15. In the first three words Ph = P, but in the use of ܐܬܬܒܥ it shows independence of P. In the second clause, ܠܡܟ ܘܥ̄ܙ Ph = LXX in the use of ܕܝܢ (=δέ) and in the number expressed (= Hex). The use of ܠ (as in Ph here) to express the multiplication of numbers (i.e., = "times") is apparently older than the use of ܥܦ̈ܝܦ or ܒܥܦܝܦܘܬܐ (as in Hex).[420]
16. Comment on this quotation must be tempered by the fact that Ph does not mark it as a quotation in any way. For this reason, the first two words must be discounted as belonging to Ph's style. The use of ܦܩܕ marks the influence of LXX.
17. Ph is acquainted with P in the first word and especially in the use of the indeterminate phrase ܕܒܪ ܘܢܩܒܐ. In 34v 14, Ph reverts also to ܕܡܘܬܗ of P in place of ܨܠܡ in 33v 25. Otherwise, Ph reflects LXX.
18. Ph = P except that the participle ܐܫܕ (replacing the imperfect ܢܐܫܘܕ of P) corresponds to the LXX participle ἐκχέων.
19. Ph = P except for omission of ܗܐ (twice) and the addition of ܕ (twice), which is nothing more than a matter of style, although we note that the second ܗܐ = ἰδού is omitted from LXX.
20. The phrase [illegible] in Ph is based on LXX. The variant ܐܬܗܦܟ has no textual or versional warrant, and may simply appear in this context because the author wished to vary the vocabulary. ܐܫܬܢܝ (in P and Hex) is used two lines down (27v 13).
21. Although this is a conflation of part of Exodus 4:23 with a phrase (in brackets) from 4:22, it is clear that Ph used P with the addition of ܠܝ for which there is no apparent precedent.
22. Ph = P, except for the phrase ܪܡܐ ܒܪܘܡܐ (cf. ܒܪܘܡܐ in P) which echoes Isaiah 6:1 (P) cited in the same context (5r 27).

23. Ph = P, except that Ph used ܐܠܗ̈ܐ for ܐܠܗܝܢ, and curiously adds ܚܕ ܡܢ. In the second stichos of Ps. 82:7, the phrase ܚܕ ܡܢ ܪ̈ܘܪܒܢܐ occurs, and it is likely that the insertion of these two words in Ph was conditioned by the author's memory of the whole verse. In *Inhabitation*, p. 56, the two verses (Ps. 82:6-7) are correctly quoted in full from P, but with the same spelling ܐܠܗ̈ܐ as in Ph.
24. Ph = Heb where Ph differs from P. Hex (= LXX) has not been exhibited here because it is not close to Ph.
25. Ph = P except that he substitutes ܚܘܒܐ for ܘܠܡܚܒܐ. This substitution may have been based on an understanding of LXX, though Hex (retaining the infinitive) does not make it, but is more likely in this context of Ph to be tendentious, for it suits Philoxenus' argument.
26. Ph = P. ܟܠܟ in Ph is a misspelling for ܟܠܟ (cf. 8v 11 where it is spelt correctly). The variant ܗܠܟ is stylistic and inconsequential. LXX and Hex are obviously different from Ph and have not been exhibited.
27. Ph = P with a change in the position of ܪܓܠܐ and the omission of ܗܘ (twice).
28. Although Ph is badly damaged, it contains four significant modifications of P while basically adhering to it: the omission of ܠܡܫܒܪܗ (it is impossible to fit this word into the lacuna where one would expect it), the addition of ܒܟܠ ܗܕܐ, the addition of ܒܪ ܢܫܐ, and the substitution of the verb ܢܐܬܪ (Ph) for the noun ܬܘܪܐ (P). All these modifications to P have been made on the basis of readings found in LXX which Philoxenus (or a Syriac version he used) adopted.
29. The omission of ܠܠܠܐ and changing of the feminine participle ܐܬܝܐ (P) to masculine thus making ܪܘܚܐ refer to the Holy Spirit, is tendentious and has no textual or versional warrant. Otherwise Ph = P (the omission of ܕ is insignificant).
30. Ph = P, except for the first two words which repeat the first two words of the preceding citation from Ezekiel 1:4.
31. Ph = P, except for the first word ܚܙܐ which the author has used to introduce all six examples of biblical visions in 5r 23 - 5v 9, with or without scriptural warrant.

32. Ph alters the word-order of the first clause, placing the first three words of P after the verb and its subject. He transposes ܒܣܪܐ from the second half of the verse in P replacing ܒܐܠܐ with it and making the last eliptical. The same wording for the first half of the verse in Ph is found in the *Discourses*. In spite of these changes, Ph depends on P.
33. As in the preceding text from Wisdom, Ph here does not slavishly adhere to P, though he obviously depends on it. The omission of ܕܝܢ in Ph is merely stylistic.
34. As Vööbus has pointed out and our exhibit shows, Ph uses an older Syriac idiom to express multiplication involving ܒܠ = the later use of ܐܥ̈ܦܝܢ in P (and also in Har). Vööbus contends that this quotation in Ph is a fragment of an old Syriac Gospel text type used by Tatian in creating the Diatessaron.[421] Ph's use of ܒܠܚܘܕ is not in any of the versions, and is probably stylistic.
35. Ph and *Senun* twice omit the repetitious ܐܠܗܐ, but apart from that they part company. Ph follows P, while *Senun* is closer to Har. The addition of the last clause in Ph is more than the author's whim in conflating Matthew 22:32 and Luke 20:37-38; it, in fact, reflects exactly the wording of the Diatessaron (34:20-21).[422] The remarkable difference between Ph and *Senun* is explained by the fact that Ph was copied in A.D. 511 as its colophon states, *Senun* was written ten years later,[423] and in the meantime (we submit) Philoxenus had been slowly accustoming himself to the new translation of the New Testament which he sponsored and which was published by his chorepiscopus, Polycarp, in 508. *Senun* quotes in a somewhat condensed fashion from the Philoxenian version of Matthew 22:32. Exhibit 35b illustrates the kind of revision of the Philoxenian version Har is, especially in the spelling of names where Har slavishly and barbarically follows the Greek.
36. All Syriac versions except Pal omit the last clause of Ph. It is also omitted in some Greek MSS. In the Syriac versions of Mark 13:32 it is included, but it is unlikely that Philoxenus had the Markan version in mind here. His use of the preposition lamadh in place of ܥܠ used in the

other Syriac versions may preserve the use of an Old Syriac version now lost. The omission of ܕܫܡܝܐ in Ph is another example of his tendency to eliminate repetition in a text he is quoting.

37. Except for the addition of ܡܢ ܠܘܬܗܘܢ and the omission of ܟܠܗ, both in the first clause, Ph = P. The omission can be ascribed to the author's tendency to abbreviate quotations, but the addition is not so readily explained. Sin was included in the exhibit because the ܟܠܗܘܢ in the first clause is similar to Ph. That first clause in Sin corresponds to Diatessaron 48:7. In this light, we may have in Ph here another quotation from the Old Syriac Diatessaron.[424]

38. Ph = P, except for the addition of ܕ to ܒܫܡܝܐ. This addition occurs also in Eph who wrote a commentary on the Diatessaron. Vööbus cites several Syriac patristic sources where this same reading occurs, and adds to the evidence he has accumulated for an Old Syriac Gospel tradition distinct from Sin and Cur and reflected in the now lost Syriac Diatessaron.[425]

39. Ph = P, except for the change to the masculine form which is in keeping with Philoxenus' tendency to treat ܪܘܚܐ as masculine if it refers in any way to the Holy Spirit.[426] This masculinization of ܪܘܚܐ, upon which our author insisted, must have been a feature of his version as it was of the Harklean. Philoxenus uses P also in quoting part of the verse in his "Letters to the Monks of Beth Gaugal" and in his "Ten Discourses on How One of the Trinity Became Incarnate." De Halleux, on other grounds, gives both these works an early date in the career of our author (c. 484), and the evidence of this quotation adds some weight to that conclusion.[427] This suggests that while the manuscript before us was copied in 511, it was originally composed earlier than that date.

On the other hand, *Tractatus* and *Senun* were written after the publication of the Philoxenian version in 508 as de Halleux has shown, *Senun* being perhaps the last work to be written by our author.[428] These quote from the Philoxenian version as Exhibit 39b makes clear. We note that the earlier work (*Tractatus*) still retains the older expression for Holy Spirit, while *Senun* has adopted the newer one.[429] In Ph, the older expression is the rule throughout the manuscript except for two occurrences of ܪܘܚܐ ܩܕܝܫܐ in Fragment 3, which (as we have already shown) does not belong to the manuscript.[430] On the basis of such an abundance of evidence, we must conclude that Philoxenus deliberately changed from one expression to the other to conform to his (or rather, Polycarp's) new Syriac version of 508. It was not Thomas of Harkel who first rendered πνεῦμα ἅγιον as ܪܘܚܐ ܩܕܝܫܐ (as Zuntz thought); it was Polycarp a century earlier.[431]

We have also exhibited this quotation as it is found in Philoxenus' sermon on the Annunciation, here symbolized as *Ann* (Luke 1:26-35). Because of the obvious development in the citing of Luke 1:35, we conclude that *Ann* was written late in our author's life, perhaps just before he was taken into exile in 519, and certainly not long before he wrote *Senun* in 521. We see in this exhibit that the addition of ܒܠܚܡ after ܘܐܡܪ and the change from ܠܠܗܐ to ܡܪܝܡܐ were also Polycarp's.[432] We conclude that the Philoxenian version of Luke 1:35 is quoted correctly in *Ann*. The variant ܗܕܐ in Sen[1] is scribal, being influenced by the later Har tradition, which tradition also caused the scribe to insert ܘܐܦ in Sen.[2] The only change which Har made to the Philoxenian of this verse was that of substituting ܐܦ for ܘ, corresponding to the postpositive use of καὶ in the Greek. A corollary to our conclusion is that the whole passage in *Ann* which quotes most of Luke 1:28-35 is taken from the Philoxenian version.[433] Evidence in *Tractatus* and *Senun* bears this out.[434]

40. Ph is a condensed form of P.
41. Ph = P, but with the omission of ܕܝܢ and 3 m.s. pronominal suffix (twice). The latter omission occurs also in Pal and (apparently) in the Diatessaron.[435] All Syriac versions (and the Diatessaron) follow the order of P, except Har which follows the Greek order (i.e., "in wisdom, and stature, and favour, etc.").

42. Ph cites Luke as his source (33r 5), yet his quotation = P of Matthew 3:17 ("P [Mt.]"). The use of 3rd m.s. in Luke 3:22 is found in one 14th century Greek MS (1574), and one Bohairic MS, as well as in the Diatessaron and the Acts of Pilate.[436] It may be that Philoxenus had the Syriac Diatessaron in mind as we have noted in other citations. In one of his early letters (Let), he uses ܨܒܝܬ which is used by Cur and Sin both in Matthew 3:17 and Luke 3:22.[437] The Ph wording is repeated exactly in *Senun* 7:12-13, but in the previous page (6:17-18) we have the wording exhibited as Sen which uses ܐܝܬ (plus a suffix) in the same way that Har does (though without the latter's verbosity). Once again, we have an example of Philoxenus attempting to adapt himself in his final years to the wording of the version he sponsored, but lapsing back into the old familiar phraseology. Nevertheless, we see that the extensive use of ܐܝܬ as a copula in Har was a feature of the Philoxenian version before it.

43. Ph's modification of P by the phrase ܕܐܝܬܘܗܝ seems to reflect the Philoxenian version; but, while that phrase is included, Har's wording is quite different. The more likely model is Sin (cf. also Pal Codex B) which then suggests an old Syriac source.

44. Ph's use of ܡܟܝܠ is unique here and may belong to his style.[438] The rest of the quotation follows Cur-Sin rather than P, as Vööbus has already pointed out, providing another fragment of evidence for an Old Syriac version.[439] Har, though verbose, follows P and is not exhibited here.

45. Ph is closest to Cur-Sin in omitting ܡܢ ܫܘܪܝܐ. On the other hand, Har (not exhibited) follows P, but qualifies ܡܠܬܐ as follows: ܡܠܬܐ ܕܐܝܬܝܗ ܡܢ ܫܘܪܝܐ.

46. Ph quotes the whole of John 1:1 and only the first word varies in spelling from that of P. This variant occurs also in the *Book on Selected Passages from the Gospels*. In other places Philoxenus quotes exactly from P; i.e., *Letters* = *Tractatus* = *Senun* = P. In other contexts in Ph, he makes use of the indeterminate ܒܪܫܝܬ.[440] It is significant that this anomalous spelling is found in two of the "orphan" fragments which (as suggested in Comment 39

above) are probably from a later work (or works) than Ph.[441] The fact that the same form is found in the *Book on Selected Passages* suggests some sort of affinity with that work, and it certainly indicates that the variant is no accident. The fact that Har begins with ܒܪܫܐ lends support to the proposal that in the Philoxenian version ܒܪܫܝܬܐ was the first word of John's Gospel. More evidence is needed, however, before we can maintain that with any assurance, especially since ܒܪܫܝܬ alone is found in *Tractatus* and *Senun*.

47. We have found that this verse is cited six times in Philoxenus' works (including Ph). Only *Letters*, p. 137 = Ph exactly. The omission of ܐܠܗܐ in these two is due to the author's tendency to condense his quotations. One of the three citations in *Tractatus* (215:16-17) uses ܢܬܠ of P, while the others use ܢܗܒ of Cur-Sin. Only *Senun* has ܕܝܠܗ = Har, though in a different position. All six add ܚܠܦܘܗܝ This last phenomenon is well attested in Syriac literature, and as Vööbus has pointed out, belongs to "an Old Syriac reading, and a popular one" at that.[442] From the evidence before us, it is difficult not to conclude that ܚܠܦܘܗܝ was carried into the Philoxenian version, but dropped from Har because there was no Greek warrant for it. Because of the developing pattern of Gospel citations in the works of Philoxenus which we have been noting (namely, that he used P and Old Syriac versions in his works prior to the publication of his version in 508 and after that he slowly began to incorporate the new translation into his writings), and because *Senun* is particularly close to Har, we submit that Sen = Philoxenian version of John 3:16a.

48. Ph basically follows P. The omission of ܓܝܪ is stylistic and insignificant, and the omission of the first ܕܒܒܠ is due to Ph's abbreviating tendency. The change to the masculine construction for ܪܘܚܐ has already been noted as a feature of Philoxenus' works as it was of his version reflected in Har. The qualifying ܕܩܘܕܫܐ in Ph (≡ Har) is well attested in many Greek MSS, πνεῦμα ἅγιον, as in Pal, though the older Greek tradition omits the qualifier as do P and Cur-Sin. We can be sure it

was included in the Philoxenian version.

49. Ph = P except for ܪܓܫܬܐ-- a preference in Ph (as already noted in Comment 46) which was no doubt carried into the Philoxenian version (rendered ܡܢ ܓܘܪܝܐ in Har).

50. Ph = Har = Philoxenian version. Significantly, this quotation is found in "orphan" Fragment 4 and its use of the new Syriac version indicates that it was written later than Ph. It also appears to be later than *Tractatus* which = P except for the addition of ܠܒܪܐ ܐܠܗܐ in both citations. This addition in *Tractatus* may simply be the author's way of recalling the wider context of this statement, for the phrase is used in John 9:35 of the Syriac versions.

51. Ph = P except for the change in gender in the demonstrative pronoun ܗܢܐ – ܗܕܐ.

52. Ph ≡ P with the addition of ܠܢܦܫ. Vööbus sees this addition as evidence of the lost Old Syriac version.[443] This may well be the case, but we should not rule out the possibility of the author's device for recalling the context of his quotation by repeating an antecedent to bring out the full meaning intended. The use of ܠ in the *Letters* quotation to modify it is especially relevant here ("I have power *with respect to* my soul to lay it down"), and may indicate a similar explicative use of the preposition lamadh in Ph and *Senun*. However, the fact that ܢܦܫܐ is repeated in Ph and elsewhere favours Vööbus's conclusion. This addition is not attested in the Greek text or the versions.

53. Ph's single variant ܐܒܐ = Greek = Sin = Pal. Har follows P in using ܐܒܝ. Ph agrees with the more ancient tradition.

54. In the mind of Philoxenus, this is a dominical saying of the first order as the context in Ph makes clear ("Jesus said to His disciples . . . ."), and as its appearance three times in *Tractatus* in exactly the same form underscores that fact. Yet it is not to be found in the New Testament, although there are sayings like it. Although it is most like Ephesians 1:4, it is quite distinct from it, for that verse is cited along with it.[444]

It is placed here with John 15:16 and 17:24, with which it has some affinity, but it is obviously quite distinct from both. Did it belong to an Old Syriac Gospel tradition now lost? We may suggest it, but there is nothing to substantiate such a suggestion. It remains an enigma.

55. Once again, it is an "orphan" fragment that provides us with part of a verse from the Philoxenian version. ܠܪܚܡܐ had to be written over an erasure as though the writer had written ܪܚܡܬܐ out of his familiarity with P and then changed it to conform to the new version.[445] The use of lamadh to mark the accusative is a characteristic of Har, but the possessive particle in place of a suffix seems to have belonged to the Philoxenian version. We note also that ܐܠܐ is expanded to ܐܢ ܠܐ corresponding to the two words of the Greek, ἐὰν μὴ.

56. Ph follows P with the addition of ܢܦܫܐ and consequent change in the gender of the verb. The addition (found in Har) must have been included in the Philoxenian, but whether ܒܣܪܐ (Har and Pal) replaced ܦܓܪܐ (P and Ph) is not known.

57. Ph = P. The addition of ܗܘܘ ܫܠܝܚܐ recalls the subject from the biblical context and adjusts the tense to the context of Ph.

58. Ph is closer to Har than to P. *Senun* and *Tractatus* provide us with another clause from the Philoxenian, as the exhibit makes clear.[446] The fact that *Letters* quotes P exactly demonstrates once again that in the earlier writings Philoxenus used P, while the evidence before us reveals how he adapted himself to the new version after 508.

59. Ph = P. Ph quotes both verses in full and only one word deviates from P: the first word of verse 4 is 3 m.pl. rather than 1 pl. because the writer was influenced by the 2 m.pl. of the same verb correctly quoted from Colossians 2:12 (21r 21-23) immediately before the present quotation. He also seems to prefer the more direct and forceful "you" to the less forceful "us" as his quotation from Ephesians 1:4 shows (Exhibit 63).

60. While in the second part of this verse (quoted in 38r 20-21) Ph = P, in the first part (38r 10-12) Ph is closer

to Har: the phrasing of the opening clause is essentially the same and both show dissatisfaction with P's rendering of συμμόρφους by ܒܕܡܘܬܐ. It appears that Har was also dissatisfied with the Syriac idiom ܒܢ̈ܝ ܕܡܘܬܐ of Ph (which we suggest belonged to the Philoxenian) and changed it to the more technically correct phrase ܫܘ̈ܝ ܕܡܘܬܐ where ܫܘ̈ܝ ≡ συν-. This is another example of the distinction between Har and the Philoxenian. The former revised the latter in the following ways: (1) by the addition of lamadh to mark the accusative (ܠܗܘܢ), (2) by changing ܘ to ܐܦ where καί seems to be enclitic, (3) by preferring a "literal" (i.e., word for word) translation as noted above in the case of ܫܘ̈ܝ = συν-, (4) by substituting the possessive particle (here ܕܝܠܗ) for the possessive suffix, and (5) by adhering rigidly to the Greek word-order (ܒܣܓܝ̈ܐܐ ܐܚ̈ܐ = ἐν πολλοῖς ἀδελφοῖς). The Philoxenian version was much more idiomatic.

61. In all four examples Ph abbreviates in accordance with his style. The copulas added in Ph[1] and Ph[3] are also part of our author's style. The 3 m.s. suffix is grammatically necessary in the first three examples but unnecessary in Ph[4] where ܕܐܠܗܐ comes at the end of the phrase. Since Har = P, we can assume that the Philoxenian = P.

62. Ph = P, except for the first word of Ph which probably reflects the Philoxenian since Har uses the cognate -- ܡܫܠܡܘܬܐ (Ph) = ܡܫܠܡܐ. All the other additions of Har are markedly Harklean. Apart from the reversing of the two clauses peculiar to Ph (probably due to a lapse in the author's memory), we suggest that the text as here quoted belongs to the Philoxenian version.

63. Ph ≡ P, but substitutes the 2 m.pl. suffix for the 1 pl. of the Greek and P (= Har). It may be a misreading of the Greek (for ἡμᾶς he [or his source] read ὑμᾶς); or he may have preferred the more direct and forceful "you" as he did in Romans 6:4 (Exhibit 59); or he may have been influenced by the unidentified dominical saying exhibited above (54) which he cites immediately after this quotation.

64. Ph ≡ P except for the addition of ܠܡܘܬܐ which is obviously taken from Romans 6:4 quoted immediately after

this quotation.

65. Ph ≡ P except for the change in the verb from 3 m.s. to 2 m.s. and the consequent dropping of the subject ܐܠܗܐ. The author seems to be quoting from memory as there is no other warrant for this change.
66. Ph has very neatly reduced the first two clauses of Hebrews 2:14 to one by using ܐܝܟ and changing the verb from 3 m. pl. to 3 m.s. Ph's order of the last two words = P's order, but lamadh replaces beth as it does in *Tractatus* and Har. In one of the three places in *Tractatus* where this verse is quoted, the order of the last two words = Ph = P (*Tractatus*, 237:4-5). In the other two places, their order = that of Har (= that of Greek). While the quotation is allusive in *Dissertatione* (an early work), it alone follows P exactly in quoting the last two words: ܒܒܣܪܐ ܘܕܡܐ. This exhibit conforms to the pattern of development our study has now established, and we can say with some confidence that "Tra" is based on the Philoxenian version.
67. Ph = P. The change from 3 m.s. to 3 m. pl. in the participle and auxiliary is conditioned by the context of Ph.
68. Ph follows P but adds ܐܢܐ (*Tractatus* does not add it), omits ܗܢܐ and ܗܝ, and spells out P's ܠܘܬܗ. The addition of ܐܢܐ may be from the Philoxenian since *Tractatus* (an earlier work) does not have it.

B. *RESULTS OF THIS ANALYSIS*

The preceding analysis identifies one hundred and eight separate quotations from the Bible in the fourteen fragments of our manuscript. This number does not include any repetitions of the same biblical sentence or phrase, but such repetitions have always been noted along with the single reference. Only by isolating these quotations and examining them individually can we hope to discover their nature in relation to the texts and versions and in the process learn what Philoxenus' habits were in citing the Bible.

One thing is clear: Philoxenus quotes from the Bible carefully and accurately and when there is any deviation from known versions the reason is almost always an obvious one.

His high view of the Scriptures would lead us to believe it,[447] and the evidence before us confirms it. That evidence includes the following facts: (1) forty of the one hundred and eight quote the Peshitta verbatim,[448] (2) another twenty-six vary only slightly from the Peshitta but still reflect careful citation,[449] and (3) another fourteen (while differing significantly from the Peshitta) are repeated in whole or in part in this manuscript or in some other Philoxenian work with exactly the same wording as is found in the Exhibits.[450] Thus, Philoxenus' care in quoting from the Bible is well attested in seventy-four percent of all the quotations in the manuscript before us. We may assume that he exercised the same care in citing the Bible throughout, unless the evidence in particular instances is to the contrary.[451] This is borne out even by a cursory examination of the quotations in the other works of our author. Budge's assessment in this regard (quoted at the beginning of this chapter) is simply not adequate: every one of Philoxenus' quotations is not only of interest, but their wording must be taken as seriously as he took it.

An examination of his quotations from the Old Testament reveals certain patterns. Of the forty-three verses (or parts of verses) quoted from the Old Testament twenty-nine are from Genesis, five from Isaiah, two from Wisdom, and one each from Exodus, 1 Kings, Psalms, Jeremiah, Ezekiel, Daniel, and Amos. Our analysis shows that the Peshitta was consistently the source of the quotations from all these books except Genesis and Isaiah. Since the Peshitta books cited are represented only by a single quotation from each (except Wisdom which has two), such scant evidence can only suggest a pattern of dependence on the Peshitta Old Testament that requires more information before it can be established.[452]

The distribution of quotations from Genesis and Isaiah is of more than passing interest. In Genesis, twelve are from the Peshitta,[453] thirteen are based on the Septuagint,[454] one falls between the two,[455] one may be based on the Hebrew or the Septuagint,[456] one is clearly based on the Hebrew,[457] and one is a misquotation.[458] In Isaiah, three are from the Peshitta,[459] one from the Septuagint,[460] and one reflects the Hebrew.[461]

Such a high proportion of readings which are independent of the Peshitta suggests either that Philoxenus had a Syriac version of the Old Testament (or at least of Genesis and Isaiah) now lost, or that he himself had access to the Hebrew text and Greek version. In favour of the first alternative, we have the claim of Eli of Qartamin that the Philoxenian version included the Old as well as the New Testament,[462] and the statement in the Milanese manuscript of the Syro-Hexaplar that an alternate reading of Isaiah 9:6 is from "the version that was translated by the care of the holy Philoxenus."[463] Moreover, the pattern of translation seen in these quotations is similar to that found in the New Testament quotations, which stands between the Peshitta and the Harklean version. However, no ancient writer (as far as we can tell) has ever suggested that Paul of Tella had a Philoxenian Old Testament before him when he produced his version. The fact that several of the "Septuagint" quotations are repeated in exactly the same form favours the existence of a Syriac version available for Philoxenus which was distinct from the Peshitta.[464]

The second alternative (that Philoxenus had access to the Hebrew and Greek Old Testament) must also be taken seriously. To assert this is to run counter to the consensus of scholarly opinion which, since Lebon published his *Monophysitisme Sévérien* in 1909, has assumed that Philoxenus did not know Greek.[465] De Halleux cites the confusion between γένεσις and γέννησις in British Mus. Add. 14,534 as further proof of this assumed ignorance, but the confusion may have been the scribe's and not Philoxenus'.[466] That our author was aware of the distinction is surely an indication that he knew some Greek. Moreover, his concern for a new translation was born of his desire for a more accurate rendering of the text into Syriac than any translation then currently in use.[467] That concern is more understandable if he himself knew the Greek text than if he was ignorant of it. Indeed, it is difficult to imagine how a man of Philoxenus' nature and influence could have remained ignorant of Greek while maintaining close contact with the Greek-speaking world of the Eastern Empire and with its emperors and prelates. And it must not be forgotten that he received his early training in the

Persian School of Edessa which, in Philoxenus' youth, was a centre for translating Greek works into Syriac.

While Philoxenus' knowledge of Greek has been open to doubt, his knowledge of Hebrew has never been suggested; nor do we have enough evidence to support such a suggestion. Nowhere in his extant writings does he appeal to the Hebrew text of the Old Testament in any way. From his use of Wisdom in this manuscript and of some of the other apocryphal books elsewhere in his writings, it is clear that he accepted the canon of the Greek Old Testament,[468] and we have every reason to believe that he regarded the Greek version as normative.[469] The apparent affinities which Exhibits 4 and 24 have with the Hebrew text must be explained on the basis of a Greek or Syriac version available to him which was closer to the Hebrew of these exhibited quotations than existing versions are. But the evidence of our manuscript is simply not sufficient to be conclusive.[470] In citing the Old Testament, Philoxenus may have had the Peshitta and a Greek version before him, or he may have used some unknown (and now lost) Syriac version which stood between the Peshitta and the Syro-Hexaplaric version produced by Paul of Tella a century later.

The analysis of the sixty-five New Testament quotations shows that thirty are exactly the same as the Peshitta and ten are very close to it,[471] one (cited as a dominical saying) has no New Testament warrant for the form in which it is quoted,[472] and the remaining twenty-four provide significant patterns of variants which bear witness to two lost Syriac versions: the Old Syriac and the Philoxenian. Professor Vööbus has done the pioneer work in identifying the existence of an Old Syriac version of the Gospels close to, but distinct from, that of the Curetonian and the Sinaitic.[473] Some nine of the twenty-two quotations from the Gospels in this manuscript support Vööbus's findings,[474] four of them having been already identified by him as belonging to an Old Syriac Gospel-text.[475] It may well be that this was the version to which Philoxenus was first exposed and its phrasing remained with him throughout his life. To this Old Syriac version may have belonged the unidentified dominical saying of Exhibit 54.

The comparative analysis of New Testament texts in our

manuscript and their relation to similar texts in other works by Philoxenus (as well as to the Harklean version) has brought the nature of the Philoxenian version into focus. Some sixteen different quotations are involved.[476] The features of that version published in A.D. 508 may be summarized as follows:

1) It was a version quite distinct from the Harklean produced a century later. What Thomas of Harkel meant in his colophon was that he revised the translation made under the patronage and supervision of Philoxenus a century earlier,[477] which is precisely what Bar Hebraeus believed.[478] What Zuntz concluded from his study of quotations in *Tractatus* is borne out by the above analysis; viz., "Behind these Philoxenian citations there lies a definite text, different from, and intermediate between, the Peshitta and the Harklean."[479]

2) Its New Testament canon was coterminous with that of the Peshitta; that is, it did *not* include 2 Peter, 2 and 3 John, Jude, and Revelation. There is no evidence to show that Philoxenus ever regarded these five books as canonical.[480]

3) It was a revision of the Peshitta rather than a completely new translation from Greek to Syriac. Our study supports Vööbus's conclusion that "Polycarp's contribution belongs to the stream of revision-work so characteristic of the Syrian biblical studies which, time after time, by means of Greek philology went over the previous versions and produced newer and more exact translations."[481] We concur with Gwynn's assessment of the Philoxenian version that "it does not appear that the translation showed, or was ever impugned as showing, a doctrinal bias."[482]

4) When ܪܘܚܐ refers to the Holy Spirit, Philoxenus always treats it as a masculine noun, and we may be sure that it was so treated consistently in the version which bears his name.[483] In the Peshitta, ܪܘܚܐ is feminine throughout.[484] Philoxenus retained the usual Peshitta phrase ܪܘܚܐ ܕܩܘܕܫܐ for "Holy Spirit," but Thomas of Harkel substituted ܪܘܚܐ ܩܕܝܫܐ.

5) The Philoxenian version retained the Semitic spelling of proper names, whereas the Harklean sought to reproduce the Greek spelling. This is clearly illustrated in Exhibits 35 (Abraham, Isaac, Jacob) and 43 (Joseph). It is also

illustrated in the spelling of ܫܡܥܘܢ (lr 4) which the Harklean variously spells ܣܝܡܘܢ (Matthew 10:2), ܣܝܡܘܢ (Mark 3:16) and ܣܝܡܘܢܐ (Luke 6:14). Philoxenus refused to use ܟܐܦܐ of the Peshitta, but substituted the Greek ܦܛܪܘܣ.[485] This substitution was incorporated into his version and retained by Thomas of Harkel.[486]

6) In one instance, Philoxenus prefers the Greek word of the text to the Syriac of the Peshitta.[487] While it is unreasonable to generalize on the basis of one example, we note that this kind of preference is a characteristic of the Harklean version and Exhibit 55 suggests that that tendency had its beginnings in the Philoxenian version.

7) Four Exhibits (35, 42, 43, 50) reveal a greater use of ܐܝܬ as a copula in the Philoxenian, a use that was to become much more extensive in the Harklean.

8) The use of the pronominal particle (ܕܝܠ and a pronominal suffix) in place of the pronominal suffix became the rule in the Harklean version, but the movement in that direction was reflected in the Philoxenian as Exhibits 47, 55 and 56 show.[488]

The biblical quotations extracted from the fragments of the Philoxenian codex before us are but gleanings from a corner of the field. Nevertheless, they are important, for they provide clues necessary for the correct understanding of the Philoxenian version. They also point the way for further research. This study makes clear that the chronological sequence of Philoxenus' writings must be held in full view in any careful analysis of the biblical quotations they contain, especially if those quotations are to be used for the reconstruction of the version he sponsored. Such a comprehensive analysis is beyond the scope of this dissertation, but it must be made before anything definite can be said about that version.

CHAPTER V

PHILOXENUS' METHOD OF BIBLICAL INTERPRETATION AS SEEN IN THIS MANUSCRIPT

Philoxenus had a high view of scripture. He believed that the Bible was the principal authority in all matters of Christian doctrine and practice.[489] He wrote in the *Discourses*, "Behold the orthodox canon which has been inscribed for us in the Holy Scriptures!"[490] "I do not speak these things of myself, but I follow the will of the Holy Scriptures."[491] "While reading our discourse, it is right for the reader to examine the Holy Scriptures and see whether these words in their contexts are thus understood."[492] To the question, "Does the Holy Spirit leave a man when he sins and return to him when he repents?" Philoxenus prefaces his answer by saying: "On questions like these, it is not right for us to answer those who ask from our own thinking, but from the teaching of the Holy Scriptures; for in them is the correct answer to every question which is asked in faith."[493] In the fragments before us, he affirms a blind faith in the written text of scripture: "We believe these things because they are written, and not because they are comprehensible to those who hear them."[494] "Its reading is its explanation and faith accepts this."[495] These sentiments are not of course peculiar to Philoxenus. They belong to a tradition which was well established in the Church before his time. What is noteworthy is that, while he held the Councils of Nicea (A.D. 325) and Constantinople (A.D. 381) in the highest regard,[496] he did not appeal to them as ultimately authoritative in matters of the Christian faith. The tenor of all his writings assumes the scriptures to be the final court of appeal.

The affirmation of scriptural authority is of course no guarantee that the scriptures so affirmed will be universally understood and interpreted in the same way. Religious history provides many examples illustrative of that fact. How, then, did Philoxenus interpret the Bible? His own answer to that question is to be found in one of his statements quoted above: "Its reading is its explanation and faith accepts this."[497] For him, the meaning of the text was self-evident. All that was required was that it be accepted in its own terms. For this reason, he sponsored a new translation of the New Testament into Syriac, the purpose of which was to express as clearly as possible the meaning of the original Greek.[498] Having done that, he is content to maintain the mystery and incomprehensibility of a given biblical text rather than seek an explanation which the text does not warrant: "We only adhere to that which is written and we do not penetrate into the innermost part of the word by questioning, lest error confront us instead of knowledge, and deception instead of truth."[499] Again, he writes, "Christians who believe accept it, not by understanding it, but because it is written."[500]

The operative words in all these quotations are "faith" and its cognates. It is faith which accepts the "reading" as the explanation. Wisdom and the understanding of scriptures can only come to the true believer.[501] The heretic, then, cannot possibly receive and understand the divine wisdom in scripture. In one of his *Discourses*, Philoxenus develops the idea that it takes the eye of faith to see these things, for "the eye of the body is too small for the sight of our mysteries."[502] In this, he simply restates St. Paul's dictum, "The unspiritual man does not receive the gifts of the Spirit of God, for they are folly to him, and he is not able to understand them because they are spiritually discerned."[503] As our author sees it, "Not every man can hear and receive that wisdom."[504] It takes faith because it necessarily involves accepting a divine mystery.

Philoxenus never loses sight of the mystery (ܐܪܙܐ) which enshrouds the revelation of God. Fundamentally, it is the mystery of the Incarnation.[505] This divine mystery was first given when God created Adam in His image,[506] was transmitted to Seth and through Seth and the people listed in the Lucan genealogy to Christ,[507] who perfected it by His divine action.[508] Thus, Philoxenus can speak of "the mystery of His growth,"[509] of His baptism,[510] and of His earthly ministry (ܡܫܡܫܢܘܬܐ).[511] Sometimes he applies the word "mystery" to biblical statements about these realities. The Christian "remembers the proclaimed word of the mystery," "accepts it, not by understanding it but because it is written," and yields himself to God's authority.[512] These statements are inscribed in the Old Testament,[513] and are not just a pious hope, for "disciples . . . have also died and are dying in various ways for Him."[514] The Johannine description of the Incarnation is itself called a "mystery."[515] The divine promise and its fulfilment both contain the mystery of the real presence of God as that presence is revealed in those who transmitted His image from Adam to Christ and in the words of holy scripture, but supremely in the incarnate Son of God Himself. In Philoxenus' view, monophysitism maintained the mystery by its refusal to define the Person of Christ in other than scriptural ways, while the Chalcedonian and Nestorian doctrines of two distinct natures denied it.

With such a view of scripture, one might expect Philoxenus to eschew any exposition of or commentary on the Bible. But such is not the case. In the manuscript before us are fragments of expository discourses on topics from the first three chapters of Luke, and in some of his other writings he reverts time and again to biblical themes not merely to quote them but to interpret them. Obviously, "the reading" is *not* always "its explanation." Biblical texts require interpretation and Philoxenus is not slow to provide it. Nevertheless, his fundamental respect for scripture saves him from espousing the allegorizing methods of the Alexandrian school so prevalent in Western Christendom in his day and for a millenium after.

His first principle of interpretation is that the text must be understood literally or on its own terms. "The reading is its explanation" may overstate this principle, but it does put it in bold relief. Because of this conviction, he sees significance in the repetition of words, phrases and ideas in scriptures, "especially since it is unusual for the written word to have one clear meaning repeated."[516] The fact that he imports trinitarian concepts into his interpretation of Genesis 1:26-27 (the context of this last quotation) simply reveals what he presupposes the nature of God to be, and does not detract from the basic intention of his approach to the text. There is no evidence in his writings, however, for his dealing with such repetitions in a slavishly mechanical way, as though he were duty-bound to give a meaning to every repetition he found. Moreover, in this particular context, he combats the interpretation of these two verses which says in effect that because there is repetition they represent two distinct acts of God (i.e., "God said, Let us make man, etc.," then [later], "God made man, etc."). Philoxenus regards the repetition as simply reinforcing the main meaning.[517]

To interpret literally is to understand the context of a biblical text. In the thirteenth fragment, he sees the Lucan genealogy as "explaining the voice of the Father calling to His Son" in the Baptism narrative which immediately precedes it.[518] For him, the genealogy is not an unrelated unit fortuitously inserted into the third Gospel. On the contrary, he believes that its position in the narrative immediately after Jesus' Baptism has significance for its interpretation. Its context is important. Another example of contextual exposition is found in Fragment 7. There the focus is Luke 2:51b ("His mother kept all these things in her heart."), which he relates both to preceding statements (Luke 2:19, 33, 40, 51a) and to the verse which follows.[519] The result is a running commentary on related statements leading up to an exposition of Luke 2:52.

A form of running commentary which Philoxenus found particularly suited to his style was that of the extended paraphrase. In the first fragment, he explains the divine sentence pronounced on Cain (Genesis 4:15) by a long paraphrase in which God speaks in the first person, and this is even marked in the margin as a direct quotation.[520] Similar examples are found in his ascetic *Discourses*. In the *Eighth Discourse*, he expands Jesus' retort to His mother in John 2:4 ("Woman, what have you to do with me?") into some fourteen lines of printed text purporting to be the words of Jesus in order to give it the meaning he believes it to have.[521] The *Ninth Discourse* extends Matthew 11:28 to forty-six lines of printed text.[522] Other instances could also be cited illustrating the same paraphrastic style of expository discourse.[523] Extended paraphrases are also found in midrashic sections of some of the targums, but this does not necessarily mean that the roots of Philoxenus' usage are to be sought there. More probably it indicates that this was an effective method of interpreting the scriptures orally, for it lends itself well to teaching and preaching. The homilies of Chrysostom contain examples of this style of interpretation.[524]

It is noteworthy that following this single example in our manuscript of his use of extended paraphrase, Philoxenus still considers further interpretation to be necessary. In this case, he gives five alternative explanations for the sentence, "Whoever kills Cain shall release seven penalties" (Genesis 4:15), without stating which in his view is the best one.[525] I have been unable to find in Philoxenus' works any other instance of this kind of exegesis which merely lists the alternatives without drawing any conclusion. It certainly demonstrates that where no doctrinal issue is at stake, he is willing to leave the matter unresolved. It also shows very clearly that he did not always hold to his own dictum, "Its reading is its explanation."

Fragment 1 also illustrates another facet of Philoxenus' approach to the interpretation of scripture. In the space of two folios he moves exegetically from Matthew 18:22 to Genesis 4:24 to Genesis 4:15-17 (with a digression on John 8:44) to the building programs of Hezekiah, David and Solomon (in that order) where the fragment breaks off.[526] The contrast drawn by Philoxenus between the call to forgiveness in Matthew 18:22 ("not seven times but seventy times seven") and the threatened vengeance multiplied seven times in Genesis 4:15 and "seventy times seven" times in Genesis 4:24 (LXX), has been noted by interpreters ancient and modern, and is exegetically sound.[527] His digressions in the remainder of the fragment, however, have no apparent bearing on Matthew 18:22. Instead, their interrelationship depends on the associations they have with one another in the mind of the interpreter. The interpretation is always literal (with only a hint of typology at the end of the fragment).[528] Its development seems undisciplined and to that extent uncharacteristic of Philoxenus; but it is merely a wide-ranging contextual approach to a given text which in this instance, sees the whole Bible as the legitimate context.[529]

In this light, it is not unlike the contextual exposition found in Fragment 7 (referred to above), the difference there being that the associated texts were all in the same chapter of Luke.

Philoxenus' second principle of interpretation is that a biblical text may be understood typologically. This is never stated explicitly, but it is implicit in his use of the word ܛܘܦܣܐ and in some of his expositions. It is an approach to scripture which is theologically grounded. God, the Father, is the "Archetype" (ܪܫ ܛܘܦܣܐ), enshrouded in the mystery of His being, whose self-revelations were in types and shadows until the full revelation was made when the Word became flesh in Jesus.[530] Our author tells us, for example, that the divine likeness in man is a "type" of Him who is the Archetype;[531] that is to say, the likeness has factual reality in itself, yet it points beyond itself. To understand this is to understand Philoxenus' typological use of the Bible, and especially of the Old Testament. In this important way, it is distinguished from allegorical interpretation for which the factual content of a passage is irrelevant to the hidden or spiritual meaning which it is said to contain.

In our manuscript, several examples of his typological use of the Old Testament occur. He believes that "types and mysteries of (Christ) were . . . formed and inscribed in the Old Testament," and these are distinct from the predictions which prophets made concerning Him.[532] The first fragment remarks parenthetically that the Davidic kingdom was given to Solomon "as a type"; but no development of this thought survives, for the fragment ends in the next line.[533] In Fragment 11, Philoxenus sees in Jacob's dream of the ladder to heaven on which angels ascended and descended, a type of the two Gospel genealogies of Christ: the one "descending" from Abraham to Christ (Matthew 1:1-16), and the other "ascending" from Christ to Adam (Luke 3:23-38).[534] In his comment, he acknowledges the legitimacy of a literal and contextual interpretation of the dream having application to Jacob's going down to Laban's house and returning ("ascending") from it. The type in the Old Testament event foreshadows the divine archetype in an aspect (that of the genealogies) of the full revelation of God in the Incarnation. In an entirely different context, our author uses the same dream to illustrate the ascending experience of a man devoted to the ascetic life, but makes no suggestion that it has either a literal or a typological meaning.[535] In that instance, the context of his interpretation is parenetic and "Jacob's ladder" becomes a useful metaphor which, in the enthusiasm of the author, is extended to the point of allegory. Dreams, by their very nature, invite all sorts of interpretations; so his allegorizing tendency at this point must not be overstressed.

In more general terms, but still adhering to his understanding of Old Testament typology, Philoxenus sees God's adoption of Israel as a type, with all the things associated with the Israelites as "shadows prefiguring the reality."[536] The reality is the revelation of God in Christ of whose body Christian believers are members; "for we are not known as children apart from the Person of the Son, but He is the head and we are members of His body."[537] The reality of adoption in Christ is the reality of the Incarnation.[538] On the other hand, the adoption of Israel was nominal. They were called "first-born" (Exodus 4:22) to "teach that others would come after them"; that is, "the Gentiles were to be accepted in their place."[539] Israel's calling was historically factual within the context of the old covenant with God, but it was also a type, a foreshadowing, of the divine reality of the Church as the body of Christ.

As far as this fragmentary work is concerned, the New Testament offers no "types," for its main witness is to the revelation of God, the Archetype. The types and shadows of the Old Testament are replaced by the full light of the New. However, his treatment of baptism suggests that a new typology is to be found in the sacramental activity of the Church, although this idea remains largely undeveloped. In Fragment 10, he considers baptism to be "a type of death and resurrection"; while in Fragment 12, it is "a type of (the world's) consummation in that when He was baptized Jesus fulfilled His Father's will, and created all things new, both visible and invisible."[540] The Church's practice of baptism, then, typifies in retrospect Christ's baptism, death and resurrection, and in prospect the final consummation of the world, as well as initiating the baptized into the body of Christ.

In this double approach, literal and typological, to the interpretation of the Bible, Philoxenus followed the School of Antioch; yet he regarded as heretics those who were its greatest exponents -- Diodore of Tarsus and his famous students, Theodore of Mopsuestia, Theodoret of Cyrrhus, and Nestorius -- accusing them all of Nestorianism.[541] John Chrysostom, another of Diodore's students, a friend of Theodore and a great popularizer of Antiochian hermeneutics, escaped the monophysite charge of heresy, and instead was held in high regard as a biblical exegete.[542] Philoxenus was well enough acquainted with the works of Chrysostom to cite them some thirty times in his treatise on how "One Person of the Holy Spirit Became Incarnate and Suffered for Us."[543] In his "Letter to the Monks of Palestine," Philoxenus appeals to "Athanasius, Theophilus, the Gregories, John, Cyril and the blessed Ephrem"; and of course "John" refers to Chrysostom.[544] He is not mentioned by name in the manuscript before us, but in our analysis we have noted several parallels suggesting that Philoxenus not only knew the homilies of Chrysostom, but some of his expositions were influenced by them.[545] His apparent choice of Chrysostom as a model is very much in keeping with his strong preference for the principles of Antiochian exegesis.

CONCLUDING POSTSCRIPT

Since Wright published his *Catalogue* in 1872, British Museum Manuscript Add. 17,126 has usually been referred to as the "Fragments of the Commentaries of Philoxenus on the Gospels of S. Matthew and S. Luke," and the meaning of the term has been generally assumed to mean "exegetical commentary." Our study has shown that the Philoxenian "commentary" was in the nature of a homiletical discourse based on a chosen text of scripture. The original codex contained five homilies on texts selected from the first three chapters of Luke's Gospel. Fragments of four of these are preserved in this manuscript, along with a fragment (no. 1) from a discourse on Matthew 18:22 (probably) and three fragments (nos. 3, 4, 5) from a polemic against the Nestorians. Philoxenus was the author of all the fragments. On the basis of our examination not only of this manuscript but also the remains of the other Philoxenian "commentaries," we conclude that it is more accurate to speak of the "homilies" of Philoxenus on the Gospels.

Our analysis of all the scriptural quotations in these fragments confirms the general conclusions of Zuntz (followed by Vööbus) that the Philoxenian version of the New Testament in 508 was a revision of the Peshitta, and that it in turn was revised by Thomas of Harkel in 616. We have demonstrated the necessity of holding to a strict chronological sequence of Philoxenus' works in order to determine which deviations from the Peshitta may reasonably be regarded as belonging to the version of 508, and which to some other version such as an Old Syriac. We have thus been able to isolate a few of the features of the lost Philoxenian. But we recognize that the biblical quotations in all the writings of our author still need to be analyzed. In this regard, ours has been merely a sounding, albeit an important one.

In spite of its fragmentary condition, this manuscript has proved to be of value in determining Philoxenus' method of biblical interpretation. He adopted the method of the School of Antioch and made it an expression of his theology.

While one fragmentary codex has been the focus of this dissertation, always looming in the background has been the much larger *Book on Selected Passages from the Gospels* (British Museum Add. 14,534), produced during Philoxenus' lifetime in the same scriptorium at Mabbug. Consisting of one hundred and ninety-nine folios, it is more than five times larger than the manuscript edited here and in much better condition, but it remains unedited. Its publication and analysis is a challenge for future study.

NOTES

1. Wright, *Catalogue*, p. 526. Wright's *Short History of Syriac Literature*, published twenty-two years later (i.e., in 1894) maintained somewhat vaguely the same conclusion: "Portions of his (Philoxenus') commentaries are contained in two mss.(i.e., Add. 17,126 and 14,534) in the British Museum." (p. 74).

2. Wright, *Catalogue*, p. 526.

3. See ch. 3 below.

4. Budge, *Discourses*, II, p. xlix.

5. Baumstark, *Evangelienexegese*.

6. *Ibid.*, p. 162.

7. Baumstark, *Geschichte*, p. 141: "Von seinen bedeutendsten literarischen Arbeiten eröffnet ein nur sehr unvollständig erhaltener grosser Evangelienkommentar die exegetische Literatur des aramäischen Monophysitismus."

8. Lebon, *Philoxénienne*.

9. *Ibid.*, p. 436. Note: "La version polycarpienne" = the Philoxenian version.

10. Zuntz, *Harklean*, p. 41.

11. *Ditto*.

12. Vööbus, *New Data*, p. 178. This study is substantially repeated in Vööbus, *Early*, pp. 103-121, where he gives additional examples from the manuscript.

13. Vööbus, *New Data*, p. 179. Cf. *Early*, p. 111; and *Studies*, pp. 198 f.

14. De Halleux, *Vie*.

15. *Ibid.*, pp. 128-162.

16. Throughout this dissertation, the name "Philoxenus" is used because the monophysite bishop of Mabbug (485-519) is most commonly known by it both in Syriac and Greek writings. Less often, he is known as Aksenaia (ܐܟܣܢܝܐ = Ξεναΐας = ξένος = a stranger). For a full discussion of the name, see de Halleux, *Vie*, pp. 9-12.

17. Scholars have generally followed the Romanized spelling

"Tahal" of Assemanus, *B.O.*, II, p. 10, but the word appears as both in the *Anonymous Notice on Philoxenus* in MS. Vat. Syr. 155, fol. 5r, a - b (Vaschalde, *Three Letters*, p. 175) and in Eli of Qartamin's *Memra on the Holy Mar Philoxenus of Mabbug* (ed. by A. de Halleux in *C.S.C.O.*, C, pp. 2, 11, 33, 36, and 38). De Halleux vacillates in his transcription of the word: in his French translation of the Memra (1963), he uses "Tahil" (*C.S.C.O.*, XCIX, p. 2); while in his biography of Philoxenus, he uses "Taḥel" (*Vie* [1963], p. 13). A. Mingana, in his translation of a parallel Memra on Philoxenus, transcribes the word as "Taḥl," but does not provide a copy of the text which he translated (*New Documents*, p. 151). In order to retain some indication of the presence of the yudh in the spelling cited above (ܛܚܝܠ), I have used the transcription "Taḥil." The modern identification of the village is unknown. I would suggest that the village of Tarjil, ten kilometres south of Kirkuk in modern Iraq, may well be the same place.

18. So Hoffman, *Auszüge*, pp. 253 f. Hoffman's description is followed by Vaschalde, *Three Letters*, p. 3; by Duval, *Littérature*, map; by R. P. G. Levenq in *D.H.G.E.*, VIII, cols. 1230-1; and by de Halleux, *Vie*, p. 13. Mingana, *New Documents*, p. 151, fn. 1, is surely wrong in suggesting that the "Great Zab" was one of the boundaries of Beth-Garmai. The Greater Zab was the northern boundary of the region of Adiabene (as Mingana, *Early Spread*, p. 5, correctly notes), the neighbouring region to the north of Beth-Garmai.

19. Canon 21 of the Synod held at Seleucia-Ctesiphon in 410 under the presidency of the Catholicos, Isaac (Chabot, *Synodicon*, p. 272).

20. Abbeloos, *Acta*, p. 35.

21. Zorell, *Chronica*, p. 28. Mingana, *Early Spread*, pp. 4-5, states: "The date 225 is referred to in connection with the epoch-making year in which the first Sassanian king gained a decisive victory over Artaban, the last monarch of the Parthian dynasty."

22. De Halleux, *Vie*, p. 13, fn. 13, summarizes the diversity of scholarly opinion as follows: "Les modernes situent la naissance de Philoxène au deuxième quart du Ve siècle (Vaschalde, *Three Letters*, p. 3; Kruger, *Philoxenos*, p. 367), vers 440 (Rücker, *Philoxenus*, col. 248; Bergsträsser, *Monophysitismus*, p. 15, fn. 2), vers le lilieu du Ve siècle (Lebon, *Christologie*, p. 426, fn. 3) ou dans son troisième quart (Budge, *Discourses*, II, p. xvii)."

23. De Halleux, *Memra*, p. 2, ll. 39-44. A similar passage is translated in Mingana, *New Documents*, p. 151, but it omits any reference to persecution as the reason for the migration of Philoxenus' family to Tur 'Abdin.

24. Mingana, *New Documents*, p. 151, claims that the cell was a

mile away from his home.

25. Hoffman, *Auszüge*, pp. 53 ff., which is a German translation of the work published in Moesinger, *Monumenta*. Sykes, *History*, I, p. 471, inaccurately gives the date of this persecution as "455 or 456."

26. Hoffman, *Auszüge*, p. 54.

27. Sykes, *History*, I, p. 471.

28. De Urbina, *Patrologia*, p. 99, Assemanus *B.O.*, I, pp. 351 ff.

29. Assemanus, *B.O.*, I, pp. 352-353.

30. For text and French translation, see de Halleux, *Senun*.

31. De Halleux, *Senun*, versio, p. VI.

32. *Ibid.*, p. III.

33. The account of Philoxenus' early adoption of the ascetic life in Eli of Qartamin's *Memra* has the marks of pious legend connecting the name of a great monophysite with the establishing of the monastery of Qartamin. Perhaps the kernel of truth in the legend is nothing more than Philoxenus' instinct as an adolescent to establish his personal independence.

34. His brother, Addai, who also belonged to this minority, remains a shadowy figure. The *Memra* (l. 35) states that Addai was a teacher in the village of Taḫil, thus suggesting that he was older than Philoxenus. Did Addai become a junior teacher or tutor in the Edessene school while Philoxenus was a student there? The extant sources provide no answer. According to Michael the Syrian, Philoxenus also had a sister whose son, named Philoxenus, became suffragan bishop of Doliche under his uncle in Mabbug (which was the metropolitan see). See Michel, *Chronique*, IX, 29, p. 308 (cited by de Halleux, *Vie*, p. 15).

35. See especially Vööbus, *Nisibis*, pp. 13-30, on the "Character of the School of Edessa."

36. Vööbus, *Nisibis*, p. 14.

37. It was because Ḥiba was identified with Theodore of Mopsuestia, and thus with Nestorius, that he was deposed as bishop of 449 (only to be reinstated by the Council of Chalcedon in 451).

38. Vööbus, *Nisibis*, pp. 20 f.

39. De Halleux, *Vie*, pp. 30 f., fn. 52, ". . . les notions d'aristotélisme et de sciences profanes que l'on rencontre dans ses oeuvres (par ex. dans le *Commentaire de Jean I*, 1-17, f. 47v - 59v, etc.)."

40. Quoted by de Halleux, *Vie*, p. 29; cf. pp. 201 f.

41. *Ibid.*, p. 30. De Halleux goes so far as to call this reaction of Philoxenus a "conversion."

42. So Theodorus Lector, *Ecclesiasticae Historicae* (*Migna P.G.*, t. 86, col. 216), Theophanes Abbas, *Chronographia (Migne P.G.*, t. 108, cols. 325 f.), Evagrius Scholasticus, *Historiae Ecclesiasticae*, Bk. III, ch. XVI (*Migne P.G.*, t. 86, cols. 2657 f.), and Georgius Cendrinus, *Historiarum Compendium* (*Migne P.G.*, t. 121, col. 675).

43. De Halleux, *Senun*, 94:27 f.

44. De Halleux, *Vie*, pp. 189-200, where de Halleux shows that five Philoxenian letters were written during this period.

45. Brière, *Dissertationes*, p. 452.

46. Peter the Fuller had been deposed twice before. He was a strong supporter of Zeno's *Henoticon*.

47. De Halleux, *Memra*, ll. 347 f. In l. 154, Eli of Qartamin states that he received the name Philoxenus on his elevation to the episcopacy (so also Assemanus, *B.O.*, II, p. 10). Vööbus, *Legislation*, p. 51, claims that Philoxenus was made chorepiscopus of Mabbug before becoming the bishop, citing "ms. sin. syr. 10, fol. 48a" as his authority, but he provides no further information. In his discussion of Philoxenus' consecration, de Halleux, *Vie*, pp. 40 f., ignores the above-quoted source in Vööbus, *Legislation*. Instead, he makes reference to a similar tradition in *Chronicon Anonymum* 846, p. 200, but he feels that "rien ne permet de contrôler cette affirmation." Mabbug (also transliterated Mabbôgh, Mabug, Mabbog -- ܡܒܘܓ) was the Syriac name for Hierapolis, for a full account of which see Goosens, *Hiérapolis*.

48. Honigmann, *Évêques*, pp. 66-75.

49. *Chronicle 846*, p. 220. For more on Flavian II, patriarch of Antioch, see below.

50. Wright, *Chronicle*, p. 21.

51. Why Philoxenus was in Edessa at that time, is not stated. He was out of his own territory, which may partly explain his reticence to speak out against Edessan paganism. It was the year when Cyr, bishop of Edessa, died. Perhaps Philoxenus exercised some episcopal oversight during the interim period prior to the election of Cyr's successor, Peter.

52. Budge, *Discourses*, II, p. l. xxiii.

53. So Theophanes Abbas, *Chronographia* (*Migne P.G.*, t. 108, col. 341).

54. So Liberatus (*Migne, P. L.*, t. 68, col. 1030).

55. De Halleux, *Vie*, pp. 49 ff., gives a full account of the struggle.

56. Sykes, *History*, I, pp. 478 f.; Vaschalde, *Three Letters*, p. 17.

57. De Halleux, *Senun*, p. 95, l. 1 ff..

58. De Halleux, *Vie*, p. 76.

59. Zacharius, *Life os Severus*, p. 115.

60. *Camb. Med. Hist.*, I, p. 518.

61. De Halleux, *Vie*, pp. 217-223, dates the following letters in this period: *The Second Letter to the Monks of Teleda, A Letter in Defence of Dioscurus* (addressed to some monks), *A Letter to All the Orthodox Monks of the East, A Letter to Simeon of Teleda,* and *A Letter to the Monks of Senun.* Cf. Vaschalde, *Three Letters*, p. 20.

62. De Halleux, *Vie*, pp. 96-97, points out that Gangra is on the way to Philippopolis. He considers the *Chronicle of Se'ert*, p. 139, to be correct in stating that Philippopolis was the place of Philoxenus' death. This, de Halleux claims, is supported by the witness of two Philoxenian letters (*To the Monks of Senun*, and *To Simeon of Teleda*). The traditional view that Philoxenus was asphyxiated in Gangra is supported by the *Memra of Eli of Qartamin* (and the parallel document published by Mingana, *New Documents*), *The Anonymous Notice* (published by Vaschalde, *Three Letters*), and Zacharius Rhetor, *Eccl. Hist.*, VIII:5. This traditional view is followed by Assemanus (*B.O.*, II, pp. 19-20), Budge (*Disc ourses*, II, pp. xxv-xxvi), Vaschalde (*Three Letters*, pp. 19-20), and Honigmann (*Évêques*. p. 67).

63. See above, p. 9.

64. Sykes, *History*, I, p. 471. *Camb. Med. Hist.*, I, p. 466.

65. Sykes, *History*, I, pp. 437, 448, 468.

66. Labourte, *Christianisme*, pp. 123 f.

67. The exact date of the founding of the School of Nisibis is not known. After discussing the problem fully, Vööbus, *Nisibis*, p. 41. concludes that the date was sometime after 571.

68. Assuming the migration from Persia was in fact during the persecution of Yezdigird II in 446 as suggested in pp. 11 f. above.

69. Sellars, *Chalcedon*, pp. 3-29.

70. *Ibid.*, p. 66.

71. E.g., Brit. Mus. Ms. Add. 17,126, fol. 4r 20,21. See also the list of Philoxenus' works in Budge, *Discourses*, II, pp. liii ff.

72. Sellars, *Chalcedon*, p. 110.

73. *Ibid.*, pp. 97, 103. *Cam. Med. Hist.*, I, pp. 506 ff.

74. Budge, *Discourses*, II, pp. xxxiii ff., has a translation of Philoxenus' statement anathematizing the Council of Chalcedon (the Syriac text is found in pp. xcviii ff.).

75. *Camb. Med. Hist.*, I, pp. 515 ff.

76. The Greek text of the *Henoticon* is given by Evagrius Scholasticus, *Hist. Eccles.*, III:14.

77. Sellars, *Chalcedon*, p. 277.

78. Quoted in Budge, *Discourses*, II, p. xxxviii (translation) and p. cxxi (Syriac text).

79. *Ditto*.

80. Evagrius Scholasticus, *Hist. Eccles.*, III:32. This document was deposited in the archives of the Church of St. Sophia. Later, Anastasius tried to secure it from Euphemius, but he refused to hand it over to the emperor. This led to his being deposed from his see in 495 (So Theodorus Lector, *Eccles. Hist.* (*Migne, P.G.*, t. 86, cols. 188 f.).

81. Lebon, *Monophysitisme*, p. 41.

82. Labourt, *Christianisme*, p. 158.

83. Lebon, *Monophysitisme*, p. 44.

84. Vasiliev, *Justin*, pp. 132 ff.

85. *Ibid.*, p. 135 et passim.

86. De Halleux, *Memra*, l. 468, uses "Justinian" (ܝܘܣܛܝܢܐ) for "Justin." As Vasiliev, *Justin*, p. 26, notes, this is "usual in Syriac Chronicles."

87. Brit. Mus. Add. 14,534 = *Book on Selected Passages from the Gospels* (unpublished), fol. 38 a-b. See Appendix "A" for a copy of the text from which I have made this translation. A French translation of part of this passage appears in de Halleux, *Vie*, p. 121, fn. 20. He calls the manuscript "Commentaire de Jean 1:1-17."

88. Rom. 1:3 where the Peshitta reads:
ܐܬܝܠܕ ܒܒܣܪ ܡܢ ܙܪܥܐ ܕܒܝܬ ܕܘܝܕ.
It would appear that Philoxenus was explicitly taking issue with the Peshitta, both here and in what follows.

89. Matt. 1:1, where the Peshitta reads:
ܟܬܒܐ ܕܝܠܝܕܘܬܗ ܕܝܫܘܥ ܡܫܝܚܐ.

90. Matt. 1:18, where the Peshitta reads:
ܝܠܕܗ ܕܝܢ ܕܝܫܘܥ ܡܫܝܚܐ ܗܟܢܐ ܗܘܐ.
Philoxenus' apparent invertion of the word order follows exactly the word order of the Greek. Early in this manuscript (Brit. Mus. Add. 14,534), the author insists that the proper Syriac rendering of γένεσις is ܗܘܝܐ, and chides the translators for their careless use of ܝܠܝܕܘܬܐ and ܝܠܕܐ. These last two words render γέννησις . In folio 31b, he says he does not know why the translator should have used these words instead of ܗܘܝܐ. In folio 32a, he suggests that the confusion comes because the two Greek words γένεσις and γέννησις are similar; then, as de Halleux has observed (*Vie*, p. 22), he proceeds to confuse them himself! In folio 34b, he writes: "No one should think that it is irrelevant for us to consider here a matter which is on this subject, although we take issue with the translator; for (in saying), more than the truth which was written, he used words which he supposed suited the Syriac language, or which he thought proper to God, as if he knew more than He what things suited Him." (See also de Halleux, *Vie*, p. 122, fn. 23).

91. Brit. Mus. Add. 14,534, fol. 39b.

92. Assemanus, *B.O.*, II, p. 82.

93. Vööbus, *New Data*, p. 173, fn. 28, does not believe that the Psalms were included in the new translation, but he does not say why. He simply states: "These words (i.e., "and of David") are between brackets because they seem to be, if not an interpolation, then a corruption."

94. The colophon to the Harklean Gospels gives this date(= A. Gr. 927). See Hatch, *Subscriptions*, p. 149 ff., for full text of the subscription. The date given by Gwynn, *Remnants*, p. xxii, is "A. Gr. 925 (= A.D. 614)." The translation of the colophon here given is based on Hatch's text.

95. Cf. Payne-Smith, *Thesaurus*. See also Vööbus, *Early Versions*, p. 108, and *New Data*, p. 174.

96. Vööbus, *New Data*, pp. 170 ff., gives a useful summary of the variety of ways in which the colophon has been interpreted, ranging from White, *Versio Philoxenia*, who understood the colophon to mean that Thomas of Harkel merely copied the Philoxenian version to which he added marginal notes (thus claiming that the Harklean version = the Philoxenian), to Gwynn, *Remnants*, who insisted that the surviving Harklean version was a thorough revision of the Philoxenian and quite different from it, and that the older version was lost except for the four Minor Catholic Epistles and the Book of Revelation which he published. It is noteworthy that the recent edition of the *Greek New*

Testament edited by Kurt Aland et al. (1966), p. xxix, assumes that Gwynn's conclusions are correct.

97. Bar Hebraeus, *O. T. Scholia*, p. 5.

98. De Halleux, *Memra*, ll. 130-134, claims that Philoxenus did the work of translation himself; but no other witness writes in this way, and Philoxenus' competence in Greek remains in some doubt (see de Halleux, *Vie*, p. 22).

99. See above, p. 20.

100. Above, p. 20.

101. Above, p. 20.

102. Above, p. 21.

103. Quoted in Gwynn, *Remnants*, p. xxxi, from Cod. Ambros. c. 313.

104. *Ibid.* Ceriani identified fragments of a Syriac version of Isaiah as Philoxenian, but such an identification needs to be re-examined.

105. Gwynn, *Remnants*, p. xxxii, et passim; *Apocalypse*, pp. xcvii ff.

106. The consensus of modern scholarly opinion is reflected in the recent edition of the *Greek New Testament* edited by Kurt Aland et al. (1966), p. xxix, where the siglum "syr^{ph} = Philoxenian (Gwynn)."

107. Lebon, *Philoxénienne*, pp. 415 ff. De Halleux, *Vie*, p. 118, makes the same point.

108. I have also examined the Biblical quotations in Brit. Mus. Add. 15,534 (*Book on Selected Passages from the Gospels*) and have not found any quotations from the Minor Catholic Epistles or Revelation.

109. It should be added, however, that Severus, who was the monophysite patriarch of Antioch during the last decade of Philoxenus' life, clearly regarded 2 Peter and 2 and 3 John as canonical, ascribing apostolic authority to them in his extant letters. While these letters exist almost entirely in the Syriac version of Athanasius of Nisibis, Severus wrote in Greek and his biblical quotations originally in Greek throw no light on the Syriac versions of his day. He apparently adopted the western canon, though quotations from Jude and Revelation are lacking in his published letters. For quotations from 2 Peter and 2 and 3 John, see Brooks, *Letters*, I (text), pp. 182, 257, 296, 298, 302, 306, 326, 394, 449.

110. Zuntz, *Harklean N.T.*, p. 40. Vööbus, *New Data*, pp. 176 f.; *Early Versions*, pp. 109 f.; and de Halleux, *Vie*, pp. 120 f.

111. This abbreviates the title which Budge gives the work: *Three Discourses on the Trinity and the Incarnation* (Budge, *Discourses*, II, p. (ii). Vaschalde *(Tractatus)* called it *Tractatus Tres de Trinitate et Incarnatione*. Both are translations of a Syriac title attached to the work, though apparently not original with Philoxenus. Zuntz, for reasons not given, calls it *De Uno et Trinitate* (*Harklean N.T.*, pp. 39-58). De Halleux confuses matters further by naming it *Le libre des sentences* (*Vie*, pp. 240-6), for good reasons, however, which he states fully.

112. Zuntz, *Harklean N.T.*, p. 57.

113. *Op. cit.*, p. 41. See also de Halleux,*Vie*, p. 120 f.

114. Vööbus, *Studies*, pp. 88-92, 197-201; *New Data*, pp. 169-186; *Early Versions*, pp. 103-121.

115. See especially the statement in Budge, *Discourses*, II, pp. xcviii f. In his statement, "Against every Nestorian" (*op. cit.*, pp. cxx ff.), he affirms the creeds of the Councils of Nicea and Constantinople, and the *Henoticon*.

116. The quotation from his *Book on Selected Passages from the Gospels*, folio 38 a-b, translated on pp. 20 f. above, illustrates this concern.

117. Brit. Mus. Add. 17,126, the subject of the dissertation.

118. Brit. Mus. Add. 14,534. The title I use here and throughout is based on the colophon which states: "The end of the writing of this book on passages (or, perhaps, "topics") selected from the Evangelists and made by the holy Philoxenus, Bishop of Mabbug." (The Syriac is quoted in Wright, *Catalogue*, p. 527, col. 2). De Halleux calls this book "Commentaire de Jean 1:1-17."

It should be added here that O. H. Parry, *Monastery* (1895), p. 370, reported seeing a manuscript dated A.D. 1001 containing a "Commentary on the Gospels by Philoxenus and Abraham of Malatia" in the Monastery of Deir az-Za'faran near Mardin in modern Turkey (cf. Badger, *Nestorians*, I, pp. 433-435). De Halleux, *Vie* (1963), p. 128, refers to Parry's note, but without further comment. Vööbus, *Kanon* (1970), pp. 320-1, fn. 39, states that after considerable trouble he has been unable to find any trace of this manuscript. There the matter stands. Perhaps some day soon this monastery will open up its literary treasures (if, indeed, it has any) to the scrutiny of the scholarly world.

119. Assemanus, *B.O.*, II, p. 23.

120. De Halleux, *Vie*, p. 128. In pp. 134-162, he provides the details which need not be repeated here.

121. *Ibid.*, pp. 128 ff. Wright, *Catalogue*, p. 1000, col. 2, indicates a fragmentary comment by Philoxenus on 1 John 5:6 in Brit. Mus. Add. 17,193, fol. 94b; but this does not

mean that a commentary on 1 John existed as Budge, *Discourses*, II, pp. xlixl, seems to imply. Certainly he is overstating the evidence when he suggests that Philoxenus wrote a Commentary on the New Testament. Moreover, de Halleux, *Senun*, I, pp. XII-XIII, has shown that the comment on 1 John 5:6 comes from Philoxenus' *Letter to the Monks of Senun* (See *Senun*, I, p. 8, ll. 2-5).

122. De Halleux, *Vie*, pp. 134-162. The question marks indicate de Halleux' uncertainty as to whether the Gospel reference used is the basis for the commentary cited. In such cases he suggests alternative references.

123. *Ibid*., pp. 140 f.

124. ܕܡܦܫܩܐ ܗܘܐ ܐܘܢܓܠܝܐ ܡܢ ܟܬܒܐ ܕܦܘܫܩܐ ܕܡܬܝ. -- from Brit. Mus. Add. 14,613, fol. 162r = Add. 14,649 fol. 202va (on Matt. 3:1-16). Similar statements are found in Brit. Mus. Add. 12,154, fol. 64r (Matt. 3:14-15, or 11:11); Mingana 9, p. 267a (Matt. 11:25-27 or 13:16-17 or 16:17); Vatican syr. 100, fol. 34ra (Matt. 22:29-32[?]); Brit. Mus. Add. 12,155, fol. 78vb = Add. 14,532, fol. 74ra = Add. 14,538, fol. 113r (Matt. 26:36-44); and Brit. Mus. Add. 17,193, fol. 97r (Matt. 17:1-8 or 27:45-53).

125. Brit. Mus. Add. 12,154, fol. 50v, refers to chapter five (ܡܢ ܪܝܫܐ ܕܗ̄ - Matt. 2:1), chapter six (ܕܘ̄ = Matt. 2:14-15), and chapter seven (ܕܙ̄ = Matt. 3:1). Mingana, syr. 9, p. 267, cited chapter twenty-two (ܦܠܟܣܢܘܣ ܕܡܢ ܒܦܘܫܩܐ ܕܡܬܝ ܒܩܦܠܐܘܢ ܕܟܒ̄ = Matt. 11:25-27 or 13:16-17 or 16:17). Chapter twenty-nine is given as the source for two distinct expository passages; which may, indeed, come from the same "chapter," since both are based on the Matthew passion narrative. The first is found in three manuscripts which say that it is from "the second book": Brit. Mus. Add. 12,155, fol. 78vb = Add. 14,532, fol. 74ra = Add. 14,538, fol. 113r (ܕܡܪܝ ܐܟܣܢܝܐ ܡܢ ܟܬܒܐ ܕܬܪܝܢ ܕܦܘܫܩܐ ܕܡܬܝ ܡܢ ܪܝܫܐ ܕܟܛ̄ ܘܬܫܒܚܬܐ). The second is found in Brit. Mus. Add. 17,193, fol. 97r-v (ܕܡܦܫܩܐ ܦܠܟܣܢܘܣ. ܡܢ ܦܘܫܩܐ ܕܡܬܝ ܒܩܦܠܐܘܢ ܕܟܛ̄).

126. Brit. Mus. Add. 17,126, fol. 38v. 822 of Alexander = A.D. 511.

127. Reference to Luke 2:7. Brit. Mus. Add. 12,154, fol. 50r reads: ܡܢ ܪܝܫܐ ܕܟܒ̄. ܦܘܫܩܐ ܡܛܠ ܗܝ ܕܐܬܐܡܪ ܡܢ ܒܡܥܪܬܐ ܘܐܬܬܣܝܡ ܒܐܘܪܝܐ.

128. Brit. Mus. Add. 12,154, fol. 49v: ܡܢ ܪܝܫܐ ܕܟܗ̄ ܕܠܘܩܐ ܘܬܪ̈ܝܢ. ܦܘܫܩܐ ܕܡܠܝ ܕܗ̈ܘܝ ܡܢ ܠܘܩܐ.

129. The argument is weakened somewhat by the fact that one reference repeated in three manuscripts (see note 107 above) speaks of the twenty-ninth chapter of the second book, while the fourth book of five chapters apparently covered either chs. 31-35 or 32-36 (or parts of Luke 2 and 3) leaving the "lost" third book to cover one or (at most)

two chapters: so we are left assuming that books 1 and 2 together contained twenty-nine chapters, book 3 one or two chapters, and book 4 five chapters -- which patently is an unlikely distribution of chapters.

130. Brit. Mus. Add. 17,126, fol. 38v.

131. De Halleux, *Vie*, pp. 22, 120-123, 150-158, 285, 460, 462, 465, 470. Wright, *Catalogue*, p. 526, states that "it contains the Commentary of Philoxenus on selected passages of the Gospels, more especially on ch. 1:1-18 of the Gospel of S. John" (see note 118 above). Budge, *Discourses*, II, p. 1 (= roman 50), apparently relying on a quotation from the manuscript in Wright, *loc. cit.*, speaks of "fragments of the Commentary on Saint John preserved in Add. 14,534, fol. 16a ff." That quotation simply says: "I tell Diodore and Theodore to debate with the Arians from the words which are placed at the beginning of the book of John." (Add. 14,534 fol. 16r -- see Wright, *Catalogue*, p. 527).

132. *Ibid.*, p. 152.

133. The manuscript is defective with the first three quires missing and the fourth imperfect (Wright, *Catalogue*, p. 526). De Halleux, *Vie*, p. 151, reckons that the total number of folios missing from the beginning is between twenty-five and thirty-one.

134. The Syriac is quoted in Wright, *Catalogue*, p. 527.

135. De Halleux, *Vie*, pp. 150-162.

136. *Ibid.*, p. 150.

137. *Ibid.*, pp. 158-161. Bar Salibi's *Commentary on John's Gospel* is found in Vatican (Biblioteca Apostolica) syr. 155 and is unpublished and unavailable to me. I have relied on de Halleux' description for my comments here. See also Assemanus, *Catalogue*, III, p. 297.

138. De Halleux, *Vie*, p. 159. Brit. Mus. Add. 14,538, fol. 23v (Wright, *Catalogue*, p. 1005): ܡܢ ܡܐܡܪܐ ܕܒ̄ ܕܦܘܫܩܐ ܕܝܘܚܢܢ

139. De Halleux, *Vie*, p. 161. Brit. Mus. Add. 12,155, fol. 76r = Add. 14,532, fol. 67r = Add. 14,533, fol. 68r = Add. 14,538, fol. 110r (Wright, *Catalogue*, pp. 932, 960, 969): ܡܢ ܡܐܡܪܐ ܕܝܒ̄ ܗܘ ܕܐܡܪ ܡܪܢ. ܐܢܐ ܐܢܐ ܠܚܡܐ ܕܚܝܐ ܘܓ̄

140. De Halleux, *Vie*, pp. 161-162, finds these fragments in an Armenian work he calls "Sceau de la foi" (= Knik' hawatoy, ed. by K. Ter Mkertc'ean). I have been unable to consult this work, and rely on the information provided by de Halleux.

141. Budge, *Discourses*, II, p. clxxi. Cf. also. p. clv where Budge quotes from the Peshitta of Mark 10:15 to compare it with Philoxenus' quotation which varies from it. The fact

is that the Peshitta of Luke 18:17 is closer to Philoxenus' citation than its Marcan equivalent.

142. De Halleux, *Senun*, II, p. 82.

143. I.e., "Matthew-Luke" (Brit. Mus. Add. 17,126) and "John 1:1-17" (Add. 14,534).

144. Vaschalde, *Tractatus*, p. 237 (176). In the *Three Letters*, pp. 171 and 183, Vaschalde cites Mark 15:34 as being quoted by Philoxenus, but the equivalent in Matthew 27:46 could just as easily be his source.

145. So F. C. Grant, "Gospel of Matthew," article in *Interpreter's Dictionary of the Bible*, III, p. 303. H. B. Swete, *The Gospel According to St. Mark*, pp. xxxiv ff., believes that a low estimate of Mark (in comparison with the other three Gospels) existed from the second century, and was due in part to the view that Mark was merely an abridgement of Matthew.

146. The percentages are Streeter's (*Four Gospels*, p. 151). Goodspeed (*Matthew*, p. 40) credits Streeter with an estimate of 95% rather than 90%, but provides no reference.

147. Payne-Smith, *Thesaurus*, II, col. 3327.

148. Brit. Mus. Add. 14,534. See p. 20 above.

149. Brit. Mus. Add. 17,126, 9r 19, 20, 25; 11r 13; 28r 24; and 32r 15.

150. The colophon reads in part: "In this book is a commentary (ܦܘܫܩܐ) of five chapters (ܪ̈ܫܐ) taken from the Evangelist, Luke . . . . The end of the fourth book of commentary of the Evangelists, Matthew and Luke, which was made by Philoxenus . . ." (Brit. Mus. Ms. Add. 17,126, fol. 38v 11-15). ܦܘܫܩܐ is not used in the contemporary colophon of the *Book on Selected Passages of the Gospels*, Brit. Mus. Add. 14,534.

151. De Halleux, *Vie*, pp. 134-162.

152. As has been shown above, the existence of Philoxenian commentary on John's Gospel has not been demonstrated. The title of only one out of thirteen Johannine fragments uses the term "commentary," and it exists only in an Armenian translation (so de Halleux, *Vie*, p. 162) which is not available to the present writer. De Halleux considers folios 11-13 of our document part of a Johannine commentary (*ibid.*, p. 150).

153. So Oxford (Bodleian Library), Marsh 101, fol. 57r. The same fragment occurs in two manuscripts in the Mingana collection, but in both it is said to come from a "section or an explanatory note" (ܒܘܗܪܐ) by Philoxenus (Mingana syr. 105, fol. 2215 = Mingana syr. 480, fol. 400v).

154. It should be stressed that this analysis takes de Halleux' account of the extant literature at face value. The bare analysis indicates that that account must be modified.

155. De Halleux, *Vie*, pp. 135 f., where he designates this fragment as no. 5 of the Matthean Commentary.

156. The fragment in Brit. Mus. Add. 14,613 is 23 pages long and each page has 22 lines.

157. The folio numbers are those of the Brit. Mus. Add. 14,613.

158. Brit. Mus. Add. 14,613, fol. 172v.

159. Budge, *Discourses*, I, pp. 7 f., II, pp. 5 f.

160. Wright, *Catalogue*, p. 813, calls it "extracts from the commentary of Philoxenus of Mabbug on the Gospel of S. Matthew" which merely expands the title given in the manuscript itself.

161. So Wright, *Ethiopic*, p. 201. See also de Halleux, *Vie*, p. 137. The manuscript is Brit. Mus. Orient. 736.

162. Brit. Mus. Orient. 731 and 732. I depend here on Wright, *Ethiopic*, pp. 199-203. Wright does not state whether the two later manuscripts, Orient. 735 and 734 (from the 18th and 19th centuries respectively), name Philoxenus or not. According to de Halleux, *Vie*, p. 136, fn. 3, the colophon of Orient. 732 suggests that this catena was translated from Syriac into Arabic at the beginning of the 11th century, and from Arabic into Ge'ez in the 16th century.

163. *Op. cit.*, p. 137. I have to rely on this résumé since I do not read Ethiopic.

164. I.e., Brit. Mus. Add. 17,126.

165. I.e., Budge, *Discourses*, I, p. 620, II, p. 592.

166. Budge, *Discourses*, I, pp. 431 ff., II, pp. 413-415.

167. *Op. cit.*, p. 137.

168. Brit. Mus. Add. 12,164 = Vatican Syr. 138. The folios cited are those of Add. 12,164. The subject of this work is "How One Person of the Holy Trinity Became Incarnate and Suffered for us." (See Wright, *Catalogue*, pp. 527 f., Budge, *Discourses*, II, pp. li-lii, and de Halleux, *Vie*, pp. 225 ff.) This work is in ten memre, only two of which have been as yet published (with a Latin translation -- see Brière, *Dissertationes*).

169. I.e., Budge, *Discourses*, I, pp. 249 ff., II, pp. 239 ff.

170. Budge, *Discourses*, II, p. 240.

171. Wright, *Catalogue*, pp. 976 ff. De Halleux, *Vie*, p. 137.

172. Why de Halleux feels it necessary to suggest Marr. 3:14-15 is not clear, for this passage is not mentioned in the fragment.

173. Budge, *Discourses*, I, pp. 300 ff.; II, pp. 287 ff. The other parallel cited by de Halleux from *Discourses*, I, pp. 484 f., II, p. 463, is a comment on Matt. 9:14 ff. and is not directly relevant to the fragment before use.

174. See Matthean fragments 10, 12, 13, 15, and 16, and Lucan fragment 3 in de Halleux, *Vie*, pp. 137-139 and 143. I was unable to examine Matthean fragment 12 because it exists in only one manuscript -- Vatican Syr. 100 -- and it was unavailable to me. Matthean fragment 13 is written in Karshuni with which I am not familiar, but I have tried to examine it as best I can. Budge, *Discourses*, II, p. li, lists it as "an exposition on the parable of the ten talents."

175. Following de Halleux' schema (*Vie*, pp. 134 ff.), these fragments are Nos. 1, 2, and 3 of the proposed "introduction to the commentary," Nos. 2, 3, and 4 of the Matthean commentary, and Nos. 5 and 9 of the Lucan commentary.

176. P. 27 above.

177. A: 1,2,3; B: 2 (5th ch.), 3 (6th ch.), 4 (7th ch.), 9 (22nd ch.), 15 (29th ch.), 16 (27th ch.); C: 3 (32nd ch.), 9 (35th ch.), and 14. See de Halleux, *Vie*, pp. 134 ff.

178. Payne-Smith, *Dictionary*, p. 539.

179. Budge has published the texts of the following: *Ten "Chapters" Against Those Who Divide Our Lord (Discourses*, II, pp. c-civ), *Twelve "Chapters" Against Those Who Say There Are Two Natures in Christ and One Person* (*Discourses*, II, pp. civ-cxx), *Special "Chapters" Against Every Nestorian* (*Discourses*, II, pp. cxx-cxxiii), and *Twenty "Chapters"* (ܩܦܠܐܐ) *Against Nestorius* (*Discourses*, II, pp. cxxiii-cxxxvi). De Halleux, *Vie*, pp. 181 ff., describes two more polemical works by Philoxenus which Budge only lists (*Discourses*, II, pp. liv-lv): [*Seven*] *Special "Chapters" etc.*,and *The First* [*Three*] *"Chapters" Against Heresies*.

180. In the title of the *Twenty "Chapters"* the Greek term ܩܦܠܐܘܢ occurs. It also is used in the colophon of the *Twenty "Chapters"*, illustrating the fact that it is synonymous with ܪ̈ܫܐ.

181. Budge, *Discourses*, II, pp. c-civ (text); partly translated on pp. xxxvi f. The MS containing this work is dated A.D. 569.

182. The quotation is from the LXX and not the MT or the Peshitta. It is similar to but not identical with the Syro-Hexaplar.

183. A comparison of texts here is noteworthy:
Philoxenus here: ܘܐܫܬܚܠܦ ܠܥܝܢܝܗܘܢ
Peshitta Matthew 17:2 ܚܙܘܗ ܩܕܡܝܗܘܢ "
Peshitta Mark 9:2 ܠܥܝܢܝܗܘܢ "
Philoxenus uses the Greek ܐܣܟܝܡܗ where the Peshitta (as always) uses ܚܙܘܐ.

184. So two MSS, Mingana syr. 480, fol. 400v, and 105, fol. 221r. A third containing the same text, Oxford, Marsh 101, fol. 57r, uses only the first word, ܦܠܚܐ. Evidently, the author of the title understood the two words to be synonymous, as his use of ܘܐܟܘܬ shows.

185. Mingana 105, fols. 221v, 222r.

186. De Halleux, *Vie*, p. 143.

187. Brit. Mus. Add. 12,155 (8th century) = Add. 14,532 (8th century) = Add. 14,533 (8th-9th centuries) = Add. 14,538 (10th century). See Wright, *Catalogue*, pp. 921 ff., 955 ff., and 967 ff., and 1003 ff.

188. Wright, *Catalogue*, p. 937.

189. Budge, *Discourses*, I, p. 3.

190. Lucan fragments 1 and 11. De Halleux, *Vie*, pp. 142, 147.

191. Ortiz, *Patrologia*, p. 159, simply lists this memra as a separate item under "Dogmatica."

192. ܟܬܒܐ ܕܝܠ ܡܬܪܬܝܢܘܬܐ ܕܕܘܒܪܐ ܕܡܫܝܚܝܘܬܐ ܠܬܠܡܝܕܐ ܗܘ، ܦܝܠܘܟܣܢܘܣ ܐܦܝܣܩܘܦܐ ܕܡܒܘܓ : ܘܡܐܡܪܐ
Budge, *Discourses*, contains the text and translation of the thirteen extant discourses. Part of the title quoted above is from *op. cit.*, I, p. 3. De Halleux, *Vie*, pp. 280-290, provides a list of all the extant copies of these discourses with a brief discussion of them. The title uses the term ܟܬܒܐ -- a term which Philoxenus uses twice in the Prologue to describe these writings (Budge, *Discourses*, I, pp. 10, 25), but each discourse is called a "memra" both in its title and in its concluding note. De Halleux refers to these discourses as "Les memre parénétiques."

193. Budge, *Discourses*, I, p. 10.

194. De Halleux, *Vie*, pp. 285 f.

195. Budge, *Discourses*, I, pp. 14-15, and 25.

196. This work is preserved in two MSS: Vatican syr. 138 (which has the Syriac title translated here), and Brit. Mus. Add. 12,164. Several fragments of the work also exist (see de Halleux, *Vie*, pp. 225-238). The first two discourses (memre) have been published by Brière, *Dissertationes*. The term ܦܢܩܝܬܐ (volume) occurs at the end of the first discourse (Brière, *op. cit.*, p. 491).

197. For this reason, de Halleux, *Vie, loc. cit.*, calls the work, "Memre contre Ḥabib."

198. Following de Halleux, *Vie*, p. 227.

199. Vaschalde, *Three Letters*, p. 94. The letter is edited and translated in this book by Vaschalde. See also de Halleux, *Vie*, pp. 189 ff.

200. Brit. Mus. Add. 12,164, fols. 120v-125v; so de Halleux, *Vie*, pp. 225 ff.

201. See note 196 above.

202. *Ibid.*, fols. 130r-141r. A description of the MS is found in Wright, *Catalogue*, pp. 527 ff. See also de Halleux, *Vie, loc. cit.*

203. Edited with a Latin translation in Vaschalde, *Tractatus Tres*. De Halleux, *Vie*, pp. 240 ff., calls it "Le livre des sentences" because the second and third memre are divided into numbered sub-sections called ܪܝܫܐ -- "sentences or maxims," which are between ten and thirty printed pages in length.

204. De Halleux, *Vie*, pp. 241 f.

205. See especially Zuntz, *Harklean N.T.*, pp. 41-58.

206. Edited with a German translation in Krüger, *Annuntiatione*.

207. De Halleux, *Vie*, p. 142.

208. Krüger, *Annuntiatione*, p. 158, l. 18.

209. Wright, *Catalogue*, pp. 886 ff. This MS (Add. 14,727) throws light on the use of the term ܦܘܫܩܐ, for it is applied to the homilies of some of the Fathers (e.g., Cyril of Alexandria and John Chrysostom), and does not presuppose a "commentary" in any technical sense. Similarly, this same MS contains a Philoxenian fragment "from the commentary (ܦܘܫܩܐ) on the Gospel of Luke," but all the other patristic selections are from homilies (cf. de Halleux, *Vie*, p. 144, where he takes this fragment as a commentary on Luke 2:24-39).

210. Only de Halleux does so. Budge, *Discourses*, II, p. lvi, lists it with other discourses. Ortiz, *Patrologia*, p. 159, classifies it under the heading, "Dogmatica." Baumstark, *Geschichte*, p. 143, calls it "eine Predigt."

211. Edited with a French translation in Tanghe, *Inhabitation*.

212. De Halleux, *Vie*, p. 276.

213. Budge, *Discourses*, II, p. lvi; Wright, *Catalogue*, p. 993; Baumstark, *Geschichte*, p. 143 ("Abhandlung"); Tanghe, *Inhabitation*, p. 50 (Memra) and de Halleux, *Vie*, p. 276

(Memra).

214. Tanghe, *Inhabitation*, p. 57.

215. Ortiz, *Patrologia*, p. 159.

216. De Halleux, *Vie*, pp. 126 f.

217. *Ibid*., p. 147.

218. *Ibid*., pp. 246 ff. This work is very like the "Three Discourses on the Trinity and on the Incarnation" (see note 203).

219. *Ibid*., pp. 238 ff.

220. See pp. 33 ff. above. Budge, *Discourses*, II, p. liv, no. XVI, lists one polemical discourse "against the Nestorians and Eutychians" without giving any reference. I have been unable to trace this work.

221. For text, see Budge, *Discourses*, II, pp. cxxxvi ff. De Halleux, *Vie*, p. 175, translates ܦܘܪܫܐ by "catalogue," but its root idea is that of "separating," or "setting apart."

222. Budge, *op. cit*., p. cxxxvii, l. 18 f.

223. The text is edited in Budge, *Discourses*, II, pp. xcviii f.

224. Edited text in Budge, *Discourses*, II, pp. xcvi ff. The abrupt end to the fragment suggests that the whole text of the original was not quoted in the MS.

225. Budge, *Discourses*, II, pp. lv f., lists a total of six confessions of faith (nos. XXII -XXVI). De Halleux, *Vie*, pp. 168-178, discusses the genre and the Philoxenian fragments fully.

226. Edited text in de Halleux, *Memra*, I, p. 8, l. 195 f. Eli of Qartamin may have counted the two letters to the Monks of Teleda and the two letters to the monks of Beth Gogal as single volumes.

227. Budge, *Discourses*, II, pp. lviii ff. De Halleux, *Vie*. pp. 187-223 and 253-274. The latter questions the authenticity of "une lettre sur les trois degrés de la vie monastique" (pp. 269-274).

228. De Halleux, *Vie*, p. 188, has found references to four distinct Philoxenian letters none of which has been preserved even in fragmentary form.

229. Edited with a French translation in Lavenant, *Patricius*.

230. Edited with a French translation in de Halleux, *Senun*.

231. Lavenant, *Patricius*, p. 848, ll. 2-3.

232. De Halleux, *Senun*, pp. 1-2. Here Philoxenus quotes from Acts 14:22.

233. Enough letters have been published to justify the generalizations made in this section; viz., "First Letter to the Monks of Beth-Gogal," "Letter to Monks," "Letter to Zeno" (all in Vaschalde, *Three Letters*), "First Letter to the Monks of Teleda" (in Guidi, *Tell 'Adda*), "Letter to the Monks of Amid" -- a fragment (in Vööbus, *Legislation*), "Letter to Abu Nafir" (in Mingana, *Early Spread*), "Letter to Monks in Palestine," "Prefatory Letter to the 'Synodicon' of Ephesus" -- two fragments (in de Halleux, *Textes*, I), "Letter to the Orthodox Monks of the East" -- in six fragments (fragments 1-3 in Lebon, *Textes*, and fragments 4-6 in de Halleux, *Textes II*), "Letter to Maron, the Lector, of Anazarba," "Letter to Monks on Behalf of Dioscorus" -- a fragment, "Letter to Simon, the Archimandrite of Teleda" -- in four fragments (in Lebon, *Textes*), "Letter to the Monks of Senun" (in de Halleux, *Senun*), "Letter to Patricius" (in Lavenant, *Patricius*), "Letter to Abraham and Orestes" (in Frothingham, *Bar Sudayli*), "Letter to a Novice" (in Olinder, *Novice*), "Letter to a Convert from Judaism" (translation only in Albert, *Juif*), and "Letter to a Lawyer Who Has Become a Monk" (translation only in Graffin, *Avocat*).

234. For text, see de Halleux, *Senun*, pp. 55-61.

235. For text, see Lavenant, *Patricius*, p. 848 128.

236. De Halleux, *Vie*, p. 254. I have chosen these two letters as examples because they are complete, and each represents one or the other of Philoxenus' two major themes in his writings -- right doctrine, and strict asceticism.

237. Assemanus, *B.O.*, II, p. 24; Budge, *Discourses*, II, pp. lvii ff.; de Halleux, *Vie*, pp. 293 ff. De Halleux points out that several of the prayers listed by Budge are duplicates of one another.

238. Ortiz, *Patrologia*, p. 160. This work was published in 1965, while de Halleux, *Vie*, was published in 1963.

239. Assemanus, *B.O.*, II, pp. 24 f.; Budge, *Discourses*, II, pp. l-li; de Halleux, *Vie*, pp. 303 ff.; Raes, *Anaphorae*, I, p. xliii.

240. Budge, *Discourses*, II, p. lxiv. The footnote on this item is misnumbered, the correct one being no. 1 on the opposite page. De Halleux concludes: "Il ne semble pas que l'évêque de Mabbog ait jamais écrit autrement qu'en prose."

241. Vööbus, *Legislation*, pp. 51-54.

242. De Halleux, *Vie*, pp. 197 f.

243. See note 118 above.

244. Wright, *Catalogue*, p. iv.

245. *Ibid.*, p. xv.

246. Cureton, *Athanasius*, p. xiii. Cureton had described the deplorable condition of some 315 MSS acquired by H. Tattam five years before: "The manuscripts arrived in the British Museum on the 1st of March, 1843. Upon opening the cases very few only of the volumes were found to be in a perfect state. From some the beginning was torn away, from some the end, from others both the beginning and the end; some had fallen to pieces into loose quires, many were completely broken up into separate leaves, and all these blended together. Nearly two hundred volumes of manuscripts, torn into separate leaves, and mixed up together by time and chance more completely than the greatest ingenuity could have effected, presented a spectacle of confusion which at first seemed almost to preclude hope. To select from this mass such loose fragments as belonged to those manuscripts which were imperfect, and to separate the rest, and collect them into volumes, was the labour of months. To arrange all those leaves now collected into volumes, in their proper consecutive order, will be the labour of years. Without the aid either of pagination or catchwords, it will be requisite to read almost every leaf, and not only to read it, but to study accurately the context, so as to seize the full sense of the author. Where there are two copies of the same book, or where it is the translation of some Greek work still existing, this labour will be in some measure diminished; but in other instances nothing less than the most careful perusal of every leaf will render it possible to arrange the work, and make it complete."

247. In July, 1971, I spent three weeks in the British Museum examining this MS and others related to it. I am grateful to the Museum Director and his staff in the Department of Oriental Printed Books and Manuscripts for the many courtesies extended to me at that time.

248. These numbers and the few other extraneous notes do not, of course, appear in the edited text here presented.

249. These tiny numbers seem to be in the same hand as the "stroked-out" sets, but their size (about 1/16 inch high) prevents them from being compared with absolute certainty with the other figures (about ¼ inch high).

250. Wright, *Catalogue*, p. xxxiii.

251. De Halleux, *Vie*, p. 145, fn. 11, disputes the existence of this yudh to which Wright, *Catalogue*, p. 526, refers. An examination of the MS confirmed its existence. Fragment 14 is, therefore, the last quire of the original volume since it concludes with the colophon.

252. Wright, *Catalogue*, p. 526, Brit. Mus. Add. 14,534 = *The Book on Selected Passages from the Gospels*.

253. De Halleux, *Vie*, p. 150.

254. The colophon of Add. 14,534 does not state where or when the manuscript was written, but it has so many things in common with Add. 17,126 that we must conclude that it also was written in Mabbug at the beginning of the sixth century. As de Halleux, *Vie*, p. 151, notes, the lower part of the last folio of Add. 14,534 has been torn off. It may have contained a colophon stating the place and time of writing.

255. The "silver" may have been some other colour when it was penned. This punctuation mark differs in Fragment 5 (13r 4 and 17, and 13v 4), where in all three occurrences it appears as /...⌒../ -- a further indication that this fragment does not belong in the MS.

256. See Appendix B for untouched copies of three typical pages.

257. Where there is a gap in the text and no square brackets, it simply means that the gap was original to it and nothing is lost. The gap is there either because of the scribal tradition requiring the last word of every line to end at the left margin (e.f., folio 1r, 11, 12), or because of a natural hole originally in the vellum (e.g., folio 18r and v, middle of l. 1).

258. Wright, *Catalogue*, p. 526.

259. 38v 14 ff.

260. See p. 47 above.

261. Wright, *Catalogue*, p. 526.

262. De Halleux, *Vie*, p. 149.

263. *Patr. Syr. 1*, col. 76.

264. Comparisons of Biblical texts quoted in this MS with Syriac versions will be made in the next chapter.

265. Olinder, *Friend*, p. 12. See also Vööbus, *Studies*, p. 197. De Halleux, *Vie*, pp. 269-274, questions the authenticity of this letter, but leaves the matter open. The unusual form of this quotation from Matthew favours a Philoxenian authorship. The Philoxenian works examined for the purpose of this dissertation are all the published discourses, letters, and other fragments (see bibliography), and the unpublished fragmentary "commentaries" discussed in ch. 1.

266. *Patr. Syr. III*, cols. 120, 276, 425. Col. 41 reverses the word-order: ܫܒܥ ܥܠ ܫܒ̈ܥܝܢ. Col. 492 explicitly states that the number is 490!

267. Leloir, *L'Évangile*, pp. 35-36.

268. *Loc. cit.*, fn. 66.

269. Budge, *Discourses*, I, p. 140 (on John 21:15 = Curetonian. Peshitta and Greek add "Peter"), p. 234 (on Marr. 17:24-27 = Curetonian. Peshitta and Greek read "Peter" in v. 24 and "Simon" in v. 27), p. 317 (on Matt. 19:27; Curetonian has "Simon Peter" and Peshitta and Greek have "Peter), and p. 324 (on John 6:68; Greek text and Syriac versions read "Simon Peter"). This preference for "Simon" is also seen in citations from Acts (*Discourses*, I, p. 486; see also p. 132). Philoxenus apparently never used ܟܐܦܐ for "Peter" (which is the rule in the Peshitta), but always ܦܛܪܘܣ (see de Halleux, *Senun*, pp. 31, 32, 77-78; Budge, *Discourses*, I, p. 600 -- the last refers to 1 Peter which the Peshitta also designates by ܦܛܪܘܣ). In the quotation from Matt. 16:16 ff. in *Senun*, pp. 77-78, Philoxenus deliberately avoids the use of the term ܟܐܦܐ and in its place uses ܫܘܥܐ which seems to play on the sound of the word ܫܡܥܘܢ. ܫܘܥܐ in this context is not found in any of the Syriac versions, though they use it elsewhere (e.g., Matt. 7:24, 13:5, Mark 15:46, Acts 27:29).

270. *De Oratione* (P.L.I., col. 1163). Origen, *Matthew*, XIV:5, also relates the two texts to one another and understands in both "seventy-seven times," but says the meaning is obscure.

271. Some examples of this paraphrastic style of exegesis are found in Budge, *Discourses*, I, p. 228 (on Matt. 5:24), pp. 251-252 (on John 2:4), pp. 271-273 (on Matt. 11:28), pp. 484-485 (on Matt. 9:14), and p. 556 (on Matt. 5:28).

272. This verse is quite different in the Peshitta, and is missing in the available Hebrew text.

273. Cf. the collection of rabbinic comments in Kasher, *Encyclopedia I*, pp. 158 ff. Josephus, *Antiquities*, I:58, merely says that God "threatened to punish his posterity in the seventh generation." Patristic commentators throw no light on this passage in Philoxenus (cf., e.g., Chrysostom on Genesis in *P.G.*, LIII, col. 166, where seven sins of Cain are enumerated).

274. See Kasher and Josephus, *loc. cit.*

275. Genesis 2:15; 3:23, 24.

276. Burkitt, *Evangelion*, II, p. 138. The Sinaitic and Peshitta versions read "Paradise," Leloir, *Diatessaron*, p. 96. *Patr. Syr. I*, cols. 628, 1037.

277. In both the Ceriani and Nestorian (Trinitarian Bible Society) editions.

278. De Halleux, *Vie*, p. 149, makes this statement concerning the last fragment (folios 33-38), but by inference he seems to suggest that it applies also to this first fragment since he would place it immediately before the

last in his scheme of rearranging the fragments.

279. See colophon, 38v 11, 12.

280. See p. 46 above.

281. Of 21 quires in Add. 14,534, 18 have 10 folios each, 2 have 8 each, and the last quire has 4.

282. Except codex Laudianus and codices 383 and 614 (see Clark, *Acts*, p. 12).

283. Vaschalde, *Tractatus*, p. 187 (text).

284. Justin Martyr, *Apologia* I.26.6, understood Simon Magus to be possessed by demons and links his name with Menander and Marcion, heretics who flourished in his time. Eusebius, *Church History*, II, 13, 1-8, said that Simon was the author of all heresy, which is what this fragment indicates.

285. Frothingham, *Bar Sudayli*, p. 30.

286. Vaschalde, *Tractatus*, p. 205 (text).

287. Budge, *Discourses*, II, pp. cxxxvi ff. See also above and note 221.

288. The text and Latin translation of only two of the ten discourses have been published in Brière, *Dissertationes* (see pp. 16, 24, 47, 95, and 103). The others are as yet unavailable.

289. Vaschalde, *Three Letters*, pp. 149, 159, 160 respectively.

290. Vaschalde, *Three Letters*, p. 179, also translates by "likeness."

291. Smith, *Exegesis*, I, pp. 300-309 and 321-351, gives catenae of quotations from ante-Nicene writers on the subject. The following quotation from Hegemonius (as quoted in Smith, *op. cit.*, p. 209) is suggestive of the background: "Archelaus quotes these verses as a proof that Jesus was truly born of the Virgin -- not simply appearing *as* a man while not being man. *Manes* replies that if He is simply a man born of Mary, and received by the Spirit in baptism, He will appear to be Son by advancement and not by nature. If to speak of Him as man means He was truly man of flesh and blood, then the Spirit Who appeared as a dove will be a literal dove. Archelaus replies that a true dove will not enter a true man; Jesus is true man, the Spirit was only '*as* a dove'."

In his "Letter to Zeno," Philoxenus makes reference to the same theme: "The Son was baptized as a man and not in the likeness (of a man). It was the Holy Spirit who possessed the likeness of a dove." (Vaschalde, *Three Letters*, p. 169).

292. We quote the following paragraph from Chrysostom's sermon on John 1:28, 29 (Homily XVII in Marriott's translation published in the *Nicene and Post-Nicene Fathers* (first series vol. XIV, New York, 1890, pp. 60-61) because it not only throws light on this statement but also on the development of the argument in this fragment:
"But," says one, "how then did not the Jews believe? for it was not John only that saw the Spirit in the likeness of a dove." It was, because, even if they did see, such things require not only the eyes of the body, but more than these, the vision of the understanding, to prevent men from supposing the whole to be a vain illusion. For if when they saw Him working wonders, touching with His own hands the sick and the dead, and so bringing them back to life, and health, they were so drunk with malice as to declare the contrary of what they say; how could they shake off their unbelief by the descent of the Spirit only? And some say, that they did not all see it, but only John and those of them who were better disposed. Because, even though it were possible with fleshly eyes to see the Spirit descending as in the likeness of a dove, still not for this was it absolutely necessary that the circumstance should be visible to all. For Zacharias saw many things in a sensible form, as did Daniel and Ezekiel, and had none to share in what they saw; Moses also saw many things such as none other hath seen; nor did all the disciples enjoy the view of the Transfiguration on the mount, nor did they all alike behold Him at the time of the Resurrection. And this Luke plainly shows, when he says, that He showed Himself "to witnesses chosen before of God." (Acts X. 41)

293. De Halleux, *Vie*, p. 320, fn. 9. De Halleux calls the *Ten Discourses* "Memre contre Habib." This quotation is taken from the tenth discourse which remains unpublished.

294. ܐܠܐ ܗܘܐ ܓܝܪ ܘܠܝܬ ܡܠܐܟܐ ܕܫܘܬܐ ܥܡ ܐܠܗܐ.
-- Krüger, *Annuntiatione*, p. 159.

295. See p. 182 above on 4r 23-26 and 4r 27.

296. E.g., in his "Letter to the Monks of Beth-Gogal": "The disciple who does not confess that the Impassible One suffered, and the Immortal One died for us, is pagan and not a disciple." (Vaschalde, *Three Letters*. p. 153). Cf. the longer statement in his "Letter to Zeno" (*op. cit.*, p. 170).

297. Quoted from the title of the work as printed in Budge, *Discourses*, II, pp. liv-lv. (See also de Halleux, *Vie*, pp. 179 ff.)

298. See p. 47 above.

299. E.g., in the "Letter to the Monks of Senun," Philoxenus speaks of Diodore and Theodore as the teachers of Nestorius (de Halleux, *Senun*, p. 95).

300. The same term (ܡܪܟܒܐ) is used in his "Letter to Zeno" (Vaschalde, *Three Letters*, p. 165): "I see with the eye of faith a spiritual being who without changing became a physical being. Mary gave birth, not to a *composite being* as Nestorius has said, but to the Only-Begotten, Incarnate One, who is not half God and half man, but completely God because He is of the Father and completely man because He came into being by the Virgin."

301. The slight change in writing may simply be due to the limitations imposed by writing over an erasure; e.g., the ink tends to blot or spread more readily on the erased surface, so the scribe makes allowances by writing somewhat larger. The variant form of the waw may in fact be a small blot which causes the right end of the letter to turn to the left -- ܘ for ܘ .

302. But see his two eucharistic prayers, one of which begins, "I carry you, O living God, for you have become embodied in bread" (Budge, *Discourses*, II, p. 1, Wright, *Catalogue*, p. 124, de Halleux, *Vie*, pp. 285 f.); also, his references to the Eucharist in "Letters to the Monks of Senun" (de Halleux, *Senun*, I, pp. 5, 6, 8, 9). In his "Letter to Monks," Philoxenus writes, ". . . not tangible, we handle Him; not capable of being eaten, we eat Him; not capable of being tasted, we drink Him." (Vaschalde, *Three Letters*, p. 140.)

303. This is also the tradition of Vulgate, and it is that which is translated in the New English Bible (see R. V. G. Tasker, *The Greek New Testament* [Oxford, 1964], p. 177).

304. Philoxenus nowhere cites 1 Corinthians 2:14, but in *Senun* (de Halleux), p. 70, he quotes 1 Corinthians 2:12-13.

305. De Halleux, *Senun*, pp. 3-4.

306. I.e., ܐܠܗܐ ܪܘܚܐ. In this MS the phrase ܐܠܗܐ ܡܠܬܐ often occurs.

307. See pp. 29 f. above.

308. De Halleux, *Senun*, p. 3. Cf. 26r 14, 18 of the MS before us.

309. See pp. 29 f. and 33 f. above. De Halleux, *Vie*, p. 150, considered them part of a commentary on John 1:14 (following Wright's suggestion in his *Catalogue*, p. 526). This fifth fragment has John 20:19 and 26 as its biblical basis for the polemic and not John 1:14.

310. See those listed in de Halleux, *Vie*, pp. 134, 135, 144, 147.

311. De Halleux, *Senun*, p. 46. While the statement in the Apostles' Creed, "He descended into hell," was not added until about the beginning of the sixth century, it was part of the creedal language of the Syriac Church much

earlier. J. N. D. Kelly in his *Early Christian Creeds* (p. 379) writes: "There is a good deal of evidence pointing to the probability that the Descent figured very early in Eastern creed material," and he goes on to cite the doxology of the Syriac *Didascalia* and the homilies of Aphrahat.

312. Tanghe, *Inhabitation*, pp. 46 f.

313. See p. 180 above.

314. Tanghe, *Inhabitation*, p. 62, fn. 29, has pointed out that in this Philoxenus differs from Aphrahat: "Pour Aphraate, nier Dieu c'est ne pas ses commandements."

315. *Ibid.*, p. 57, fn. 1.

316. Vaschalde, *Tractatus*, p. 67, and Budge, *Discourses*, I, p. 139.

317. Budge, *loc. cit.*

318. Vaschalde, *Three Letters*, p. 154. A similar identification is found in his "Letter to the Monks of Senun." After quoting Luke 1:34-35, he writes: "If then the Lord, who was both the Word of God and the Son of God, the Power of the Most High and the Holy One, came into being with Mary, how can Jesus who was born of the Virgin Mary to be other than the Word of God?" (de Halleux, *Senun*, p. 60).

319. The "résumé" of Fragment 8 in de Halleux, *Vie*, p. 146, is quite irrelevant (we quote it in full): "En Luc, II, 52, Jésus est sorti de l'enfance ([illegible] , de sept à douze ans), dans laquelle il se trouvait encore en Luc, II, 40." Whether this fragment belongs with Fragment 10 (as he suggests) will also be considered later.

320. In his prologue to the *Discourses*, Philoxenus writes: "The disciple of God therefore shall seek to have the remembrance of his Master Jesus Christ fixed in his soul and to meditate on it day and night." (Budge, *op. cit.*, I, p. 6, II, p. 4). Cf., e.g., *op. cit.*, I, pp. 432 f., on Christ's fasting in the wilderness.

321. Or, did Philoxenus understand John the Baptist to have lived in more than one desert (cf. Luke 3:2-3)?

322. See the next chapter for a comparison with the Peshitta.

323. De Halleux, *Vie*, pp. 284-285. His references in brackets are to Budge, *Discourses*, I.

324. A ḥeth at the foot of folio 19r marks the beginning of the quire and a ṭeth occurs in the same position on 29r, indicating that folios 19-28 form a complete quire.

325. This assumption is based not only on the size of quire

ḥeth, but also on the fact that Brit. Mus. Add. 14,534 (*Book on Selected Passages from the Gospels*) consists of eighteen quires of ten folios each and only two quires of eight folios each (the first quire has four folios), and it has close affinities with our manuscript.

326. Philoxenus refers to the "blessed," "great" and "renowned" Athanasius some twelve times in his "Letter to the Monks of *Senun*" (de Halleux, *Senun*). In his *Ten Discourses on the One Person of the Trinity*, etc., he cites Athanasius eight times (so de Halleux, *Vie*, p. 233).

327. See also 10r 8, 12r 24, 16v 4.

328. As translated in Hill, *Diatessaron*, pp. 179-180.

329. Tanghe, *Inhabitation*, p. 56. We note in passing that in the fragment before us Philoxenus cites "the prophets" as the source of this quotation from the Psalter!

330. The Hebrew reads אכן כאדם תמותון, where the singular אדם is like Philoxenus' singular phrase. However, the quotation as found in his "Letter" = Peshitta (which = Greek) except that the Peshitta reads ܐܠܗܝܢ for ܐܠܗ̈ܐ in the "Letter" and also here in 21v 14 and 22r 17.

331. Vaschalde, *Tractatus*, I, pp. 95, 177, 212.

332. *Nicene and Post-Nicene Fathers*, series 2, vol. 4, p. 422. The context of this quotation is in part as follows: "Now Luke says, 'And Jesus advanced in wisdom and stature, and in grace with God and man'. This then is the passage, and since they stumble in it, we are compelled to ask them, like the Pharisees and the Sadducees, of the person concerning whom Luke speaks. And the case stands thus. Is Jesus Christ man, as all other men, or is He God bearing flesh? If then He is an ordinary man as the rest, then let Him, as a man, advance; this however is the sentiment of the Samosatene, which virtually indeed you entertain also, though in name you deny it because of men. But if He be God bearing flesh, as He truly is, and 'the Word became flesh', and being God descended upon earth, what advance had He who existed equal to God? or how had the Son increase, being ever in the Father? For if He who was ever in the Father, advanced, what, I ask, is there beyond the Father from which His advance might be made? Next it is suitable here to repeat what was said upon the point of His receiving and being glorified. If He advanced when He became man, it is plain that before He became man, He was imperfect; and rather the flesh became to Him a cause of perfection than He to the flesh. And again, if as being the Word, He advances, what has He more to become than Word and Wisdom and Son and God's Power? For the Word is all these. . . . How did Wisdom advance in wisdom? or how did He who to others gives grace (as Paul says in every Epistle, knowing that through Him grace is given, 'The grace of our Lord Jesus Christ be with you all'), how did He advance in grace? for either let them

say that the Apostle is untrue, and presume to say that the Son is not Wisdom, or else if He is Wisdom as Solomon said, and if Paul wrote, 'Christ God's Power and God's Wisdom', of what advance did Wisdom admit further? . . .

. . . To men then belongs advance; but the Son of God, since He could not advance, being perfect in the Father, humbled Himself for us, that in His humbling we on the other hand might be able to increase. And our increase is no other than the renouncing things sensible, and coming to the Word Himself; since His humbling is nothing else than His taking our flesh. It was not then the Word, considered as the Word, who advanced; who is perfect from the perfect Father, who needs nothing, nay brings forward others to an advance; but humanly is He here also said to advance, since advance belongs to man. Hence the Evangelist, speaking with cautious exactness, has mentioned stature in the advance; but being Word and God He is not measured by stature, which belongs to bodies. . . .

. . . Thus, the body increasing in stature, there developed in it the manifestation of the Godhead also, and to all was it displayed that the body was God's Temple, and that God was in the body. And if they urge, that 'The Word become flesh' is called Jesus, and refer to Him the term 'advanced', they must be told that neither does this impair the Father's Light, which is the Son, but that it still shews that the Word has become man, and bore true flesh. And as we said that He suffered in the flesh, and hungered in the flesh, and was fatigued in the flesh, so also reasonably may He be said to have advanced in the flesh. . . . Neither then was the advance the Word's, nor was the flesh Wisdom, but the flesh became the body of Wisdom. Therefore, as we have already said, not Wisdom, as Wisdom, advanced in respect of Itself; but the manhood advanced in Wisdom, transcending by degrees human nature, and being defiled, and becoming and appearing to all as the organ of Wisdom for the operation and the shining forth of the Godhead. Wherefore neither said he, 'The Word advanced', but Jesus, by which Name the Lord was called when He became man; so that the advance is of the human nature in such wise as we explained above." (*Ibid.*, pp. 421-422).

333. Cf. his attack on Chalcedon in his "Confession of Faith . . . Against the Council of Chalcedon" (Budge, *Discourses*, II, pp. xcviii f.

334. Vaschalde, *Three Letters*, p. 181.

335. See note 332 above.

336. These controversial texts include Psalm 45:7-8 (ch. 12), Prov. 8:22 (chs. 16-22), Matt. 11:27 (ch. 27), Mark 13:32 (ch. 28), Luke 2:52 (ch. 28), John 10:30 (ch. 25), 14:10 (ch. 23), 17:3 (ch. 24), Acts 2:36 (ch. 15), Phil. 2:9-10 (ch. 11), Hebrews 1:4 (ch. 13), and 3:2 (ch. 14). The numbering of the chapters is continuous through the four "Discourses Against the Arians" (English edition in the

Library of Nicene and Post-Nicene Fathers, series 2, vol. 4, New York, 1892).

337. De Halleux, *Vie*, p. 148.

338. *Nicene and Post-Nicene Fathers*, ser. 1, vol. 10, pp. 10 f.

339. I have been unable to find a trace of such a 'literal' interpretation in rabbinic or patristic literature. In his seventh *Discourse* (Budge, pp. 185 f.), he uses the example of Jacob's ladder to illustrate the ascending experience of the man who has devoted himself to the ascetic life.

340. It may be too that ܠܚܡܬ suggests ܠܚܡܐ ܕܚܝ̈ܐ of John 6:35, 41, which "came down" (ܢܚܬ) from heaven.

341. 4r 5, 20; 8r 25; 9r 8; 20v 17; 20r 3.

342. *Nicene and Post-Nicene Fathers*, ser. i, vol. 10, p. 10.

343. *Ibid.*, p. 12.

344. The present order may be due to the fact that Fragment 13 contains phrasing which is repeated at the beginning of Fragment 14 (cf. 32r 17-18 with 33r 8-10). There is no apparent reason for the unexplained sequence in de Halleux, *Vie*, p. 148 (i.e., 13, 12, 11); unless it is that Fragment 11 refers to Seth, Enoch, etc., and Fragment 14 also deals with these names.

345. See p. 46 above.

346. An exact copy of all parts of the colophon is found in Wright, *Catalogue*, p. 526.

347. Cf. Peshitta and Old Syriac of John 1:14.

348. *The Greek New Testament* (ed. by K. Aland et al., United Bible Societies, 1966), p. 214, cites four secondary witnesses to the use of the third person singular in Luke 3:22. They are a 14th century Greek MS (1475), one Bohairic MS, the Diatessaron and the Acts of Pilate.

349. See the comment on the quotation from Rom. 8:29 in the ch. 4 where it becomes clear that the expression must have belonged to the Philoxenian version.

350. Cf. pp. 178 f. above.

351. Cf. p. 178 above. De Halleux, *Vie*, p. 149, suggests that Fragment 1 be placed immediately before Fragment 14, but it cannot possibly fit there and, indeed, must be from another work altogether.

352. Cf. the long discussion on "La mort de Dieu" in de Halleux, *Vie*, pp. 484-505.

353. Payne-Smith, *Thesaurus*, I, col. 289, "ars medendi, medicina . . . sanatio."

354. Cf. pp. 29 and 33 above.

355. Nine quires of ten folios each, and the last quire with six folios. See pp. 268f. above for the details.

356. See pp. 197 ff. above.

357. See p. 190 above.

358. Cf. p. 192 above where we suggested that Fragment 8 may have belonged to some other work.

359. 14r 27 - 14r 5. The reference to growth "in the Spirit" recalls Luke 2:40 (rather than 2:52) where the Peshitta reads ܘܡܬܚܝܠ ܪܘܚܐ.

360. De Halleux, *Vie*, pp. 147-148.

361. That evidence turns on the existence of the quire number ܒ at the foot of folio 33r, which we reaffirm with Wright, *Catalogue*, p. 525, is clearly discernible in spite of de Halleux's statement to the contrary. See note 251 above.

362. See Exhibit 39 in ch. 4 for a complete list of known citations in the Philoxenian corpus.

363. Krüger, *Annuntiatione*.

364. As de Halleux, *Vie*, pp. 142-143, maintains.

365. Bar-Salibi, *N.T. Commentaries* (on Luke), pp. 241 and 248, Bar-Hebraeus, *Sanctuary Lamp*, Base VIII, pp. ܟܒ - ܟܐ.

366. Budge, *Discourses*, II, pp. ix-x.

367. See our discussion above, pp. 19-24.

368. Zuntz, *Harklean N.T.*, pp. 40-62.

369. = Vaschalde, *Tractatus*.

370. Zuntz, *op. cit.*, p. 41: "It is tempting to test one work of Philoxenus before all others; viz., the fragments of his commentary on the Gospels. They are preserved in two manuscripts in the British Museum, written in Mabbug, one of them certainly (A.D. 510/11), the other probably, during his episcopate and after the completion of Polycarp's version." (He is referring to Add. 17,126 and Add. 14,534 respectively.)

371. Vööbus, *New Data*, pp. 176 ff. (where he focuses on Johannine quotations from Add. 14,534), and *Early Versions*, pp. 109 ff. and 197 ff.

372. I have used the editions in Lagarde, *Syro-Hexaplar*, and in Middeldorpf, *Syro-Hexaplar*. The photo-lithographic edition of *Codex Syro-Hexaplaris Ambrosianus* published by A. M. Ceriani (Milan, 1874) was unavailable to me.

373. For the Old Testament, I have used Ceriani, *O.T. Peshitta*, and Emerton, *Wisdom*, and for the New Testament Gwilliam, *Gospels*, and *Peshitta N.T.* I have also consulted Lee, *Peshitta*, for both Testaments.

374. The texts are found in Lewis, *Gospel Lectionary*, *Palestinian Lectionary*, and *Syriac Texts*.

375. Also *Tractatus*, I, p. 156.

376. Ph has ܐܪܡܫܐ for ܪܡܫܐ. The prosthetic alaph is not significant (cf. ܐܪܙܐ/ܪܙܐ in this MS).

377. Also *Tractatus*, p. 135, and *Three Letters*, p. 169. Matt. 3:17 is cited twice in *Senun* (pp. 6 and 7), each citation differing from the other and both different from the Peshitta which Philoxenus quotes exactly in *Tractatus*, *Three Letters* and here. It is also noteworthy that while he quotes Matt. 3:17, the context is Luke 3:22-23 where the words spoken by the voice from heaven are somewhat different:
Matt. 3:17 ܗܢܘ ܒܪܝ ܚܒܝܒܐ ܕܒܗ ܐܨܛܒܝܬ
Luke 3:22 ܐܢܬ ܗܘ " " ܕܒܟ "

378. Also *Tractatus*, I, p. 187.

379. *Ibid.*, p. 239.

380. Also *Senun*, pp. 4, 37, 62, 63, 64; *Dissertatione*, p. 463; *Three Letters*, p. 166. In *Tractatus*, pp. 39, 143, 239, ܡܠܬܐ is preceded by ܗܘ but on p. 47 the ܗܘ is omitted. The inclusion of ܗܘ in the *Tractatus* citations seems to be an attempt to reflect the article in Greek, ὁ λόγος ; cf. John 1:1 where ܗܘ ܡܠܬܐ occurs in the Syriac versions. In his "Letter to the Monks of Tell 'Adda" (Guidi, *Tell 'Adda*, p. 456), Philoxenus uses ܦܓܪܐ of the Old Syriac version in place of ܒܣܪܐ, but this is anomalous.

381. Also in *Senun*, p. 8, except that the latter has ܥܢ̈ܒܘܗܝ (sheep) in place of ܥܢܗ of Peshitta. (Cf. the variations referred to in note 375 above.)

382. Also *Discourses*, pp. 38, 433-434.

383. Also *Dissertationes*, p. 523, and *Tractatus*, pp. 143 and 237; pp. 247-248 of the latter have the same quotation but with ܡܠܟ instead of ܡܠܟܬܗ̇.

384. Also *Patricius*, p. 106; *Three Letters*, pp. 137, 152 (in the latter instance the word order is slightly different). *Tractatus*, p. 215, and *Senun*, p. 28, read the first clause as follows: ܠܐ ܒܪܐ ܕܠܗ ܠܗ ܢܣܒ (ܐܠܗܐ)

P. et al. -- ܟܠ ܒܪܐ ܕܠܗ ܠܗ ܗܘ.
Senun also adds ܐܠܗܐ , indicating a citation ad sensum.

385. Also *Patricius*, p. 66.

386. Ph's spelling ܐܟܒܪ is simply a variant of ܟܒܪ.

387. Also *Tractatus*, pp. 47, 143, 194, 237, 245, 247; *Patricius*, p. 48; *Dissertationes*, pp. 462-463, 523.

388. Also *Discourses*, I, p. 241; *Tractatus*, pp. 69, 96, 182; *Dissertationes*, p. 523.

389. Also *Tractatus*, p. 243.

390. Also *Tractatus*, p. 243.

391. Also *Tractatus*, p. 156.

392. Also *Tractatus*, p. 156.

393. Genesis 1:26a is also found in 30r 1-2, 34r 26-27, 35r 2-3, 8-9, 35v 23-24, 37r 21-22 and *Tractatus*, p. 28. All have the same wording as that cited here.

394. Also 34r 17.

395. Also 35r 11. In 34:2-3, ܒܨܠܡܗ is omitted making this citation equivalent to Pal and LXX.

396. Also 36v 6-8 and Genesis 2:7b in *Inhabitation*, p. 52.

397. Cf. *Tractatus*, p. 235.

398. Also Genesis 4:16b in 2r 13-14.

399. Cf. 34v 13-15.

400. Also 22r 16-17 and *Inhabitation*, p. 56.

401. Also *Discourses*, p. 123. The variant ܒܒܢ̈ܝܬܐ found in some MSS of P also occurs in two MSS of *Discourses*.

402. Cf. Olinder, *Friend*, p. 12. Vööbus, *Studies*, p. 201, quotes Cambr. MS. Add. 1999 containing some of this text (*Friend*) in which the order of numbers is reversed ܥܣܪ ܟܠ ܥܣܪܝܢ but Olinder's text = Ph.

403. Also 11r 12-13, *Dissertatione*, p. 523, and *Letters*, p. 154.

404. In this exhibit, "Ann" = *Annuntiatione* (Krüger), p. 156, "Sen[1]" = *Senun*, p. 39, "Sen[2]" = *Senun*, p. 60 and "Trac" = *Tractatus*, pp. 38, 55, 58, 95, 236 (p. 236 has ܒܚܝܠ (= P) for ܘܚܝܠ. "Trac" = "De Uno et Trinitate" in Zuntz, *Harklean N.T.*, pp. 42 ff., where he deals inadequately with the citation from Luke 1:35.

405. Also 16r 13-15, 27r 3-4, and *Patricius*, 118:22-23.

406. Also 33r 12 and *Tractatus*, 135:18-19 (with addition of ܗܘ after ܒܪܝ).

407. Also in part 31v 9, 28.

408. Also *Letters*, p. 152; *Tractatus*, 72:9-11; 170:131-171:1; 239:16-17; *Senun*, 62:25-26; and Br. Mus. Add. 14,534, fol. 15r 21-22.

409. Also *Letters*, p. 137. Cf. *Tractatus*, 97:31-98:1; 215: 16-17; 220:9-11; and *Senun*, 28:15-17 (here exhibited as "Sen").

410. Also *Tractatus*, 259:29-30 (= "Tra" in exhibit).

411. Also *Senun*, 8:27-28. Cf. *Letters*, p. 171 (here exhibited as "Let").

412. Also in part *Tractatus*, 187:23-24.

413. Also in *Tractatus*, 85:26, 177:3-4, 212:28-29.

414. Also *Tractatus*, 215:14-15 and *Senun*, 28:12-13. Cf. *Letters*, p. 137. In *Tractatus*, ܐܬܪܚܡܢ is without its pronominal suffix perhaps through haplography. *Letters* = P exactly.

415. Exhibited are all four occurrences of this quotation in Ph: viz., Ph^1 = 16r 17, Ph^2 = 25v 10-11, Ph^3 = 29v 23, and Ph^4 = 26v 10-11.

416. Ph_2 = 24r 12-13 = *Tractatus*, 67:29 = *Discourses*, 139:10-11. The numbers in the exhibit mark the two clauses of the verse, since Ph reverses the order of P and Har; thus, the first clause of Ph (Ph_1) corresponds to the second clause of P and Har (P_2, Har_2).

417. Cf. *Dissertatione*, p. 517 (allusion), and *Tractatus*, 39:17-18; 47:24-25; and 237:4-5.

418. Also *Discourses*, 75:20-21.

419. Also *Tractatus*, 237:10-11.

420. Cf. Vööbus, *Studies*, pp. 197 and 201.

421. Vööbus, *Studies*, pp. 197, 201.

422. Hill, *Diatessaron*, pp. 179-180. All references to the Diatessaron are from this work.

423. De Halleux, *Vie*, p. 223.

424. See on Luke 22:42 below.

425. Vööbus, *Studies*, p. 198.

426. See, e.g., Comment 29 on Ezekiel 1:4. Cf. Vaschalde, *Letters*, p. 111, where Philoxenus anathematizes those who say that the "Power of the Most High" is not God the Word.

427. De Halleux, *Vie*, p. 200, dates the (First) Letter to Beth-Gaugal to just before September 484; and p. 238, fn. 70, places the "Ten Discourses" (or *Dissertatione*, or "Memre contre Habib") in the same period.

428. De Halleux, *Vie*, p. 245, shows that *Tractatus* (also called "Le libre des sentences") was written after 509, and p. 223 gives the autumn of 521 as the date of *Senun*.

429. *Senun* always uses ܪܘܚܐ ܩܕܝܫܐ for "Holy Spirit" (de Halleux, *Senun*, I, 7:8, 8:13; 11:4; 13:18; 25:14; 31:17; 32:2; 41:25; 42:6; 48:25; 50:3, 9; 58:9; 68:2, 5, 14; 71: 22, 24; 83:14; 96:11). *Tractatus* uses ܪܘܚܐ ܕܩܘܕܫܐ (Vaschalde, *Tractatus*, I, 24:27; 25:1; 28:29; 30:1; 44:10; 51:9; 55:17, 24; 58:9; 61:15; 63:1, 3; 90:14; 95:2; 131: 23; 143:19; 144:26; 171:22; 236:27, 28, 29; 237:13; 262: 1, 15; 263:9) more than twice as often as ܪܘܚܐ ܩܕܝܫܐ (*op. cit.*, 27:20; 95:24; 118:23; 194:24; 261:12; 262:16; 263:16; 264:3, 13; 265:29; 268:5; 271:32). Such a distribution may indicate either that the last part of *Tractatus* was written later in the author's career, or was edited by a monophysite scribe who made the expression conform to the phrase adopted by the Philoxenian and Harklean versions.

430. ܪܘܚܐ ܕܩܘܕܫܐ occurs in Ph 4v 4, 19; 5v 10; 14v 12; 15r 23; 16r 20; 17r 7; 17v 11; 19v 11; 30v 15, 20, 23, 26. ܪܘܚܐ ܩܕܝܫܐ in Ph 11r 3, 7 (= Fragment 3).

431. Zuntz, *Harklean N.T.*, pp. 43 f.

432. Philoxenus vacillated in his use of ܥܠܝܐ/ܡܪܝܡܐ. In Ph Fragment 3, each occurs once (11r 4, 13). In *Tractatus*, he uses ܡܪܝܡܐ when quoting Luke 1:35 (55:24; 58:9; 95:2; 236:29), but in other contexts, ܥܠܝܐ is used (57:28; 97:13; 103:12; 181:17). Even in *Senun* (his latest work), ܥܠܝܐ occurs once (10:1), but not in quoting Luke 1:35 directly; in other places, ܡܪܝܡܐ occurs.

433. Krüger, *Annuntiatione*, pp. 156-157.

434. De Halleux, *Senun*, I, pp. 30, 39, 55, 58, 59, 60; and Vaschalde, *Tractatus*, pp. 55, 58, 95, 236, *237, 265.

435. Cf. Hill, *Diatessaron*, p. 53.

436. So *Greek New Testament*, p. 214.

437. Vaschalde, *Letters*, p. 169.

438. Cf. 5r 3; 15v 22; 21v 15; 36r 7.

439. Vööbus, *Studies*, p. 198. Vööbus mistranscribed this quotation in Ph. The redundant possessive suffix with the

possessive particle which he saw only in P of Mark 14:36 is in fact here too.

440. See 33r 10; 35r 24.

441. 1v 4 (cf. John 8:39 in P) and here in 11v 21.

442. Vööbus, *Studies*, p. 197, where he lists the Syriac writings which include this reading.

443. Vööbus, *Studies*, p. 185, does not cite these three examples from Philoxenus, but refers to "Syriac Theophania, III, 43 and also Ms. Br. Mus. Add. 12,161, fol. 76a."

444. Vaschalde, *loc. cit.*, cites Ephesians 1:4 as its probable origin, but indicates some doubt.

445. What was under the erasure is completely obliterated.

446. Zuntz, *Harklean N.T.*, pp. 49-50, deals with this verse with only the *Tractatus* evidence in view.

447. See the next chapter for a statement on his view of the Scriptures.

448. See pp. 212 f. above.

449. See Exhibits 2, 5, 19, 21, 22, 23, 25, 26, 27, 29, 30, 31, 32, 33, 38, 39, 40, 41, 42, 51, 57, 59, 63, 64, 65, 67.

450. Exhibits 1, 7, 9, 10, 13, 34, 43, 46, 52, 53, 54, 58, 62, 68. Exact wordings of Peshitta texts are repeated in nineteen instances: Gen. 1:3, Matt. 3:17b, 26:38, Luke 1:37, John 1:14a, Rom. 4:17, 8:3, 8:32, 1 Corin. 1:18a, Gal. 4:4, Phil. 2:7b, Heb. 2:11-12; and Exhibits 2, 23, 32, 39a, 41, 42, 67.

451. The misquotation of Exhibit 3 is easily explained from the context. Exhibit 8 shows some ambivalence in the use of ܒܪܐ/ܥܒܕ. Exhibit 54 remains an enigma.

452. We note, however, that the only exact Peshitta quotation (Jerem. 51:15a) is found in Fragment 3 which (on internal evidence) is later than the work to which it has become attached (cf. the comment on Exhibit 50 on p. 238).

453. Nine are from the Peshitta, and three (Exhibits 2, 5, 19) are close to it.

454. Exhibits 6, 7, 8, 9, 10, 11, 12, 13, 14, 15, 16, 17, 20.

455. Exhibit 18.

456. Exhibit 1, which is repeated exactly in *Tractatus*.

457. Exhibit 4.

458. Exhibit 3.

459. Exhibits 25, 26, 27.

460. Exhibit 28.

461. Exhibit 24.

462. De Halleux, *Memra*, II, ll. 130-135; cf. Mingana, *New Documents*, pp. 152-153. Eli of Qartamin further claims that Philoxenus translated both Testaments himself.

463. Quoted in Gwynn, *Remnants*, p. xxxi. See

464. See Exhibits 1, 7, 8, 9, 13.

465. Lebon, *Monophysitisme*, p. 145; *Philoxénienne*, p. 417; Vööbus, *New Data*, p. 184; *Early*, p. 114; de Halleux, *Vie*, p. 22.

466. De Halleux, *Vie*, p. 22.

467. See his stated intention quoted on p. 20 above. De Halleux, *Vie*, p. 123, is unfair in characterizing the Philoxenian version thus: "elle visait à des fins exclusivement dogmatiques, et concrètement à fournir des lieux d'argumentation plus corrects aux polémistes antidiphysites." On the other hand, Gwynn states: "It does not appear that the (Philoxenian) translation shewed, or was ever impugned as shewing, a doctrinal bias." (*Dictionary of Christian Biography*, IV, p. 432).

468. E.g., Sirach 17:19 and 23:19 in *Discourses*, pp. 182 and 595; and Baruch 3:38 in *Tractatus*, p. 169, and in *Dissertatione*, p. 519.

469. Did Philoxenus regard one Greek version as normative? If so, which one? The question has no ready-made answer.

470. I have found nothing in Old Testament quotations in the published works of Philoxenus which would modify this opinion. A thorough examination of the Biblical quotations in all his works is, however, beyond the scope of this dissertation.

471. Exhibits 40, 41, 42, 51, 57, 59, 63, 64, 65, 67.

472. Exhibit 54.

473. See especially Vööbus, *New Data*, *Studies*, and *Contemplation*.

474. Exhibits 34, 37, 38, 43, 44, 45, 47, 52, 53.

475. Exhibits 34, 38, 44, 47 in Vööbus, *Studies*, pp. 197, 198, and 201.

476. See Exhibits 35, 36, 39, 46, 47, 48, 49, 50, 55, 56, 58, 60, 61, 62, 66, 68.

477. The translated text of the colophon is on p. 21 above.

478. See p. 21 above.

479. Zuntz, *Harklean N.T.*, p. 57.

480. See pp. 22 f. above. The evidence which Gwynn gathered to prove that the version of these five books which he edited was Philoxenian, only indicates that it was made prior to the Harklean version (Gwynn, *Remnants*, pp. xxxii ff.), not that it was part of Polycarp's work published in A.D. 508.

481. Vööbus, *New Data*, p. 185.

482. In *Dictionary of Christian Biography*, IV, p. 432. Perhaps the only exception to this is the deliberate masculinization of ܪܘܚܐ in every instance where it is thought to refer to the Holy Spirit. De Halleux' judgment in this regard has no real basis in fact: "La philoxeniénne n'avait pas un caractère proprement philologique, mais elle visait à des fins exclusivement dogmatiques, et concrètement à polémesties antidiphysites." (*Vie*, p. 123).

483. See, e.g., Exhibit 48.

484. In the Lee edition of the Peshitta, ܪܘܚܐ ܩܕܝܫܐ occurs in Ephesians 4:30; but the British and Foreign Bible Society edition of 1919 reads ܪܘܚܐ ܩܕܝܫܬܐ. I have not found any other instance of ܪܘܚܐ treated as a masculine in the Peshitta.

485. See p. 178 and note 269 above.

486. The Harklean version, however, is inconsistent in its spelling; e.g., ܦܛܪܘܣ (Matt. 10:2), ܦܐܛܪܘܣ (Matt. 16:23), ܦܗܛܪܘܣ (Matt. 18:21) and ܦܛܪܐ (Luke 22:34, where the use is vocative).

487. See Exhibit 55.

488. Cf. Exhibit 58.

489. As already pointed out, his Bible included the Old Testament Apocrypha and excluded the Minor Catholic Epistles and Revelation.

490. Budge, *Discourses*, I, p. 237.

491. *Ibid.*, p. 238.

492. *Ibid.*, p. 254.

493. Tanghe, *Inhabitation*, p. 42.

494. 25v 16 ff.; cf. 26v 1-2, "Christians who believe accept it, not by understanding it but because it is written."

495. 9r 25. He also makes clear that the acceptance of the word of scripture by faith results in obedient action on the part of the believer (*Discourses*, I, pp. 4-5).

496. Budge, *Discourses*, II, p. xxxviii.

497. 9r 25.

498. See p. 20 above for a full expression of this concern of his.

499. 7r 18 ff.

500. 26v 1-2.

501. 28v 5 ff.

502. Budge, *Discourses*, I, p. 65. Aphrahat uses the same figure of speech in his address on "Faith": "Hear, then, my beloved, and open to me the internal eyes of your heart and the spiritual perceptions of your understanding to that which I say to you." (Quoted in Budge, *Discourses*, II, p. clvvv.)

503. 1 Corinthians 2:14.

504. Budge, *Discourses*, I, p. 83.

505. 7v 6, 24, 26; 8v 18; 9r 5; 11r 9; 15r 21; 26r 10; 35v 7. De Halleux, *Vie*, pp. 319-330, deals at length with "Le mystère du devenir divin" in Philoxenus' theology. He writes: "Philoxène regarde le devenir sans changement de Dieu Verbe comme le mystère de la foi par excellence." (*Op. cit.*, p. 325.)

506. 33r 10.

507. 33r 17 ff.

508. 37v 27.

509. 16r 26.

510. 31r 25 ff.

511. 25v 17, 21.

512. 36v 1-5.

513. 7v 4.

514. 7v 13 ff.

515. John 1:14; cf. 9r 5.

516. 34r 21-22. In 37r 23-25, he writes: "If words are written which are like one another, they make known in the first words what they intend."

517. 34r 13 ff.

518. 32r 14 ff. Cf. Luke 3:21-22 (Baptism) and 23-38 (genealogy).

519. 15r-v. See also p. 206 above.

520. 1r 10-18.

521. Budge, *Discourses*, I, pp. 251-252.

522. *Op. cit.*, pp. 271-273.

523. E.g., *op. cit.*, pp. 228, 284-285, 556.

524. See, e.g., Chrysostom on Matt. 16:13 ff. and on John 2:4 (translation in *Nicene and Post-Nicene Fathers of the Christian Church*, ser. 1, vol. 10, p. 333, and vol. 14, pp. 76 f., respectively).

525. 1r 20-28.

526. 1r - 2v.

527. For ante-Nicene exegesis, see Smith,*Exegesis*, vol. 3, pp. 246-249. The same contrast is noted by W. C. Allen, *Commentary on Matthew* (I.C.C.), p. 199.

528. 2v 25-26 says that the Davidic kingdom "was given to (Solomon) as a type."

529. The undisciplined nature of this rambling fragment of exegesis is not characteristic of Philoxenus, and it led me to re-examine the fragment to see whether there were any definite signs of a non-Philoxenian origin. The results of such re-examination only confirm Philoxenus as the author.

530. 33r 22, 34v 6. In 7v 3, Philoxenus speaks of "the types and mysteries of (Christ) found and inscribed in the Old Testament." Cf. 20v 3. In 6r 20 ff., he combats the idea that the Word in Jesus was a mere "shadow." Gregory of Nazianzus referred to God as the "Archetype" ("First Homily on Easter Night," 4); but he did not develop the concept in relation to biblical typology.

531. 34v 6.

532. 7v 1-4.

533. 2v 26.

534. 30r 14-23.

535. Budge, *Discourses*, I, pp. 192-193. In this passage, Philoxenus presses the analogy so much that the type becomes an allegory. Significantly, in this context he does not call the dream a "type."

536. 20v 1 - 21r 4.

537. 20v 5 ff.

538. 20v 9 ff.

539. 20v 24 f., 21r 1 f.

540. 22v 3, 31r 25.

541. 11r 2, 13v 5, 20r 2, 23r 24. Cf. Budge, *Discourses*, II, p. cxxxvii.

542. Baumstark, *Evangelienexegese*, p. 155: "Johannes Chrysostomos ist wie für die Auslegung der Paulusbriefe so auch für die Matthäus-und die Johanneserklärung recht eigentlich die erste exegetische Autorität in der jakoblitischen Kirche geworden."

543. So de Halleux, *Vie*, p. 233, who calls this work "Le volume contre Habib." Only the first two Memre have been published -- see Brière, *Dissertationes*.

544. De Halleux, *Textes*, I, p. 38; cf. *Vie*, p. 323. I know of no other Philoxenian works in which Chrysostom is mentioned.

545. See pp. 183, 198, and 200 above.

BIBLIOGRAPHY (WITH ABBREVIATIONS)

The works are listed alphabetically according to the abbreviations used throughout this dissertation. Thus, the abbreviation comes first in each case, followed by a dash (--) and a full description of the source (author, title, etc.).

Abbeloos, *Acta* -- J. B. Abbeloos. *Acta Sancti Maris.* Brussels, 1885.

Albert, *Disciple* -- M. Albert. "Lettre inédite de Philoxène de Mabboug à l'un de ses disciples." *L'Orient syrien*, t. 6 (1961), pp. 243-254.

Albert, *Juif* -- M. Albert. "Une lettre inédite de Philoxène de Mabboug à un Juif converti engagé dans la vie parfaite." *L'Orient syrien*, t. 6 (1961), pp. 41-50.

Altaner, *Patrology* -- B. Altaner. *Patrology.* Trans. by Hilda C. Graef. New York: Herder and Herder, 1960.

Assemanus, *B.O.* -- J. S. Assemanus. *Bibliotheca Orientalis Clementino-Vaticanae.* 2 vols. Rome, 1719 and 1721.

Assemanus, *Catalogus* -- S. E. and J. S. Assemanus. *Bibliothecae Apostolicae Vaticanae Codicum Manuscriptorum Catalogus.* 3 vols. Rome, 1756-59.

Atiya, *History* -- A. S. Atiya. *A History of Eastern Christianity.* London, 1968.

Baars, *Texts* -- W. Baars. *New Syro-Hexaplaric Texts.* Leiden, 1968.

Badger, *Nestorians* -- G. P. Badger. *The Nestorians and Their Rituals.* London, 1852; reprinted 1969.

Baethgen, *Glauben* -- F. Baethgen. "Philoxenus von Mabug über den Glauben." *Zeitschrift für Kirchengeschichte*, t. 5 (1882), pp. 122-138.

Bar-Bahlul, *Lexicon* -- Hassan Bar-Bahlul. *Lexicon Syriacum*, ed. R. Duval. 3 vols. Paris, 1901.

Bardenhewer, *Geschichte* -- O. Bardenhewer. *Geschichte der altkirchlichen Literatur*, t. 4. Fribough-en-Br., 1924.

Bardy, *Anastase* -- G. Bardy, "Sous le régime de l'Hénotique: la politique religieuse d'Anastase" in A. Fliche and V. Martin, *Histoire de l'Église*, t. 4 (Paris, 1931), pp. 299-320.

Bardy, *Sévère* -- G. Bardy. "Sévère d'Antioche." *Dictionnaire de théologie catholique*, t. 14 (1941), cols. 1988-2000.

Bar-Hebraeus, *Gospel Commentary* -- Gregory Abu'l Faraj. *Commentary on the Gospels from the Horreum Mysteriorum*, ed. W. E. W. Carr. London, 1925.

Bar-Hebraeus, *O.T. Scholia* -- M. Sprengling and W. C. Graham. *Bar-Hebraeus' Scholia on the Old Testament*. Part I: Genesis-II Samuel. Chicago, 1931.

Bar-Hebraeus, *Sanctuary Lamp, Base VIII* -- Gregory Abu'l Faraj. *Candélabre des sanctuaires*, éd. J. Bakos. *Psychologie de Grégoire Aboulfaradj, dit Barhébraeus, d'après la huitième base de l'ouvrage*. Leiden, 1948.

Bar-Salibi, *N.T. Commentaries* -- Dionysius Bar-Salibi. *Commentarii in evangelia*, Matt. 1:1-20:34, ed. I. Sedlacek and J. B. Cabot in *C.S.C.O.* Syr. II, 98^1 (1906) and 98^2 (1922); *ibid.*, Matt. 21:1-Luke 24:53, ed. A. Vaschalde in *C.S.C.O.*, Syr. II, 99^1 (1933) and 99^2 (1940); in *Apocalypsim, Actus et Epistulas Catholicas*, ed. I. Sedlacek in *C.S.C.O.* Syr. II, 101 (1910).

Baumstark, *Evangelienexegese* -- A. Baumstark. "Die Evangelienexegese der syrischen Monophysiten." *Oriens Christianus*, t. 2 (1902), pp. 151-169 and 358-389.

Baumstark, *Geschichte* -- A. Baumstark. *Geschichte der syrischen Literatur*. Bonn, 1922.

Beck, *Philoxenos* -- E. Beck, "Philoxenos und Ephräm." *Oriens Christianus*, t. 46 (1962), pp. 61-76.

Bedjan, *Acta* -- P. Bedjan. *Acta Martyrum et Sanctorum*. 7 vols. Paris, 1890-7.

Bensley, *Four Gospels* -- R. L. Bensley et al. *The Four Gospels in Syriac Transcribed from a Sinaitic Palimpsest*. Cambridge, 1894.

Bensley, *Harklean* -- R. L. Bensley, *The Harklean Version of the Epistle to the Hebrews*. Cambridge, 1889.

Bergsträsser, *Monophysitismus* -- E. Bergsträsser. *Monophysitismus und Paulustradition bei Philoxenos von Mabbug*. Erlangen, 1953.

Bergsträsser, *Philoxenos* -- E. Bergsträsser, "Philoxenos von Mabbug: Zur Frage einer monophysitischen Soteriologie." *Gedenkschrift für D. Werner Elert*. Berlin, 1955. Pp. 43-61.

Bewer, *Gospel Texts* -- J. A. Bewer. "A Collation of the Gospel Text of Aphraates with that of the Sinaitic, Curetonian and Peshitta Text." *American Journal of Semitic Languages*, XVI (Jan. 1900), pp. 110-123.

Brière, *Dissertationes* -- M. Brière, ed. *Sancti Philoxeni episcopi Mabbugensis dissertationes decem de une e sancta Trinitate incorporato et passo.* Diss. I et II in *Patrologia Orientalis*, t. 15 (1920), pp. 439-542.

Brockelmann, *Lexicon* -- K. Brockelmann. *Lexicon Syriacum.* 2nd ed. Halle, 1928.

Brooks, *Hymns* -- E. W. Brooks. *The Hymns of Severus and Others in the Syriac Version of Paul of Edessa, as Revised by James of Edessa*, in *Patrologia Orientalis*, t. 6 (1911), pp. 1-179, and t. 7 (1911), pp. 593-802.

Brooks, *Letters* -- E. W. Brooks. *The Sixth Book of the Selected Letters of Severus*, vol. 1 (Syriac text), vol. 2 (English translation). London and Oxford, 1902-4.

Budge, *Discourses* -- E. A. W. Budge. *The Discourses of Philoxenus, Bishop of Mabbogh*, vol. 1 (Syriac text), vol. 2 (English translation, etc.). London, 1894.

Budge, *Nile* -- E. A. W. Budge. *By Nile and Tigris.* 2 vols. London, 1920.

Burkitt, *Ephraim* -- F. C. Burkitt. "St. Ephraim's Quotations from the Gospel." *Texts and Studies*, VII, no. 2 (Cambridge, 1901).

Burkitt, *Evangelion* -- F. C. Burkitt. *Evangelion Da-Mepharresha, the Curetonian Version of the Four Gospels.* 2 vols. Cambridge, 1904.

Bury, *Later Empire* -- J. B. Bury. *The History of the Later Roman Empire from the Death of Theodosius I to the Death of Justinian.* 2 vols. London, 1931.

Camb. Hist. Bible -- *The Cambridge History of the Bible.* 3 vols. London, 1963-70.

Camb. Med. Hist. -- *Cambridge Medieval History, vol. I: The Christian Roman Empire and the Foundation of the Teutonic Kingdoms.* New York, 1911.

Ceriani, *O.T. Peshitta* -- A. M. Ceriani, ed. *Tranlatio Syra Pescitto Veteris Testamenti ex Codice Ambrosiano.* Milan, 1879-83.

Chabot, *Documenta* -- J.-B. Chabot, *Documenta ad Origines Monophysitarum Illustrandas*, in *C.S.C.O.*, Syr. II, 37 (Louvain, 1907, 1933).

Chabot, *Littérature* -- J.-B. Chabot. *Littérature Syriaque.* Paris, 1934.

Chabot, *Synodicon* -- J.-B. Chabot. *Synodicon orientale, ou recueil de synodes nestoriens.* Paris, 1902.

Charanis, *Anastasius* -- P. Charanis. *Church and State in the*

Later Roman Empire: The Religious Policy of Anastasius I. Madison, 1939.

Christensen, *Iran* -- A. Christensen. *L'Iran sous les Sassanides.* 2nd ed. Copenhagen, 1944.

Chronica Minora -- *Scriptores Syri, Textus et Versio: Chronica Minora*, ed. I. Guidi et al in *C.S.C.O.*, Syr. III, vol. 4 (Paris, 1903).

Chronicle 846 -- *Chronicon Anonymum ad A.D. 846 pertinens*, ed. E. W. Brooks and J.-B. Chabot, in *C.S.C.O.*, Syr. III, vol. 4 (Paris, 1903).

Chronicle 1234 *Anonymi Auctoris Chronicon ad A.D. 1234 pertinens*, ed. J.-B. Chabot, in *C.S.C.O.*, Syr. III, vol. 15 (Louvain, 1937).

Clark, *Acts* -- A. C. Clark. *The Acts of the Apostles -- A Critical Edition.* Oxford, 1933.

Clarke, *Isho bar Nun* -- E. G. Clarke. *The Selected Questions of Isho bar Nun on the Pentateuch.* Leiden, 1962.

C.S.C.O. -- *Corpus Scriptorum Christianorum Orientalium*, editum consilio Universitatis Catholicae Americae et Universitatis Catholicae Lovaniensis (Louvain).

Cureton, *Athanasius* -- W. Cureton, ed. *The Festal Letters of Athanasius* (discovered in an ancient Syriac version). London, 1848.

Cureton, *Gospels* -- W. Cureton. *Remains of a Very Ancient Recension of the Four Gospels in Syriac Hitherto Unknown in Europe.* London, 1858.

Cureton, *MSS* -- W. Cureton. "British Museum Manuscripts from the Egyptian Monasteries." Article II in *The Quarterly Review*, No. CLIII (Dec. 1845), Vol. LXXVII.

Cyril, *On Luke* -- *S. Cyrilli Alexandrini, Commentarius in Lucam*, ed. R. Payne Smith, vol. I (text), vol. II, Parts 1 and 2 (English translation. Oxford, 1858, 1859.

De Halleux, *Memra* -- A. de Halleux. *Éli de Qartamin, Memra sur S. Mar Philoxène de Mabbog*, in *C.S.C.O.*, Syr. 100-101 (Louvain, 1963).

De Halleux, *Senun* -- A. de Halleux. *Philoxène de Mabbog, Lettre aux moines de Senoun*, in *C.S.C.O.*, Syr. 98-99 (Louvain, 1963).

De Halleux, *Textes I* -- A. de Halleux. "Nouveaux textes inédits de Philoxène de Mabbog. I: Lettre aux moines de Palestine; Lettre liminaire au synodicon d' Éphèse." *Le Muséon*, t. 75 (1962), pp. 31-62.

De Halleux, *Textes II* -- A. de Halleux. "Nouveaux Textes

inédits de Philoxène de Mabbog. II: Lettre aux moines orthodoxes d'Orient." *Le Muséon*, t. 76 (1963), pp. 5-26.

De Halleux, *Vie* -- A. de Halleux. *Philoxène de Mabbog: sa vie, ses écrits, sa théologie.* Louvain, 1963.

Devreese, *Antioche* -- R. Devreese. *Le patriarcat d'Antioche depuis la paix de l'Église jusqu'à la conquête arabe.* Paris, 1945.

De Vries, *Primacy* -- W. de Vries. "Primacy, Communion, and Church in the Early Syrian Monophysites." *Orientalia Christiana Periodica* (1952), pp. 52-88.

D.H.G.E. -- A. Bandrillart, ed. *Dictionnaire d'histoire et de géographie ecclésiastiques.* Paris, 1912+.

Draguet, *Julien* -- R. Draguet. *Julien d'Halicarnasse et sa controverse avec Sévère d'Antioche sur l'incorruptibilité du corps du Christ.* Louvain, 1924.

Driver, *Bazaar* -- G. R. Driver and L. Hodgson. *Nestorius: The Bazaar of Heraclides.* Oxford, 1925.

Duval, *Littérature* -- R. Duval. *Littérature syriaque.* 1st ed. Paris, 1899.

Emerton, *Wisdom* -- J. A. Emerton. *The Peshitta of the Wisdom of Solomon.* Leiden, 1959.

Eynde, *Isho'dad* -- C. van den Eynde. *Commentaire d'Isho'dad de Merv sur l'ancient testament*, in *C.S.C.O.*, vols. 67 (1950) and 75 (1955).

Flemming, *Ephesus 449* -- "Akten der ephesinischen Synode vom Jahre 449," ed. J. Flemming and G. Hoffman, in *Abhandlungen der königlichen Gesellschaft der Wissenschaften zu Göttingen*, Neue Folge, Bd. XV, No. 1.

Frend, *Monophysite* -- W. H. C. Frend. *The Rise of the Monophysite Movement.* Cambridge, 1972.

Frothingham, *Bar Sudayli* -- A. L. Frothingham. *Stephen Bar Sudayli, the Syrian Mystic, and the Book of Hierotheos.* Leyde, 1886.

Goodspeed, *Matthew* -- E. J. Goodspeed. *Matthew, Apostle and Evangelist.* Philadelphia, 1959.

Goodspeed, *New Testament* -- E. J. Goodspeed. *The Formation of the New Testament.* Chicago, 1926.

Goosens, *Hiérapolis* -- G. Goosens. *Hiérapolis de Syrie: Essai de monographie historique.* Louvain, 1943.

Graffin, *Avocat* -- F. Graffin. "Une lettre inédite de Philoxène de Mabboug à un avocat, devenu moine, tenté par Satan." *L'Orient syrien*, t. 5 (1960), pp. 183-196.

Graffin, *Supérieur* -- F. Graffin. "La Lettre de Philoxène de Mabboug à un supérieur de monastère sur la vie monastique." *L'Orient syrien*, t. 6 (1961), pp. 317-352, 455-486; t. 7 (1962), pp. 77-102.

Gribomont, *Messalianisme* -- J. Gribomont. "Les homélies ascétiques de Philoxene de Mabboug et l'écho du Messalianisme." *L'Orient syrien*, t. 2 (1957), pp. 419-432.

Grillmeier, *Chalcedon* -- *Das Konzil von Chalkedon, Geschichte und Gegenwart*, ed. A. Grillmeier and H. Bacht. 3 vols. Wurzbourg, 1951-54.

Guidi, *Tell 'Adda* -- I. Guidi. "La lettera di Filossena ai monaci di Tell 'Adda." *Atti della Reale Accademia dei Lincei* (classe di science morali, III, 12) (Rome, 1884).

Gwilliam, *Gospels* -- P. E. Pusey and G. H. Gwilliam. *Tetraevangelium Sanctum juxta simplicem syrorem versionem.* Oxford, 1901.

Gwilliam, *Materials* -- G. H. Gwilliam. "The Materials for the Criticism of the Peshitta New Testament with Specimens of the Syriac Massorah." *Studia Biblica et Ecclesiastica*, III (Oxford, 1891), pp. 47-104.

Gwilliam, *Peshitta N.T.* -- G. H. Gwilliam and J. Pinkerton. *The New Testament in Syriac.* London: British and Foreign Bible Society, 1919.

Gwilliam, *Place* -- G. W. Gwilliam. "The Place of the Peshitta Version in the Apparatus Criticus of the Greek New Testament." *Studia Biblica et Ecclesiastica*, V, Part 3, pp. 187-236.

Gwynn, *Apocalypse* -- J. Gwynn. *The Apocalypse of St. John in Syriac.* London, 1897.

Gwynn, *Remnants* -- J. Gwynn. *Remnants of the Later Syriac Versions of the Bible.* London, 1909.

Hamilton, *Zachariah* -- F. J. Hamilton and E. W. Brooks. *The Syriac Chronicle Known as That of Zachariah of Mitylene.* London, 1899.

Harb, *L'Attitude* -- P. Harb. "L'Attitude de Philoxene a l'égard de la spiritualité 'savante' d'Évagre le Pontique." *Memorial Monseigneur Gabriel Khouri-Sarkis*, pp. 135-155 (Louvain, 1969).

Harb, *Conception* -- P. Harb. "La Conception pneumatologique chez Philoxène de Mabbûg." *Recherches Orientales*, t. 5 (1969), pp. 5-15.

Hatch, *Album* -- W. H. P. Hatch. *An Album od Dated Syriac Manuscripts.* Boston, 1946.

Hatch, *Subscriptions* -- W. H. P. Hatch. "The Subscriptions in the Chester Beatty Manuscript of the Harclean Gospels." *Harvard Theological Review*, XXX (1937), pp. 148-151.

Hausherr, *Contemplation* -- I. Hausherr, "Contemplation et sainteté: une remarquable mise au point par Philoxène de Mabboug." *Revue d'ascétique et de mystique*, t. 14 (1933), pp. 171-195.

Hausherr, *Spiritualité* -- I. Hausherr. "Spiritualité syrienne." *Orientalia christiana periodica*, t. 23 (1957), pp. 171-185.

Hill, *Diatessaron* -- J. H. Hill. *The Earliest Life of Christ . . . Being the Diatessaron of Tatian* (literally translated from the Arabic version). Edinburgh, 1894.

Hobson, *Diatessaron* -- A. A. Hobson. *The Diatessaron of Tatian and the Synoptic Problem.* Chicago, 1904.

Hoffmann, *Auszüge* -- G. Hoffman. *Auszüge aus syrischen Akten Persischer Märtyrer.* Leipsig, 1880.

Honigmann, *Évêques* -- E. Honigmann. *Évêques et évêchés monophysites d'Asie antérieure au VIe siècle. C.S.C.O.*, Subsidia 2 (Louvain, 1951).

Jennings, *Lexicon* -- W. Jennings. *Lexicon to the Syriac New Testament* (Peshitta). Rev. by U. Gantillon. Oxford, 1926.

Kahle, *Geniza* -- P. Kahle. *The Cairo Geniza.* 2nd ed. Oxford, 1959.

Kidd, *Churches* -- B. J. Kidd. *The Churches of Eastern Christendom.* London, 1927.

Krüger, *Annuntiatione* -- P. Krüger. "Der Sermo des Philoxenos von Mabbug de annuntiatione Dei Genetricis Mariae." *Orientalia Christiana Periodica*, t. 20 (1954), pp. 153-165.

Krüger, *Mönchtum* -- P. Krüger. "Das syrisch-monophysitische Mönchtum in Tur-Abdin von seinen Aufängen bis zur Mitte des 12. Jahrhunderts." *Orientalia Christiana Periodica*, t. 4 (1938), pp. 5-46.

Krüger, *Philoxeniana* -- P. Krüger. "Philoxeniana inedita." *Oriens Christianus*, 48 (1964), pp. 150-162.

Labourt, *Christianisme* -- J. Labourt. *Le christianisme dans l'empire perse sous la dynastie sassanide.* Paris, 1904.

Lagarde, *Analecta* -- P. de Lagarde, *Analecta Syriaca.* 1858.

Lagarde, *Syro-Hexaplar* -- P. de Lagarde. *Veteris Testamenti ab Origene recensiti fragmenta apud Syros servata quinque.* 1880.

Land, *Anecdota* -- J. P. N. Land. *Anecdota Syriaca.* 4 vols. Leiden, 1862-75.

Lavenant, *Patricius* -- R. Lavenant. "La lettre à Patricius d'Édesse de Philoxène de Mabboug." *Patrologie Orientalis*, t. 30 (1963), pp. 723-873.

Lebon, *Monophysitisme* -- J. Lebon. *Le monophysitisme sévérien.* Louvain, 1909.

Lebon, *Philoxénienne* -- J. Lebon. "La version philoxénienne de la Bible." *Revue d'histoire ecclésiastique*, t. 12 (1911), pp. 413-436.

Lebon, *Textes* -- J. Lebon. "Textes inédits de Philoxène de Mabboug." *Le Muséon*, t. 30 (1930), pp. 17-84, and 149-220.

Lee, *Peshitta* -- S. Lee, ed. *The Peshitta Bible.* London, 1823.

Leloir, *Ephraem* -- L. Leloir. *Doctrines et méthodes de S. Éphrem d'après son commentaire de l'évangile concordant*, in *C.S.C.O.*, Subsidia 18 (1961).

Leloir, *Diatessaron* -- L. Leloir. *Le temoignage d'Éphrem sur le Diatessaron*, in *C.S.C.O.*, Subsidia 19 (1962).

Leloir, *L'Évangile* -- *L'Évangile d'Éphrem d'après les oeuvres éditées, recueil des textes*, in *C.S.C.O.*, Subsidia 12 (1958).

Lemoine, *Homélies* -- E. Lemoine. *Philoxène de Mabboug: Homélies.* Paris, 1956.

Lemoine, *Physionomie* -- E. Lemoine. "Physionomie d'un moine syrien: Philoxène de Mabboug." *L'Orient syrien*, t. 3 (1958), pp. 91-102.

Lemoine, *Spiritualité* -- E. Lemoine. "La spiritualité de Philoxène de Mabboug." *L'Orient syrien*, t. 2 (1957), pp. 351-366.

Levene, *Genesis* -- A. Levene. *The Early Syrian Fathers on Genesis.* London, 1951.

Lewis, *Catalogue* -- A. S. Lewis. *Catalogue of the Syriac Manuscripts in the Convent of St. Catherine on Mt. Sinai.* London, 1894.

Lewis, *Codex* -- A. S. Lewis. *Codex Climaci Rescriptus.* Cambridge, 1909.

Lewis, *Four Gospels* A. S. Lewis. *A Translation of the Four Gospels from the Syriac of the Sinaitic Palimpsest.* London, 1894.

Lewis, *Gospel Lectionary* -- A. S. Lewis and M. D. Gibson. *The*

Palestinian Syriac Lectionary of the Gospels. London, 1899.

Lewis, *Palestinian Lectionary* -- A. S. Lewis. *A Palestinian Syriac Lectionary,* in *Studia Sinaitica No. 6* (London, 1897).

Lewis, *Syriac Texts* A. S. Lewis and M. D. Gibson. *Palestinian Syriac Texts from Palimpsest Fragments.* London, 1900.

Margoliouth, *List* -- G. Margoliouth. *Descriptive List of the Syriac and Karshuni Manuscripts in the British Museum Acquired Since 1873.* London, 1899.

Michael, *Chronicle* -- J.-B. Chabot. *Le chronique de Michel le Syrien, patriarche jacobite d'Antioche (1166-1199).* 4 vols. Paris, 1899-1910.

Middeldorpf, *Hexaplar* -- H. Middeldorpf. *Codex Syriaco-Hexaplaris.* Berlin, 1835.

Migne, *P. G.* -- J. P. Migne. *Patrologiae Cursus Completus: series graeca.* Paris, 1857-1866.

Migne, *P. L.* -- J. P. Migne. *Patrologiae Cursus Completus: series latina.* Paris, 1844-1890.

Mingana, *Catalogue* -- A. Mingana et al. *Catalogue of the Mingana Collection of Manuscripts* (now in the possession of the Trustees of the Woodbrooke Settlement, Selly Oak, Birmingham). 3 vols. Cambridge, 1933-39.

Mingana, *Early Spread* -- A. Mingana. *The Early Spread of Christianity in Central Asia and the Far East: A New Document.* Manchester, 1925.

Mingana, *New Documents* -- A. Mingana. "New Documents on Philoxenus of Hierapolis, and on the Philoxenian Version of the Bible." *The Expositor,* XIX (1920), pp. 149-160.

Mingana, *Nicene Creed* -- A. Mingana. *Commentary of Theodore of Mopsuestia on the Nicene Creed in Woodbrooke Studies.* Vol. V. Cambridge, 1932.

Molitor, *Diatessaron* -- J. Molitor. "Tatians Diatessaron und sein Verhältnis zur altsyrichen und altgeorgischen Überlieferung." *Oriens Christianus,* vol. 53 (1969), pp. 1-88; vol. 54 (1970), pp. 1-75; vol. 55 (1971), pp. 1-61

Moss, *Catalogue* -- C. Moss. *Catalogue of Syriac Printed Books and Related Literature in the British Museum.* London, 1962.

Muyldermans, *Evagriana* -- J. Muyldermans. *Evagriana Syriaca: Textes inédits du British Museum et de la Vaticane.* Louvain, 1952.

Nau, *Documents* -- F. Nau. "Documents pour servir à l'histoire de l'église nestorienne." *Patrologia Orientalis*, t. 13 (1919), pp. 111-326.

Nau, Notice -- F. Nau. "Notice inédite sur Philoxène, évêque de Mabboug (485-519)." *Revue de l'Orient chrétien*, t. 8 (1903), pp. 630-633.

Nau, *Opuscules* -- F. Nau. *Opuscules Maronites*. Paris, 1899.

Nau, *Plérophories* -- F. Nau. "Jean Rufus, Plérophories, témoignages et révélations contre le concile de Chalcédoine." *Patrologia Orientalis*, t. 8 (1912), pp. 1-168.

Nöldeke, *Grammar* -- J. Nöldeke. *Compendious Syriac Grammar*. Translated by J. A. Crichton. London, 1904.

Olinder, *Friend* -- G. Olinder. *A Letter of Philoxenus of Mabbug Sent to a Friend*. Götesborg, 1950.

Olinder, *Novice* -- G. Olinder. *A Letter of Philoxenus of Mabbug Sent to a Novice*. Götesborg, 1941.

Origen, *Matthew* -- Origen. "Commentary on Matthew," in E. Klostermann, ed., *Origenes Werke*. Band X. Leipzig, 1935.

Ortiz, *Patrologia* -- I. Ortiz de Urbina. *Patrologia Syriaca*. Rome, 1965.

Parry, *Monastery* -- O. H. Parry. *Six Months in a Syrian Monastery*. London, 1895.

Patr. Syr. -- *Patrologia Syriaca, I, II, and III*. Ed. by R. R. Graffin. Paris, 1894, 1907, and 1926.

Payne Smith, *Catalogus* -- R. Payne Smith. *Catalogus Codices Manuscripts Syriacos, Carshunicos, Mandaeos Bibliothecae Bodleianae Complectens*. Oxford, 1864.

Payne Smith, *Dictionary* -- J. Payne Smith (Mrs. Margoliouth). *A Compendius Syriac Dictionary*. Oxford, 1903.

Payne Smith, *Thesaurus* -- R. Payne Smith. *Thesaurus Syriacus*. 2 vols. Oxford, 1879 and 1901. Supplement by J. Payne Smith (Margoliouth). Oxford, 1927.

Peshitta Psalms -- W. E. Barnes. *The Peshitta Psalter According to the West Syrian Text*. Edited with an apparatus criticus. Cambridge, 1904.

Raes, *Anaphorae* -- A. Raes et al. *Anaphorae Syriacae*. Vol. I, fasc. 1 and 2. Rome, 1939.

Rücker, *Philoxenus* -- A. Rücker. "Philoxenus," article in *Lexicon für Theologie und Kirche*, 1st ed., t. 8 (1936), cols. 248-249.

Sachau, *Arbela* -- E. Sachau. *Die Chronik von Arbela*. Berlin, 1915.

Sachau, *Verzeichniss* -- E. Sachau. *Verzeichnis der syrischen Handschriften der köninglichen Bibliothek zu Berlin*. 2 vols. Berlin, 1899.

Sarkissian, *Chalcedon* -- K. Sarkissian. *The Council of Chalcedon and the Armenian Church*. London, 1965.

Segal, *Edessa* -- J. B. Segal. *Edessa: The Blessed City*. Oxford, 1970.

Segal, *Syriac* -- J. B. Segal. *The Diacritical Point and the Accents in Syriac*. Oxford, 1953.

Sellars, *Chalcedon* -- R. V. Sellars. *The Council of Chalcedon: A Historical and Doctrinal Survey*. London, 1961.

Severus, *Letters* -- E. W. Brooks. *Severus of Antioch: A Collection of Letters from Numerous Syriac Manuscripts*, in *Patrologia Orientalis*, t. 12 (1919), pp. 163-342, and t. 14 (1920), pp. 1-310.

Smith, *Exegesis* -- H. Smith. *Ante-Nicene Exegesis of the Gospels*. 6 vols. London, 1925.

Streeter, *Four Gospels* -- B. H. Streeter. *The Four Gospels: A Study in Origins*. London, 1936.

Strothmann, *Tetraevangelium* -- W. Strothmann. *Das Wolfenbütteler Tetraevangelium Syriacum*. Wiesbaden, 1971.

Sykes, *History* -- P. M. Sykes. *A History of Persia*. 2 vols. London, 1915.

Tanghe, *Inhabitation* -- A. Tanghe. "Memra de Philoxène de Mabboug sur l'inhabitation du *Saint-Ésprit*," in *Le Muséon*, t. 73 (1960), pp. 39-71.

Tisserant, *Philoxène* -- E. Tisserant. "Philoxène de Mabboug." Article in *Dictionnaire de théologie catholique*, t. 12 (1935), cols. 1509-1532.

Tisserant, *Specimena* -- E. Tisserant. *Specimena Codicum Orientalium*. Bonn, Oxford, and Rome, 1914.

Tixeront, *Abou Niphir* -- J. Tixeront. "La lettre de Philoxène à 'Abou-Niphir." *Revue de l'Orient chrétien*, t. 8 (1903), pp. 623-630.

Vaschalde, *Three Letters* -- A. A. Vaschalde. *Three Letters of Philoxenus, Bishop of Mabbogh*. Rome, 1902.

Vaschalde, *Tractatus* -- A. A. Vaschalde. *Philoxeni Mabbugensis: Tractatus Tres de Trinitate et Incarnatione*, in *C.S.C.O.*, Syr. II, vol. 27 (Paris, 1907).

Vasiliev, *Justin* -- A. A. Vasiliev. *Justin the First: An Introduction to Epoch of Justinian the Great.* Cambridge, Mass., 1950.

Vööbus, *Alter* -- A. Vööbus. "Das Alter der Peschitta." *Oriens Christianus*, XXXVIII (1954), pp. 1-10.

Vööbus, *Angaben* -- A. Vööbus. "Neue Angaben über die Textgeschichtlichen Zustände in Edessa in den Jahren ca. 326-340." *Papers of the Estonian Theological Society in Exile*, No. 3 (Stockholm, 1951).

Vööbus, *Asceticism* -- A. Vööbus. *History of Asceticism in the Syrian Orient*, vol. 1 in *C.S.C.O.*, Syr. Subsidia 14 (Louvain, 1958); vol. 2 in *C.S.C.O.*, Syr. Subsidia 17 (Louvain, 1960).

Vööbus, *Completion* -- A. Vööbus. "Completion of the Vetus Syra Project." *Biblical Research*, VII (1962), pp. 49-56.

Vööbus, *Early* -- A. Vööbus. "Early Versions of the New Testament--Manuscript Studies." *Papers of the Estonian Theological Society in Exile*, No. 6 (Stockholm, 1954).

Vööbus, *Ergebnisse* -- A. Vööbus. "Neue Ergebnisse in der Erforshung der Geschichte der Evangelientexte im Syrischen (Kurze Mitteilung)." *Contributions of Baltic University*, No. 65 (Pinneberg, 1948).

Vööbus, *Investigations* -- A. Vööbus. "Investigations into the Text of the New Testament Used by Rabbula of Edessa." *Contributions of Baltic University*, No. 59 (Pinneberg, 1947).

Vööbus, *Kanon* -- A. Vööbus. *Syrische Kanonessammlungen*, in *C.S.C.O.*, Syr. Subsidia 35 and 38 (Louvain, 1970).

Vööbus, *Legislation* -- A. Vööbus. "Syriac and Arabic Documents Regarding Legislation Relative to Syrian Asceticism." *Papers of the Estonian Theological Society in Exile*, No. 11 (Stockholm, 1960).

Vööbus, *Materialien* -- A. Vööbus. "Neue Materialien zur Geschichte der Vetus Syra in den Evangelienhandschriften. *Papers of the Estonian Theological Society in Exile*, No. 5 (Stockholm, 1953).

Vööbus, *New Data* -- A. Vööbus. "New Data for the Solution of the Problem Concerning the Philoxenian Version." *Spiritus et Veritas: Festschrift Carolo Kundzinš* (Eutin, 1953).

Vööbus, *Nisibis* -- A. Vööbus. *History of the School of Nisibis*, in *C.S.C.O.*, Syr. Subsidia 26 (Louvain, 1965).

Vööbus, *Researches* -- A. Vööbus. "Researches on the Circulation of the Peshitta in the Middle of the Fifth Century." *Contributions of Baltic University*, No. 64

(Pinneberg, 1948).

Vööbus, *Studies* -- A. Vööbus. *Studies in the History of the Gospel Text in Syriac*, in *C.S.C.O.*, Syr. Subsidia 3 (Louvain, 1951).

Vööbus, *Syrische*-- A. Vööbus. "Syrische Bibelübersetzungen." *Lexicon für Theologie und Kirche*, II (1958), cols. 386-392.

Vööbus, *Targumim* -- A. Vööbus. "Peschitta und Targumim des Pentateuchs." *Papers of the Estonian Theological Society in Exile*, No. 9 (Stockholm, 1958).

Vosté, *Catalogue* -- J. M. Vosté. "Catalogue de la bibliothèque syro-chaldéenne du couvent de N.-D. des Semences, près d'Alqoš." *Angelicum*, t. 5 (1928), pp. 3-36, 161-194, 325-358, 481-498.

White, *Harklean N.T.* -- Joseph White. *Sacrorum Evangeliorum, Versio Syriaca Philoxeniana*. 1 vol. Oxford, 1778; and *Actuum Apostolorum et Epistolarum, Versio Syriaca Philoxeniana*. 2 vols. in 1. Oxford, 1799 and 1803.

White, *Monasteries* -- H. G. E. White. *The Monasteries of Wadi 'N Natrun*. 3 vols. New York, 1926-33.

Wigram, *Assyrian Church* -- W. A. Wigram. *An Introduction to the History of the Assyrian Church: Or, The Church of the Sassanid Persian Empire, 100-640 A.D.* London, 1910.

Wood, *Ephrem* -- F. H. Wood. "An Examination of the New Testament Quotations of Ephrem Syrus." *Studia Biblica et Ecclesiastica*, III (Oxford, 1891), pp. 105-138.

Wright, *Catalogue* -- W. Wright. *Catalogue of Syriac Manuscripts in the British Museum Acquired Since the Year 1838*. 3 parts. London, 1870-72.

Wright, *Chronicle* -- W. Wright. *The Chronicle of Joshua the Stylite*. Cambridge, 1882.

Wright, *Ethiopic* -- W. Wright. *Catalogue of the Ethiopic Manuscripts in the British Museum Acquired Since the Year 1847*. London, 1877.

Wright, *Literature* -- W. Wright. *A Short History of Syriac Literature*. London, 1894.

Zorell, *Chronicon* -- F. Zorell. "Chronicon Ecclesiae Arbelensis." *Orientalia Christiana*, XIII:4, No. 31 (Rome, 1927).

Zuntz, *Études* -- G. Zuntz. "Études harkléennes." *Revue Biblique*, t. 57 (1950), pp. 550-582.

Zuntz, *Harklean N.T.* -- G. Zuntz. *The Ancestry of the Harklean New Testament*. London, 1945.

APPENDIX A

The following page contains a trascribed extract from British Museum MS. Add. 14,534, folio 38r line 25 to 38v line 28. The beginning of each fifth line of the manuscript is marked by an asterisk and noted in the margin. A translation of this extract is given on page 20.

....ܐܦ ܕܝܢ ܗܕܐ ܐܫܬܟܚܘ ܚܢܢ ܕܦܫܩܘ:
ܕܠܐ ܢܦܩܘܢ ܕܢܬܬܦܫܩ ܒܠܫܢܐ ܣܘܪܝܝܐ ܗܘܢܐ
ܕܡܫܝܚܐ. ܐܘ ܕܐܠܗܐ: ܐܘ ܕܒܪܢܫܐ: ܘܗܢ ܗܘܢܐ
ܠܗܘܢ ܠܡܒܥ. ܕܠܘ ܕܐܢܫܝܢ ܡ̈ܠܐ ܠܒܢ̈ܝ *ܠܟܠ ܚܕ
ܡܢ ܠܒܢܐ. ܘܠܐ ܠܡܟܬܒܘ ܠܗܘܢ ܕܢܬܒܥ ܕܢܣܒܪܐ
ܢܦܫܗ. ܐܠܐ ܠܡܟܬܒܐ ܕܐܢܫܝܢ ܐܝܬܝܗܘܢ ܦܬܓܡܐ
ܘܫܪܒܐ. ܗܢܘܢ ܕܝܢ ܐܠܗܐ ܐܘ ܡܢ ܪܘܚܗ: ܒܗܝ
*ܒܢ̈ܝܐ ܘܫ̈ܠܝܚܐ ܐܬܡܠܠܘ. ܡܛܠ ܕܠܘ ܢܟܪܝܐ ܕܡܫ̈ܝܚܐ
ܐܢ̈ܫܐ ܐܝܬܝܗܘܢ ܗܠܝܢ ܕܗܢ̈ܘܢ ܒܟܬ̈ܒܐ ܡܢܝܢܐ.
ܕܒܗ ܢܒܥܘ ܐܝܟܢܐ ܐܝܬܝܐ ܢܦܩܠܘ ܬܘܪܓܡܐ ܐܘ ܬܘܕܝܬܐ.
ܠܬܬ ܕܝܢ ܢܦܫܐ. ܟܠ ܚܕܐ ܡܢ ܗܠܝܢ *ܡ̈ܠܐ ܘܫܪ̈ܒܐ
ܕܐܬܡܠܠܝܢ ܕܐܬܐܡܪ ܡܢ ܐܢܬܓܠܘܣܐ ܘܡܢ ܫܠܝܚܐ.
ܗܟܢܐ ܦܝܫܝܢ ܐܝܟ ܡܐ ܕܐܬܐܡܪ ܡܢܝ. ܕܗܘܐ ܡܢ
ܘܪܟܐ ܕܗܘܐ ܒܒܣܪ: ܘܠܘ ܕܐܬܬܠܕ ܒܒܣܪ. ܘܬܘܒ
ܒܬܪܟܐ ܕܗܘܐ *ܕܢܫܒܘܩ ܡܫܝܚܐ. ܘܕܢܫܒܘܩ ܡܫܝܚܐ
ܗܘܐ ܗܟܢܐ ܐܝܬܘܗܝ. ܘܡܛܠ ܕܒܠܫܢܐ ܕܢܫܠܡܘܢ
ܐܬܡܠܠܘ ܒܬܪܟܐ ܕܕܢܬܦܫܐ ܚܕܬܐ. ܠܗܠܝܢ ܕܠܬܗܘܢ
ܦܢܝܢ ܘܠܐ ܢܬܪܐܝܬ ܠܡܬܕܝܢܘ. *ܘܠܘ ܠܐܢܫܝܢ ܕܝܢ
ܡܢ ܕܗܘ ܐܬܦܫܩ. ܗܠܝܢ ܕܐܢܫܝܢ ܕܡܫܒܚܘܬܐ
ܕܠܗܢ. ܘܠܘ ܕܢܠܦܫܐ ܕܝܢ ܪܘܚܐ......ܐܝܬܘܗܝ
ܡܕܝܢ ܟܠ ܡܢ ܕܢܫܡܠܐ: ܐܘ ܫܦܫܡ ܐܢܫܝܢܬܐ
ܡ̈ܠܐ ܘܫܪ̈ܒܐ *ܕܐܬܡܠܠܘ ܡܢ ܪܘܚܐ. ܠܘ ܒܠܚܘܕ
ܒܕܠܐ ܘܡܥܪܒ. ܐܠܐ ܐܦ ܢܫܬܡܥ ܘܢܬܦܫܩ.
ܘܫܘܦܐ ܕܡܫܝܚܘܬܐ ܘܕܢ̈ܫܝܢܐ. --------

(from Brit. Mus. Add. 14,534, 38r 25 - 38v 28)

APPENDIX B

The following three pages are unrestored photo copies of British Museum MS. Add. 17,126, folios 2r, 22r and 38v respectively, and illustrate the present condition of the text.

20 ܗܘ̇ ܕܪܘܚܐ ܘܕܗܘ ܕܒܗ̈ܘܢ. ܕܒܠܒܬܐ
ܕܗܘܐ ܒܪܘܚܐ. ܘܕܒܢ̈ܝܫܐ ܕܗܘܘ ܒܢ̈ܫܐ.
ܘܐܝܟ ܕܐܬܪ̈ܐ ܗܘܬ ܕܒܬܠܡܝܕܝܢ ܒ̈ܢܝ ܐܢܫܐ
ܡܢ ܒܪܘܚܐ ܕܒܢܫܐ. ܒܬܪ̈ܬܐ ܘܡܫܡܫܢܘܬܐ
ܡܘܕܝܢ ܒ̈ܢܝܐ ܐܠܐ ܡܢ ܒܪܘܚܐ
[illegible]

INDEX